Intimate Relationships across the Lifespan

Intimate Relationships across the Lifespan

Formation, Development, Enrichment, and Maintenance

Abdul Khaleque

Foreword by Ronald P. Rohner

 PRAEGER™

An Imprint of ABC-CLIO, LLC

Santa Barbara, California • Denver, Colorado

Library of Congress Cataloging-in-Publication Data

Names: Khaleque, Abdul, Ph.D. author.
Title: Intimate relationships across the lifespan : formation, development, enrichment, and maintenance / Abdul Khaleque ; foreword by Ronald P. Rohner.
Description: Santa Barbara, California : Praeger, an imprint of ABC-CLIO, LLC, [2018] | Includes bibliographical references and index.
Identifiers: LCCN 2017037296 (print) | LCCN 2017046746 (ebook) | ISBN 9781440861413 (ebook) | ISBN 9781440861406 (hardcopy : acid-free paper)
Subjects: LCSH: Intimacy (Psychology) | Interpersonal relations.
Classification: LCC BF575.I5 (ebook) | LCC BF575.I5 K48 2018 (print) | DDC 158.2—dc23
LC record available at https://lccn.loc.gov/2017037296

ISBN: 978-1-4408-6140-6 (print)
      978-1-4408-6141-3 (ebook)

22 21 20 19 18   1 2 3 4 5

This book is also available as an eBook.

Praeger
An Imprint of ABC-CLIO, LLC

ABC-CLIO, LLC
130 Cremona Drive, P.O. Box 1911
Santa Barbara, California 93116-1911

www.abc-clio.com

This book is printed on acid-free paper ∞

Manufactured in the United States of America

Contents

Foreword

Abdul Khaleque has written an unusual and important book because, among other things, it covers topics not ordinarily included in a book on intimate relationships. For example, the book is unique in its focus on life-span and cross-cultural perspectives in the origin, development, enrichment, and maintenance of intimate relationships. The book also provides timely information about nontraditional areas of intimate relationships such as in lesbian, gay, and transgender relationships. Moreover, the text contains evidence-based information about the implications of age, gender, and culture in intimate relationships. And importantly, it discusses the implications of intimate relationships for health, well-being, and quality of life across cultures and gender.

Given the breadth and depth of its coverage, the volume will be useful not only to undergraduate students, but will be a useful resource for graduate students, professional academics, and practitioners.

Good reading,

Ronald P. Rohner, Professor Emeritus and Director
Ronald and Nancy Rohner Center for the Study of
Interpersonal Acceptance and Rejection
University of Connecticut

Preface

Writing a book on intimate relationships across the lifespan is an enormously challenging undertaking because of the ever-growing body of research literature in this field that continuously expands our knowledge. This book focuses on the lifespan and cross-cultural perspectives. It is a comprehensive, research-based, next-generation core textbook for undergraduate students, and a resource book for graduate students, faculties, and practitioners. The text will likely also be of interest to a general readership, because intimate relationships—including friendship, love, intimacy, marriage, and sexuality—are some of the important and attractive topics to general readers. Detailed information is provided about friendship, love, sexuality, stability, and conflicts, in both marital and nonmarital intimate relationships. The text also focuses on how to manage conflicts and violence in marital and nonmarital relationships, and how to improve relational satisfaction and the quality of life of couples.

A unique feature here is comprehensive attention to the formation, development, enrichment, and maintenance of intimate relationships. There is also a focus on the implications of intimate relationships for health, well-being, and happiness throughout people's lifespan, across cultures and gender. Integrated, evidenced-based, and cutting-edge information is provided on almost all aspects of intimate relationships including concepts, history, theory, research methods and tools of measurement, major components, communication, formation, development, maintenance, conflict, violence, abuse, maladjustment, depression, deterioration, dissolution, reconstruction, and enrichment of marital and nonmarital intimate relationships over the lifespan across cultures and gender.

The chapters are organized in such a way to impart information about the origin, formation, development, enrichment, and maintenance of intimate relationships sequentially, systematically, and coherently.

Chapters 1 through 4 present information about the origin and meaning of intimacy, elements of intimacy, definition of intimate relationships, dynamics and dimensions of intimate relationships; major concepts of research, operational definition of concepts, types of research, research designs, characteristics of scientific research; various aspects of intimate relationships across the lifespan from childhood through old age; and historical and theoretical perspectives of intimate relationships including psychoanalytic theory, psychosocial theory, humanistic theory, and bio-ecological theory.

Chapters 5 and 6 focus on interpersonal acceptance-rejection theory and attachment theory including origin and basic tenets, and implications of these two theories on intimate relationship research; and reviews intimate relationship research literature and adult intimate relationship measures in interpersonal acceptance-rejection theory and attachment theory.

Chapters 7 and 8 address issues relating to communication in intimate relationships, especially characteristics of effective communication, and techniques for removing barriers to effective communication; and foundations, determinants, and types of attraction in intimate relationships for people across age, gender, and cultures.

Chapters 9 through 11 contain discussions about the foundations of intimate relationships including friendship, love, and sexuality; basis and components of friendship, and characteristics of a good friend; components and patterns of love, individual differences in love, and different perspectives on love; and sexuality including sexual attitudes and behavior across cultures, gender, and the lifespan.

Chapters 12 and 13 include discussions about intimate relationships in marital and alternative lifestyles including marital quality, satisfaction, happiness, and determinants of stable marriage; causes, correlates, and consequences of divorce; and intimate relationships in cohabiting, lesbian, gay, bisexual, and transgender relationships.

Chapters 14 through 16 focus on conflict, abuse, and violence in intimate relationships; deterioration and loss of intimate relationships; and reconstruction, enrichment, and maintenance of intimate relationships.

Acknowledgments

This book is the outcome of encouragement, support, and help of a number of individuals. I wish to express my deepest appreciation to all of them. I am deeply grateful to Professor Ronald P. Rohner for his generous support and valuable guidance from beginning through the completion of this book. He provided me with countless suggestions to improve the quality of the book. His devotion and commitment to the highest quality of scientific work encouraged me to reach my potential for excellence in this work. I am especially grateful to him for writing the Foreword.

Nancy Rohner, Sumbleen Ali, Carla Gomez, and Janice Berriault deserve thanks for their technical help and support for preparing tables and figures for this book. Sumbleen deserves special thanks for preparing several figures. I am also thankful to researchers and scholars whose research works are cited to make this book evidenced-based and informative. They are too numerous to acknowledge individually. I would like to thank Kevin Downing, editorial director, and Debbie Carvalko, senior acquisitions editor, ABC-CLIO/Praeger Publishers, for their vital help and support in producing this book.

Last but not certainly the least, I am indebted to my wife, Ferdous Jahan, for her understanding, support, and sacrifices. She shared the burden of this work with me more than anyone else. Above all, I am thankful to Almighty God for His infinite mercy that enabled me to complete this work.

My efforts for completing this project will be successful, if students, teachers, researchers, and practitioners find this book to be a useful resource for learning, teaching, research, and application. Finally, I hope that readers enjoy the book.

CHAPTER ONE

Introduction

Origin and Meaning of Intimacy

The word *intimacy* originates from the Latin word "intimus," which means the most internal or deepest nature of loving relationships between two individuals. Intimacy, generally, refers to very close or deep personal relationships between two individuals marked by emotional attachment, warmth, affection, and love.

Elements of Intimacy

The essential elements of intimacy include emotional attachment and close personal relationships characterized by close physical, psychological, and social contact; friendliness, positive attitudes, mutual cherishing, appreciation, and interest; intense likings, feeling of warmth, affection, care, and concern for the loved ones; and responsiveness to one another's needs (Mikulincer & Shaver, 2008; Prager et al., 2013; Rohner, 2008). In addition, they include mutual self-disclosure, unreserved communication, trust, confidence, commitment, interdependence, mutual acceptance, feelings of pleasure when together with the partner, and feelings of distress when separated (Berscheid, Snyder, & Omoto, 2004; Collins & Miller, 1994; Hazan & Shaver, 1987; Mikulincer & Shaver, 2007).

Douglas and Heer (2013) have broken down intimacy into the following five elements:

1. *Honor.* Showing honor to one's intimate partner means treating him/her with due regard and respect. Not to say or do anything that may harm his/her

self-esteem. Respecting partner's opinions, values, beliefs, and faiths regardless of whether they are similar to or different from one's own (Simpson, 2007a).

2. *Trust.* Believing in the honesty, integrity, and sincerity of the intimate partner. However, trust does not necessarily mean blind faith. But baseless suspicion is harmful to developing trust between partners. Trust depends on the confidence that the partner will do and choose what is right for both of them and will not deceive (Reis, 2014).

3. *Allowance.* Allowance means believing in the freedom of thought, expression, and activities of the intimate partner. Allowing to let the partner live his/her life the way he/she chooses, and accepting different viewpoints with an open mind. Allowance means not to try to control the partner, to let the partner be his/her own self with a unique sense of identity.

4. *Vulnerability.* Vulnerability means not to create any barriers between partners. That means not to try to separate or defend good or bad habits or behaviors of the partner, but rather accept the partner in totality and have free and fair communion with him/her.

5. *Gratitude.* Gratitude means showing gratefulness to one's partner for who he/she is, and for what he/she does, taking care of the partner as an enjoyable attachment figure without expecting any return, and focusing more on giving to the partner than on getting in return from the partner.

Intimate Relationships

An intimate relationship refers to an individual's emotionally close and deep personal relationship with a partner. This is a kind of attachment relationship that is characterized by mutual love, affection, care, concern, sense of happiness, well-being, and emotional security between intimate partners. An intimate partner is a significant other as well as an attachment figure (Khaleque, 2001).

Significant other. Significant others are individuals with whom one has a relatively long-lasting and important emotional bond. The significant other is viewed as a unique, irreplaceable person, interchangeable with no one else (Rohner, 2005; Rohner & Khaleque, 2010).

Attachment figure. An attachment figure refers to a person with whom one has a uniquely important emotional bond like significant others, but also where the individual's sense of emotional security, comfort, and well-being are dependent to some degree on the quality of the relationship (positive or negative relationship) with his/her attachment figure (Ainsworth, 1989, 1991).

Note that the significant other and attachment figure are overlapping concepts with one major distinction between them. Specifically, the two social categories are hierarchically arranged so that the concept of an attachment figure contains all the defining attributes of a significant other, plus one additional attribute. That is, in an attachment relationship one's sense of well-being, emotional security, and happiness are dependent to some degree on the perceived quality of the relationship with one's attachment figure. But this is not true of a significant other. Thus all attachment figures are also significant others, but not all significant others are attachment figures (Khaleque, 2001; Rohner & Khaleque, 2008).

Dynamics and Dimensions of Intimate Relationships

As intimate relationships develop over individuals' lifespan, the nature of relationships changes from casual to close, and the relationships become increasingly multidimensional. Several authors (Cassidy & Shaver, 2008; Feeney, 2008) have suggested that the following changes take place as the relationship become close:

1. Frequency, duration and settings of interaction increase.
2. Individuals gain more in-depth knowledge about the personality and behavior of partners.
3. Individuals become more skilled in identifying and predicting partners' opinions and behaviors.
4. Individuals increase their investment in the intimate relationship.
5. Interdependence and sense of belongingness to one another increase.
6. Partners start feeling that their separate interests are inextricably linked to the outcome of their relationship.
7. The magnitude of positive feeling toward one another such as liking, loving, caring, commitment, and trust increases.
8. Partners increasingly like to stay in close proximity and avoid separation.
9. Partners perceive their relationships as unique and irreplaceable.

Dimensions of Intimate Relationships

Several authors have suggested that as intimacy grows, the dimensions of intimate relationships expand to the following domains of life (Augsburger, 1988; Chapman, 2004; Rohner & Khaleque, 2005):

Physical intimacy. Physical intimacy includes a variety of physical interactions between partners such as hugging, kissing, fondling, caressing, and other sexual activities. But physical intimacy is neither limited to sexual intercourse nor ends with it. This is much more than just sexual intercourse, because individuals' sexual potency and performance can diminish due to physical and psychological problems, ill health, and old age. Despite these problems, physical intimacy between partners can continue lifelong.

Emotional intimacy. Emotional intimacy refers to positive attachment bonds expressed through feelings and behaviors characterized by warmth, affection, love, care, concern, and support for one another. Emotional intimacy is also revealed by the spontaneity, comfort, and ease with which a partner is able to respond emotionally to another partner. The degree of comfort and mutual experience of closeness might indicate the magnitude of emotional intimacy between partners. Emotional intimacy is a psychological phenomenon that can be achieved when the level of trust and communication between two partners are such that it fosters the mutual sharing of one another's deepest selves. Emotional intimacy depends mainly on trust, and confidence that the partners can share their dreams, and positive and negative characteristics without the fear of losing emotional intimacy. Emotional intimacy is different from sexual intimacy. Because sexual intimacy can take place with or without emotional intimacy. Similarly, emotional intimacy can also occur with or without sexual intimacy. Partners may come across tough moments in life when intimate relationships can be at a breaking point. But this risk can be overcome with patience and sincere communication of feelings to show how much each partner cares for the other (Reis, 2013).

Intellectual intimacy. This form of intimacy is also called cognitive intimacy, where intimate partners exchange opinions, share thoughts and ideas with open minds, and accept and enjoy similarities and differences between their viewpoints. If partners interact comfortably in creative and problem-solving activities, they can develop good intellectual intimacy.

Spiritual intimacy. This kind of intimacy depends on sharing and practicing common faiths, beliefs, and values, and working together to develop intimacy through spiritual growth. However, if religious and spiritual beliefs of partners are different, they should respect and appreciate each other's spiritual needs, beliefs, and values.

Parenting intimacy. When intimate partners become parents, their intimate relationships enter into a new phase called parenting intimacy. Parenting intimacy largely depends on performing shared responsibilities of parenting duties by being supportive to each other while helping the child to grow in socially desirable ways. Parenting is a process that includes nourishing, protecting, and guiding the child through the course of development jointly by both parents. Parents should provide the child with self-help skills, age appropriate toilet training, and social and intellectual learning. Parenting intimacy grows if parents help each other in performing these duties.

Work intimacy. This kind of intimacy involves helping the partner in maintaining the home, family income and expenses, and social and occupational activities. Supporting each other in achieving common goals can lead to a high work intimacy between partners.

Conflict and crisis management intimacy. This kind of intimacy depends on partners' attitude and ability to compromise and sort out differences in a fair and amicable way, and reach mutually agreeable and satisfactory solutions, especially in time of family crisis. The most important factor that can enhance conflict and crisis management intimacy is recognizing and accepting the fact that there are no perfect solutions to human problems.

Play intimacy. Play intimacy depends on partners' ability to have fun together through recreation, humor, and relaxation in home or out of home during vacation.

Aesthetic intimacy. This intimacy depends on enjoying and supporting each other's aesthetic pleasures. Aesthetic intimacy can be obtained from listening to music, visiting museums and historic places, viewing arts and natural scenes, and so on.

Finally, the nature and dynamics of intimate relationships are very complex. All the components discussed previously are not absolutely essential for intimate relationships to occur. These components are not mutually interdependent. Intimate relationships can occur and exist even in the absence of some components. Generally, intimacy exists to a higher degree when a greater number of components are present and to a lesser degree when a smaller number of components are present (Fletcher & Kerr, 2013).

Fear of Intimacy

The concept fear of intimacy (FOI) refers to a psychological condition where an individual is afraid of forming or anxious about forming an intimate relationship with another individual who is significantly important to her/him. According to interpersonal acceptance-rejection theory (IPARTheory), FOI refers to an individual's anxiousness or reluctance about disclosing and exchanging deeply personal thoughts and feelings with a significant other with whom the individual has a significant emotional tie, who is uniquely important to the individual, and exchangeable with no one else (Rohner, 2005).

According to Sherman and Thelen (1996), fear of intimacy involves three essential elements:

1. **Communication.** Exchange of deeply personal information between partners.
2. **Strong feelings.** Partners have very close or deep personal relationship characterized by emotional attachment, warmth, affection, and love.
3. **Unique importance.** Each partner is uniquely important to the other and exchangeable with no one else.

Descutner and Thelen (1991) reported that individuals who are high in FOI are more likely to be psychologically maladjusted, anxious, depressed, and to have low self-esteem than individuals who are low in FOI. Similarly, evidence from IPARTheory-based research has shown that adults' remembered childhood rejection tends worldwide to be not only related with many of the problems reported by Descutner and Thelen, but also with negative self-adequacy, anger, emotional unresponsiveness, emotional instability, dependence, and negative world view (Khaleque & Rohner, 2012; Rohner & Britner, 2002). In addition, a number of studies conducted in different countries including Bangladesh (Uddin et al., 2016), Croatia (Glavak-Tkalic, Vulic-Prtoric, & Zoroja, 2016), Greece (Giovazolias & Goitsa, 2016), Pakistan (Butt, Malik, & Faran, 2016), and the United States (Lindsey & Khan, 2016) showed that experiences and memories of parental rejection in childhood have significant relations with fear of intimacy, psychological maladjustment, and anxiety of adults in these countries. Moreover, remembered parental rejection and psychological maladjustment of adults have independent effects on their fear of intimacy, and in most cases psychological maladjustment and relational anxiety mediated the relationship between parental rejection and fear of intimacy.

Correlates of Intimate Relationships

Some of the important factors that have been found to have significant association with intimate relationships are culture, ethnicity, personality, experience, and gender. The patterns of association between intimate relationships and these factors are discussed in somewhat more detail in the following section.

Culture and Ethnicity

Several researchers have indicated that cultural background, cultural values, and attachment styles have a profound impact on the way people think, feel, and behave in intimate relationships (Hatfield & Rapson, 2005, 2010; Schmitt, 2008). Research findings have also revealed that culture and ethnicity have a significant impact on people's romantic preferences, comfort in romantic commitments, and on the reaction and behavior in marital and nonmarital romantic relationships (Hatfield & Rapson, 2010). In a landmark study of 17,000 men and women from 56 nations, Schmitt (2008) found that most people in most cultures claim to have a secure attachment style. In another study on Americans, Russians, and Japanese, Sprecher et al. (1994) found that in all three cultures, men and women generally identified themselves as secure in their love relationships. Doherty and colleagues (1994), who interviewed Americans of Chinese, European, Japanese, and Pacific Islander ancestry, found similar results. Culture also does have some impact on how men and women classify themselves as secure or insecure in their attachment relationships. Sprecher et al. (1994), for example, found that American men are more likely than Russian or Japanese men to possess a secure attachment schema. On the other hand, Japanese women are more likely to possess secure schemas than do Russian women.

Schmitt (2008) suggested that insecure romantic attachments were most prevalent in societies afflicted with political, economic and social uncertainties, where quality of life is poor and life expectancy is low. Chisholm (1999) tried to provide an evolutionary explanation for socio-cultural differences in people's love schemas. He argued that in affluent cultures with abundant resources, people can afford to plan to invest in long-term secure romantic attachments, monogamy, and a small number of high-quality offspring. By contrast, in cultures characterized with poverty, people are forced to adapt to short-term temporal horizons. In such societies, the optimal mating strategy is to engage in promiscuous sexual affairs, to reproduce more children in short time, and to invest minimally in any single romantic relationship. But this explanation is not supported by current evidence. For example, the United States, an economically affluent country, has a very high divorce rate. Currently, about 50 percent of marriages in the United States end in divorce each year (Cruz, 2013). Only about 65 percent of married couples in the United States stay together for about 10 years, and the average length of marriage is only 18 years (Elliot & Simmons, 2011).

Personality Characteristics

According to Freud (1949), a human being's first intimate relationship is the mother-child bond during infancy through the act of breast-feeding, which has a profound influence on shaping individuals' personality throughout the lifespan. Although Freud focused more on the impact of early parent-child relationships on the development of abnormal personality, a couple of other theorists including Bowlby and Ainsworth (pioneers of attachment theory), and Rohner (pioneer of interpersonal acceptance-rejection theory) have predicted that childhood experiences of attachment and love by parents shape individuals' whole range of personality characteristics throughout the lifespan. Attachment theory postulates that child-parent secure attachment relationship leads to the development of positive personality characteristics of an individual (Ainsworth & Bowlby, 1991). Note- that attachment theory and interpersonal acceptance-rejection theory (IPARTheory) are discussed extensively in Chapter 5.

Interpersonal acceptance-rejection theory postulates that parental acceptance or love is likely to lead to the development of psychological adjustment and positive personality dispositions, and parental rejection or love withdrawal is likely to lead to the development of psychological maladjustment and negative personality dispositions in children (Rohner, 1986/2000; Rohner & Khaleque, 2015). In particular, the personality subtheory of the IPARTheory postulates that children, adolescents, and adult offspring who perceive themselves to be accepted or loved by their parents are likely to develop (1) low hostility and aggression, (2) independence, (3) positive self-esteem, (4) positive self-adequacy, (5) emotional stability, (6) emotional responsiveness, and (7) positive worldview. A meta-analysis was performed to test if children's perceptions of parental warmth or love were related to their positive personality dispositions (Khaleque, 2013a). The meta-analysis was based on 30 studies from 16 countries in five continents involving 12,087 children. Results showed that perceived parental warmth/affection correlated significantly with all seven of the postulated positive personality dispositions of children across ethnicities, cultures, gender, and geographical boundaries.

On the other hand, the subtheory postulates that children who perceive themselves to be rejected or not loved by their parents are likely to develop (1) hostility and aggression, (2) dependence or defensive independence, (3) negative self-esteem, (4) negative self-adequacy, (5) emotional instability, (6) emotional unresponsiveness, and (7) negative worldview. Results of another meta-analysis based on 33 studies from 15 countries in four continents involving 11,755 children showed that perceived maternal and paternal indifference and neglect correlated significantly with negative personality dispositions of children across cultures (Khaleque, 2015c). Findings of another meta-analysis based on 36 studies involving 8,573 children and 1,370 adults from 18 countries showed that both maternal and paternal acceptance in childhood correlated significantly in all countries with almost all of the seven personality dispositions of children and adult offspring (Khaleque & Rohner, 2011).

Several researchers found that quality of interpersonal relationships often varies because of variations in individuals' personality dispositions and behavioral functioning (Kandler, 2012; Soto et al., 2011). People characterized with extraverted, agreeable, conscientious, and friendly personality traits tend to have happier relationships with their partners (Hill, Nickel, & Roberts, 2014).

Personal Experiences

According to attachment theory, the parent-infant attachment relationship is critical for the subsequent cognitive and socioemotional development of children (Ainsworth & Bowlby, 1991). Attachment theory proposes that the following four types of parent-child attachment relationships have a profound influence on children's socioemotional and interpersonal relationships development.

The types of attachments are as follows: (1) secure-attachment (mothers/ primary caregivers who foster security are more responsive), (2) insecure attachment (mothers/caregivers whose behaviors foster insecurity are less responsive), (3) avoidant attachment (insecure attachment) in which the children show little separation anxiety, and (4) ambivalent attachment in which children show both likes and dislikes for parents. Children with secure attachment tend to develop positive psychosocial characteristics, and children with insecure attachment tend to develop negative psychological characteristics. Prompt and consistent attention and response from parents or caregivers to the children's needs and comforts during the first three months help the development of basic trust between parents and children (Bowlby, 1994). The child's degree of trust about parents, other people, and the world at large depends, to a considerable extent, on the quality of care he/she receives during the first year of life (Erikson, 1950/1963). For example, the infants whose needs are met when they arise, discomforts are quickly removed, and who are fondled and played with develop a feeling that the environment is safe and the people around them are dependable.

Parental acceptance-rejection has a profound influence in shaping children's personality development over the lifespan. A meta-analysis showed that regardless of culture, ethnicity, or geographic location, approximately 26 percent of the variability in children's psychological well-being and 21 percent of the variability in adults' psychological well-being are accounted for by perceived parental acceptance-rejection (Khaleque & Rohner, 2002a). Experience of parental rejection is expected to lead to negative personality outcomes in children and adults including hostility, aggression, dependence, impaired self-esteem, impaired self-adequacy, emotional unresponsiveness, emotional instability, and negative worldview. Rejected children are likely to feel anxious and insecure (Khaleque, 2017a).

Effects of rejection are apt to linger into adulthood, placing people at greater risk of social and emotional problems throughout life (Rohner & Khaleque, 2015). Nearly 80 percent of children and adults—irrespective of geographic location, race, and ethnicity—tend to be negatively affected by the experience of parental rejection (Khaleque & Rohner, 2002a, 2012; Rohner & Khaleque, 2015). A study on Finnish adults' experience of partner acceptance and partner control showed that controlling intimate partners are perceived to be less accepting than more permissive intimate partners, and more accepting and less controlling intimate partners are perceived to provide more emotional security than less accepting and more controlling intimate partners (Khaleque, Rohner, & Laukkala, 2008). Recent reviews showed that adult intimate relationships have significant impact on the psychological adjustment and well-being of partners (Cassidy & Shaver, 1999; Rohner & Khaleque, 2010). Psychological and behavioral outcomes of intimate relationship problems are found in adults who have difficulty in forming and maintaining intimate relationships (Hendrick & Hendrick, 2000). Individuals often experience negative consequences of disrupted intimate relationships on their mental health and well-being (Roberts & Pragner, 1997; Rohner, 2008). Since intimate relationships satisfy certain psychological needs, individuals who are not involved in such relationships are likely to feel lonely, anxious, or depressed (Solano, 1986). Several empirical studies show that disrupted intimate adult relationships tend to make individuals susceptible to many psychological problems including stress, anxiety, substance abuse, suicide, and other forms of psychopathology (Bloom, Asher, & White, 1978; Goodwin et al., 1987; Lynch, 1977; Uchino, Cacioppo, & Kielcolt-Glaser, 1996). Experience of perceived rejection by a partner has been found to be associated with adult women's poor quality of life (Khaleque, 2004).

Gender Difference

Gender differences refer to psychological, social, and behavioral differences between men and women within any single culture and between different cultures (Muchlenhard & Peterson, 2011). In intimate relationships—like any other interpersonal relationships—power, position, role, status, and expectations of men and women may be quite different.

An increasing number of studies show that perceived paternal acceptance often has as strong as or even stronger implications than perceived maternal acceptance for children's positive developmental outcomes, including psychological adjustment and behavioral functioning (Rohner & Veneziano, 2001). Results of a recent meta-analytic review based on 66 studies involving 19,511 respondents from 22 countries in five continents showed that father love tends to have a significantly stronger relationship with children's psychological adjustment than the relationship between mother love and children's psychological adjustment cross-culturally (Khaleque & Rohner, 2012). Moreover, in a review of a large number of cross-cultural studies, Rohner and Britner (2002) found that perceived paternal rejection tends to have stronger negative implications than perceived maternal rejection for the development of depression, conduct disorder, and substance abuse. On the other hand, some studies have indicated that maternal acceptance-rejection sometimes has significantly stronger implications for children's psychological adjustment, personality, and behavioral development than paternal acceptance-rejection (e.g., Ripoll-Nunez & Alvarez, 2008; Rohner et al., 2008). A meta-analytic review has shown that both paternal and maternal acceptance-rejection often make independent contributions to the psychological adjustment and personality development of children (Khaleque, 2013a).

From the previously mentioned research findings it remains unclear why father love sometimes has a stronger influence on offspring's psychological adjustment than mother love, why in other cases just the opposite is true, and still in other cases why both parents appear to make approximately equal contributions to offspring's adjustment and development? Some researchers have suggested that children's perceptions of differences in their parents' interpersonal power and prestige in the family may explain the differential outcomes of paternal and maternal acceptance-rejection on children's psychological adjustment and personality development (Rohner & Veneziano, 2001; Sultana & Khaleque, 2016; Veneziano, 2008; Wentzel & Feldman, 1996).

To address this issue, an international research project in 11 different countries of the world, including Bangladesh, China, Croatia, Greece,

Korea, Pakistan, Poland, Portugal, Spain, Turkey, and the United Kingdom, was conducted under the title International Father Acceptance-Rejection Project (Rohner, 2014). Results showed that adults in 6 of the 11 nations reported that their social systems were more or less patriarchal (i.e., institutionalized gender inequality), where a woman's primary role is to maintain family, rear children, and to give social-emotional support to family members. On the contrary, a male member, generally a father, is the undisputed head of the family, who controls resources and enjoys more power and prestige in the family as well as in the society. These countries are Bangladesh, China, Korea, Pakistan, Portugal, and Turkey. Adults in the other five countries considered their countries as being more-or-less egalitarian (having gender equity). These include Croatia, Greece, Poland (marginal), Spain, and the United Kingdom. Results also showed males and females within a given country differed significantly in their perceptions of parental power. For example, in Crete (Greece), Poland, Portugal, and Turkey, males reported both parents as being approximately equal in interpersonal power, but females reported their mothers as having somewhat more power than their fathers. In all the other countries males and females perceived both parents to be approximately equal in interpersonal power and prestige.

Results of this analysis revealed that both parents made independent contributions to the psychological adjustment of male and female offspring in six countries. These include Bangladesh, Croatia, Pakistan, Portugal, Spain, and the United Kingdom. Both parents also made independent contributions to the adjustment of adult sons (but not of daughters) in China and Crete (Greece). Interestingly, only mothers made independent contribution to daughters' adjustment in Crete (Greece) and Turkey. Finally, only mothers' acceptance contributed uniquely to the adjustment of both sons and daughters in Korea, whereas only fathers' acceptance did this in Poland. These results confirm conclusions that sometimes only mothers' love-related behaviors are significantly associated with variations in offspring's psychological adjustment, whereas in other instances, it is only fathers' love-related behaviors that are associated with offspring adjustment (Rohner, 1998; Rohner & Veneziano, 2001). But in the majority of cases, the love-related behaviors of both parents are independently associated with offspring's adjustment (Rohner, 2014).

As noted earlier that not only power and position, and role and status, but also attitudes, beliefs, values, and expectations of men and women in interpersonal relationships including friendship, love, and marriage can be quite different. Cultural norms, roles, and sense of identity generally vary according to gender. Gender roles refer to cultural norms or expectations for appropriate male and female behavior, interest, attitudes, and personality traits. Gender identity refers to the awareness of what it means to be a male or a female in a society. Traditionally, men are expected to develop masculine characteristics such as active, assertive, aggressive, autonomous, and dominant. Women are expected to develop feminine characteristics such as emotional, nurturing, submissive, and empathic (Kite, Deaux, & Haines, 2008). According to Bem (1993), people of both sexes have a mixture of masculinity and femininity. Bem places people in one of the four categories in terms of personality characteristics:

Masculine. Having predominantly manly characteristics.
Feminine. Having predominantly womanly characteristics.
Androgynous. High in both masculinity and femininity.
Undifferentiated. Low in both masculinity and femininity.

Figure 1.1 shows different combinations of masculinity and femininity. However, regardless of gender, some people can be high in some typical

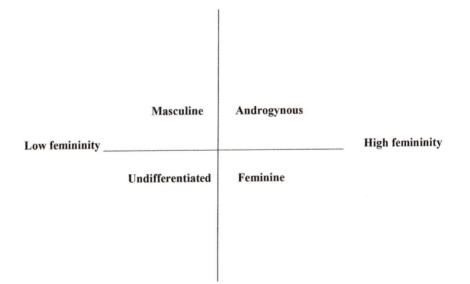

Figure 1.1   Mixture of Masculinity and Femininity (Adapted from Bem, 1993)

masculine characteristics and low in some typical feminine characteristics and vice versa (Choi, Fuqua, & Newman, 2007). There is considerable evidence that people become more androgynous in midlife. Middle-aged men tend to be more open about feelings, more interested in intimate relationships, and more nurturing than young men. Middle-aged women tend to be more assertive, active, self-confident, and achievement oriented than young women (Costa & McCrae, 1994).

Several researchers have suggested that regardless of cultures, women typically tend to be more caring, express more emotion, and define themselves more in terms of relations than men. Men and women also tend to differ in social dominance and aggression. For example, men's communicating style reflects concern for social power and dominance, whereas women's communicating style reflects connectedness and team spirit (Anderson & Leaper, 1998; Pratto et al., 1997). Concerning aggressive activities, men have about 20 times higher record of aggressive activities than do women globally (Daly & Wilson, 1989). In the United States, the man-to-woman arrest rate is 9 to 1 for murder, and 4 to 1 for assault (U.S. Census Bureau, 2000). Men and women also differ in attitudes and behaviors about friendship, love, and sexuality (Clark & Hatfield, 2003). For example, women typically have more intimate friends than men and may share more personal information with friends than do men. On the other hand, men are more likely to share professional but not confidential personal matters with friends (Rosenbluth & Steil, 1995). About sexual attitudes and behavior, one study showed that approximately 60 percent of men and only 12 percent of women born before 1910 admit to having premarital sex (Papalia, 2012). Although by the 1980s, women had nearly as much premarital sexual experience as did men (Smith, 1994). Yet another study showed that 48 percent of men and 12 percent of women reported that they feel comfortable and enjoy casual sex with different partners. Results of a review of 177 studies on an aggregate sample of 130,000 revealed that men are much more willing to accept casual sex than women (Oliver & Hyde, 1993). In a recent study on a multicultural sample, men were found more likely than women to accept sexual offers (Tappé et al., 2013). Men and women also have different expectations about intimacy, sex, and marriage. For example, to women marital intimacy entails sharing of emotional feelings, trust, and confidence, but men tend to express intimacy through sex and practical help (Thompson & Walker, 1989). A similar trend in gender difference is found in adolescents' intimacy, love, and sexual behavior. Generally, adolescent girls are less permissive about premarital sex than boys; and unlike adolescent boys, girls prefer to stick to a single partner with whom they have an intimate relationship. Teenage girls tend to give more emphasis on the quality of intimate relationships before sexual intercourse occurs. But teenage boys are more likely than teenage girls to separate sex from love (Wilson & Medora, 1990).

Gender stereotypes and traditional roles of men and women have important implications for building intimate relationships because they often create more incompatibility than compatibility in the relationships between partners (Ickes, 1993). A review of research on relationships between traditional gender-role adherence and sexuality for heterosexual men and women revealed negative effects of traditional gender-role adherence for couples' romantic relationships, particularly for women's sexual problems and satisfaction (Sanchez, Fetterolf, & Rudman, 2012). Spouses who adhere to stereotyped gender roles are generally less happy in their marital relationships than spouses who follow nontraditional gender roles (Helms et al., 2006; Marshall, 2010). However, due to gradual social changes, especially in the United States, young men and women are increasingly becoming more egalitarian than middle-aged and aging men and women (Parker & Wang, 2013).

CHAPTER SUMMARY

Chapter 1 focuses on the origin and meaning of intimacy, elements of intimacy, definition of intimate relationships, dynamics and dimensions of intimate relationships, fear of intimacy, and correlates of intimate relationships including culture, ethnicity, personality, and gender.

Origin and meaning of intimacy. The word *intimacy* originates from the Latin word "intimus," which means deepest loving relationships between two individuals.

Elements of intimacy. The core components of intimacy include emotional attachment and deep personal relationships characterized by close physical, psychological, and social contact; and intense feeling of warmth, affection, care, and concern for loved ones.

Intimate relationship. This is a kind of attachment relationship, characterized by mutual love, affection, care, concern, and emotional security between intimate partners. An intimate partner is a significant other as well as an attachment figure.

Dimensions of intimate relationship. As intimacy grows, the dimensions of an intimate relationship expand to different domains of life including physical, psychological, and social.

Fear of intimacy. It is a psychological condition of being afraid of forming an intimate relationship with any individuals.

Correlates of intimate relationship. Culture, ethnicity, personality, and gender are some of the important correlates of an intimate relationship.

REFLECTIVE QUESTIONS

1. Define intimate relationship. Discuss the origin, meaning, and elements of intimacy.

2. Explain how dimensions of intimate relationships grow with the level of intimacy.

3. How do cultural background, cultural values, and attachment styles impact the way people think, feel, and behave in an intimate relationship?

4. How do different types of parent-child attachment relationships influence socioemotional and interpersonal relationship development in childhood and adulthood?

5. How are different combinations of masculinity and femininity related with different attitudes and behaviors about friendship, love, and sexuality?

CHAPTER TWO

Research Methods

This chapter discusses the fundamentals of social research methods and procedures. It contains clear and concise description of research methods. As a relational science, intimate relationship researchers use more or less the same methods used in other social sciences research. However, descriptions and discussions about specific measures of intimate relationships are provided in Chapter 6.

Major Concepts

Here are the major concepts of research:

Research. A research generally refers to a systematic study or investigation in some fields of knowledge, which is undertaken to discover, explain, and establish facts or principles or a theory.

Behavioral research. This type of research is concerned with investigation or study that aims at understanding and explaining behavior.

Research methods. Research methods refer to procedures and techniques applied to conduct a research.

Research design. Research design is an overall detailed plan for obtaining, analyzing, and interpreting research data.

Characteristics of Research

A scientific research has the following basic characteristics:

Objectivity. A scientific research is intended to find unbiased evidence or facts.

Verifiability. Findings of a scientific research can be verified through repetition or replication.

Reliability. Reliability refers to the consistency of a research measures and findings. A scientific research provides more or less similar findings if it is repeated or replicated. There are four major types of reliability: (1) *Interrater reliability* is a measure of the degree to which different raters give consistent estimates of the same phenomenon. (2) *Test-retest reliability* is an assessment of the consistency of a measure used at different times. (3) *Parallel-forms reliability* is used to assess the consistency of the results of two tests or questionnaires constructed from the same content domain. (4) *Internal consistency reliability* is used to assess the consistency of results across items within a questionnaire or a test.

Validity. Validity refers to the accuracy of a research. Validity is an indication of how sound a research is including its design, method, measures, data analysis, and findings. Major types of validity are: (1) *Face validity* is an indication of apparent validity of a measure. It is concerned with the query, whether a test or a questionnaire appears to measure what it is intended to measure. It is a crude form of validity. (2) *Content validity* is an index of how relevant is the content of a questionnaire or a test to what it intends to measure. (3) *Construct validity* is an indication of whether a measure truly reflects the underlying concepts or constructs. (4) *Predictive validity* refers to the correlation between a test score and a criterion measure. For example, if a test accurately predicts academic performance or job performance of a target group. (5) *Convergent validity* refers to the degree to which two measures of constructs that should be theoretically related are in fact related. (6) *Discriminant validity* refers to the degree to which two measures of constructs that are not supposed to be related are, in fact, unrelated.

Research Objectives

Any scientific research, especially behavioral research, has five objectives or goals. These are to:

1. describe behavior;
2. determine the causes of behavior;
3. understand and explain behavior;
4. test theories, laws, and principles related to behavior; and
5. predict behavior.

Starting a Research

The motivation to start a scientific research often originates from a *natural curiosity* about something or some issues. For example, "I wonder why and how people develop pathological behavior?" This curiosity or question may be the starting point of a research on pathological behavior.

How Is Research Done?

The following steps are generally followed in doing a scientific research:

1. Asking or framing questions about any research problems.
2. Formulating a hypothesis or probable explanation.
3. Collecting data using the scientific method.
4. Analyzing data with appropriate statistical techniques.
5. Formulating or confirming a theory, based on findings.
6. Using the theory to make predictions.
7. Testing those predictions by future research.
8. Modifying the theory in the light of available results.

Research Information

There are two important sources of obtaining research information. These are:

1. **Primary sources.** Journal articles, dissertations, conference papers, research books, research monograms, etc.
2. **Secondary sources.** Handbooks of research, encyclopedias, yearbooks, scholarly books, government records, magazine and newspaper articles, etc.

Locating Sources of Information

Sources of research information can be located electronically through computer-based Internet search using PsycNET, Current Contents, Dissertation Abstract International, Social Work Abstract, Sociological Abstracts, Anthropological Literature, Sociofile, Child Development Abstracts, National Council on Family Relations, ERIC data systems, etc.

Research Topic and Proposal

For selecting a research topic and making a proposal a researcher should focus on the following points:

Steps for choosing a research topic. Topic selection process include the following steps: identification of promising topics, selection of a specific topic, and refinement of the selected topic.

Topic selection criteria. Topic selection is generally made on the basis of the following criteria: interest, importance, newness, time required, difficulty, availability of instruments, and cost involved.

Content of research proposal. Content includes introduction, literature review, statement of the problem, significance of the problem, rationale of the research, research questions or hypotheses, definitions of concepts, research methods, data collection and analyses, concluding comments about the implications of the research. If it is a funded research, the research proposal should also include duration and the budget.

Hypothesis

A hypothesis is a statement that predicts the relationships between two or more variables. Most research studies attempt to test one or more hypotheses—tentative ideas or questions that might be supported or rejected by facts or evidence. Most hypotheses are formulated on the basis of findings of past research or theory. Hypotheses can be of two types:

Experimental hypothesis. It is a statement about prediction of cause and effect relationship between two or more variables.

Nonexperimental hypothesis. It is a statement about prediction of relationships (not about a causal relationship) between at least two variables.

Characteristics of an Experimental Hypothesis

An experimental hypothesis ideally should have the following characteristics:

Synthetic statement. A statement that can be either true or false.

Testable statement. A statement that can be tested or verified.

Parsimonious statement. A statement that is simple and does not require many supporting assumptions.

Fruitful statement. A statement that leads to new ideas.

Models of Formulating a Hypothesis

There are two types of models on the basis of which hypotheses are formulated:

Inductive model. This model refers to a process of reasoning from specific cases to more general principles to formulate a hypothesis.

Deductive model. This model refers to a process of reasoning from general principles to specific instances for formulating a hypothesis.

Prediction

A prediction usually involves formation of a hypothesis.

- In formulating a hypothesis, a researcher is likely to make a specific prediction (a belief of what may happen). If the prediction is supported by the findings of the study, the hypothesis is confirmed.
- In behavioral sciences, a hypothesis is either supported or rejected, not proved or disproved.
- If the same hypothesis is supported by results of different studies at different times and in different places using different methods, the hypothesis might be accepted as a test of theory or as a general principle for explaining any issue, event, or behavior.

Types of Research

There are different types of classification of research, which are sometimes overlapping. The most common classification are:

Basic research. Basic research is done to answer fundamental questions or theoretical issues relating to human behavior and development.

Applied research. On the other hand, applied research is conducted to address issues relating to practical problems and potential solutions.

Qualitative research. This type of research is mainly based on narrative (verbal and descriptive) data. It provides more intensive (in-depth) but less extensive and less objective information than quantitative research.

Quantitative research. Quantitative research, on the other hand, is mainly based on numerical data. It provides more extensive and objective information than qualitative research. In comparison to qualitative research, quantitative research provides better precision and greater opportunity for replication.

Research Designs

A research design refers to the plan and structure of research investigation used to collect data for finding answers to research questions. The

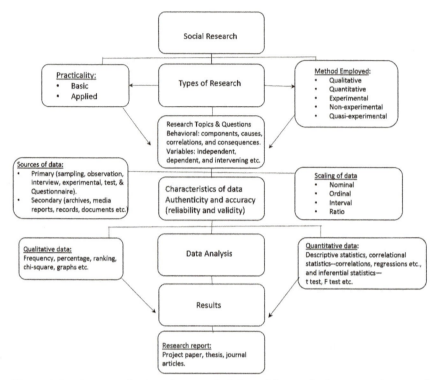

Figure 2.1   A Design for Social Research (adapted from Charles & Mertler, 2002)

design describes the procedures for conducting a study including when, how, and from whom data will be collected and how data will be analyzed? Figure 2.1 depicts a design of research in social sciences.

Major Types of Research Designs

There are five major types of research design. These are:

Experimental design. There are three types of experimental design, such as between subjects, within subjects, and mixed designs.

Quasi-experimental design. This type of design is partially experimental and partially non experimental.

Nonexperimental design. This type of design includes phenomenology, case studies, field studies, and survey research.

Qualitative design. This type of design includes ethnographic design (observation, interview, and document analysis for in-depth understanding), and analytical design (such as concept analysis, historical analysis, and legal analysis).

Quantitative design. This type of design is intended to collect large-scale numerical data in a field condition through observation or survey method including questionnaires, interviews, or both, and/or archival data from different organizations such as census report, historical records, etc.

Nonexperimental Designs

Since nonexperimental design is more common in social sciences than experimental design, this section contains a little more elaborate description of the nonexperimental design. Nonexperimental designs or approaches of research are generally used in situations where experiments are neither feasible nor desirable. Common nonexperimental approaches include phenomenology, case studies, field studies, and survey research.

Phenomenology. Phenomenology refers to the descriptions of one's own immediate experiences. Here subjective experience is the main source of data. This method has the following limitations:

• Experiences may not be accurate and objective.
• Experiences differ from person to person.
• One's experiences might not be generalizable to others.
• Phenomenology describes a behavior but cannot explain it in terms of cause and effect relationship.

Case Study. A case study is a descriptive record of an individual's experiences and behaviors kept by an outside observer or an organization. It is more objective than phenomenology. Clinical psychologists use it frequently and rely heavily on this method. Case studies can be useful sources of ideas, inferences, hypotheses, theories, and research. A case study can lead to new therapeutic techniques. This method can also be used to study rare phenomena. However, case studies often rely on retrospective data that are not always accurate.

Field Studies. A field study method is used to collect data in real-life settings. It includes a variety of techniques:

• **Naturalistic observation.** Observing behaviors as they occur spontaneously in natural settings.
• **Systematic observation.** Recording behaviors using specific rules and guidelines.

- *Participant observation.* Observing the activities of a group by becoming a part of it as an actual member of the group.

Limitations of Field Studies

Field studies have the following limitations:

- Researchers have limited control over the situations, events, or behaviors that they are observing.
- The occurrence of situations, events, or behaviors cannot be repeated for verification or reexamination.
- The observers can be biased either positively or negatively.

Survey Research

In survey research, data are collected by asking questions to a sample of individuals who are supposed to be representative of the population being studied. Techniques of data collection in a survey method include (1) questionnaires and/or (2) interviews.

Questionnaires and interviews can be of the following types:

Close-ended questions. This type of questions can be answered by saying "yes" or "no," "agree" or "disagree." Close-ended questions are more structured and easier to code and score than open-ended questions. They are also more useful when dimensions of variables are well defined.

Open-ended questions. This type of questions is designed to obtain respondents' clarifications or explanations for any opinions. Open-ended questions are less structured and more difficult to code and score. But open-ended questions are more useful than close-ended questions in getting in-depth information about people's thinking.

Mixed questions. These questions consist of a combination of both open-ended and close-ended questions.

Wording of Questions. Important considerations for wording questions include:

Simplicity. Questions should be easy to understand and reply.

Clarity or unambiguity. Respondents should easily understand what response is wanted.

Length. Questions should not take a great deal of time to respond.

Loaded questions. Questions should not lead to a negative or a hurtful emotional effect.

Administration of Questionnaires. A questionnaire can be administered in any one or a combination of the following ways:

Group administration. A questionnaire can be administered in a group situation such as in a class of students or in a meeting of a group of employees. A researcher or a representative of the researcher is usually present during administration, so that respondents can ask questions and she/he can explain that.

Mail survey. In a mail survey, questionnaires are sent by mail to a listed group of respondents. But a mail survey has a low response rate, and no one is present to help if the questions are not clear.

Internet survey. This is an online survey technique. An online survey is a less expensive and quicker procedure than a mail survey.

Interviews

Interviews are a direct method of data collection, but they are more expensive and time consuming than other methods. There are different types of interviews:

- Face-to-face interviews
- Telephone interviews
- Online interviews
- Focus group interviews—consist of a group of about 6 to 10 people who are selected because they have specific knowledge or interest in the topic that the researcher is studying

Variables

A variable refers to a factor that can vary or change in ways that can be observed, measured, and verified. A variable is any event, situation, or behavior that has at least two levels or values. For example, the variable gender has two levels (male and female); the variable social class has three levels (upper class, middle class, and lower class); and a numeric variable can have many levels (e.g., from 0 to 100).

Categories of Variables

One type of classification of variables in social sciences are (1) independent variable, (2) dependent variable, and (3) intervening or mediating variable. Another type of classification of variables are (1) situational variable—the characteristics of a condition or environment (such as size of the classroom); (2) response variable—behavior or reaction of an individual; (3) participant or respondent variable—characteristics of participants; and (4) mediating variable—a process that influences a particular response. For example, helping behavior may be influenced by gender and acquaintance.

Operational Definition of Variables

Variables can be defined operationally in terms of the operations or techniques that a researcher uses to measure or manipulate behaviors, situations, or events. For example, cognitive task performance may be operationally defined by the number of words correctly remembered, or the number of mathematical problems correctly solved.

Need for an Operational Definition

An operational definition is needed for the following purposes:

- Defining abstract concepts in concrete terms.
- Clarity of concepts, because concepts that are vague can't be measured.
- Communicating ideas clearly and precisely with others.

Measurement of Variables

Variables can be measured by using one of the four types of the following scales:

Nominal scale. It is the lowest level of measurement. It classifies items into different distinct categories such as Black, Hispanic, and White.

Ordinal scale. This scale refers to a measure of magnitude in which each value is measured in the form of ranks.

Interval scale. In this scale measurement of magnitudes have equal intervals between values but no true zero point.

Ratio scale. In this scale measurement of magnitudes have equal intervals between values having a true zero point.

Relationships between Variables

Relationships between two variables (having values along a numeric scale) can be of four types:

Positive linear relationship. This relationship exists when two variables vary in the same direction (increase or decrease together). When the values of two variables increase together or decrease together, they indicate a positive linear relationship. For example, if marital satisfaction increases, the stability of marriage also increases.

Negative linear relationship. When increases in values of one variable are accompanied by decreases in values of the other variable and vice versa, they indicate a negative linear relationship. Here two variables vary in the opposite directions. For example, if the rate of marital satisfaction increases, the divorce rate decreases.

Curvilinear relationship. In a curvilinear relationship, the data points increase together up to a certain point (like a positive relationship), and then as one increases, the other decreases (negative relationship) or vice versa, and the directions of relationship may change more than once. This type of relationship is called an inverted-U relationship. For example, the researchers have found that the relationship between motivation and performance is an inverted-U-type relationship, because both very low and very high motivations tend to be associated with low performance, and a moderate (neither too high nor too low) level of motivation is likely to be associated with high performance. This type of relationship is also called nonmonotonic functional relationship.

No relationship. When two variables neither go together in the same direction nor in the opposite direction, they are unrelated. Unrelated variables vary independently of one another. The graphic picture of two unrelated variables is a flat line.

Sources of Data

In any research study, data can be obtained from two main sources such as:

Primary source. The primary source refers to the first hand or direct source of information collected from a sample of subjects through questionnaires, psychological tests, interviews, observations, experiments, etc.

Secondary source. The secondary sources include media reports, archival data from different organizations, historical records, documents, autobiography, personal diary, etc.

Sampling

Most research projects involve sampling of participants or respondents from a population. A sample is a part or a subset of a target population.

Accuracy and generalizability of research findings largely depend on the representativeness and the size of the sample. The more representative and larger the sample is, the more accurate and generalizable the findings are likely to be.

Sampling Procedures

There are two basic sampling procedures:

Probability sampling. In a probability sampling procedure, each member of the population has an equal or a specifiable probability of being included in the sample.

Nonprobability sampling. In a nonprobability sampling procedure, the researcher does not know the probability of any particular member of the population of being included in the sample.

Types of Probability Sampling

The major types of probability samples are:

Simple random sampling. In this procedure, each and every member of the population has an equal chance of being selected in the sample. For example, if we select 100 individuals from a population of 1,000, every member of the population will have a 10 percent probability of being included in the sample.

Stratified random sampling. In this procedure, the population is divided into different subgroups or strata, then the random sampling procedure is used to select a sample from each stratum in proportion as they exist in the population. This procedure is useful to ensure that the sample will represent the numerical composition of various subgroups in the population.

Cluster sampling. In this procedure, the researchers divide the sampling areas into certain clusters (e.g., districts, counties, or zip code areas), then select a random sample from each cluster.

Nonprobability Sampling

The major types of nonprobability samples are:

Quota sampling. In this sampling procedure, a sample is selected through predetermined quotas (e.g., ethnic groups) to reflect the makeup of the population. The sample reflects the proportion of the population subgroups, but individuals are not included in the sample randomly. Therefore, the sample has low external validity.

Convenient sampling. In this procedure, respondents are selected from a group of individuals who happen to be available at a particular time and place—for example, people present in a church, in a classroom, or in a supermarket. This is the most convenient and less expensive method of sampling. But it has limited reliability and validity because the sample is unlikely to be representative of the whole population.

Data Analysis and Research Findings

In any research, data can be either qualitative or quantitative or a combination of these two types. Purposes of data analysis, regardless of the types of data, are:

1. to find answers to research questions and/or
2. to test hypotheses.

Analysis of Qualitative Data

Qualitative data are expressed in words and analyzed logically to identify topics, cluster topics into categories, form categories into patterns, make explanations from the patterns, and use explanations for answering research questions.

Tests for Qualitative Data

Qualitative data are analyzed using frequency distributions, percentage, chi-square, ranking, and other nonparametric statistical techniques.

Analyzing Quantitative Data

Quantitative data are expressed numerically and analyzed statistically using the following statistical techniques:

Descriptive analysis. Descriptive analyses are done by computing central tendency—mean, median, and mode; variability—variance, standard deviation, etc.; relative standing—percentile and percentile ranks; and graphic presentations—histograms, polygons, bar graphs, pie charts, etc.

Exploring relationships. Relations between variables are explored using correlations—Spearman rank order correlation, Pearson product moment correlation, partial correlation; and regressions—multiple regressions including standard regression equation, stepwise regression, hierarchical regression, etc.

Exploring causal relations. Causal relations between variables are tested using inferential statics, such as *t* tests, *F* tests, etc.

Preparing a Research Report

A research report can be in one of the three formats:

1. Thesis or dissertation
2. Project paper
3. Journal article

The thesis format usually has the following parts:

Front Materials

- Title page
- Abstract page
- Acknowledgement page
- Table of contents
- List of tables
- List of figures

Body

Usually the body consists of the following sections:

- **Introduction.** This includes background of the study, statement of the problem, importance of the problem, hypotheses and/or research questions, and definition of concepts or terms.
- **Review of literature.** This includes reviews of previous studies—old and current studies relevant to the present study.
- **Methods.** This includes research design, sample, measures, and procedures of data collections.
- **Results.** This includes analysis of data using relevant statistical tests and presentation of findings using tables and figures.
- **Discussion and conclusions.** This includes explanations of results, relating and contrasting of results with findings of other relevant studies, discussions about implications, generalizations and limitations of the findings, and suggestions for future research.

Back Materials

- Bibliography
- Appendices

Writing Styles of a Thesis or a Dissertation

- Descriptive, objective, analytic, factual, and evidence-based.
- Clear, consistent, unambiguous, and unloaded.
- Overall consistency.
- Suggestive and tentative conclusions.
- Emphasis on implications (theoretical and practical), limitations, and future research.

CHAPTER SUMMARY

Chapter 2 includes major concepts of research; operational definition of concepts; types of research—basic, applied, quantitative, and qualitative research; research designs—experimental, nonexperimental, quasi-experimental, and field studies; characteristics of scientific research—reliability, validity, objectivity, and verifiability; sampling procedures—probability and nonprobability samples; data collection and analyses; and report writing.

Research. Research refers to any systematic study or investigation in some fields of knowledge, which is undertaken to discover, explain, and establish facts or principles or a theory.

Research method. A research method refers to procedures and techniques applied to conduct a research.

Research design. It is a detailed plan for collecting, analyzing, and interpreting research data.

Characteristics of research. The basic characteristics of a scientific research include reliability, validity, objectivity, and verifiability.

Variables. A variable is a factor that can vary or change in ways that can be observed, measured, and verified.

Hypothesis. A hypothesis is a tentative idea that predicts relationships between two or more variables. A hypothesis might be supported or rejected by facts or evidence.

REFLECTIVE QUESTIONS

1. Discuss major concepts, characteristics, and objectives of social research.

2. How is research done? What are the major sources of research information, and how are they located?

3. What is a hypothesis and what are its different types? Discuss different models of formulating a hypothesis.

4. What is a research design, and what are the objectives of a research design? Discuss different types of research designs and their merits and demerits.

5. What is a sample? Why does a researcher need to select a sample? Critically discuss different types of samples.

CHAPTER THREE

Intimate Relationships across the Lifespan

Goals for intimate relationships and the decision to enter into such relationships vary widely across the life courses of people (Sassler, 2010). This chapter focuses on the nature and dynamics of intimate relationships over an individual's lifespan, extending from childhood through adolescence and adulthood. Intimate relationships during childhood are characterized by nonromantic love, warmth, and affection between children and their parents and other attachment figures. But inmate relationships during adolescence and adulthood are characterized by both nonromantic and romantic relationships with their attachment figures including peers, friends, and partners.

Major Lifespan Premises

There are three major lifespan-developmental premises with regard to intimate relationships (Diamond, Fagundes, & Butterworth, 2010). First, the quality and functioning of intimate relationships as shaped by the individual's developmental conditions. Second, influences of intimate relationships on the individual's social, psychological, and behavioral development. Third, effects of intimate relations on the individual's mental health, well-being, and adjustment over the lifespan. An important model that focuses on the lifespan-developmental premises with regard to intimate relationships is the convoy model of social relationships.

Convoy Model of Social Relationships

The convoy model of social relationships presents a framework for explaining the nature, characteristics, and dynamics of intimate relationships, and other forms of close relationships over the individual's lifespan (Antonucci, Birditt, & Ajrouch, 2011; Kahn & Antonucci, 1980). The model incorporates both a lifespan perspective and a multigenerational perspective and focuses on a wide range of close relationships.

The convoy of intimate relationships can shape and share individuals' life experiences, challenges, successes, and disappointments (Antonucci et al., 2010). Convoy of intimate relationships can have positive or negative effects on individuals' lifespan development. For example, in an ideal situation, the convoy can help the individual learn, grow, and mature in a prosocial manner. However, in a suboptimal condition, the convoy can also have negative effects on individuals' efforts, aspirations, and successes by creating problems rather than solving them.

Like attachment figures, the convoy can provide the same secure base for individuals' lifespan development. The convoy of very close attachment relationships includes mother, father, other caregivers, siblings, grandparents, spouse, and intimate partners. In case of less but still close relationships, the convoy may include peers, other relatives, friends, and even coworkers or classmates (Antonucci, Ajrouch, & Birditt, 2014). According to the convoy model, the intimate relationship convoy represents three levels of close circles. These are inner, middle, and outer circles. These circles indicate different degrees of closeness. According to Kahn and Antonucci (1980), inner circle members of a person are so close and important that it is hard for him/her to imagine life without them. Next to the inner circle in degree of closeness are respectively the members of middle and outer circles, who are not as close as the members of the inner circle, but nonetheless, they are quite close and important members of a person's convoy relations.

The convoy model predicts relative stability and changes in convoy memberships with the changing positions of the individual, family, and social life cycles. The model also assumes a curvilinear pattern in convoy relations over the lifespan of individuals. For example, young children have few convoy members, but the number keeps growing during young adulthood and middle adulthood as roles and family size increase, and the number begins decreasing with older adulthood, when aging people's roles and families become limited. Findings of a study (Antonucci, Akiyama, & Takahashi, 2004) support the notion that there are both consistency as well as clear changes in social relationships at different stages of an individual's life cycle.

Thus the convoy model emphasizes the lifespan nature of social relations focusing on the stability and change of convoy relations throughout the individual's life course of development. However, certain relationships, such as the parent-child relationship, especially the mother-child relationship, are consistently present over the life course. The mother-child relationship usually occupies the top position among the closest relationships during childhood, followed by other developmentally appropriate relationships, such as peer relationships among teens, spousal relationships among adults, and finally relationships with adult offspring and grandchildren as the individual ages (Antonucci, Akiyama, & Takahashi, 2004).

The convoy model (Antonucci, Ajrouch, & Birditt, 2014) also attempts to explain how personal and situational factors influence social relationships and how these, in turn, influence the individual's mental health, well-being, and life satisfaction. As individuals grow from infancy through adulthood, important life circumstances influence their developmental processes. The convoy of close relations usually influence individuals over time by helping and supporting them to face challenges of life. Contrarily, the convoy can also disrupt their development and ability to successfully meet challenges of life.

Childhood Attachment Relationships

Human development theorists and researchers have observed that humans have phylogenetically acquired the need for positive response or love from people most important to them. This need in childhood is for parental warmth, affection, care, comfort, support, nurturance, and love (Rohner, 1986/2000, 2015) or attachment (Ainsworth, 1973; Baumeister & Leary, 1995; Bowlby, 1969/1982, 1994). According to Rohner (1999), individuals who can best satisfy this need for infants and children are their parents, but for adolescents and adults this number expands to include significant others, such as peers and intimate partners. Similarly, attachment researchers have shown that the exclusive mother-child relationship during infancy normally expands to include fathers, siblings, grandparents, and other relatives in early childhood. Children's later relationships development largely depends on their relationships with parents (Bowlby, 1969/1982; Rohner, 1986/2000). Children tend to behave, throughout the lifespan, in ways that are similar to their parents' behaviors. Children's relationships with their siblings may also influence their relationships with peers. Children with closer relationships to their siblings tend to have closer relationships with their friends as well.

Attachment and other close social relationships are likely to expand further in later childhood through adolescence and adulthood to include peers, friends, spouse, adult offspring, and grandchildren. Several attachment researchers have documented these changes in children and adolescence (Bretherton & Waters, 1985), and also in adults including older adults (e.g., Antonucci, 1994; Consedine & Magai, 2003; Magai et al., 2001).

Quality of Childhood Attachment Relationships

One of the most powerful factors in children's growth and development is the quality of attachment relationship between parents and children (Ainsworth & Bowlby, 1991). Good quality attachment relationship depends on how quickly and adequately parents respond to children's needs for care, comfort, and security. Moreover, it depends on the feelings of children, and not of parents, about parental care, love, and affection.

Types of Child-Parent Attachment Relationships

Child-parent attachment relationships can be of two types: (1) primary attachment relationships and (2) secondary attachment relationships. The parent(s) or any other caregiver who provides most direct, continuous, and responsive care to a child becomes the primary attachment figure to the child. Individuals who provide occasional care and support to a child in the absence of a primary caregiver become secondary attachment figures to a child. An array of secondary attachment figures can include siblings, grandparents, aunts, uncles, etc.

Attachment Styles

Attachment theorists (Ainsworth & Bowlby, 1991) suggest two major forms or styles of attachment relationships: (1) secure attachment and (2) insecure attachment. Insecure attachment has the following three subtypes:

Resistant/ambivalent attachment. This is a subtype of insecure attachment, which is characterized by anxiousness and frustration of children with their parental responses toward them. They seek parental love but get upset with parental behavior.

Avoidant attachment. This subtype of attachment is characterized by children's willingness to avoid or ignore parents' presence and responses toward them.

Disorganized attachment. This subtype of attachment is characterized by children who show unpredictable behavior. They feel uncomfortable, sometimes scared, and confused with parental responses toward them.

Developmental Outcomes of Attachment Styles

Different types of attachment styles indicate the overall quality of parent-child relationships, depending on children's feeling of security and comfort with parental or other caregivers' responses to their needs. The attachment styles have important lifespan-developmental outcomes for children. Prompt and consistent care, attention, and active response from parents or caregivers to the children's needs and comforts, especially during the first three months, help the development of the basic trust between parents and children (Bell & Ainsworth, 1972). The child's degree of trust about parents, other people, and the world depends, to a large extent, on the quality of care she/he receives during the first year of life (Erikson, 1950/1963). A number of attachment researchers have shown that parent-child secure attachment can help children to explore their environment more actively and confidently, develop healthy peer relations, and positive social interactions with other children (Waters, Hamilton, & Weinfield, 2000). In addition, children with secure attachment demonstrate greater emotional stability, ability to express their feelings more easily, and handle their stress more effectively than do children with insecure parent-child attachment (Goldberg, 2000). The role of gender in childhood friendships is often overestimated. For example, although there are some differences in friendship behaviors between male and female children, there are also substantial similarities. Differences in behavior such as aggression and nurturing may be largely due to differences in circumstances that males and females may encounter with their friends. Behaviors of male and female children are likely to be similar in the same circumstances.

Development of Childhood Attachment Styles

Development of good quality attachment styles between parents and children depends on several factors including a child's developmental history (such as abuse and traumatic experiences), and a child's perception of reliability of parental behavior in providing warmth, affection, support, comfort, and security. The following parental-child interactions have been found to promote attachment relationships (Rohner, 1986/2000):

Physical: Touch, kiss, hug, fondle, etc.
Verbal: Praise, compliments, say nice things, etc.

Attachment Relationships during Adolescence

Adolescence is a distinct and critical stage of development. This is the period of transition from late childhood to the beginning of adulthood. Many significant physical, psychological, and social developments occur during adolescence. This is a stage of life when an individual becomes an emerging adult physically, emotionally, cognitively, and socially.

Two important developmental characteristics emerge during adolescence. These are: (1) sexual maturity and (2) psychological and social independence. One of the most important factors for adolescents' psychosocial development is identity development, including the formation of values, beliefs, and ideals that guide the adolescents' behaviors (Rice & Dolgin, 2005). This is a stage of life when an individual attains puberty, the period during which an adolescent reaches sexual maturity and becomes capable of reproduction.

Physical Development

The following significant physical developments occur in an adolescent during puberty:

1. The period of sexual maturation during which an adolescent becomes capable of reproduction.
2. Puberty follows a surge of hormones which trigger a two-year period of rapid physical development, usually beginning at about age 11 in girls and 13 in boys. This is called a period of growth spurt.
3. Primary sex characteristics development. For example, the reproductive organs (ovaries, testes, and external genital) develop dramatically and make sexual reproduction possible.
4. Secondary sex characteristics: development of nonreproductive sexual characteristics, such as female breasts and hips, male voice quality, and pubic hairs in both male and female.
5. Two important physical developments occur at the onset of puberty: (a) beginning of menstrual cycle in girls usually around the age of 13 years, and (b) beginning of ejaculation in boys about the age of 14 years.

Adolescent Peer Relationships

Social development of adolescents is marked by an expansion of peer network, increased importance of close friendships, and the emergence of romantic relationships (La Greca & Harrison, 2005). Two distinguishing features characterize adolescents' social network: (1) increasing number and importance of peers in social network, and (2) beginning of heterosexual romantic relationships. As adolescents move from middle school to high school their peer networks increase significantly, and peer crowd affiliation becomes an important characteristic of peer relations (La Greca & Prinstein, 1999). Moreover, adolescents gradually decrease conformity to parents and increase conformity to peers. Influences of peers become more important than influences of parents in adolescents' self-concept and identity development, and close friends begin to surpass parents as adolescents' primary source of social support (Furman & Buhrmester, 1992). Interaction with family members decreases substantially during adolescence. Research findings show that ninth graders spend 50 percent less time with family members than fifth graders do (Larson & Richards, 1991). Similarly, ratings of support show that adolescents' perceptions of support from mothers, fathers, and siblings decreases and support from friends and romantic partners increases. For example, in elementary school, parents are perceived as the most supportive; in middle school or junior high school both friends and parents are perceived as almost equally supportive; and in high school friends and romantic partners are perceived as the most supportive (Furman & Buhrmester, 1992).

Dunphy (1963) identified two types of peer group networks that precede adolescents' romantic relationship development. According to Dunphy, these networks are (1) small groups of same-sex close friends, which he termed as "cliques," and (2) large mixed-sex networks, which he labeled as "crowds." These peer networks differ in size as well as in developmental functions. Peer cliques are smaller in size than peer crowds. He proposed that same-sex cliques of adolescent boys and girls merged together to form mixed-sex cliques. The combination of several mixed-sex cliques make mixed-sex crowds. Dunphy argued that the major function of these mixed-sex peer crowds is to channel adolescents' heterosexual romantic relations by providing access to romantic partners and context for initial dating. Similarly, another study has shown that small groups of same-sex peer networks are the foundations of large groups of mixed-sex peer networks, which in turn are predictive of the emergence of future romantic relationships among adolescents (Connolly, Furnman, & Konarski, 2000). One study indicated that adolescent romantic relationships occur across group boundaries when they are exposed to new sets of peers and group norms through their romantic partners (Kreager, Haynie, & Hopfer, 2013).

Friendships

Friendships refer to voluntary dyadic relationships in which each member has positive emotional feelings toward the other. In most cases adolescents' friendships begin with peers of the same-sex and gradually extending to other-sex friendships with transition from early to late adolescence.

Difference between friendships and family relationships. Friendships can differ from family relationships in several important ways. Unlike family relationships, friendships are reciprocal and voluntary, where each person has equal status. Friendships appear to be as important or even more important than sibling relationships, because good friendships can often make up for poor sibling relationships, but good sibling relationships can rarely make up for poor friendships.

Emergence of chumships. Friendships often emerge much earlier in life, such as in childhood, and undergo significant developmental changes during preadolescence and adolescence with the emergence of chumships (Sullivan, 1953). Chumship refers to a reciprocal relationship, in which each individual adjusts his/her behavior to meet the needs of the other in order to attain satisfying and shared outcomes. An important aspect of such relationships is characterized by extensive self-disclosure. The need for such intimate relationships is thought to be motivated by the expectation to experience love and avoid loneliness (Buhrmester & Furman, 1986). The focus of chumships or friendships during preadolescence is often based on frequent shared activities with a child's best friend. Frequent activity with the same person often promotes interpersonal sensitivity and feelings of self-worth (Sullivan, 1953). One of the major components of chumships and adolescent friendships is intimate self-disclosure. During preadolescence individuals begin to disclose and share thoughts and affect with their close friendships based on intimacy, trust, mutual support, and loyalty within these close relationships (Youniss & Volpe, 1978). Such intimate disclosures of emotional experiences are associated with less lonely feelings (Franzoi & Davis, 1985). In addition, supportive interactions with friends are associated with lower level of social anxiety (La Greca & Harrison, 2005).

Contrarily, about one-third of adolescent boys report that their friendships are characterized by an absence of support (Youniss & Smollar, 1985). Conflict is not uncommon in adolescent friendships, and adolescents' relationship quality depends on the nature of conflicts (Laursen, 1993, 1995) and the manner in which conflicts are resolved (Perry, Perry, & Kennedy, 1992). Uncontrolled affective expression, power assertion techniques, and mediation through a third party may result in disengagement and poor quality of friendships (Shulman & Laursen, 2002). Though disagreements sometimes occur, open conflict is less frequent among late adolescents because of increased awareness of the negative impacts of conflict and increased skill in conflict resolution (Collins & Steinberg, 2006). In healthy late adolescent relationships, conflict resolution often involves compromise. Consequently, such resolution often leads to increased intimacy and understanding (Collins & Steinberg, 2006). Whatever may be the reasons, dissolution of friendships is frequently associated with depression, loneliness, guilt, and anger (Laursen, Hartup, & Koplas, 1996; Parker & Seal, 1996).

Changing Patterns of Peer Group Relationships

Although young adolescents prefer same-sex peers, the importance of other-sex peers increases over time with transition from early adolescence through late adolescence (Arndorfer & Stormshak, 2008). During childhood, children primarily interact with their same-sex friends and peers (Maccoby, 1998). A significant shift in peer relations occurs during early adolescence with increase in interest and interactions with other-sex peers. Although early adolescents spend time thinking about members of the other sex, actual interactions with the other-sex begin later during middle and late adolescence (Connolly et al., 2004). Compared to sixth graders, eighth graders were found to have an increased preference for other-sex peers across time. Both eighth grade boys and girls rated mixed-sex peer groups as more enjoyable than same-sex peer groups (Darling et al., 1999). This research indicates that mixed-sex peer relationships are generally preferred over same-sex peer relationships with the transition from early adolescence into late adolescence.

Romantic Relationships of Adolescents

Like friendships, adolescents' romantic relationships involve support, intimacy, and companionship (Laursen, 1996). Romantic relationships have some additional specific characteristics such as passion, commitment, and sexual intimacy, which do not exist in friendships (Connolly, Furman, & Konarski, 2000). Although romantic relationships may begin during early or middle adolescence, greater closeness with romantic partners than with best friends typically begins around late adolescence (Laursen, 1996). However, interest in and interactions with other-sex peers increases during early adolescence. Initially adolescents keep on thinking about the other-sex and start increasingly interacting with them. These interactions typically occur in mixed-sex groups (Connolly et al. 2004). As a part of adolescents' romantic behavior, dating typically begins around the age of 14 to 15 years, initially as an extension of close relationships in mixed-sex peer groups (Connolly et al., 1999; Feiring, 1996). Dating relationships typically mark the beginning of adolescents' sexual interactions with romantic partners. A large body of research has shown that adolescent dating relationships are not transitory and unimportant (Collins, 2003; Davila et al., 2004).

Sexual Behavior of Adolescents

According to the Centers for Disease Control and Prevention data (CDC, 2006):

- About 4 to 9 percent of teenagers in the United States have experienced sexual intercourse by age 13.
- About 40 percent of girls and 45 percent of boys have had sex by the tenth grade.
- About 60 percent of teenagers are sexually active during late adolescence.
- Only about 15 to 20 percent of Americans over 20 years of age are virgins.

Meaning of Adolescent Sex

A study (Laumann et al., 1994) designed to explore the meaning of adolescent sex, asked a large number of adolescent males and females the following question: Why did they have first-time sexual intercourse? Their responses with the percentage of respondents are as follows:

- 51 percent of adolescent males attributed it to readiness for sex and curiosity.
- 25 percent of males said they were in love.
- 50 percent of adolescent females said they were in love.
- 25 percent of females said readiness for sex and curiosity.
- Only a small percentage of males and females attributed it to the desire for physical pleasure.
- Majority of the adolescent males admitted that they were not in love with their first sexual partner.
- Majority of the females said they were in love.

Gender Differences in Sexual Attitudes and Behavior

About 7 percent of adolescent girls said that their first intercourse was forced by their male partners, and about 25 percent of adolescent girls said that their first intercourse was unwanted and just to please their partners (Rice & Dolgin, 2005). Approximately 70 percent of girls who were involved in sexual intercourse before 13 years of age said that their first incident was either unwanted or forced by their partners (Alan Guttmacher Institute, 1999). Teenage boys are more likely than teenage girls to separate sex from love. Most sexually active adolescents, especially girls, prefer to stick to a single partner. Adolescent females are more likely than their male peers to be involved in sexual activities with a same-sex partner. A recent analysis of national data indicated that about 10 percent of females and 5 percent of males had engaged in sexual activity with the same-sex partners, and the percentage increases as they entered into young adulthood (Mulye et al., 2009).

Correlates of Adolescent Sexual Behavior

Sexual activities of adolescents are influenced by a variety of factors. Some of the important factors that are associated with adolescent sexual behavior are as follows:

Age. The older adolescents, regardless of gender, are more likely to have had sexual intercourse than the younger adolescents (Laumann et al., 1994).

Ethnicity. The incidence of teenage sex is highest among African American adolescents followed by Hispanic Americans and European Americans. For example, a report of the U.S. high school students about sexual intercourse in 2009 showed that percentages were highest among Black males (72 percent) and females (58 percent), followed by Hispanic males (53 percent) and females (45 percent), and White males (45 percent) and females (40 percent) (Centers for Disease Control and Prevention, 2010). In comparison to adolescents of other ethnic groups, Asian American adolescents are less likely to be sexually active. They typically restrict their romantic behavior to kissing, hugging, and petting until they are married (Huang & Uba, 1992). Black youth aged 15–21 report first sexual intercourse at earlier ages than their White, Hispanic/Latino, or Asian counterparts (McCabe, Brewster, & Tillman, 2011). White youth aged 15–21 report heterosexual oral sex at higher rates than their Black, Hispanic/Latino, or Asian youth (McCabe, Brewster, & Tillman, 2011).

Religion. The adolescents, especially females, with strong religious belief have the lowest incidence of premarital sex. Religious practice is a strong determinant of sexual abstinence (Mott et al., 1996).

Boyfriend or girlfriend relationships. Adolescents who have a boyfriend or a girlfriend are more likely to have teenage sex than those who don't have any such friends (Scott-Jones & White, 1990).

Early dating. Adolescents who start dating at an early age, and have more or less stable dating relationships, are more likely to be sexually active with more partners than adolescents who begin dating at later age (Dorius, Heaton, & Steffen, 1993).

Age at first incidence. Adolescents who are younger at the first intercourse have a more permissive attitude toward teen sex and have more sexual interactions than those who are older at the first incidence (Rice & Dolgin, 2005).

Age at puberty. The younger the adolescents are during puberty, regardless of gender, the greater the probability for them to become sexually more active earlier in life than those who reach puberty at a later age (Halpern et al., 1994).

Parental control. Parental strictness and control have curvilinear relations with adolescent attitude toward sexual permissiveness and rate of sexual activity. The sexual permissiveness is highest among adolescents who perceive their parents as most liberal about premarital sex, and lowest among those who perceive their parents as neither very strict nor very liberal, and neither too high nor too low for adolescents who perceive their parents as very strict (Khaleque, 2003; Miller et al., 1986).

Peer influences. Adolescents often get involved in teenage sex when they see that their peers are involved in such behavior (Miller et al., 1997). Adolescents having deviant peer groups are more likely to engage in early sex than adolescents who are not associated with such peer groups (Underwood, Kupersmidt, & Coie, 1996).

Siblings. Adolescent girls are more frequently influenced by the sexual attitude and behavior of their same-sex older siblings than adolescent boys (East, Felice, & Morgan, 1993). However, once the younger siblings start sexual interactions, they can be sexually more active than their older siblings (Rodgers, Rowe, & Harris, 1992).

Gender. Initially adolescent girls tend to be less permissive about teenage sex than adolescent boys. However, once they start it, they become equally active like adolescent boys (De Gaston, Weed, & Jensen, 1996). In 2009, 60 percent of sexually active male high schoolers reported using condoms in intercourse, as did 44 percent of sexually active female high schoolers (Centers for Disease Control and Prevention, 2010). Adolescent females are more likely than their male peers to report a same-gender sexual partner. A recent analysis of national data estimated that roughly 10 percent of females and 5 percent of males had engaged in same-gender sexual activity, with percentages increasing as youth entered into young adulthood (Thompson & Auslander, 2011).

Problem behaviors. Teenagers with problem behaviors, such as delinquency, drug addiction, alcohol abuse, and promiscuity are more likely to engage in premarital sex than those who are not involved in such behaviors (Harvey & Springer, 1995; Weinbender & Rossignol, 1996).

Single-parent family. Teenagers, especially girls, from single parents and father-absent families are more likely to be involved in premarital sex and teen pregnancy than teenagers from two-parent intact families. Due to deprivation of parental love and affection, these teenagers get involved in sex as a means to find love and affection (Rice & Dolgin, 2005).

Broken family. Adolescents from divorced and reconstituted families tend to get more involved in early sexual behavior than adolescents from two-parent intact families (Young et al., 1991).

Parental education and socioeconomic status. Adolescents of parents with higher education and higher socioeconomic status report less premarital sex than do adolescents of parents with lower education and socioeconomic status (Murry, 1996; Sieving, McNeely, & Blum, 2000).

Gender Differences in Sexual Values

Although differences between adolescent males and females in sexual attitudes and behavior are increasingly diminishing, they still exist. For example, more males than females generally accept sex without love (Feldman, Turner, & Araujo, 1999). Moreover, women, generally get involved in sex with the desire for intimacy, love, and affection, but men typically want to have sex for pleasure and getting relief from tension (Leigh, 1989). Although the double standard in sexual attitudes and behaviors is rapidly diminishing, still many adolescents continue to believe that teenage sex, especially casual sex, is more acceptable for males than for females. Adolescents, especially females, believe that first sex then love may be acceptable for males but not for females. For females, premarital sex is more likely to be acceptable in the context of first love then sex (Rosenthal, Moore, & Brumer, 1990). Despite increasing social tolerance of premarital sex in Western culture, many adolescents still believe that teen sex is more acceptable for males than for females. Adolescent girls are more likely than boys to be concerned about their reputation, which could be adversely affected if it is known to their peers that they are sexually active, especially with multiple partners (Hiller, Harrison, & Warr, 1997; Jackson & Cram, 2003).

Sexual Aggression and Peer Victimization

Both adolescent males and females can be victims of unwanted sexual aggression. However, in most cases victims are females and harassers are males. Findings of a number of studies revealed that approximately 20 to 30 percent of adolescent females reported sexual aggression by their partners (e.g., Rhynard, Krebs, & Glober, 1997; Shrier et al., 1998), and only 10 percent of males reported having had unwanted sexual intercourse (Shrier et al., 1998). Some of the important reasons of sexual harassment are peer pressure, addiction, threat to terminate relationship, fear of losing job, verbal coercion, and date rape (Rhynard, Krebs, & Glober, 1997).

Teen Pregnancy and Abortion

A high rate of teenage sexual intercourse accompanied by negligence or unwillingness to use contraceptives has resulted in a high rate of teen pregnancy in Western countries (Rice & Dolgin, 2005). The United States has the highest rate of teen pregnancy among industrialized countries (Rodriquez & Moore, 1995) Although the teen pregnancy rate has declined in the United States during the 1990s, still the number of teen pregnancies among 15–19-year-olds girls is over one million a year, and about 1 in 5 sexually active teenage girls gets pregnant each year (Henshaw, 2003). Approximately one-half of these pregnancies get terminated either by miscarriages or by induced abortions. The teenage pregnancy rate is highest for African American teenage girls, closely followed by Hispanic girls, and next European American teenagers. The rate of teen pregnancy is the lowest among Asian American teenagers (Ventura et al., 2001).

Causes of Teen Pregnancy

According to Darroch and her colleagues (2001), some of the important causes for a high rate of teen pregnancy in the United States are (1) increase in premarital sexual intercourse; (2) lack of efficient use of contraceptives; (3) erosion in religious and moral values; (4) family breakdown (such as high divorce rate, increasing number of single-parent families, father absence, etc.); (5) high rate of poverty, school dropout, delinquency, and drug addiction; (6) increased tolerance of teen sex and pregnancy by society; and (7) inadequate education about sex and reproduction.

Several other studies (e.g., Domenico & Jones, 2007; Martin, Hamilton, & Ventura, 2011) indicate the following additional reasons for teen pregnancy: (1) experience of childhood abuse, (2) lack of parental love and supervision, (3) false belief that having a baby will improve their relations with partner, and (4) little or no idea about parental responsibilities.

Outcomes of Adolescent Peer and Romantic Relationships

Outcomes of peer relationships. Peer relationships have significant implications for adolescent social and emotional development. Peer relationships help adolescents learn how to be sensitive toward others' wishes, feelings, and needs. Moreover, positive interactions with peers enhance adolescents' skills to negotiate areas of conflict in order to maintain a relationship that is mutually satisfactory. As adolescents grow older, they start partying on weekend nights with several other-gender peers or a romantic partner, and through this process they increasingly develop positive affect. On the other hand, staying alone on the weekend nights often causes loneliness and depression (Larson & Richards, 1998).

Results of a study on multiple levels of adolescents' interpersonal functioning, including general peer relations and qualities of best friendships relationships, showed that peer crowd affiliations and positive qualities in best friendships protected adolescents against feelings of social anxiety; whereas relational victimization and negative interactions in best friendships have significant effects on high social anxiety and depressive symptoms (La Greca & Harrison, 2005).

The changes in adolescents' interactions patterns are also reflected in their affective experiences. Overall, affective states become more negative in middle school or junior high school than in late elementary school (Larson & Lampman-Petraitis, 1989). Adolescents' socioemotional development through interactions with friends or peers are relatively more positive than those with family members, and they become increasingly more positive from elementary school to high school (Larson & Richards, 1991).

Although interactions with peers are generally characterized by positive affect, peers are also a frequent source of negative affect. In fact, negative affect generated by peer interactions increases, especially by peer victimization, from preadolescence through adolescence, and for girls such negative affect occurs more often with peers than with family members during adolescence (Larson & Asmussen, 1991). Considerable evidence supports that peer victimization is associated with a host of maladjustment indices, and the consequences of victimization are long lasting (McDougall & Valliancourt, 2015). Sustained peer victimization during childhood and adolescence is associated with poor academic performance, negative views about school climates, and heightened perceptions of being at risk in school (Esbensen & Carson, 2009; Juvonen, Wang, & Espinoza, 2011). Adolescents experiencing peer victimizations at school are at increased risk of health problems including headache, loss of appetite, sleeping problems, poor quality of life, etc. (Bogart et al., 2014; Gini et al., 2014). Sustained period of peer victimization during early and middle adolescence has been found associated with relationship problems, such as loss of friends and feelings of isolation (Smith et al., 2004). Findings of several longitudinal research have shown that peer victimizations during childhood and adolescence are linked to a bunch of mental problems (internalizing disorders) including depression, anxiety, and loneliness in subsequent years (Yeung & Leadbeater, 2010; Zwierzynska, Wolke, & Lereya, 2013). In a meta-analysis of 10 longitudinal studies, Reijntjes et al. (2011) showed that peer victimization predicted increasing problems of mental health such as aggression, delinquency, and misconduct. Peer victimizations during childhood and adolescence have also been found to be associated with suicidal tendency and attempted suicide (Klomek, Sourander, & Gould, 2010).

As a process of interactions, peer relationships provide much more give and take than other relationships (Larson, 1983). Peer interactions also provide chances for growth of self-knowledge, interpersonal communication skill, and self-control (Douvan & Adelson, 1966). Because of similar developmental experiences and cohort effects, adolescent peers are typically in a better position than parents to understand the intensity and intricacies of each other's affective life.

Outcomes of romantic relationships. Adolescent romantic relationships resulting in sexual interactions have many unintended consequences. Existing evidence indicates that adolescents who are engaged in nonprotective sex are at higher than average risk for HIV, other sexually transmitted infections (STIs), unintended pregnancy, sexual abuse, and other preventable sexual health problems (McCabe, Brewster, & Tillman, 2011; Thompson & Auslander, 2011). According to the National Research Council and Institute of Medicine (2009), most adolescents who are engaged in risky behavior can develop health problems in adulthood. In the United States, HIV infections increased by 21 percent among adolescents and young adults aged 13–29, from 15,600 in 2006 to 18,800 in 2009; while within the same age group of African American males, HIV infections increased 48 percent during the same period (Prejean, Song, & Hernandez, 2011). All sexually active teens are at risk of contracting sexually transmitted diseases (STDs) due to unprotected and risky sexual behavior (Rosenthal et al., 1997). Approximately 25 percent of adolescents contract at least one STD every year (Alan Guttmacher Institute, 1994). Some STDs, such as chlamydia and gonorrhea, are more common among adolescents than adults (CDC, 2000). Adolescent girls are more likely to contract STDs than adolescent boys. For example, an adolescent boy is less likely to contract an STD after having sex with a HIV-infected girl than vice versa (Rosenthal et al., 1995). Moreover, STDs are often asymptomatic, especially in females.

Other notable outcomes of adolescent sexual intercourse are unintended teen pregnancy and abortion. Despite recent declines, teenaged birthrates in the United States remain still as much as eight times higher than the teenaged birthrates in other developed countries (Martin, Hamilton, & Ventura, 2011). The cost of adolescent childbearing is enormous. Adolescents' childbearing negatively affects adolescents' own lives, their children, adolescents' parents, and the society at large (USDHHS, 2013). Compared with their peers who delay childbearing, teen girls who have babies are (1) less likely to finish high school; (2) less likely to get good jobs; (3) more likely to be dependent on public support; (4) more likely to be pregnant again; (5) less likely to be able to establish a stable family life, because if they marry the chance of divorce will be very high; (6) more likely to be poor as adults; and (7) more likely to have children with poorer educational, behavioral, and health outcomes over their lifespan (Rice & Dolgin, 2005).

Some of the major problems of parents of adolescent mothers are (Rice & Dolgin, 2005) (1) initial shock and disappointment; (2) unpredicted disruption of their own life plans; (3) unexpected child care burden in old age; and (4) cost of food, clothes, health care, and additional space for the new child, especially if they are retired with limited income.

Major problems of the newborn include (CDC, 2015) (1) a vicious circle of increased probability of life in poverty in a single-parent family, (2) poor educational and developmental prognosis, (3) high probability of becoming adolescent parents themselves, and (4) increased probability of developing personality and behavioral problems.

Finally, the society has to bear the cost of adolescents' pregnancy. For example, the cost to the U.S. taxpayers for teen childbearing was about 9.4 billion dollars in the year 2013 (NCTUP, 2015). The average annual public cost in the United States for each child born to a teen mother each year is approximately $1,682.00 from birth to 15 years of age (NCTUP, 2015).

Adult Intimate Relationships

Intimate relationships develop and change throughout adulthood. Age-related changes in the character of intimate relationships are generally connected with the physical, psychological, and social changes that occur at different stages of adulthood. Although demarcation of different stages of adulthood varies in different times and in different societies, most human development researchers divide adulthood in three stages: (1) young adulthood (ages 20–40), (2) middle adulthood (ages 40–65), and (3) late adulthood (ages 65 and over).

Significant Changes at Different Stages of Adulthood

Descriptions of the three stages of adulthood are as follows:

Young adulthood. This stage is characterized by the height of physical and cognitive development. During this stage young adults make career choices, select intimate partners, and establish intimate relationships.

Middle adulthood. This stage is characterized by the beginning of decline in health and physical strength, height of careers, and mature thinking. Children become adult and start leaving the nest. Parents get more time and privacy for intimate interactions.

Late adulthood. This stage is characterized by continuous decline and deterioration of physical and mental abilities, retirement, chronic health problems, old age dependency, and loss of friends and loved ones.

Intimate Relationships in Young Adulthood

Young adulthood is typically the time when the vast majority of young men and women start exploring and moving in and out of romantic relationships (Sassler, 2010). According to Erikson (1950/1963) a central task during late teens and early twenties is the development of "intimacy versus isolation." Erikson believed that during young adulthood individuals learn how to develop enduring and committed intimate relationships. When young adults enter in college, friendships they had developed in high school tend to be eroded and replaced by new friendships in campus (Roberts & Dunbar, 2011). Their intimacy levels and interactions with new friends increase and gradually become deeper (Miller, 2015). Generally, young adults are sexually active, and they begin to establish romantic relationships that may continue for much of their lives or lifelong. But experiences in earlier stages of life have some effects on young adults' intimate relationship formations. For example, parent-offspring ties and parental supports during adolescence and young adulthood have been found to have positive effects on early achievement, successful transition to adulthood, and development of healthy intimate relationships (Booth et al., 2012). Several studies have shown that young adults who were involved in romantic relationships in high school during adolescence have increased likelihood of forming cohabiting and marital relationships by their early twenties (Gassanov, Nicholson, & Koch-Turner, 2008; Raley, Crissey, & Muller, 2007; Uecker & Stockes, 2008).

Entering into romantic relationships involves skill development for comfortable communication with opposite-sex partners. Young people need to become familiar with the process of making initial overtures, communicating their needs to partners, managing conflicts, and repairing or terminating problematic relationships successfully (Booth et al., 2012). Young women are generally more competent and confident than young men in navigating intimate communication (Giordano, Longmore, & Manning, 2006). But young men often score higher in self-esteem and self-efficacy than young women (Gecas & Longmore, 2003). Some scholars have suggested that while young women are likely to become highly emotionally involved in their romantic entanglements, young men tend to avoid softer emotions (Eder, Evans, & Parker, 1995). In contrast to these views, recent findings show that regardless of gender both young men and women tend to develop positive emotional feelings and meanings in their romantic relationships (Korobov & Thorne, 2006; Giordano, Longmore, & Manning, 2006).

Partnering for romantic relationships during young adulthood may take different forms. Individuals select from an array of romantic options, including entering into casual or short-term sexual relationships; dating for finding a long-term partner; entering into shared living with a romantic partner in a cohabitation as a substitute for marriage or "trial marriage"; and finally settling into a formal marital union (Sassler, 2010). Cohabiting adults more often tend to marry their partner than do single adults who are not cohabiting with a romantic partner (Lichter, Batson, & Brown, 2004; McGinnis, 2003). Although the marriage rate is decreasing, especially in Western countries, still it remains one of the most venerated options (Cherlin, 2004). In 2001, about 35 percent of U.S. young adults aged 18 to 25 were dating, 20 percent were cohabiting, and 20 percent were married (Scott et al., 2011).

Adolescents and emerging adults who seek long-term partnerships have different attitudes and show different behavior patterns than the young adults who look for short-term partnerships. For example, both young women and men are less selective about desired attributes (such as physical attractiveness, personality, education) for short-term partnerships than for long-term partnerships (Buunk et al., 2002; Stewart, Stinnett, & Rosenfeld, 2000). Emerging adults who intend to enter into marital relationships with their partners in their early twenties engage in different relationship patterns than do those who intend to marry later. For example, they tend to be more conservative in sexual attitudes as they are less likely to be involved in premarital sexual activity (Gaughan, 2002; Uecker, 2008). Moreover, they are engaged in fewer risky behaviors, such as binge drinking and drug addictions (Carroll et al., 2007).

Adolescents and young adults often get involved in intimate interactions characterized by different styles. According to Orlofsky (1993) these styles are: pre-intimate, intimate, stereotyped, pseudo-intimate, and isolated style.

Pre-intimate style. This style is marked by love without long lasting and without obligations.

Intimate style. This style is characterized by deep and enduring love relationships between partners.

Stereotyped style. This style refers to a superficial friendly relationship between same-sex individuals rather than between opposite individuals.

Pseudo-intimate style. In this style individuals maintain a long-lasting sexual relationship without real love, affection, and intimacy.

Isolated style. In this style individuals have no consistent love, affection, and attachment for the partners. They often discontinue or withdraw intimate interactions, if and when they want.

Influences of Ethnicity, Gender, and Nativity on Young Adults' Intimate Relationships

Several researchers have found ethnic and racial differences in dating behavior, mate selection, entrance in cohabiting and marital unions, and marital expectations (Crissey, 2005; Vaquera & Kao, 2005). Romantic relationships among younger adults, like those of older adults, tend to be ethnically homogenous (Blackwell & Lichter, 2004). But younger adults are the more likely to participate in cross ethnic intimate relationships than older adults (Joyner & Kao, 2005). However, involvement in interethnic relationships may have some long-lasting effects (Sassler, 2010). Several studies have shown that young adults in interethnic relationships receive less social support from families and friends than they receive in ethnically homogenous unions, and their relationships are less likely to be stable (Vaquera & Kao, 2005; Wang, Kao, & Joyner, 2006). Interethnic romantic involvement may also influence subsequent partner choice. For example, adolescent women whose first sexual experience was with a partner of a different race were significantly more willing than women without such experience to enter in interracial marriages as adults (King &

Bratter, 2007), although interracial couples experience more instability in marriages (Bratter & King, 2008; Zhang & Van Hook, 2009).

Generational status is another factor that has been found to affect intimate relationship processes. Foreign-born (first generation) youth were found significantly less likely as adolescents to enter in romantic relationships than their second generation counterparts; and the second generation were still less likely than their third generation counterparts to form such relationships (King & Harris, 2007). Research also reported substantial ethnic variations in intimate relationship progression patterns (O'Sullivan et al., 2007). A study on some Hispanic groups (e.g., Mexicans and Puerto Ricans) showed that the likelihood of cohabitation increases among Hispanic young adults with each successive generation in the United States (Brown, Van Hook, & Glick, 2008).

Intimate Relationships in Middle Adulthood

A vast majority of middle-aged adults are involved in intimate relationships through marital union. According to the 2000 U.S. Census report (U.S. Census Bureau, 2003), more than 70 percent of men and 66 percent of women aged 45 through 64 years were married. As a distinctive relationship with social and legal recognitions, marriage between heterosexual individuals remains the most common form of intimate relationship during the middle and late adulthood (Bookwala, 2012).

Relationship Quality and Satisfaction in Middle Adulthood

The quality of intimate relationships in marital couples often takes the shape of a U-curve. That means marital satisfaction is generally high during the early years then goes down during the middle years and again goes up during the later years (Rollins & Feldman, 1970). But some later studies do not support this view (Vaillant & Vaillant, 1993). Several cross sectional studies, comparing marital quality across adulthood, have found support for a U-shaped trend with marital satisfaction and happiness. For example, marital satisfaction and happiness were found to be lower among middle-aged adults compared to younger or older adults (e.g., Van Laningham, Johnson, & Amato, 2001). However, a number of longitudinal studies have found that marital satisfaction and happiness typically decline after the newlywed young adults enter into middle adulthood, and later on either stabilize or continue to decline (Umberson et al., 2006; Van Laningham, Johnson, & Amato, 2001).

The course of intimacy and love changes across adulthood. The changes often become evident in midlife. The ideal form of love in adulthood consists of three components—passion, intimacy, and commitment. But in many cases, passion begins to diminish during middle adulthood, transforming marital love into companionate love based only on two components—intimacy and commitment. For some middle-aged couples the end of passion in a marital relationship may signal the beginning of marital dissatisfaction and unhappiness, which may finally lead to divorce or extramarital relationship.

Problems in Marital Relationships in Midlife

Like young and older adults, middle adults are not immune to problems in the marital relationship. About 50 percent of all marriages in the United States end in divorce. Marital relationships may end for a variety of reasons, including poor communication between couples, couples' inability to manage personal and family crises in midlife, interpersonal conflicts and couples' inability to resolve conflicts equitably, lack of purpose and emotional stress in midlife due to "empty nest" (children leaving home as they grow adult), and so on. However, for some marital satisfaction increases when children leave home, because couples get more time and better privacy to get involved in a romantic relationship. But those couples who are relatively dissatisfied, the possibility of divorce increases when their children leave home.

Transition to empty nest in middle age can in some cases play an important role in marital disruption (Bookwala, 2012). A longitudinal study found that the empty nest is associated with an increased risk of marital disruption, which varies by the duration of the marriage (Hiedemann, Suhomlinova, & O'Rand, 1998). The transition to the empty nest significantly increased the probability of divorce or separation for couples who experienced the empty nest relatively early in their marriages than those who arrived at this life stage relatively late in their marriages (Heidemann, Suhomlinova, & O'Rand, 1998). They also found that women who were employed during the empty-nest transition were at a greater risk for divorce presumably because of their economic independence due to employment that permitted them to end poor marriages after the children had left home. Other reasons for midlife divorce found in a large-scale survey by the American Association of Retired Persons (AARP, 2004) include some form of abuse (e.g., physical, verbal, or emotional), inconsistency and conflict between spouses in terms of values or lifestyles, lack of trust, and infidelity. The AARP survey also found that midlife divorce is often initiated more by women than men, and men are sometimes caught by surprise by the divorce decision of their long-term married partners.

Lasting Marital Relationships in Midlife

Long-term loving relationships depend on several factors including, among others, both partners' commitment for long-term relationship; mutual trust and reliability; physical and verbal expression of appreciation, admiration and love to each other; partners offering emotional supports to each other to deal with midlife crises; and both considering one another as the best intimate partner. In addition, sex also plays a major role in marital relationships in midlife. For example, in a longitudinal study on 283 middle-aged married couples, Yeh et al. (2006) found that higher sexual satisfaction was related to greater marital satisfaction, with lower marital instability among middle-aged couples.

Nonmarital Intimate Relationships in Midlife

Although marriage is still the main form of partnered relationship during middle adulthood, an increasing number of middle adults are opting for intimate relationships other than traditional marriage (Amato et al., 2007). Common nonmarital partnered relationships during middle adulthood include heterosexual or same-sex intimate relationships with or without cohabitation. Middle-aged and older adults, particularly widows, are often unwilling to remarry because of losing freedom and financial benefits (Davidson, 2001). For these and other reasons, remarriage is uncommon in later life (Carr, 2004). But middle-aged and older singles are more often inclined to forming alternative relationships, dating, and establishing long-term supportive companionships that are not cohabitating but are termed as living apart together (LAT) (Strohm et al., 2009).

The living apart together (LAT) relationship is an emerging form of non-cohabiting intimate relationships in Western societies (Levin, 2004). In a LAT relationship a couple does not share the same household. But the two individuals consider themselves a couple because of their deep personal relationship including romantic relationship (Levin & Trost, 1999). More than 4 percent of the Swedish population aged 18 to 74 are engaged in LAT relationships, while even larger numbers are engaged in LAT relationships in other Western European countries such as France and Germany (Levin & Trost, 1999). A study reported that 32 percent of Dutch elders who started a new partnered relationship after dissolution of marriage enter into a LAT relationship (De Jong Gierveld & Peeters, 2003). A national survey report, using national data from 1996 and 1998, showed that 6 percent of men and 7 percent of women aged 23 to 70 were in LAT relationships in the United States (Strohm et al., 2009). Using data from California in 2004–2005, the same report showed that the prevalence rates of LAT relationships were even higher than the national average for those who are in both heterosexual relationships (13 percent of men, 12 percent of women) and same-sex relationships (17 percent of gay men, 15 percent of lesbians) in California. Although research focusing on LAT relationships, especially among middle-aged and older adults is lacking in the United States (Casalanti & Kiecolt, 2007), researchers in Western Europe have recognized this issue as a growing phenomenon in these age groups (Bookwala, 2012).

The LAT relationship is primarily serving as a vehicle for giving and receiving emotional support without the duties and obligations associated with marital relationship (Bookwala, 2012). Thus the LAT relationships provide opportunity to combine intimacy with autonomy. Some common reasons for entering in a LAT relationship are having minor children living with one or both of them in the home, giving care to one or both parents or to another person, pursuing education or working in different places, and living in their own homes after retirement (Levin & Trost, 1999). Motives for involvement in LAT relationships vary by gender. Women are more interested and active than men for being in LAT relationships (Bookwala, 2012). The main reasons for women to prefer LAT relationships are the desire for and privilege of keeping and living in their own homes and enjoying intimate relationships without the duties and obligations of marital relationships.

Intimate Relationships in Late Life

Adults' desire for intimacy continues through late life, because of social changes, especially in Western culture. There is no age at which intimacy, including physical intimacy, is considered to be inappropriate. However, the patterns of intimacy can change with aging. For example, the socio-emotional selectivity theory argues that people become more selective in their attachment relations in late life and develop a tendency to reduce the number of individuals with whom they would maintain a close relationship (Carstensen, 1992). Several researchers suggested that in attachment and other close relationships aging people tend to follow an overall preferred social relations convoy (e.g., spouse, family, and friends only) (Antonucci, Akiyama, & Takahashi, 2004).

   Sex and intimacy patterns of older men and women differ from that of young men and women for many reasons such as health, hormonal changes, interest, privacy, and culture. In some societies there are negative stereotypes toward aging sex. Physical and psychological changes that often occur with aging can interfere with developing and maintaining romantic relationships. The physical aspect of intimacy increasingly becomes less important in old age than psychological aspects such as love, warmth, affection, care, support, and companionship. Communication and expression of feelings through touching, kissing, and fondling indicate reassurance, love, and support.

   Intimacy, especially physical intimacy, may be diminished or lost in old age because of the following reasons:

- *Loss of a partner.* Death or absence of a partner is one of most common age-related problems of intimacy in late life. Some aging people, especially women, may not find a new partner for romantic relationship after the death of spouse.

- *Health problems.* Various health problems that become more common with aging can interfere with physical intimacy. Cardiovascular diseases, diabetes, and prostate enlargement can cause erectile dysfunction; and arthritis can affect movements and make life painful. The pain, discomfort, drugs, anxiety, and tension associated with different health-related disorders can diminish the desire for physical intimacy. Moreover, moderate to severe cognitive impairment complicates issues of consent to and comfort during intercourse.

- *Use of drugs.* The aging people, especially males, who take drugs (e.g., antihypertensive and psychoactive drugs) may develop erectile dysfunction and consequently become unable to have sexual intercourse.

- *Age-related reproductive changes.* Levels of sex hormones decrease with aging may cause changes in sex organs, especially in aging women (e.g., vaginal atrophy due to menopause), that make sexual intercourse uncomfortable or difficult. As a result the desire for sex may decrease.

- *Reluctance to discuss age-related changes.* It is likely that elderly people will develop age-related changes in body, especially in their reproductive organs (e.g., erectile dysfunction or lack of firmness in erection in male, vaginal dryness in postmenopausal women), which may interfere with their physical intimacy with partners. They should be willing to discuss these changes with their partners and with health care practitioners to find solutions. For many older adults there may not be enough scope for sex education and counseling. Sometimes older clients feel shy of expressing their sex problems.

- *Negative stereotypes about sexuality in late life.* Even some healthy elderly people may develop negative stereotypes and start thinking that sexuality is not appropriate or normal in old age.
- *Discrepancy in attitudes and expectations between partners.* One partner may have a positive attitude and want to continue with physical intimacy in late life, but the other may have a negative attitude and does not want it. Some older people may feel bored after having sex for about 30 to 40 years with the same partner.
- *Lack of privacy.* Sometimes elderly couples want to continue their intimate physical relations in late life, but they can't do it because of lack of privacy. For example, those elderly couples who live with family members or in a long-term care facility have little or no opportunity for physical intimacy.
- *Shift to other forms of intimacy.* For some older adults, passions for physical intimacy may decrease after years of living together with the same partner. Consequently, sexual intercourse may become less frequent or ultimately stop. However, many elderly couples tend to develop other forms of intimacy (e.g., touching, hugging, massaging, kissing, verbal expressions of affection) that express warmth, love, affection, care, and concern for their partner.

Despite pervasive negative stereotypes, sex is an ongoing process, and many older adults consider sexual intercourse an important part of their life and continue to have healthy sexual activity in marital or nonmarital relationships during much of their later years. Although frequency of sex may decrease with age, however, it varies from person to person. Sometimes older men perform better and have higher sexual satisfaction than younger men. Moreover, some postmenopausal women enjoy sex more than young women because there is no fear of pregnancy and better privacy at home due to empty nest. In a study on the importance of sex in late life, Gott and Hinchcliff (2003) showed that partnered elders rated sex from somewhat important to be very or extremely important; and only unpartnered elders rated sex to be of no importance at all. In a large national study of premenopausal women in the United States, Cain et al. (2003) found that 76 percent of the women reported that sex was of moderate or greater importance, and 86 percent of those who had engaged in sexual activity in the preceding six-month period, regardless of menopausal status, reported feeling moderate to greater emotional satisfaction. Indeed, sexual intimacy and satisfaction play an important role in positive relationship evaluations in the later years (Bookwala, 2012). In another study of elders between 45 and 94 years of age, DeLamater and Moorman (2007) found that more frequent sexual activity was associated with more positive evaluations of intimate relationships.

Age is typically negatively related with sexual activity and satisfaction in late life. For example, several studies showed that frequency of sexual activity is lower for older adults than younger adults (Burgess, 2004; Lindau et al., 2007). However, there was considerable variability among older adults in their sexual activity. This variability was associated with relationship status, such as partnered elders were more likely to report sexual engagement than their single counterparts.

But some studies suggest, however, that rates of sexual activity in older adults are in fact increasing among both married and unmarried cohorts with a much greater proportional increase among unmarried elders (Peplau, Fingerhut, & Beals, 2004). Moreover, these studies also showed that later-born aging cohorts reported higher satisfaction with their sexual activity, fewer sexual dysfunctions, and more positive attitudes toward sexuality in later life than earlier-born cohorts. In their review of a number of studies on gay and lesbian sexuality, Peplau and her colleagues (2004) noted that being older was significantly associated with lower frequency of sexual activity. They also noted that like heterosexual couples, higher sexual frequency was associated with higher sexual satisfaction and relationship satisfaction among the same-sex couples. Although old age is widely viewed as a broad-based explanation for decline in sexual interest and activity, this relationship may be far from simple. For example, DeLamater and Moorman (2007) suggested that declines in sexual activity in old age can be better understood by looking through biopsychosocial perspectives. In a study on sexuality in late life using secondary data from nearly 1,400 individuals aged 45+years (mean age approximately 60 years), the same researchers found that age was negatively associated with frequency of partnered and unpartnered older adults' sexual activity, and the sexual frequency was also significantly mediated by biological and psychosocial factors.

Gender and Sexuality in Late Life

Research evidence showed that significantly more older men than women reported engaging in sexual activity (DeLamater & Moorman, 2007; Lindau et al., 2007). For example, DeLamater and Moorman found that 71 percent of men aged 60 to 69 years and 64 percent of men aged 70 to 79 years reported sexual activity at least once in a month; for women of the same age range, the corresponding percentages were 47 percent and 26 percent, respectively. It is important to note that these studies typically defined sexual activity broadly to include behaviors ranging from masturbation to coital sexual intercourse. The higher levels of sexual activity reported in these studies for older men than women may be partially explained by other factors, such as age variations among the male older adults, sexual performance–enhancing drugs that are available to them, and also more opportunity for aging men to partner with younger women than older women to partner with younger men. Nonetheless, research evidence generally shows that women have lower sexual excitation and higher sexual inhibition than men, but sexual inhibition can also increase in men due to the occurrence of erectile problems (e.g., Bancroft et al., 2009).

According to Dennerstein, Alexander, and Kotz (2003) the postmenopausal stage is characterized by declines in sexual arousal and interest and increases in sexual dysfunction of women. Similarly, Mansfield, Voda, and Koch (1998) reported that 40 percent of their sample consisting of postmenopausal women experienced change in sexual responses characterized by decline in desire, arousal, ease in orgasm, enjoyment, and frequency of sexual activity. Several researchers, however, have suggested that the changes in sexual activity and interest in postmenopausal women may be influenced by other factors such as those related to sexual intimacy in the relationship (Birnbaum, Cohen, & Wertheimer, 2007), and women's desire for change in sexual qualities (Mansfield, Voda, & Kotch, 1998). The most common reasons reported by the 90 percent of postmenopausal women for engaging in sex were the expression of love or the experience of pleasure and enjoyment (Cain et al., 2003).

Many elderly people, especially aging women who live alone, find satisfaction and a sense of companionship in interactions with pets. Caring for pets can give them a sense of caregiving, support, nurturance, and connectedness.

Marriage and Health in Late Life

Numerous studies point to the health protective benefit of the marital relationship in middle and late adulthood (Bookwala & Jacobs, 2004). Mancini and Bonanno (2006) found that greater marital closeness in late life was associated with lower levels of depressive symptoms, less anxiety, and greater self-esteem among married older adults. Staying married during the retirement years has a wide array of health benefits including lower prevalence of fatal and nonfatal chronic diseases, higher functional levels, and lower disability (Pienta, Hayward, & Jenkins, 2000). Murphy, Glaser, and Grundy (1997) found that long-term illness rates are lowest among individuals in first marriages compared with all other marital status categories (widowed, remarried, divorced, and never married) for adults about 70 years old. Similarly, Prigerson, Maciejewski, and Rosenheck (2000) found that married middle-aged and older people reported fewer chronic illnesses, better functional health, fewer nursing home days, and fewer physician visits than widowed or divorced individuals in the same age group. In a longitudinal study, Zhang and Hayward (2006) found that the frequency of cardiovascular disease was higher among middle-aged and older women and men who experienced some form of marital loss including widowhood or divorce in comparison to continuously married individuals. They also found that women who experienced marital loss were at higher risk of developing cardiovascular disease than men. But cohabiting elders do not enjoy the same health privileges as their married counterparts do. A literature review on the relationship between the marital quality and health showed that in general, psychological well-being in one or both partners was higher when the marital relationship was marked by intimacy, support, and closeness; whereas psychological well-being was lower when the marital relationship was marked by disagreement, conflict, and dissatisfaction (Brown, Lee, & Bulanda, 2006).

Marital Quality and Health

A recent literature review on the relationship between characteristics of the marital relationship and health of both members of late-life couples confirmed a link between marital quality and psychological well-being. Walker and Luszcz (2009) found that, in general, psychological well-being in one or both partners in the marriage was higher when the marital relationship was marked by support and closeness, whereas psychological well-being was lower when the marital relationship was marked by dissatisfaction or conflict. In a study on the marital quality and physical health, Bookwala (2005) found that poor quality of marriage of middle-aged and older adults was consistently related to multiple physical health indicators including physical disability, higher physical symptomatology, more chronic health conditions, and poorer self-rated health. A longitudinal study revealed that middle-aged and elderly women in less satisfying marriages were at higher risk of cardiovascular diseases than women in more satisfying marital relationships (Gallo et al., 2003).

In addition, a good-quality marriage can act as a buffer in the face of stress during the middle-aged and subsequent years. These buffering effects are clearly linked with functional disability and psychological well-being. For example, Bookwala and Franks (2005) found that older adults who were more functionally disabled but in a better quality of marital relationships experienced lower levels of depressive symptoms than those with similar levels of functional disability but in worse marital relationships. Another study showed that older adults who were more functionally disabled and reported high marital closeness experienced lower levels of depressive and anxiety symptoms and higher self-esteem than their functionally disabled counterparts whose marriages were marked by low levels of closeness (Mancini & Bonanno, 2006). In addition, several authors have suggested that the negative impact of stress can be buffered by supportive social relationships including good-quality marital relationships (Carstensen, Isaacowitz, & Charles, 1999; Cohen & Wills, 1985).

Marriage and Mortality

Researchers have found relations between marital status and survival across the adult lifespan. For example, Kaplan and Kronick (2006) found that the risk of mortality was lower for married elders than their unmarried or never married counterparts. Cohabiting partners do not have the same protective benefits for survival like that of married couples. Moustgaard and Martikainen (2009) showed that cohabiting elderly partners had a higher mortality risk than their married counterparts. Results of a meta-analysis on 53 studies based on a sample of 250,000 elders confirmed that the longevity of the married couples was significantly greater than that of widowed, divorced, and never married elders. A longitudinal study showed that continuously married individuals, regardless of gender, survived longer than those who had experienced a marital disruption even if the latter had remarried (Tucker et al., 1996).

Intimate Relationship as a Source of Support in Late Life

Adult intimate relationship, especially during old age, serves as a significant source of support in times of stress (Antonucci, Lansford, & Akiyama, 2001). Here support refers to a partner's responsiveness to a loved one's needs and involvement with acts that are connected with caring and facilitating adaptive coping during stress (Cutrona, 1996). Several studies confirmed the health-promoting support of intimate relationships in older couples (e.g., Franks et al., 2004; Fekete et al., 2007). Positive partnered relationships in late life can promote older adults' ability to optimize their cognitive performance and compensate for losses they may experience in the cognitive domain (Meegan & Berg, 2002; Strough & Margrett, 2002). The benefits of supports are, however, not limited to the domain of cognition only. Berg and her colleagues (2008), for example, showed that there are significant correlations between perceived positive support from spouses and psychological well-being of older couples dealing with husbands' prostate cancer.

CHAPTER SUMMARY

Chapter 3 contains discussions about the major lifespan premises including an important model of attachment premises, childhood attachment relationships, attachment styles, and developmental outcomes of childhood attachment styles; attachment relationships during adolescence, adolescent peer relationships, changing patterns of peer group relationships, romantic relationships of adolescents, adolescent sexual behavior, correlates and consequences of adolescent sexual behavior, gender differences in adolescent sexual values, sexual aggression and peer victimization, and teen pregnancy and abortion; and adult intimate relationships including ethnicity, gender, and cultural differences among young, middle, and older adults.

Intimate relationship across the lifespan. The parent-child attachment relationship in childhood expands further through adolescence and adulthood in the form of close relationships between peers, friends, spouses, and a variety of couple relationships.

Convoy model of social relationships. This model presents a framework for explaining the nature, characteristics, and dynamics of intimate relationships, and other forms of close relationships over the individual's lifespan.

Major lifespan premises. Three major lifespan-developmental premises with regard to intimate relationships are the quality and functioning of intimate relationships as shaped by the individual's developmental conditions; influences of intimate relationships on the individual's social, psychological, and behavioral development; and effects of intimate relations on the individual's mental health, well-being, and adjustment over the lifespan.

REFLECTIVE QUESTIONS

1. Discuss the major types of child-parent attachment relationships.
2. What are different attachment styles? Discuss the developmental outcomes of attachment styles.
3. Discuss changing patterns of peer group relationships during adolescence including gender differences in sexual attitudes, values, and behavior.
4. What are the correlates and consequences of adolescent sexual behavior?
5. Discuss significant changes in adult intimate relationships at different stages of adulthood from young adulthood through old age.

Historical and Theoretical Perspectives of Intimate Relationships

Historical Perspective

The history of intimate relationships, as a part of the broader field of interpersonal relationships, goes back to the ancient Greek philosophers Plato and Aristotle. The oldest known historical discourse on intimate relationships was written by Plato approximately 2,300 years ago. But the views expressed by Plato in his discourse were more mythical than real (Fletcher et al., 2013). Aristotle started contemplating about interpersonal relationships around the same time. He believed that humans are social beings and gregarious by nature. From infancy through old age they spend most of their time with other humans. Aristotle suggested that people are attracted to three kinds of relationships that provide (1) utility, (2) sense of belongingness, and (3) feeling of pleasure. However, he thought that relationships between partners based on utility and pleasure are short-lived, if benefits provided by one partner are not reciprocated by the other partner. Aristotle also suggested that intimate relationships last long if the partners are attracted by the virtuous characteristics of one another. Although Aristotle's views about interpersonal relationships dominated the analysis of intimate relationships until the late 1880s, his thoughts and ideas did not go far enough to develop systematic knowledge, theory, and research on this topic (Perlman, 2007).

With the emergence of modern psychology and sociology in late 19th century, theorists including Sigmund Freud, William James, Emile Durkheim, and others began to focus on intimate relationships as a part of their own theories. Freud explained in his theory how childhood relationships with parents influence an individual's adult intimate relationships and psychosexual development. Freud also suggested that an individual prefers to select a marital partner who has close similarity with his/her opposite-sex parent (Vangelisti & Perlman, 2006). William James thought that a person's self-concept is influenced by his/her relationships with other persons (Perlman, 2007). Durkheim explained how social alienation and isolation negatively affect interpersonal relationships (Vangelisti & Perlman, 2006). Consent and engagement of both partners are necessary to form and maintain dyadic relationships, although the relationship can be terminated by only one partner (Miller & Perlman, 2008). Note that although the theorists just mentioned made significant contributions to build up the conceptual foundation of intimate relationships during 1880s to early 1990s, they could provide little empirical support for their views (Miller & Perlman, 2008).

A significant shift in the study of intimate relationships from theoretical explanations to empirical evidence began during the 1890s. A study by Monroe (1898) on 2,336 children to identify their traits and habits to select a friend is considered one of the first empirical studies on intimate relationships (Vangelisti & Perlman, 2006). Two other landmark events that helped the growth and development of the relationship science are the publication of the *Journal of Social and Personal Relationships* in 1984 and the formation of the International Association for Relationship Research (IARR) in 2004 (Miller & Perlman, 2008).

Currently, much research on intimate relationships is being conducted globally from different perspectives or approaches. The major approaches are:

1. *The lifespan approach.* This approach is concerned with the development of emotional bond or attachment relationships with parents or other caregivers, and transformation of them into adult romantic and nonromantic intimate relationships throughout the lifespan.

2. *Evolutionary approach.* This approach focuses on the evolutionary origins (remote or distant causes) of human mating, courting, sexual relationships, and parent-child attachment relationships.

3. *Social psychological approach.* This approach focuses on influences of individuals' interpersonal relations and personal factors including personality, and behavior on intimate relationships.

4. *Anthropological and sociological approaches.* These approaches focus on social and cultural factors such as social institutions, values, norms, and cross-cultural and ethnic variables that influence intimate relationships.

However, note that these approaches—although different but not completely independent of one another—are interrelated to one another. For example, research based on interpersonal acceptance-rejection theory and attachment theory focuses on all of the above perspectives as they are interrelated, although each theory has its own viewpoints.

Theoretical Perspective

As noted earlier, psychologists and sociologists have formulated many theories about family relations and human development. Some of these theories that have made important contributions to the development of conceptual foundations of intimate relationships include Freudian psychoanalytic theory, Erickson's psychosocial theory, Maslow's humanistic theory, and Bronfenbrenner's bioecological theory. These theories are briefly discussed in the following section. In addition, predictions, postulates, research tools, and literature of Rohner's interpersonal acceptance-rejection theory and Bowlby's attachment theory have made significant contributions to the development of intimate relationships as an empirical science. These two theories are discussed in detail in Chapter 5.

Psychoanalytic Theory

Sigmund Freud (1856–1939) is the originator of psychoanalytic theory of human psychosexual development. According to Freud, many aspects of an individual's personality development occur in response to childhood sexual instincts and parent-child interactions. He proposed five stages of human development based on sources of psychosexual pleasure (Freud, 1949). These stages are:

1. *Oral stage.* This stage extends from birth to 1 year of age. In this stage a child's main source of pleasure is oral activity—for example, sucking mother's breasts. The mouth is the center of psychosexual pleasure in the oral stage.
2. *Anal stage.* This stage extends from 2 to 3 years of age. In this stage children seek pleasure through anal activity and elimination of waste. The anal region is the center of psychosexual pleasure in this stage.
3. *Phallic stage.* This stage extends from 4 to 6 years of age. In this stage children develop interest in their own bodies and start exploring their sex organs. The genital area becomes the chief source of pleasure. The opposite-sex parent becomes the center of attraction.
4. *Latency stage.* This stage extends from 6 to 12 years of age. In this stage sexual interest remains hidden, children's sources of pleasure are shifted from self to others, and they seek friendship with peers, especially, those of the same sex.

5. ***Genital stage.*** This stage extends from 13 years to adulthood. According to Freud, at this stage individuals attain puberty and maturation of sex organs. They seek gratification of psychosexual pleasure through actual sexual activities. They try to find right person(s) for sexual activity, usually members of the opposite sex. According to Freud, puberty is the culmination of a series of changes giving sexual life its final and normal form. He described adolescence as a period of sexual excitement, anxiety, and sometimes personality disturbance. Freud believed that sexual urges and pleasures are the primary determinants of behavior.

Development of Personality Complex

Freud suggested that during the process of psychosexual development (starting from the phallic stage), boys develop an Oedipus complex (sexual attraction for the mother and envy against the father), and girls develop an Electra complex (sexual attraction for the father and envy against the mother). These complexes are resolved through the identification with fathers (by boys) and mothers (by girls) and thus absorbing their beliefs, values, and behaviors in socially desirable ways.

Freud believed that every individual is inherently bisexual. That is why each person is attracted to members of the same sex as well to members of the opposite sex. He thought that each person has a constitutional basis for homosexuality, although the homosexual impulses remain dormant for most people.

Freud suggested that the basic structure of personality is pretty well formed during childhood (by the end of the fifth year), and the later development is just the extension of the basic structure. He considered that "the child is the father of the man." He placed a great deal of importance on children's basic needs fulfilment, especially on the ability of parents to effectively gratify those needs. He considered the mother as the primary caregiver to children's healthy and continuous development.

Structures of Personality

According to Freud, there are three structures of personality. They are:

1. **Id.** According to Freud the id is the irrational component of personality. It is completely unconscious. The id seeks satisfaction of instinctual urges and is ruled by the pleasure principle.
2. **Ego.** The ego is the rational component of personality. It regulates an individual's thoughts and behavior realistically. The ego maintains a balance between the id and the superego. The ego is ruled by the reality principle.

3. ***Superego.*** The superego is the moral component of personality. It is formed by internalizing parental and social values. The superego is ruled by moral principles. An individual's mental health depends on keeping a balance among these three components of personality.

Ego Defense Mechanism

If a realistic solution of the conflicting demands of the id and the super-ego is not possible, an individual experiences anxiety and tension. The ego may try to reduce anxiety and tension by distorting thoughts and perceptions. Freud called this process an ego defense mechanism. These mechanisms include repression, displacement, sublimation, rationalization, projection, reaction formation, and denial.

Criticisms of the Psychoanalytic Theory

Few psychologists endorse Freud's pansexual views that sexual urges and pleasures are the primary determinants of all kinds of human behavior. His theory is limited in scope with an overemphasis on sexual motives as the basis of behavior, and the resolution of psychosexual conflict as the key to healthy behavior. He exaggerated the importance of early childhood psychosexual development. Psychologists find it difficult to accept his proposition that any kind of pleasure is related to sex. Another strong criticism against his theory is that it was based more on imagination and less on empirical evidence. Most of the postulates and predictions of Freudian theory have never been scientifically tested. A number of authors have argued that Freudian psychoanalysis is imperfect as a science, but it has stood the test of time as an influential source of psychotherapy (e.g., Michels, 1983; Tryon & Tryon, 2011). Several critics of psychoanalysis believed that the theory was based too little on quantitative and experimental research, and too much on the clinical case study (e.g., Horvath, 2001; Webster, 1996). Despite these criticisms, Freudian psychoanalysis, without a doubt, was a groundbreaking theory that profoundly influenced later theories of human development.

Psychosocial Theory

Erik Erikson (1902–1994) is the originator of the psychosocial theory of human development. Erikson is often regarded as the first lifespan-developmental psychologist. As a follower of the Freudian psychoanalytic school, he started focusing on the ego as the central component in the individual's developmental process. However, over the years, Erikson has widened the concept of human development from the Freudian view of psychosexual development centering on the early life to a broader concept of psychosocial development covering the entire lifespan. Thus, unlike Freud, Erikson has gone beyond early life and expanded the concept of development to the entire lifespan of the individual. He emphasized the psychosocial perspective of human development and formulated his own theory. Erikson's theory of human development is often considered as the reflection of his own life. So for a better understanding of his theory, it seems necessary to discuss briefly his life and the contextual factors that influenced the development of the theory.

Background of the Theory

Erikson experienced many conflicts, confusions, and crises during his lifetime that had a distinct influence on the development of his theoretical concept (Hall & Lindzey, 1978/1997). His life and work have been the subject of two full-length books, one written by Robert Coles (1970) and the other by Paul Roazen (1997).

Erikson was born in Frankfurt, Germany, in 1902. The identity of Erikson's real father was not known, because his parents were separated before his birth. His mother later remarried. Erikson was formerly known as Erick Homburger after the name of his stepfather. However, later in 1939, when he became an American citizen, he added Erikson with his earlier name and came to be known as Erick Homburger Erikson. He did not know at that time the identity of his real father, because neither his mother nor his stepfather informed him about his biological father. As Erikson grew up from childhood to adolescence, he started feeling increasingly alienated from his family (Roazen, 1997). After graduation, he was undecided what to do. His stepfather urged him to become a pediatrician like him. But Erikson deliberately rejected his advice. He spent a year wandering through Europe in search for a direction of life. Finally, he decided to get enrolled in an art school.

In 1927, at the age of 25, Erikson joined as a teacher in a small progressive school in Vienna, where the Montessori method was followed. Erikson became so interested that he attended a training program in the Montessori method. This experience had a profound influence on him. Some of the children in this school were in a therapeutic treatment program under the psychoanalyst Anna Freud (Freud's daughter). Anna Freud invited Erikson to become a child psychoanalyst and he agreed. Thus Erikson underwent a training program in psychoanalysis with Anna Freud at the

Vienna Psychoanalytic Institute from where he graduated in 1933. Erikson's acquaintance with Anna Freud became a turning point in his life. In 1933, Erikson came to the United States and started a psychoanalytic practice in Boston. He was the first child psychoanalyst in that city. Then he joined the faculty of Harvard Medical School. At that time he became associated with Henry Murray at the Harvard Psychological Clinic. While in Harvard, Erikson studied the way the ego or consciousness operates to develop a well-ordered individual. In 1936, he left Harvard and joined the Institute of Human Relations at Yale University. In 1938, he began to study cultural influences on the psychological development of native Indian children. He conducted further studies on them with anthropologist Alfred Kroeber, and findings of these studies eventually contributed to the formulation of his theory of psychosocial development. During the 1940s he wrote a number of essays explaining his views about human psychosocial development that were collected and published in his first and the most important book *Childhood and Society* (Erikson, 1950/1963). The book had a far-reaching impact on Erikson's professional growth and eminence. Though he has written seven other books, *Childhood and Society* is generally considered the most outstanding book as it lays down the basic foundation of his theory of human development. In this book, Erikson extended the Freudian concept of childhood by emphasizing the interactions of biological, psychological, and social factors in lifespan development. He studied young people and developed his theoretical formulation about identity formation and identity crisis.

Basic Postulates of Erikson's Theory

Erikson proposed that an individual passes through the following eight stages of lifespan development from infancy through old age (Erikson, 1950/1963, 1980/1982):

1. **Infants.** Age range is from birth to 2 years, and the critical issue at this stage is the development of basic trusts versus mistrust.
2. **Toddlers.** Age range is from 2 to 4 years, and the critical issue at this stage is autonomy versus shame.
3. **Preschoolers.** Age range is from 4 to 6 years, and the critical issue at this stage is initiative versus guilt.
4. **Grade schoolers.** Age range is from 6 to 11 years, and the critical issue at this stage is industry versus inferiority.
5. **Adolescents.** Age range is from 11 to 20 years, and the critical issue at this stage is identity versus diffusion.

6. **Young adults.** Age range is from 20 to 40 years, and the critical issue at this stage is intimacy versus isolation.

7. **Middle-aged adults.** Age range is from 40 to 65 years, and the critical issue at this stage is generativity versus stagnation.

8. **Aging adults.** Age is 65+ years, and the critical issue at this stage is ego integrity versus despair.

At each stage of life an individual faces a unique developmental task and a major crisis or a critical issue that must be resolved. These crises are not catastrophes but turning points in an individual's life with increased vulnerability or enhanced potential. The more successfully an individual can resolve the crises, the healthier is his/her developmental trajectory. According to Erikson, the success in resolution of a crisis at any stage of life depends on how effectively an individual can face the challenges of that stage (Erikson, 1968). However, some people can resolve the major psychosocial crisis at every stage satisfactorily and go ahead to face new challenges, while others cannot completely resolve these conflicts and have to continue to deal with them at later stages of development (Miller, 2011). For instance, many adults have yet to resolve the identity crisis of their adolescent stage (Slavin, 2012).

Erikson emphasized the adolescent stage for its significance on adult development because it is the transitional stage between childhood and adulthood. For example, identity formulation, identity confusion, and identity crisis in adolescence are the most significant factors for adult development. Note that Erikson did not propose any fixed chronological timetable for the eight consecutive stages of human development. He thought that every child has his/her own timetable, and it would be misleading to prescribe specific duration for each developmental stage. Moreover, each stage is not left behind when passed through; rather, it has a carryover effect to the next stage, and to the entire lifespan development (Erikson, 1968).

The confrontation with the primary task at each stage produces conflict with two possible outcomes:

1. If the conflict is resolved successfully, the outcome is positive personality development.

2. If the conflict persists, the outcome is negative personality development.

According to Erikson, during adolescence the critical issue is identity versus role confusion. The question "Who am I?" becomes important to them. To find an answer, adolescents turn from parents to peers. He suggested that adolescence is a time of significant physical, psychological, and social changes. During this period adolescents have to make decisions about education, career, and life partners. Teenagers often experiment with various roles including sexual, occupational, and educational roles as they try to find out who they are and who they can be. According to Erikson, those who are successful in choosing a right course of life can develop and establish a clear sense of identity and set a healthy trend of personality and psychosocial development.

Criticisms of the Theory

Erikson's theory has been criticized for not explaining how and why individuals progress from one stage to other. Erikson is also criticized for his overly optimistic view about human beings, as Freud is criticized for his overly pessimistic view. Psychoanalysts often criticize Erikson's theory for its deviation from Freudian theory for concentrating on the strengths of the ego, the rational, and the conscious instead of the id, the irrational, and the unconscious. However, this criticism is not justified because Erikson's theory should be evaluated in terms of its own merits and demerits, and not in terms of its agreement or disagreement with any other theory (Hall & Lindzey, 1978/1997).

Erikson's Contribution

Many professionals and practitioners consider Erikson's theory of psychosocial development as a useful framework for dealing with the developmental and academic problems of children, adolescents, and adults (Hall & Lindzey, 1978/1997; Salkind, 2004). Erikson's concept of identity formation, identity crisis, trust, autonomy, intimacy, and isolation are still being widely used by researchers and practitioners to explain developmental problems, including problems in parent-child relations and adult intimate relationships. Erikson's theory seems to have universal appeal, especially because his concept of development is equated with the democratic principles of freedom of choice and right to privacy.

Erikson's major contributions to developmental theory have been the extension of the developmental concept throughout the lifespan and the emphasis on the social context of development. Erickson is one of the few psychologists who believed that a child's degree of trust about parents, other people, and the world at large depends, to a considerable extent, on the quality of care she/he receives during the first year of life (Erikson, 1950/1963). The basic assumption of his theory that human development, including interpersonal relationships, depends on the interplay of biological, psychological, social, and historical forces is now widely accepted and supported by research evidence (Hall & Lindzey, 1978/1997). Appreciating Erikson's theory, Hall and Lindzey (1978/1997) viewed that Erikson made significant original contributions with his concepts of individuals' psychosocial development throughout the lifespan in general, and identity and identity crisis in particular.

Humanistic Theory

The most famous humanistic theory of development is the hierarchy of needs theory formulated by Abraham Maslow (1908–1970). According to Maslow, the primary goal of his humanistic theory is to explain human emotions, experiences, behavior, and the ways people seek and attain meaning in their lives. Maslow's humanistic theory emphasizes the idea that human beings innately strive for the development of positive self-concept and the realization of personal potentials. He focused on the concept of creative self. He believed that what a person would become mainly was dependent on his/her personal choice.

Basic Postulates of Maslow's Theory

Maslow (1967) proposed that people are innately motivated to satisfy a progression of needs that can be arranged in a hierarchical order. Physiological needs are at the bottom of the hierarchical order, which are followed successively by safety needs, belonging and love needs, esteem needs, and finally at the top of the hierarchy the need for self-actualization. Maslow's model of need hierarchy is presented in Figure 4.1.

Once the needs of the lowest level are satisfied, the individual is motivated to satisfy the needs at the next higher level, steadily progressing upward. The ultimate goal is self-actualization, the realization of a personal potential. For example, when one's physiological needs (e.g., hunger, thirst, and sex) are fulfilled, one looks for the fulfillment of safety needs (e.g., protection from hunger, disease, and danger); when the safety needs are satisfactorily fulfilled, one tries to satisfy belonging and love needs (e.g., need to love and to be loved, need to share one life with attachment figures and significant others); when belonging and love needs are adequately fulfilled, one looks for satisfaction of esteem needs (e.g., status, recognition, and respect); and when the esteem needs are reasonably fulfilled, one strives to satisfy the self-actualization need (e.g., need to fulfill individual's potentialities) and tries to become what one is capable of becoming.

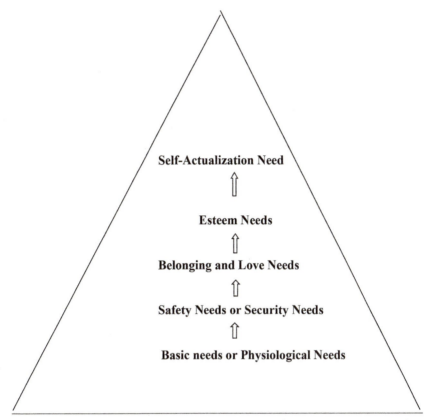

Figure 4.1 Maslow's Hierarchy of Needs (Adapted from Hergenhahn, 2000)

According to Maslow, the lower needs in the hierarchy are more basic and more similar to the needs of animals, and the higher needs are more distinctly related to humans. Maslow also believed that until the lower needs are adequately satisfied, the higher needs are not strongly felt. Once the lower needs are reasonably fulfilled, feelings about the higher needs and efforts to realize them increase in intensity.

Criticisms of the Theory

Major criticisms against Maslow's theory are (1) the majority of people don't achieve self-actualization and don't have the same urgency to achieve it, (2) motivation does not necessarily progress in a hierarchical order, and (3) people generally don't keep the satisfaction of their higher needs pending until their lower needs are fulfilled (Verhaegen, 1979). Empirical research does not support Maslow's hierarchical views that people are not motivated to fulfill the higher needs until the lower needs are adequately satisfied (Ambrose & Kulik, 1999; Hall & Nougaim, 1968). Some researchers argued that the theory makes some unrealistic assumptions about people in general such as (1) all people are alike, (2) all situations are alike, and (3) there is only one best way to meet every individual's needs (Basset-Jones & Lloyd, 2004; Kaur, 2013). Despite this criticism, the basic postulates and predictions of Maslow's theory have been found to be relevant to explain different aspects of human life, especially his concepts of belonging and love needs, and esteem needs are considered as important components of intimate relationships.

Bioecological Systems Theory

The bioecological systems theory was developed by Urie Bronfenbrenner (1917–2005) to explain how an individual's development is affected by the multiple contexts of the surrounding environment. He believed that a person's development is influenced by everything in the surrounding environment. Bronfenbrenner suggested that an individual's development is influenced by his/her relationships with a variety of people including parents, grandparents, siblings, teachers, peers, partners, and colleagues; and also by the norms, rules, and values of the surrounding institutions and organizations including families, communities, religious institutions, and socioeconomic and political institutions.

Basic Tenets of Bioecological Systems Theory

Bronfenbrenner thought that there are five different levels or systems of environment that influence an individual's lifespan development. These systems are microsystem, mesosystem, exosystem, macrosystem, and chronosystem (Bronfenbrenner, 1977, 1979). Note that Bronfenbrenner's bioecological systems theory was under continual development until he died in 2005. Bronfenbrenner (1999) argued that the 1977 and 1979 versions of the theory had been altered because it focused more on the context of development and less on the processes of human development. Later on he started focusing on the process of development—person and context interrelatedness (Bronfenbrenner, 1988). Finally, he viewed the process-person-context-time interrelationships as the essence of his theory (Bronfenbrenner, 2005). Different environmental systems that influence an individual's lifespan development are depicted in Figure 4.2.

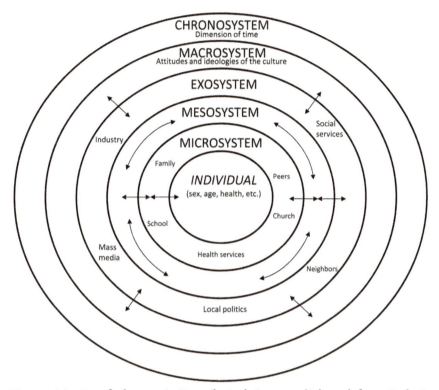

Figure 4.2 Bronfenbrenner's Bioecological Systems (Adapted from Berk & Roberts, 2009)

Microsystem

The microsystem is the closest system to the individual. It exerts direct and immediate influence on the individual. A microsystem typically includes family, friends, neighborhood, school, religious institution, and various social groups to which the individual belongs. The microsystem is the most influential level among the ecological systems. The influences of a microsystem can be bidirectional—positive or negative. A good microsystem offers positive support for an individual's healthy development.

Mesosystem

The next level of ecological systems is the mesosystem. The microsystem does not function independently. The mesosystem involves reciprocal relations and interactions among different parts of a person's microsystem—for example, interconnections between home, neighborhood, school, and work. Problems in one microsystem can affect activities in other microsystems. For example, a problem in a family can affect a child's performance in school, or a problem in a marital relationship can affect the work performance of an employee.

Exosystem

The exosystem refers to those settings in which an individual does not play an active part but still affect him or her. For example, a child has no control over the marital discord of parents or parents' job-related problems, but she/he still can be affected by such problems.

Macrosystem

The macrosystem refers to the ideologies, values, beliefs, customs, and norms of a particular culture in which an individual is born and grows up. Different cultural values are likely to have differential effects on individuals' life. The macrosystem also includes different political and economic systems. For example, consider the effects of economic hardship on the development of a child growing up in a third-world country versus the effects of economic affluence on the development of a child growing up in a Western industrialized country.

Chronosystem

The chronosystem refers to the dimension of time as it impacts human development. For example, changes in family structures, place of residence, war and peace, and economic cycles over time can have tremendous influences on individuals' lifespan development.

Implications of the Bioecological Systems Theory

Bronfenbrenner's bioecological systems theory has a great potential to provide a deep insight and understanding of the processes of human development (Tudge et al., 2009). The theory is one of the most widely accepted and applied theories for explaining and understanding the contexts, processes, and dynamics of interpersonal relationships and human development (Rice & Dolgin, 2008).

CHAPTER SUMMARY

Chapter 4 focuses on the historical development of the concept of intimate relationship and the background of the development of intimate relationship as a part of a relational science. This chapter also discusses some of the major relevant theories, including psychoanalytic theory, psychosocial theory, humanistic theory, and bioecological theory.

Historical development of the concept of intimate relationship. History of the concept of intimate relationship goes back to the ancient Greek philosophers Plato and Aristotle. The oldest known historical discourse on intimate relationships was written by Plato. Aristotle thought that people are attracted to relationships that provide utility, sense of belongingness, and feeling of pleasure. He also suggested that intimate relationships last long if partners are attracted by the virtuous characteristics of one another.

Later development. With the emergence of modern psychology in the late 19th century, theorists including Freud, Erikson, Maslow, Bronfenbrenner, and others began to focus on intimate relationships as a part of their own theories.

Freudian psychoanalytic theory. According to Freud, sexual urges and pleasures are the primary determinants of all kinds of human relations and behavior including attachment relationships from childhood through adulthood. Although few psychologists endorse Freud's pansexual views, psychoanalysis was a groundbreaking theory that profoundly influenced the later theories of human development.

Erikson's psychosocial theory. Erikson widened the concept of human development from the Freudian view of psychosexual development centering on early life to a broader concept of psychosocial development covering the entire lifespan. Erikson's concept of identity formation, identity crisis, trust, autonomy, intimacy, and isolation are still being widely used by researchers and practitioners to explain developmental problems, including problems in parent-child relations and adult intimate relationships.

Maslow's humanistic theory. Maslow proposed that people are innately motivated to satisfy a progression of needs starting with physiological needs at the bottom of the hierarchical order, which are followed successively by safety needs, belonging and love needs, esteem needs, and at the top of the hierarchy the need for self-actualization. The basic postulates and predictions of Maslow's theory, especially his concepts of belonging and love needs and esteem needs are considered important components of intimate relationships.

Bronfenbrenner's bioecological systems theory. Bronfenbrenner thought that five different levels or systems of environment influence an individual lifespan development. These systems are microsystem, mesosystem, exosystem, macrosystem, and chronosystem. Bioecological systems theory is one of the most widely accepted and applied theories for explaining and understanding the contexts, processes, and dynamics of interpersonal relationships and human development.

REFLECTIVE QUESTIONS

1. Discuss the early historical perspectives and current approaches of intimate relationships as a part of the broader field of interpersonal relationships.

2. Do you agree that Freud exaggerated the importance of early childhood psychosexual development as a basis of later development and psychological adjustment throughout an individual's lifespan? If yes, why? If not, why not?

3. Explain how Erikson has widened the concept of human development from the Freudian view of psychosexual development centering on early life to a broader concept of psychosocial development covering the entire lifespan?

4. Discuss the basic postulates of Maslow's theory. Explain why belonging or love needs and esteem needs are considered important components of intimate relationships.

5. Why is bioecological systems theory considered one of the most widely accepted and applied theories for explaining and understanding the contexts, processes, and dynamics of interpersonal relationships and human development?

CHAPTER FIVE

Interpersonal Acceptance-Rejection Theory and Attachment Theory

This chapter presents an overview of interpersonal acceptance-rejection theory (IPARTheory) and attachment theory along with a brief comparison of the two theories. Discussion of conceptual frameworks of these two theories seems to be useful for a better understanding of the theoretical relationships among interpersonal acceptance-rejection, psychological adjustment, and intimate relationships of children and adults.

Interpersonal Acceptance-Rejection Theory

Interpersonal acceptance-rejection theory (IPARTheory) was formerly known as parental acceptance-rejection theory (PARTheory). This is an evidence-based theory of socialization and lifespan development. The theory was formulated by Ronald Rohner (1935–). It aims to explain major concepts, and predict causes, correlates, and consequences of interpersonal acceptance and rejection in a variety of attachment relationships across the lifespan (Khaleque & Ali, 2017; Rohner, 1975, 1986/2000; Rohner & Khaleque, 2015b). The theory predicts that interpersonal rejection has consistent negative effects on psychological adjustment and behavioral functioning of both children and adults worldwide. Serious and chronic parental rejection in childhood, however, typically appears to have more severe and longer-lasting emotional, social, cognitive, behavioral, and neurobiological effects on children and adult offspring than do perceived rejection in other attachment relationships throughout life (Khaleque, 2017a).

Major Concepts

Parental acceptance-rejection in IPARTheory refers to a bipolar dimension of parental warmth, with parental acceptance at the positive end of the continuum and parental rejection at the negative end. *Parental acceptance* refers to warmth, affection, love, care, comfort, support, or nurturance that parents can feel or express toward their children. *Parental rejection,* on the other hand, refers to the absence or withdrawal of warmth, affection, or love. Parental rejections also include a variety of physically and psychologically hurtful behaviors of parents toward their children. Parents can express their acceptance or love through physical, verbal, and symbolic behaviors indicating their feelings of warmth and affection toward their children. On the other hand, parents can express their rejection or lack of love by being cold and unaffectionate, hostile and aggressive, or indifferent and neglecting toward their children. In addition, parental rejection can be subjectively experienced by children in the form of undifferentiated rejection. In IPARTheory, *undifferentiated rejection* refers to children's feeling that their parents do not really love them, which may or may not be objectively true.

In IPARTheory, *parental control* refers to the permissiveness-strictness continuum of parental behavior, which fits with the concept of behavioral control rather than psychological control (Rohner, 1986/2000). Conceptually, behavioral control is characterized by two separable elements. The first element has to do with the extent to which parents place limits or restrictions on their children's behavior (i.e., the extent to which parents use directives, make demands, and establish family or household rules). The second element has to do with the extent to which parents insist on compliance with these proscriptions and prescriptions. Behavioral control refers to styles of parental *discipline* (e.g., corporal punishment). Behavioral control does not, however, refer to the methods or techniques parents use to enforce compliance with their rules.

Psychological adjustment in IPARTheory refers to an individual's position on the constellation of seven personality dispositions central to IPARTheory's personality subtheory. These dispositions include hostility, aggression, passive aggression, and problems with the management of hostility and aggression; emotional unresponsiveness; dependence or defensive independence depending on the form, frequency, durations, and severity of perceived rejection; impaired self-esteem; impaired self-adequacy;

emotional instability; and negative worldview. Additionally, the theory predicts that the experience of rejection by an attachment figure is likely to induce feelings of anxiety and insecurity in children and adults. These feelings are likely to be associated with their cognitive distortions. Perceived parental warmth and acceptance, on the other hand, has been found to be associated worldwide with psychological adjustment, with positive personality and behavioral development of children and adult offspring (Khaleque, 2013a, 2015a, 2015b, 2015c; Khaleque & Rohner, 2002a, 2011, 2012).

Origin of Interpersonal Acceptance-Rejection Theory

IPARTheory is a continually evolving theory. Formulation of the theory began in the last quarter of the 1900s (Rohner, 1975, 1986/2000). Rohner began research on the worldwide antecedents, consequences, and other correlates of parental acceptance-rejection in 1960 after reading a statement by Coleman (1956, p. 117), who wrote: "In general, . . . rejected children tend to be fearful, insecure, attention seeking, jealous, hostile, and lonely. Many of these children have difficulty in later life expressing and responding to affection." After reading this, Rohner (1986/2000) conducted a small holocultural study (i.e., cross-cultural comparative research) on 19 societies scattered widely around the world (Rohner, 1960). The results of these holocultural studies inspired him to undertake another cross-cultural study on parental acceptance-rejection in three Pacific societies. Later, in 1975, he published a detailed holocultural study on 101 cultural groups (Rohner, 1975). Results of all these studies convinced Rohner about the consistent effects of parental acceptance-rejection on the personality development of children and adults across races, ethnicities, and cultures of the world. However, because holocultural research deals only with typical behaviors in stratified samples of the world's cultures, it can tell nothing about intracultural variability of behavior. As a result, Rohner felt the need to know if within-culture research on the correlates of parental acceptance-rejection would yield the same results as holocultural research. In order to explore this issue he developed and validated the Parental Acceptance-Rejection Questionnaire and the Personality Assessment Questionnaire, along with an interview format and behavior observation procedures (Rohner, 1984/1991).

Several years of research using these instruments and procedures convinced him that the correlations between perceived parental acceptance-rejection and its sequelae tend to be so robust that researchers are likely to get similar results regardless of which measurement modality they use

(Rohner, 1986/2000). Based on 20 years of reflection and research, Rohner formulated parental acceptance-rejection theory (Rohner & Rohner, 1980). Since then, hundreds of studies within the United States and internationally have tested and confirmed different aspects of the theory. To test IPARTheory's central postulates, 12 meta-analyses have been conducted on a total of 551 studies based on an aggregate sample of 149,440 respondents from 31 countries on five continents (Ali, Khaleque, & Rohner, 2013, 2015; Ali et al. 2017; Khatun, Ali, Khaleque, & Rohner, 2017; Khaleque, 2013a, 2013b, 2015c; Khaleque & Ali, 2017; Khaleque & Rohner, 2002a, 2002b, 2011, 2012; Rohner & Khaleque, 2010). Results of these meta-analyses confirm that the IPARTheory's central postulates are true for children and adults cross-culturally.

Basic Tenets of Interpersonal Acceptance-Rejection Theory

IPARTheory postulates that acceptance by attachment figures has consistent positive effects and rejection by them has consistent negative effects on the psychological adjustment and behavioral functioning of both children and adults worldwide (Rohner & Khaleque, 2015b). The theory attempts to answer five classes of questions concerning interpersonal acceptance and rejection. These questions are divided into the theory's three subtheories: personality subtheory, coping subtheory, and sociocultural systems subtheory.

Personality subtheory attempts to answer two general questions: (1) What happens to people who perceive themselves to be accepted (loved), or rejected (unloved) by their attachment figures? (2) To what extent do the effects of childhood rejection extend into adulthood and old age?

Coping subtheory tries to answer one general question: Why do some children and adults cope more effectively than others with the experience of childhood rejection?

Sociocultural systems subtheory attempts to answer two classes of questions: (1) Why are some parents warm, loving, and accepting, and others are cold, aggressive, neglecting, and rejecting? And (2) how is the total fabric of a society including the behavior and beliefs of people within the society can influence most parents in that society to be either accepting or rejecting of their children?

IPARTheory has several unique features guiding its attempt to answer these questions. First, it draws extensively from major ethnic groups in the United States as well as from worldwide cross-cultural evidence (Rohner, 1975, 1986/2000, 1999, 2014). Second, it draws from literary and historic materials going as far back as 2,000 years. Third, it draws from more than 5,000 empirical studies on interpersonal acceptance and rejection since the 1930s to form a conceptual framework for explaining the lifespan perspective incorporated in IPARTheory's three subtheories as described in the following.

Personality Subtheory of Interpersonal Acceptance-Rejection Theory

This subtheory postulates that acceptance-rejection by attachment figures have profound influence in shaping children's and adult's personality development over the lifespan. The theory begins with an apriori assumption (Rohner, 1999, p. 8):

> Humans have developed the enduring, biologically-based emotional need for positive response from the people who are most important to them. The need for positive response includes an emotional wish, desire, or yearning (whether consciously recognized or not) for comfort, support, care, concern, nurturance, and the like. In adulthood the need becomes more complex and differentiated to include the wish (recognized or unrecognized) for positive regard from people whose opinions are considered to be of value. People who can best satisfy this need for infants and children are typically their parents, but the source for adolescents and adults expands to include significant others.

The theory draws from the phylogenetic perspective (Rohner, 1975, 1986/2000). In IPARTheory, this perspective refers to the fact that humans have acquired—through the process of evolutionary development—the need for positive response or love from people most important to them. According to the theory, this need in childhood is for parental warmth, affection, care, comfort, support, nurturance, or simply love. IPARTheory's personality subtheory assumes that the emotional need for positive response from attachment figures is a powerful motivator in children and adults (Baumeister & Leary, 1995). The personality subtheory postulates that when this need is adequately met by attachment figures, children have the phylogenetically acquired tendency to develop the following positive personality dispositions: (1) low hostility and aggression, (2) independence, (3) positive self-esteem, (4) positive self-adequacy, (5) emotional stability, (6) emotional responsiveness, and (7) positive worldview. Contrarily, the subtheory assumes that when this need for positive response is not met by parents or other attachment figures, children tend to develop a specific constellation of negative personality dispositions specified in the theory's personality subtheory (Rohner, 1986/2000). In particular, the theory assumes that rejected children are likely to feel anxious and insecure. Moreover, as children grow into adulthood, these negative personality dispositions tend to form a stable negative personality pattern called rejection syndrome (Rohner, 2004). This rejection syndrome tends to have significant negative effects on the individual's psychological adjustment and behavioral functioning throughout the lifespan (Khaleque & Rohner, 2002a, 2011). Additionally, parental rejection is expected to lead to other personality outcomes in children and adults including (1) aggression or hostility, passive aggression, or problems with the management of hostility; (2) dependence or defensive independence; (3) impaired self-esteem; (4) impaired self-adequacy; (5) emotional unresponsiveness; (6) emotional instability; and (7) negative worldview.

According to IPARTheory, rejected people are likely to develop a negative worldview characterized by beliefs that people in general are unfriendly, hostile, or dangerous (Rohner, 1986/2000, 1999). Negative worldview, negative self-esteem, negative self-adequacy, and some of the other personality dispositions just described form the basis of mental representations or social cognitions of rejected people (Rohner, 1986/2000, 1999). In IPARTheory, mental representation refers to an individual's more or less coherent but usually implicit beliefs and expectations about the self and significant others that are constructed from emotionally important past and current experiences. The theory assumes that mental representation tends to influence individuals' memories, perceptions, interpersonal relations, and behaviors.

It seems important to note here that not all accepted children and adults necessarily develop in a favorable manner. Some accepted individuals develop adjustment problems similar to those of rejected individuals for reasons other than parental acceptance-rejection. Moreover, not all rejected individuals develop adjustment problems. Rohner (1999, p.11) wrote:

> Indeed some develop emotional and behavioral problems similar to those of rejected people but for reasons having nothing to do with parental acceptance and rejection per se. And some rejected people are able to remain fairly healthy—emotionally and behaviorally—despite having to live with parental rejection. [In IPARTheory, individuals in the latter group are called copers.]

Important elements of rejection are apt to linger into adulthood, placing people who were rejected as children at somewhat greater risk of social and emotional problems throughout life than people who were loved continuously. Some of the individuals who do not respond as predicted by IPARTheory's personality subtheory are called "troubled" individuals.

These troubled individuals—forming the majority of 20 percent who do not confirm IPARTheory's assumption—suffer from impaired mental health even though they felt that they had been accepted by their parents. IPARTheory researchers have so far spent little time and effort studying these troubled individuals, because it is generally believed that people can be psychologically disturbed for a variety of reasons having nothing to do with parental acceptance and rejection. More discussion about "troubled" individuals can be found under "Coping Subtheory."

Sociocultural Systems Subtheory

Sociocultural systems subtheory attempts to predict and explain major causes and sociocultural correlates of parental acceptance and rejection worldwide. The subtheory predicts, for example, that children are likely to develop cultural beliefs about the supernatural world (God and spiritual beings) as being malevolent (i.e., hostile, treacherous, destructive, or negative in some way) in societies where they tend to be rejected. Contrarily, the supernatural world is expected to be perceived as benevolent (i.e., warm, generous, protective, or positive in some other way) in societies where most children are raised with warmth and acceptance. Substantial cross-cultural evidence confirms these predictions (Batool & Najam, 2009; Rohner, 1999). IPARTheory's sociocultural subtheory also predicts, and cross-cultural evidence confirms, that parental acceptance and rejection tend to be associated worldwide with many other sociocultural correlates such as artistic preferences and job choices of individuals (Rohner, 1986/ 2000, 1999; Rohner & Khaleque, 2005).

Coping Subtheory

Not all rejected individuals develop serious adjustment problems. Some are able to cope with the impact of rejection more effectively than others. This issue is addressed in IPARTheory's coping subtheory. Studies in the United States and across the world confirm IPARTheory's assumption that nearly 80 percent of children and adults, irrespective of geographic location, race, and ethnicity, tend to be negatively affected by parental rejection (Khaleque, 2001; Khaleque & Rohner, 2002a, 2011, 2012; Khaleque, 2013a, 2015c). A small fraction of the remaining 20 percent is termed "copers" in IPARTheory. They are the people who experienced significant parental rejection in childhood but who, nonetheless, continue to be psychologically well adjusted as defined in IPARTheory's personality subtheory. According to IPARTheory's coping subtheory, copers are of two types: "affective copers" and "instrumental copers" (Rohner, 1999). Affective copers are those individuals who develop overall positive mental health despite parental rejection. Instrumental copers are those individuals who do well in their professional or occupational lives despite psychological impairment due to parental rejection in early life (Rohner, 1999). Approximately 80 percent of all respondents in most studies respond as the theory predicts. A small fraction of the remaining 20 percent of respondents do not respond as the theory predicts. They are termed "copers" in IPARTheory (see Figure 5.1).

As noted earlier, the majority of the *apparent* exceptions to IPARTheory's personality subtheory, however, are termed "troubled" individuals. These are individuals who, despite coming from loving (accepting) families, self-report the same constellation of hurtful psychological dispositions and maladjustment as do individuals who come from rejecting families.

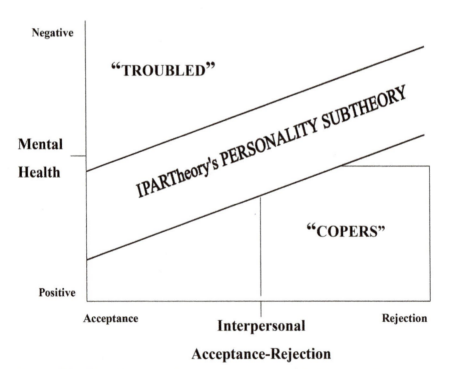

Figure 5.1   Troubled Individuals in the Context of IPARTheory's Personality Subtheory (Adapted from Rohner & Khaleque, 2005)

Paradigm Shift in Interpersonal Acceptance-Rejection Theory

Interpersonal acceptance-rejection theory emerged under the acronym IPARTheory in 2014 (Khaleque, 2017b; Rohner, 2014) after being known for well over three decades as parental acceptance-rejection theory (PARTheory). As noted earlier, PARTheory researchers, until 2000, spent little time and effort studying troubled individuals because it was generally believed that people could be psychologically disturbed for a variety of reasons having nothing to do with parental acceptance and rejection (Rohner, 1999). But research only on parental acceptance-rejection could not provide a comprehensive answer to the question: Why do some accepted people show the same constellation of personality dispositions as do rejected individuals?

Gradually, PARTheory researchers started realizing that much of what the theory postulates about the effects of perceived parental acceptance-rejection is also true about the effects of perceived acceptance-rejection in virtually all attachment relationships throughout the lifespan, although the magnitude of the effects may differ. This shift in research focus led to a major paradigm shift in IPARTheory's personality subtheory (Rohner, 2006; Khaleque, 2007).

Original PARTheory postulate. Parental rejection is associated with the specific cluster of personality dispositions noted in the personality subtheory.

Reformulated IPARTheory postulate. Perceived rejection by an *attachment figure at any point in life* is associated with the same cluster of personality dispositions found among children and adults rejected by parents in childhood.

The first empirical study to test the just noted reformulated postulate of IPARTheory was conducted by Khaleque in 2001 (Khaleque, 2001). This study examined the impact of perceived acceptance-rejection by intimate male partners on the psychological adjustment of adult females in the United States. Results showed that partner acceptance had significant impact on women's psychological adjustment. Additionally, results showed that both partners' acceptance and paternal acceptance had a significantly greater impact on women's psychological adjustment than did maternal acceptance (Rohner & Khaleque, 2008). Thus IPARTheory has gradually expanded beyond its initial concerns with *parental* acceptance-rejection, and started focusing on all aspects of *interpersonal* acceptance-rejection (Khaleque, 2007). Results of 12 meta-analyses provide compelling evidence about the worldwide generalizability of this postulate (Khaleque & Ali, 2017).

Cross-Cultural Implications of Interpersonal Acceptance-Rejection Theory

Global research evidence provided in this book and elsewhere lends credibility to IPARTheory's contention that perceived parental rejection is one of the major causes of social, emotional, cognitive, and behavioral problems of children, adolescents, and adults everywhere—regardless of race, ethnicity, culture, gender, and geographical boundary, or other such defining conditions. Having said this, it should also be noted that perceived acceptance-rejection appears to account universally for an average of about 26 percent of the variance in the psychological adjustment, personality development, and behavioral functioning of children and adults, leaving approximately 74 percent of the variance to be accounted for by other factors (Khaleque & Rohner, 2002a, 2011). Nonetheless, results of 12 meta-analytic reviews based on 551 studies involving an aggregate sample of 149,440 children and adults from 31 countries on five continents show that the central tenets of IPARTheory—especially IPARTheory's personality subtheory—are so robust and stable cross-culturally that professionals and practitioners should feel confident in using them for developing policies, practices, and intervention strategies to deal with the problems of intimate relations, psychological adjustment, personality dispositions, and behavioral functioning of children and adults globally (Khaleque, 2015a).

Criticisms of the Theory

One of the major criticisms against the interpersonal acceptance-rejection theory is that the theory is negatively designed because it focuses more on the effects of interpersonal rejection than on acceptance. But this criticism is not supported by empirical evidence. An overview of IPARTheory research literature based on 12 meta-analyses shows that during the last 40 years more studies have been conducted focusing on interpersonal acceptance than rejection globally (Khaleque, 2015a). Another criticism against the IPARTheory is about its directionality. Like most of the parent-child relational theories, IPARTheory is unidirectional as it focuses mainly on children's perceptions of parental acceptance-rejection, and little or not at all on parents' perceptions of acceptance-rejection by children.

Attachment Theory

Attachment theory is an important theoretical approach to study and understand intimate relationships over an individual's lifespan (Ainsworth & Bowlby, 1991; Bowlby, 1969/1982; Cassidy & Shaver, 1999; Colin,

1996). The theory provides important concepts and constructs for explaining intimate relationships in childhood, adolescents, and adulthood. Bowlby laid the foundation of the theory, and Ainsworth expanded it with empirical support (Bretherton, 1995). Although infant research was the original basis of attachment theory, it was later formulated as a lifespan theory (Ainsworth, 1989; Bowlby, 1979). In recent years, it has been applied to the study of adult intimate relationships (Feeney, 1999; Shaver & Clark, 1994).

Attachment theory has attracted enormous interest of intimate relationship researchers globally. According to Cassidy and Shaver (1999), for example, more than 2,000 studies have been conducted on the lifespan perspectives of attachment relationships.

Origin of the Attachment Theory

John Bowlby (1907–1990) developed the central ideas of attachment theory in the 1950s while he was working as a psychiatrist at the Tavistock Child Guidance Clinic in London. He was struck by the fact that the early histories of juvenile thieves were very often associated with severe disruptions in their relationships with the mother figures. Thus he started conducting research on the effects of temporary separation of children from their primary caregivers during the first five years of life.

In 1950 Ainsworth joined Bowlby's research team as a research associate at the Tavistock clinic and started studying the effect on personality development of separation from the mother in early childhood. In 1953 she left the Tavistock clinic and went to Uganda. There, she kept contact with Bowlby and continued working on the empirical validation of Bowlby's theoretical notions. Ainsworth observed infant development and maternal care in two different cultural settings in Uganda and the United States. In 1955, she came back to the United States and renewed her close intellectual collaboration with Bowlby. Together they defined, developed, and refined the propositions of attachment theory.

The association between John Bowlby and Mary Ainsworth was very important and fruitful for the development of attachment theory (Marrone, 1998). Some of the important elements of contemporary attachment theory were formulated by Ainsworth rather than Bowlby himself.

Basic Concepts

Bowlby constructed the basic tenets of attachment theory, drawing from the concepts of Darwinian theory, ethology, developmental psychology, and psychoanalysis. According to Bowlby (1969/1982) and Ainsworth (1973), attachment is as an enduring affective bond characterized by a tendency to seek and maintain proximity to an attachment figure, particularly under stress. As an emotional bond, Ainsworth (1989) defined attachment as a relatively long-lasting tie with the partner as a unique individual who is interchangeable with none other. According to Ainsworth (1989), attachment like all other affectional bonds includes the following elements: (1) an emotional bond, (2) an enduring relationship, (3) the need to maintain proximity, (4) the feeling of distress upon separation, (5) the pleasure in reunion, and (6) the grief at loss. Ainsworth (1989) also thought that attachment includes elements that are not necessarily present in other affectional bonds. These elements are the experience of security, comfort, and safety obtained from the relationship with the partner. However, an individual can move off from the secure base provided by the partner with confidence to engage in other activities. But because not all attachments are secure, Ainsworth (1989) proposed a modification of the secure-base criterion of attachment to imply a seeking of the closeness that would lead to a feeling of security and comfort in the relationship with the partner.

Assumptions of Attachment Theory

A brief description of attachment theory's major assumptions is given as follows:

Biological evolutionary basis. One of the fundamental assumptions of attachment theory is its evolutionary perspective focusing on the psychobiological base of attachment behavior (Bowlby, 1958, 1969/1982). Bowlby (1969/1982) formulated this theory, drawing ideas from Darwinian theory, fields of ethology, and cognitive psychology. Accordingly, attachment theory assumes that humans have a biologically based propensity to develop enduring emotional bonds with attachment figures. Human attachment bonds are subject to adaptive changes over the lifespan.

Behavioral system. In attachment theory, a behavioral system refers to a set of discrete behaviors that function in an organized way to help the individual achieve attachment. People's attachment behavior system regulates the depth (i.e., the degree of closeness or distance) of their relationships with attachment figures. Attachment theory proposes that attachment behavior is a goal-corrected behavioral system. The goal is to attain attachment, and the person goes on trying whatever will work to achieve the goal. For example, if crying does not help bring the attachment figure to the child, the child may try some alternative ways (crawl, walk, or run) to draw the attention of the attachment figure. Attachment theory assumes that the behavioral system controlling attachment tends to become active "from the cradle to the grave" (Bowlby, 1969/1982, p. 129). Attachment behavior tends to be activated in an individual either by external threatening conditions (frightening stimuli or events) or internal threatening conditions (illness and pain). The intensity of activation of attachment behavior tends to vary with the intensity of the threat (Colin, 1996).

Secure-base concept. The secure-base concept is one of the most important assumptions of attachment theory. A secure base is provided through a relationship with one or more responsive attachment figures who meet the child's needs and to whom the child can turn for security, when upset or anxious. Ainsworth provided empirical evidence to support the concept of attachment figure as a secure base from which an infant can explore the world (Ainsworth & Bowlby, 1991). Ainsworth (1989) indicated that being near the attachment figure tends to support exploration, and being away from the attachment figure tends to activate attachment behavior. In other studies in a laboratory playroom in the United States, Rheingold and Eckerman (1970) and many others showed that infants explore comfortably if mothers are present but become distressed when separated from their mothers.

Internal working model. Another important concept developed by Bowlby (1969/1982) in attachment theory is the notion of an internal working model or representational model. According to Bowlby (1994) each individual perceives events, forecasts the future, and constructs her/his plans with the help of working models of the world which she/he builds for herself/himself. A key feature of an individual's working model is her/his notion of who her/his attachment figures are, where they may be found, and how they may be expected to respond. Attachment theory assumes that internal working models of oneself and others are formed during the course of attachment-eliciting events. According to attachment theorists, internal working models begin to form during the early months of life and continue to develop and reshape in later life. Children develop certain expectations regarding their interactions with attachment figures on the basis of repeated experience. These expectations are integrated and embodied in the mental representation models or internal working models that may influence the formation and development of later models. According to attachment theory (Bowlby, 1969/1982), internal working models can be of three different types: (1) secure—in which children perceive their attachment figures as reliable—and they expect them to be responsive to their needs; (2) avoidant—in which children perceive their attachment figures as unavailable—and they defensively avoid close contact with their attachment figures; and (3) anxious/ambivalent—in which attachment figures are not consistently available or responsive to children.

Continuity and change. Attachment theory assumes continuity and change in attachment bonds and behaviors across the lifespan. The theory has proposed a set of well-integrated assumptions regarding the development of attachment bonds and intimate relationships throughout the lifespan. Many of the theory's assumptions about infancy and childhood have been well supported by research (Bretherton & Munholland, 2008). However, propositions about adult attachment and intimate relationships need more research for empirical support (Colin, 1996).

Adult Attachment

Although the initial focus of attachment theory, as noted earlier, has been infants and children, extension of the theory from childhood through adulthood mainly began with the seminal study on adult romantic relationships by Hazan and Shaver (1987). This path-breaking study has sparked increasing interests in exploring the nature and characteristics of attachment relationships in adolescence and adulthood (Berlin, Cassidy, & Appleyard, 2008; Feeney, 2008).

Based on the concepts of attachment theory, Hazan and Shaver (1987) tried to conceptualize adult intimate relationships as an attachment process. They proposed that adult romantic relationships are governed by the attachment behavioral systems, and eventually romantic partners become attachment figures. Following this initial conceptualization, adult intimate relationships research in recent years, especially research based on attachment theory, has tended to focus on three important aspects of adult attachment. First, the process of formation and maintenance of adult attachment relationships follow the same patterns of individual differences observed in child-parent attachment relationships (i.e., secure, anxious-ambivalent, and avoidant). Second, individual differences in adult attachment behaviors are likely to reflect differences in expectations, beliefs, and values (i.e., internal working models) based on differences in individuals' historical contexts of attachment development. Third, romantic love consists of three behavioral components: attachment, caregiving, and sex (Fraley & Shaver, 2000). Generally, researches on adult attachment following attachment theoretical perspective have been based on the these three assumptions (Ripoll-Núñez & Carrillo, 2016).

Comparison between Attachment Theory and IPARTheory

Both interpersonal acceptance-rejection theory and attachment theory emphasize the importance of attachment, acceptance, and intimate relationships in individuals' healthy social, emotional, and personality development over the lifespan. The two theories attempt to explain the formation and maintenance of intimate relationships with attachment figures throughout life. The theories also focused on effects of the quality of such relationships on individuals' psychological well-being and behavioral functioning. Although both the theories initially focused on the development of childhood close relationships with attachment figures, especially with parents, they have more recently been applied to the study attachment relationships in adulthood (Khaleque, 2015b; Rohner, 2008; Shaver & Mikulincer, 2008; Thompson, 2008). Because of their contributions to adult intimate relationships research, it seems relevant to analyze and compare these two theories to understand their major points of convergence and divergence.

Agreements between the Two Theories

IPARTheory and the attachment theory agree on at least five basic assumptions, which are briefly described as follows:

Evolutionary perspective. A common feature of both theories is an evolutionary perspective. Attachment theory assumes that human beings have a biologically based and phylogenetically acquired propensity to develop enduring emotional bonds of attachment with noninterchangeable attachment figures. Attachment theory emphasizes the evolutionary adaptiveness of these attachment bonds. IPARTheory, on the other hand, assumes that human beings have a phylogenetically acquired biological need for positive response (i.e., need for care, comfort, support, nurturance, love, affection, etc.) from parents, significant others, or attachment figures. In addition, IPARTheory assumes that humans have acquired over the course of hominid evolution the propensity to respond in specific negative ways when this need is not fulfilled.

Attachment theory implicitly recognizes IPARTheory's postulates that human beings have a phylogenetically acquired need for positive response. According to Bowlby (1969/1982), this need is acquired through a system of evolutionary adaptation. In this connection, Ainsworth (1990) viewed that a child who is attached to a parent has the biologically based propensity to seek proximity, security, and protection to that parent (Simpson & Belsky, 2008).

According to Rohner (1999, p. 3), "When children don't get this positive response, specific emotions and behaviors of the kind postulated in
both attachment theory and IPARTheory (i.e., insecurity, anxiety, may
be anger, dependency, etc.) begin to emerge." Worldwide cross-cultural
research supports these assumptions. For example, in a number of recent
studies, significant associations have been found between perceived parental acceptance, children's and adults' psychological adjustment, and positive personality dispositions; and on the other hand, significant associations
have been found between perceived parental rejections, children's and
adults' psychological maladjustment, and negative personality dispositions
(Ali, Khaleque, & Rohner, 2013, 2015; Khaleque, 2013a, 2013b, 2015c,
2017a; Khaleque & Rohner, 2002a, 2011, 2012; Rohner & Khaleque, 2010).

Universal propensities. Both IPARTheory and attachment theory argue
that the propensities cited previously are universal because they are thought
to be rooted in human biology.

IPARTheory draws from the logic of *anthroponomy* and the *universalist
approach* described in a number of studies by Rohner (1975, 1986/2000).
IPARTheory researchers have been employing a multimethod research
strategy across a wide range of sociocultural settings. Doing so allowed
IPARTheory researchers to explore the full range of human variability in
races, languages, ethnicities, genders, ages, and the like. The objective of
IPARTheory research is to demonstrate that the basic postulates of the theory are universally true and generalizable across all populations, regardless of geographical boundaries, as well as across different measurement
modalities (Rohner & Khaleque, 2015b). The single strongest body of evidence about the worldwide mental health correlates of interpersonal
acceptance-rejection comes from cross-cultural and intracultural studies
of IPARTheory's personality subtheory discussed earlier.

This evidence is based on the convergence of four broad paradigms of
research as well as on several discrete measurement procedures within
these paradigms. The major paradigms of research include (1) a major
holocultural study on 101 nonindustrial societies distributed widely throughout the major geographic regions and cultures of the world (Rohner,
1975); (2) a *controlled comparison* of three sociocultural groups in the
Pacific (i.e., a Maori community of New Zealand, a traditional highland
community of Bali, and the Alorese of Indonesia) where—as described
by anthropologists—children tended to be rejected by their parents
(Rohner, 1960); (3) an 18-month ethnographic and psychological *community study* in West Bengal, India (Rohner & Chaki-Sircar, 1988/2000); and
(4) more than 600 intracultural *psychological studies* in the United States

and internationally (Khaleque, 2013b; Rohner, 2014). Collectively, these studies have tested about 150,000 children and adults in more than 30 countries in five continents. These studies also included major ethnic groups in the United States, such as African Americans, Asian Americans, European Americans, Hispanic Americans, and Native Americans.

The universalist approach has been a part of attachment theory since its origins. Attachment researchers have collected empirical evidence over the past five decades from numerous cultures around the world (Ripoll-Núñez& Carrillo, 2016). On the basis of a huge amount of accumulated evidence, the attachment theorists have drawn the following universalist conclusions about the nature of attachment: (1) children everywhere tend to develop attachment relationships with their primary caregivers; (2) the quality of attachment relationships varies depending on the sensitivity and responsiveness of the caregivers to children's needs; and (3) childhood experience of attachment relationships have a significant influence on social, emotional, and personality development during adulthood (Grossman & Grossman, 2005; Van Ijzendoorn & Sagi-Schwartz, 2008).

Representational model. Both theories draw heavily from the common concept of representational model, called "mental representations" in IPARTheory, and "internal working models" in attachment theory. In attachment theory, *internal working models* are thought to be formed on the basis of individuals' early life (i.e., infancy and childhood) experiences based on daily interactions with their attachment figures (Cassidy, 2000). Similarly, in IPARTheory the formation of *mental representations* depends on individuals' experiences of interpersonal relationships with their attachment figures during childhood and adulthood (Rohner, 1986/2000; Rohner & Khaleque, 2015b).

According to Bowlby (1988), childhood mental representations are relationship specific because internal working models are constructed in interpersonal relationships. In attachment theory representations of the self and attachment figures are considered complementary (e.g., the self is lovable if the attachment figures are loving) (Bretherton & Munholland, 2008). Bowlby (1988) thought that initially relationship-specific internal representations of children become more general strategies that guide their relationships and behavior throughout lives. Because people may form different mental representations about different attachment figures, an important question arises regarding the accessibility of a working model in any given situation (Shaver & Mikulincer, 2008). According to attachment literature, the accessibility of an attachment working model depends on a number of factors such as the length of experience on which a particular working model is based, the number of times it has been applied in the past, and how relevant the working model is in a particular situation (Baldwin, 1992; Collins & Read, 1994).

The question about the specificity of mental representations has also been addressed in IPARTheory. IPARTheory coincides with attachment theory in this regard. For example, IPARTheory proposes that children's emotional security is dependent on the quality of their relationship with their parents and other attachment figures. The theory also postulates that the experience of parental acceptance and rejection during childhood has an "unparalleled influence in shaping children's personality over time" (Rohner & Khaleque, 2015b). Thus IPARTheory and attachment theory have consistent views regarding the specificity of mental representations that children construct in their relationships with caregivers.

Attachment theorists suggested that although mental representations formed in early relationships are changeable, they are fairly stable and enduring over the individual's lifespan (Shaver & Mikulincer, 2008). In this connection, Bowlby (1969/1982) argued that attachment working models formed during infancy undergo developmental changes as individuals' social and cognitive competencies develop from childhood through adulthood (Bretherton & Munholland, 2008). Bowlby also suggested that changes in the nature of attachment relationship could lead to changes of the working models. In attachment theory, this kind of discontinuity in internal working models is called *affective discontinuity* (Bretherton & Munholland, 2008).

IPARTheory also focused on the issue of stability and change of mental representations. The theory postulates that perceived parental acceptance-rejection is associated with the development of more or less stable social, emotional, and cognitive dispositions of an individual throughout the lifespan. These stable dispositions are likely to be related to the individual's ideas about self and others (Rohner & Khaleque, 2015b). IPARTheory assumes that individuals' mental representations of themselves may change as a result of rejection by an attachment figure at different times during the lifespan. Thus it may be argued that both IPARTheory and attachment theory recognize a lifelong process of stability and change in individuals' representational models.

Resistance to loss of significant relationships. According to both IPARTheory and attachment theory, children and adults tend to resist the disruption or loss of affectional bonds of attachment with parents or other attachment figures. According to IPARTheory, emotionally attached individuals usually seek emotional closeness with their attachment figures, experience distress upon separation from them, and experience grief at their loss (Rohner, 2005). Similarly, attachment theory views that children's and adults' reactions to separation and loss of an attachment figure are characterized by anxiety, anger, and denial, followed by a phase of despair in which the predominant feelings are sadness and hopelessness (Bowlby, 1980; Shaver & Fraley, 2008).

Importance of affectional bonds. Both IPARTheory and attachment theory make a distinction between general affectional bonds and specific attachment bonds. As noted earlier, persons with whom the individual has an affectional bond are in IPARTheory called "significant others." A significant other is any person with whom an individual has a relatively long-lasting emotional bond, who is uniquely important to the individual, and who is interchangeable with no one else. An attachment figure has all these characteristics but has one additional *essential* characteristic. Specifically, to be an attachment figure, as defined in IPARTheory, one's sense of emotional security, happiness, and well-being must be dependent to some degree on the quality of the relationship with the significant other person (Rohner & Khaleque, 2005). IPARTheory argues: "Parents are generally the most significant others for children because they are typically children's attachment figures—the persons with whom children have established bonds of attachment. Parents are thus uniquely important to children because children's sense of security and other psychological dispositions are dependent on the quality of relationship with the parents" (Rohner, 1999, p. 2).

Differences between the Two Theories

Despite strong similarities between the two theories, they also differ in important respects. These differences, however, do not necessarily mean disagreements. According to Rohner (1999), major differences include:

Major focus. IPARTheory traditionally focuses on the quality of parenting, especially characterized by parental acceptance-rejection (i.e., warmth/affection, hostility/aggression, indifference/neglect, and undifferentiated rejection). Attachment theory traditionally focuses on the attachment behavior of children, especially infants and toddlers, toward the parent, especially the mother, although recent focus on "caregiving" patterns in attachment relationships is also evident (e.g., George & Solomon, 1996).

Age differences. Originally, IPARTheory concentrated on school-aged children, adolescents, and adults, whereas attachment theory concentrated primarily on infants and toddlers. Now, however, both theories are trying to take a lifespan perspective, focusing on infancy through old age.

Long-term effects of infancy experiences. Historically, IPARTheory and attachment theory have different views about the role of infancy experiences on long-term socioemotional development of individuals. Although current attachment theorists do not hold deterministic views about the influence of early experiences on individuals' development, IPARTheory has always disagreed with attachment theory's original assumptions about the deterministic role of early childhood experiences.

More specifically, attachment theory originally emphasized the importance of the quality of early attachment relationships and proposed an essential stability and continuity of attachment styles from infancy to adulthood (Bowlby, 1980). Although Bowlby conceived that infants' attachment styles are changeable in response to new attachment relationship experiences, he also postulated that attachment representations tend to be more assimilating rather than accommodating to later experiences (Zhang & Labouvie-Vief, 2004). However, despite the importance attributed to early attachment experiences, many current attachment theorists suggest that the development of attachment should not be thought as a unique and linear trajectory. Instead, they propose that various paths of childhood attachment trajectory may emerge in adulthood based on the individuals' developmental characteristics, quality of their relations with attachment figures, and environmental circumstances in which those relationships evolved (Sroufe, 1995). Specific experiences with intimate partners in adulthood may either consolidate or result in variations in an initial pattern of attachment relationships (Thompson, 2008).

Similarly, IPARTheory has postulated from its beginnings that individuals' psychological adjustment in childhood and later can improve, if the forms of parenting change from rejection to acceptance (Rohner, 1999). Moreover, many adults who experience rejection by their intimate partners also tend to report the same cluster of psychological dispositions found among children who perceive themselves to be rejected by their parents (Rohner, 2008). Recognizing this fact, IPARTheory researchers have been focusing on the specific and independent contributions of intimate adult relationships on individuals' psychological adjustment (Rohner, 2008).

Differences in measurement approaches. IPARTheory tends to rely heavily (but not exclusively) on individuals' self-reports of parental treatment as revealed by questionnaires and interviews. Attachment theory, on the other hand, tends to rely heavily on behavior observations by researchers, focusing on infancy and early childhood.

Differences in approach of personality outcomes of parenting. In IPARTheory personality outcomes of parenting behaviors are viewed as dimensions or continua, which range from positive to negative. On the other hand, in attachment theory, personality outcomes are viewed as types or categories, such as secure attachment or insecure attachment.

Focus on a single primary personality outcome versus a constellation of personality outcomes of different parenting styles. IPARTheory focuses on personality as a constellation of interrelated characteristics influenced by different parenting styles. Attachment theory emphasizes different types or categories of attachment behaviors as the primary personality outcomes of different parenting styles. Despite these differences, both IPARTheory and attachment theory have made significant contributions to the understanding of the nature, characteristics, and dynamics of attachment relationships and their developmental consequences for children and adults cross-culturally (Ripoll-Núñez & Carrillo, 2016). So far numerous empirical studies have been conducted to verify the assumptions of IPARTheory and attachment theory. Research literature regarding these two theories that seems potentially relevant to intimate relationships is briefly reviewed in the next chapter.

Attachment styles. Another fundamental difference between attachment theory and IPARTheory is about the notion of attachment styles. According to attachment theorists, the specific nature of early social exchanges between the caregiver and the child results in differences in the quality of attachment relationships (Ainsworth et al., 1978; Thompson, 2008). According to attachment theory, the quality of attachment relationships with caregivers in early childhood could give rise to the following types of attachment styles: (1) secure attachment—mothers/primary caregivers who foster secure attachment are more responsive; (2) insecure attachment—mothers/primary caregivers who foster insecure attachment are less responsive. There are three different kinds of insecure attachment. They are (1) avoidant attachment—in which children show little separation anxiety; (2) ambivalent attachment—in which children show both likes and dislikes for parents; and (3) disorganized attachment—in which children show unpredictable behavior because they are uncertain and confused about the responses of parents or caregivers. Prompt and consistent attention and response from parents or caregivers to the children's needs and comforts during the first three months help the development of secure attachment between caregivers, especially parents, and children (Bell & Ainsworth, 1972). According to attachment theory, attachment styles that develop in early childhood significantly influence adult attachment styles. Attachment theory views differences in adult attachment relationships similar to secure or insecure attachment styles in childhood (Belsky, 2006).

IPARTheory, on the other hand, does not explain individual differences in adult attachment on the basis of attachment styles. Instead of classifying individuals on the basis of their attachment styles, the theory focuses on the extent to which individuals' feelings and mood are affected by—or are dependent on—the quality of the relationship between themselves and their intimate partners (Rohner, 2005). In addition, IPARTheory characterizes adult attachment on the basis of two major points: (1) perceived quality of an individual's attachment relationships and (2) an individual's need to maintain proximity with an attachment figure (e.g., the experience of distress upon inexplicable separation from the attachment figure, and joy upon reunion with the attachment figure). However, IPARTheory considers such features as correlates of the *quality* of intimate relationships and not as essential parts of intimate relationships (Rohner, 2005).

Multiple internal working models versus a single working model. Bowlby (1980) contended that defensive exclusion can have an effect on attachment working models. For example, parent's persistent rejection, neglect, or punishment of a child's intense attachment behavior can have an effect on attachment working models of the child. In such cases, the child experiences a representational conflict that may be resolved by developing two conflicting sets of working models. One set, which represents the child's negative experiences with the attachment figure, is defensively excluded from consciousness, whereas the other remains consciously accessible. Based on observations of emotionally troubled adults in therapy, Bowlby (1980) suggested that (1) defensively excluded working models formed in early life may still influence individuals' behaviors in adulthood, (2) such models are usually in conflict with consciously accessible working models, and (3) defensively excluded models may influence individuals' behavior at different stages in their lives (Bretherton & Munholland, 2008).

Contrarily, IPARTheory argues that it is unlikely for individuals to develop two radically different and incompatible internal working models of an attachment figure. Rohner (1999), for example, contended that it is not unusual for individuals to have inconsistent or conflicting sets of cognitions and feelings about their parents and other attachment figures. This does not necessarily mean that individuals have concurrently two radically different and inconsistent internal working models of an attachment figure. However, it is possible that an individual may sometime create a single internal working model with inconsistent or conflicting elements, when he/she feels ambivalent about an attachment figure.

Concluding Comments

Discussion and comparison of IPARTheory and attachment theory reveal that both the theories have made significant contributions to the understanding of the nature, characteristics, and dynamics of intimate relationships and their developmental consequences for children and adults cross-culturally (Ripoll-Núñez & Carrillo, 2016). So far numerous empirical studies have been conducted to verify the assumptions of IPARTheory and attachment theory. Research studies on these two theories that are potentially relevant to intimate relationships are reviewed in the next chapter. The review mainly focuses on contributions of these two theories, specifically on three areas of intimate relationships: (1) development of empirical knowledge, (2) assessment, and (3) nonclinical and clinical applications.

CHAPTER SUMMARY

Chapter 5 focuses on the major concepts of interpersonal acceptance-rejection theory (IPARTheory) including parental acceptance and rejection, parental control, psychological adjustment; origin of the theory, basic tenets of the theory, paradigm shift in IPARTheory, cross-cultural implications of IPARTheory, and criticisms of the theory. The chapter also discusses attachment theory, origin of the attachment theory, basic concepts of the theory, assumptions of attachment theory, adult attachment, comparison between attachment theory and IPARTheory, agreements between the two theories, and differences between the two theories.

Interpersonal acceptance-rejection theory. IPARTheory is an evidence-based theory of socialization and lifespan development.

Parental acceptance. In IPARTheory, parental acceptance refers to warmth, affection, love, care, comfort, support, or nurturance of parents toward children.

Parental rejection. Parental rejection refers to the absence or withdrawal of warmth, affection, or love, and hurtful behaviors of parents toward children.

Parental control. Parental control refers to the permissiveness-strictness continuum of parental behavior.

Origin of IPARTheory. This is a continually evolving theory. Formulation of the theory began in the last quarter of the 1900s.

Basic tenets of IPARTheory. The theory postulates that acceptance by attachment figures has consistent positive effects and rejection by them has consistent negative effects on the psychological adjustment and behavioral functioning of both children and adults worldwide.

Subtheories of IPARTheory. The theory has three subtheories: personality subtheory, coping subtheory, and sociocultural systems subtheory.

Attachment theory. This theory focuses on attachment or intimate relationships over an individual's lifespan.

Basic concepts of attachment theory. Attachment is as an enduring affective bond characterized by a tendency to seek and maintain proximity to an attachment figure.

Secure base. A secure base refers to a relationship with one or more responsive attachment figures who meet the child's needs and to whom the child can turn for security, when upset or anxious.

Internal working model. In attachment theory, internal working models are thought to be formed on the basis of individuals' early life experiences based on daily interactions with their attachment figures.

Agreements and differences between the two theories. IPARTheory and the attachment theory agree on at least five basic assumptions including evolutionary perspective, universal propensities, representational model, resistance to loss of significant relationships, and importance of affectional bonds. But they differ on major focuses including attachment styles, personality outcomes, internal representational models, and measurement approaches.

REFLECTIVE QUESTIONS

1. Discuss the origin of interpersonal acceptance-rejection theory and the paradigm shift in the theory.

2. Discuss the basic postulates and cross-cultural implications of interpersonal acceptance-rejection theory.

3. Discuss the origin and the assumptions of attachment theory.

4. Compare agreement and differences between the two theories.

5. Discuss the contributions of these two theories, specifically on intimate relationships, psychological adjustment, and lifespan development.

CHAPTER SIX

Theory-Based Research on Intimate Relationships

This chapter presents a review of theory-based empirical research on intimate relationships. The research literature is divided into two major sections. The first section contains a review of intimate relationship research based on IPARTheory. The second section contains a review of intimate relationship research based on attachment theory.

Review of IPARTheory Literature

The literature on IPARTheory's three central constructs—parental (maternal and paternal) acceptance-rejection, parental control, and psychological adjustment—is reviewed in three subsections.

Consequences of Parental Acceptance-Rejection

Since the1930s, a large number of studies have been conducted on the antecedents and the consequences of perceived parental acceptance-rejection for cognitive, emotional, and behavioral development of children, and for personality functioning of adults within the United States and worldwide (Khaleque & Rohner, 2002a; Rohner, 1986/2000, 1994, 2001). Research on parent-child relations consistently indicates that perceived parental rejection typically has serious consequences for the psychological development and personality functioning of children and adults (Rohner, 1994). In a review of available cross-cultural and intracultural studies, for example, Rohner and Britner (2002) provided evidence of worldwide correlations between parental acceptance-rejection and other mental health issues including (1) depression and depressed affect; (2) behavior problems—conduct disorders, externalizing behaviors, and delinquency; (3) substance abuse; and (4) psychological maladjustment.

Depression

Parental rejection has been found to be linked consistently with both clinical and nonclinical depression within almost all major ethnic groups in the United States, including African Americans (Crook, Raskin, & Eliot, 1981), Asian Americans (Greenberger & Chen, 1996), European Americans (Whitbeck, Conger, & Kao, 1993), and Mexican Americans (Dumka, Roosa, & Jackson, 1997). Moreover, parental rejection has been found to be associated with depression in many countries internationally, including Australia (Parker, Kiloh, & Hayward, 1987), China (Chen, Rubin, & Li, 1995), Egypt (Fattah, 1996), Germany (Richter, 1994), Hungary (Richter, 1994), Italy (Richter, 1994), Sweden (Richter, 1994), and Turkey (Erkman, 1992). It is also interesting to note that a number of longitudinal studies show that perceived parental rejection in childhood tends to be associated with the development of depressive symptoms in adolescence and adulthood (Chen, Rubin, & Li, 1995).

Behavior Problems

According to Rohner and Britner (2002) parental rejection appears to be a major predictor in almost all forms of behavior problems, including conduct disorder, externalizing behavior, and delinquency. Cross-cultural findings supporting this prediction come from many countries across the world, including Bahrain (Al-Falaij, 1991), China (Chen, Rubin, & Li, 1997), Crotia (Ajdukovic, 1990), Egypt (Ahmed, 2008), England (Maughan, Pickles, & Quinton, 1995), India (Saxena, 1992), and Norway (Pedersen, 1994). As with depression, a number of longitudinal studies in the United States (Ge et al., 1996), and internationally (Chen, Rubin, & Li, 1997) show that parental rejection also tends to precede the development of behavior problems.

Substance Abuse

Possible support for the worldwide correlation between parental acceptance-rejection and substance abuse comes from substantial research evidence in Australia (Rosenberg, 1971), Canada (Hundleby & Mercer,

1987), England (Merry, 1972), the Netherlands (Emmelkamp & Heeres, 1988), and Sweden (Vrasti et al., 1990). These studies clearly indicate that parental rejection is etiologically connected with both drug abuse and alcohol abuse. Besides these cross-national studies, parental rejection has also been found to be linked with substance abuse in most ethnic groups in the United States, including African Americans (Myers et al., 1997), Asian Americans (Shedler & Block, 1990), and Hispanics (Coombs, Paulson, & Richardson, 1991). In addition, Rohner and Britner (2002) cited a large number of studies thoroughly documenting the relation between parental rejection and substance abuse among European American middle-class and working-class Americans.

Neuropsychological Effects of Rejection

Recent studies have shown that perceived rejection is related to developmental trauma disorder (Van der Kolk, 2010) and posttraumatic stress disorder (Courtois, 2004). Moreover, emotional neglect in childhood may be a significant risk factor for cerebral infarction in old age (Wilson et al., 2012). Perceived rejection and other forms of long-term emotional trauma are often implicated in the alteration of brain chemistry (Ford & Russo, 2006). Several brain imaging (fMRI) studies reveal that specific parts of the brain (i.e., the anterior cingulate cortex and the right ventral prefrontal cortex) are activated when people feel rejected (Eisenberger, 2012). Moreover, Fisher, Aron, and Brown (2006) found that different regions of the brain were activated among adults who were accepted versus those who were rejected by their partners.

Psychological Adjustment and Maladjustment

Numerous studies conducted across the world support the postulate of a significant transcultural association between perceived parental acceptance-rejection and psychological adjustments. For example, Rohner (1975) found supportive evidence for this postulate in a holocultural study of 101 societies worldwide. Moreover, Cournoyer (2000) reported a partial list of the sociocultural groups in different countries where this finding has been replicated and reconfirmed. This list includes the United States with African Americans, European Americans, and Hispanic Americans (Rohner, 1986/2000); Bahrain (Al-Falaij, 1991); Bangladesh (Rohner et al., 2010); Egypt (Ahmed, 2008); India (Parmar & Rohner, 2010); Japan (Rohner et al., 2008); Korea (Chyung & Lee, 2008); Czechoslovakia

(Matejcek & Kadubcova, 1984); Pakistan (Malik & Rohner, 2012); Peru (Gavilano, 1988); Mexico (Rohner, Roll, & Rohner, 1980); Nigeria (Haque, 1988); St. Kitts, West Indies (Rohner, Kean, & Cournoyer, 1991); and Turkey (Erkman & Rohner, 2006). In addition, a review of a large number of cross-cultural studies showed that the predicted relations between perceived parental acceptance-rejection and psychological adjustment emerged almost invariably in all studies (Khaleque & Ali, 2017; Khaleque & Rohner, 2002a).

Meta-Analytic Studies on Interpersonal Acceptance and Psychological Adjustment

The strongest body of evidence about the worldwide relations between psychological adjustment-maladjustment and perceived parental acceptance-rejection comes from a number of cross-cultural and intracultural meta-analyses conducted to test the basic assumptions of IPARTheory's personality subtheory. So far 12 meta-analyses have been conducted to test the central postulates of IPARTheory (Khaleque, 2015a; Khaleque & Ali, 2017). These meta-analyses are based on a total of 551 studies that were conducted over a period of 41 years (1975–2016). These studies represented an aggregated sample of 149,440 respondents. These respondents were taken from 31 countries in five continents (i.e., Africa, Asia, Europe, North America, and South America). The countries are Bangladesh, Barbados, China, Colombia, Croatia, Czechoslovakia, Egypt, Estonia, Finland, Greece, India, Iran, Jamaica, Japan, Kuwait, Mexico, Nigeria, Pakistan, Peru, Poland, Portugal, Puerto Rico, Romania, South Korea, Serbia, Spain, St. Kitts, Sweden, Turkey, Ukraine, and the United States. The overall results of these meta-analyses confirmed that there are significant relations between interpersonal acceptance, and psychological adjustment, and personality dispositions of children and adults regardless of differences in race, ethnicity, culture, age, gender, and geographical boundary (Khaleque, 2015a; Khaleque & Ali, 2017).

The meta-analytic reviews of IPARTheory research specifically tested pancultural relationships between (1) perceived parental acceptance-rejection and psychological adjustment of children and adults; (2) perceived parental acceptance-rejection and personality development of children and adults; (3) perceived parental control and developmental outcomes of children and adults; and (4) perceived partner acceptance-rejection, control, and psychological adjustment of adults. Findings of these meta-analyses are discussed in the following sections.

Perceived Parental Acceptance-Rejection and Psychological Adjustment of Children and Adults

Among the 12 meta-analyses conducted so far, 8 of them have been performed to test pancultural associations between perceived maternal and parental acceptance and the overall psychological adjustment of children and adults globally (Ali et al., 2017; Khaleque, 2015a). Overall results of these meta-analyses reveal that parental acceptance-rejection has significant pancultural relations with the psychological adjustment of children and adults regardless of gender. In addition, the results showed that the effect sizes of the relation between perceived parental acceptance and psychological adjustment were significantly higher for children than for adults. Approximately 26 percent of variability in children's psychological adjustment and about 21 percent of variability in adult's psychological adjustment were accounted for by perceived parental acceptance-rejection.

Perceived Parental Acceptance-Rejection Personality Dispositions of Children and Adults

As noted earlier, IPARTheory's personality subtheory assumes that children and adults universally—irrespective of culture, race, ethnicity, gender, and socioeconomic status—are phylogenetically predisposed to develop a specific constellation of personality dispositions as a consequence of varying degrees of perceived parental acceptance or rejection (Rohner, 1986/2000, 1990, 1999). Results of one meta-analytic review, based on 30 studies from 16 countries in five continents involving 12,087 children, has shown that both paternal and maternal acceptance-rejection often make independent or unique contributions to the personality development of children (Khaleque, 2013b). Results specifically showed that perceived parental warmth correlated significantly with personality dispositions, including low hostility and aggression, independence, positive self-esteem, positive self-adequacy, emotional responsiveness, emotional stability, and positive worldview of children across ethnicities, cultures, gender, and geographical boundaries.

In addition, the experience of parental acceptance tends worldwide to be associated with the development of children's prosocial behavior (such as generosity, helpfulness, and empathy), and in adults with a sense of overall well-being and positive psychological and physical health (Rohner & Khaleque, 2014).

Results of two other meta-analyses (Khaleque, 2015a; 2017a; Khatun et al., 2017) on children have shown that both maternal and paternal indifference/neglect, hostility/aggression, and undifferentiated rejection correlated significantly with seven negative personality dispositions, including (1) hostility and aggression, (2) dependence or defensive independence, (3) negative self-esteem, (4) negative self-adequacy, (5) emotional instability, (6) emotional unresponsiveness, and (7) negative worldview of children across ethnicities, cultures, and geographical boundaries as postulated in PARTheory.

Findings of another meta-analysis have shown that both children's and adults' perceptions of paternal and maternal acceptance are transculturally associated with their positive personality dispositions, including low hostility and aggression, independence, positive self-esteem, positive self-adequacy, emotional responsiveness, emotional stability, and positive worldview (Khaleque & Rohner, 2011).

Significance of Paternal versus Maternal Acceptance-Rejection

Since the end of the 1990s, IPARTheory researchers began to recognize that paternal love has as great as or sometimes greater impact on child development than maternal love (Rohner, 1998). Many of the early studies showed that paternal love is as influential as maternal love in predicting various psychological outcomes (Rohner & Veneziano, 2001). The majority of studies that assess the relation between parental rejection and psychological maladjustment tend to focus predominantly on the influence of mothers' behavior even though fathers are often as strongly implicated as mothers in many developmental outcomes. An increasing number of studies show that perceived paternal acceptance often has as strong or even stronger implications than perceived maternal acceptance for children's positive developmental outcomes, including psychological adjustment (Rohner & Veneziano, 2001). Results of a recent meta-analytic review have shown that father love has a significantly stronger relation with children's psychological adjustment than mother love cross-culturally (Khaleque & Rohner, 2012). Findings of this and other meta-analyses partially support the IPARTheory's postulate that perceived paternal acceptance is likely to have as strong or even stronger effects on children's and adult offspring's psychological adjustment and emotional and behavioral development than perceived maternal acceptance (Khaleque & Ali, 2017). These findings also provide support to a wider body of literature showing that perceived paternal love is likely to have a greater impact on children's and adults' developmental outcomes than perceived maternal love (Li, Meier, & Adamsons, 2017; Parmar & Rohner, 2005, 2008; Schwartz et al., 2009; Sultana & Khaleque, 2016; Veneziano, 2003).

Moreover, in a review of a large number of cross-cultural studies, Rohner & Britner (2002) have found that perceived paternal rejection tends to have stronger negative implications than perceived maternal rejection for the development of depression, conduct disorder, and substance abuse.

Studies drawing the conclusion that paternal love often predicts specific child and adult outcomes better than maternal love tend to deal with the following six issues among children, adolescents, and adults (Rohner & Veneziano, 2001): (1) personality and psychological adjustment problems, (2) mental illness, (3) psychological health and well-being, (4) conduct disorder, (5) substance abuse, and (6) delinquency. The literature on paternal love shows that paternal acceptance-rejection tends to be deeply implicated in a wide variety of outcomes including cognitive, emotional, and behavioral problems, and psychological well-being of children and adult offspring. This literature further indicates that paternal love seems to affect offspring development at all ages from infancy through adulthood (Rohner & Veneziano, 2001). A recent meta-analysis shows that the outcomes of paternal versus maternal love can be different for sons and daughters. For example, remembrance of maternal love in childhood showed significantly stronger relations with adult sons' current psychological adjustment than that of adult daughters. Moreover, remembrance of paternal love in childhood showed significantly stronger relations with adult daughters' psychological adjustment than did daughters' remembrances of maternal love (Ali, Khaleque, & Rohner, 2015).

Perceived Parental Control and Developmental Outcome of Children and Adults

Parental control is another important domain of parenting having significant influence on child, adolescent, and adult development (Rohner & Pettingill, 1985). Parental control generally appears not to have a great deal of developmental impact by itself but does have its effects mostly in the context of varying degrees of perceived parental acceptance and rejection (Rohner & Khaleque, 2008, 2014). The research literature assessing the effects of parental control on specific child and adult outcomes is quite extensive because it contains a variety of conceptualizations of parental control (Barber, 1996). As explained earlier, in IPARTheory, parental control refers to the permissiveness-strictness continuum of parental behavior, which fits with the concept of behavioral control rather than psychological control (Rohner & Khaleque, 2008). Despite the fact that IPARTheory has consistently tried to empirically assess the impact of perceived parental control on individuals' development, there has been not much research literature in IPARTheory on the effects of perceived parental control on various child and adult outcomes (Rohner & Khaleque, 2014). For example, a meta-analytic study by Rohner and Khaleque (2003) reports only 11 studies on parental control in IPARTheory research literature from 1987 through 2000. The overall results of this meta-analysis show negative relationships between parental behavioral control and psychological adjustment of children and adults. But a number of recent studies have shown that parental control has no independent effects on the psychological adjustment of children and adults (Khaleque & Rohner, 2012; Khaleque, Rohner, & Rahman, 2011; Rohner & Khaleque, 2014). Findings of several international studies suggest that much of the influence of behavioral control on developmental outcomes is mediated to a large degree by perceived parental acceptance and rejection (e.g., Rohner & Khaleque, 2005, 2008). Few earlier studies showed that parental control has some other outcomes on children, adolescents, and adults, such as (1) parental warmth and control jointly tend to be better predictors of self-adequacy among adolescents than parental control alone (Saavedra, 1980); and (2) a significant positive correlation exists between parental control in childhood and job instability in adulthood (Rising, 1999).

Perceived Partner Acceptance-Rejection, Control, and Adults' Psychological Adjustment

As noted earlier, IPARTheory-based research on perceived partner acceptance-rejection, control, and adults' psychological adjustment started in 2001 (Khaleque, 2001). The first study examined the impact of perceived acceptance-rejection by intimate male partners on the psychological adjustment of heterosexual adult females in the United States. It also explored the way in which remembered childhood experiences of maternal and paternal acceptance influenced the relation between current partner acceptance and psychological adjustment. Analyses revealed that women's adjustment was impaired to the degree that they experienced their intimate partners to be rejecting. Additionally, results showed that both partners' acceptance and paternal acceptance had a significantly greater impact on women's psychological adjustment than did maternal acceptance (Khaleque & Rohner, 2004; Rohner & Khaleque, 2008). Results also revealed significant independent effects of both partner and paternal acceptance—but not maternal acceptance—on the heterosexual women's psychological adjustment. Parental and partner acceptance jointly accounted for 20 percent of the variability in the women's psychological adjustment of which partner acceptance alone accounted for approximately 16 percent, paternal acceptance about 4 percent, and maternal acceptance almost none. These findings are consistent with the findings of an increasing body of cross-cultural research that shows that perceived paternal acceptance often has as great and sometimes greater impact on child and adult development than perceived maternal acceptance (Parmar & Rohner, 2005, 2008; Rohner, 1998; Schwartz et al., 2009). The reason for the greater impact of paternal love than maternal love on adult offspring's psychological adjustment may be the fact that families all over the world are still male dominant. Consequently, children often perceive their fathers to have more power and prestige than their mothers (Khaleque, Rohner, & Laukkala, 2008; Sultana & Khaleque, 2016).

Findings of a study (Khaleque, Rohner, & Shirin, 2010) showed that adults, who remembered their fathers as having higher power and prestige than their mothers, reported better psychological adjustment than did adults who reported their fathers having lower power and prestige than their mothers. In addition, results showed a significant interaction between paternal acceptance and partner acceptance on the women's psychological adjustment. This interaction can be seen in Figure 6.1.

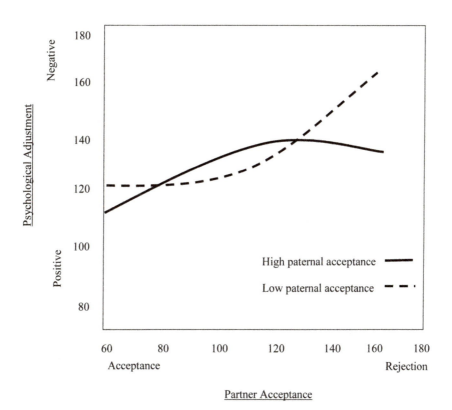

Figure 6.1 Interaction between Paternal Acceptance and Partner Acceptance in Relation to the Psychological Adjustment of Heterosexual Women (Adapted from Khaleque, 2001)

Figure 6.1 shows that heterosexual women tend to be fairly well adjusted in so far as they perceive their male partners to be warmly accepting—especially when they see their fathers as having been accepting too. As their partners become less loving, however, all the women reported more impaired psychological adjustment, but only up to a specific point for the women who had loving fathers. For them, the fact of having had a loving relationship with their fathers in childhood appears to help protect them from the more serious psychological effects of lowered partner acceptance. Women who did not experience strong paternal acceptance in childhood seem to be denied the benefit of such a protective buffer (Khaleque, 2001).

Results also revealed significant negative correlation between perceived partner control and psychological adjustment of adults. Thus results showed that more controlling partners were perceived as less accepting (loving). One of the reasons why more controlling attachment figures are perceived as less loving may be that strict behavioral control is often perceived as a form of rejection or lack of love (Khaleque, Rohner, & Shirin, 2010; Rohner & Khaleque, 2015b).

Results concerning perceived partner acceptance, partner control, and qualities of the attachment bond indicated that only perceived partner acceptance but not partner control was positively and significantly correlated with three attachment variables: (1) wishing to spend time with or be near to the partner, (2) feeling a sense of joy when reunited with the partner, and (3) feeling emotionally close to the partner. On the other hand, results revealed that partner acceptance but not partner control was negatively and significantly correlated with two attachment variables: (1) feeling insecure or anxious in relationship with the partner, and (2) wanting to avoid or ignore the partner.

This path-breaking study sparked a great deal of international interest, so much so that research on the same topic had started in more than 15 countries worldwide following that study (Khaleque, 2007). However, a meta-analysis by Rohner and Khaleque (2010) reports 17 cross-cultural studies on partner acceptance-rejection and psychological adjustment of adults in IPARTheory research literature from 2001 through 2008. This meta-analysis addressed the following questions: (1) Is perceived rejection by an intimate partner in adulthood associated with the same form of psychological maladjustment that perceived parental rejection is known to be in childhood? (2) Are adults' remembrances of parental acceptance in childhood associated with their current psychological adjustment? (3) Do such relations vary by culture or gender? The meta-analysis was based on 3,568 adults in 10 nations. Results showed that perceived partner acceptance in adulthood and remembered paternal and maternal acceptance in childhood tend to correlate highly with the current psychological adjustment of both men and women across cultures.

Childhood Parental Acceptance-Rejection, Adult Intimate Relationships, and Psychological Adjustment

This section contains more detailed discussion about relationships between childhood parental acceptance-rejection, partner acceptance-rejection, and adults' psychological adjustment. Several IPARTheory-based studies have shown that childhood experience of parental acceptance-rejection significantly mediate adult intimate relationships and psychological adjustment (e.g., Chyung & Lee, 2008; Khaleque, Rohner, & Laukkala, 2008; Parmar, Ibrahim, & Rohner, 2008; Varan, Rohner, & Eryuksel, 2008). For example, a study (Khaleque, Shirin, & Uddin, 2013) explored relations among remembered parental (paternal and maternal) acceptance in childhood, spouse acceptance and psychological adjustment of adults. It also explored whether remembered childhood experiences of parental acceptance mediate the relation between perceived spouse acceptance and psychological adjustment. The sample consisted of 354 married adult men (178) and women (176). Results have shown that the more accepting both men and women perceived their spouses to be, the better was their psychological adjustment. Similarly, the more accepting both men and women remembered their parents had been to them during childhood, the better was their current psychological adjustment. Multiple regression analyses revealed that paternal acceptance mediated the relation between perceived spouse acceptance and the psychological adjustment of both men and women. In addition, remembered maternal acceptance mediated the relation between men's (but not women's) perceived spouse acceptance and psychological adjustment. Figures 6.2 and 6.3 show the mediation effects of childhood parental acceptance or love on the adult intimate relationships and psychological adjustment.

Figure 6.2 shows significant independent effects of perceived spouse acceptance ($\beta=.27$, $t=3.57$, $p<.001$), paternal acceptance ($\beta=.26$, $t=3.22$, $p<.001$), and maternal acceptance ($\beta=.20$, $t=2.44$, $p<.01$) in men's psychological adjustment. Both paternal and maternal acceptance have significantly mediated the relation between spouse acceptance and psychological adjustment of men.

On the other hand, Figure 6.3 shows paternal (but not maternal) acceptance ($\beta=.53$, $t=8.13$, $p<.001$), and partner acceptance ($\beta=.35$, $t=5.69$, $p<.001$) has made significant contribution to women's psychological

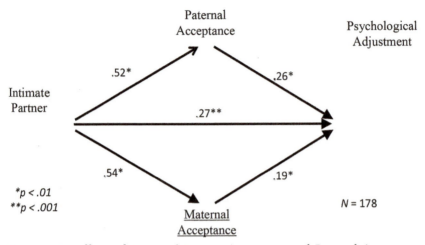

Figure 6.2 Effects of Perceived Partner Acceptance and Parental Acceptance on the Psychological Adjustment of Men (Note: Path coefficients are standardized regression. Adapted from Khaleque, Shirin, & Uddin, 2013.)

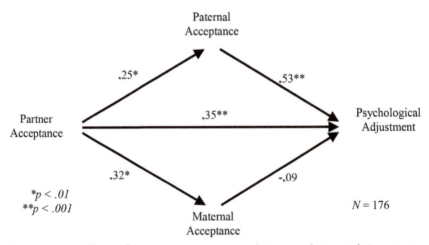

Figure 6.3 Effects of Partner Acceptance and Perceived Parental Acceptance on the Psychological Adjustment of Women (Note: Path coefficients are standardized regression. Adapted from Khaleque, Shirin, & Uddin, 2013.)

adjustment. Paternal (but not maternal) acceptance also significantly mediated the relation between spouse acceptance and psychological adjustment of women. It is interesting to note that childhood experience of paternal acceptance has accounted for greater variability in men's and women's psychological adjustment than the variability accounted for by the experience of childhood maternal acceptance.

These findings are supported by several studies on IPARTheory-based intimate adult relationship research (e.g., Khaleque, 2012; Parmar & Rohner, 2008; Ripoll-Núñez & Alvarez, 2008; Rohner, Melendez, & Kramer-Rickaby, 2008; Rohner & Melendez, 2008).

Adult Intimate Relationships, Quality of Life, and Psychological Adjustment

In addition to research on the relationships between parental acceptance, partner acceptance, and psychological adjustment, IPARTheory research also explored relationships between adult intimate relationships, quality of life, and psychological adjustment. For example, results of one study on American college students have revealed significant independent effects of intimate relationships and the quality of life on the psychological adjustment of the respondents. Results further showed that approximately 19 percent of the variability in the respondents' psychological adjustment was accounted for by intimate relationships and approximately 23 percent of the variability in psychological adjustment was accounted for by their quality of life (Khaleque, 2004). Findings of another study showed that married women reported higher perceived rejection by their partners compared to unmarried ones. It was also reported that intimate partner acceptance and resilience significantly predicted subjective well-being (Geitsidou & Giovazolias, 2016). This result confirmed previous findings that positive romantic relationships and resilience are important for people's happiness and psychological adjustment (Demir, 2008, 2010; Martin, 2005; Ong et al., 2006).

IPARTheory Measures of Adult Intimate Relationships

IPARTheory researchers have been using two standardized questionnaires for measuring adult intimate relationships. These questionnaires are (1) the Intimate Partner Acceptance-Rejection/Control Questionnaire (IPAR/CQ), and (2) the Intimate Adult Relationship Questionnaire (IARQ).

The Intimate Partner Acceptance-Rejection/Control Questionnaire (IPAR/CQ), developed by Rohner (2005), is a major instrument that is mainly being used in IPARTheory research on adult intimate relationships. This questionnaire consists of two sections: (1) The first section contains five items related to the nature of the intimate relationship along with items dealing with respondents' feelings about that relationship. (2) The second section deals with adults' reflections on the acceptance-rejection and behavioral control of their intimate partners. This section contains 73 items, 60 of which pertain to the different expressions of perceived acceptance-rejection, and 13 of which pertain to the perceived behavioral control of partners. More specifically, the acceptance-rejection portion consists of four subscales: warmth/affection ("My partner says nice things about me"); hostility/aggression ("My partner hits me"); indifference/neglect ("My partner pays no attention to me"); and undifferentiated rejection ("My partner does not really love me"). The fifth subscale measures perceived partner behavioral control (e.g., "My partner wants to control whatever I do"). All items are scored on a four-point Likert-like scale from (4) Almost Always True to (1) Almost Never True. Scores on the acceptance-rejection portion of the IPAR/CQ spread from a low of 60 to a high of 240. The higher the score the greater the perceived partner rejection.

The Intimate Adult Relationship Questionnaire (IARQ) was also developed by Rohner (2007). These two measures are almost identical except that the IARQ has an additional item to distinguish intimate partners who are true attachment figures from those who are significant others as defined in IPARTheory. Both the majors are designed in such a way that a lower score indicates higher acceptance, and a higher score indicates lower acceptance by an intimate partner.

A reliability analysis of the IPAR/CO shows that the alpha coefficient of the IPARQ portion is .80 and the test-retest reliability is .97 over a span of four weeks (Rohner, 2005).

Psychometric property of the IPAR/CO reported in Rohner and Khaleque (2005) shows that the instrument is reliable and valid for cross-culture research. An overview of IPARTheory research literature on intimate relationships has shown that alpha coefficients for the acceptance-rejection portion of the two measures ranges from .73 through .93 with a mean value of .81 (Rohner, 2008).

Concluding Comments About IPARTheory Literature

This brief review of IPARTheory literature shows the salience of parental acceptance-rejection, parental control, and psychological adjustment for various child and adult outcomes. The review indicates that attachment in early life has important implications for psychological adjustment and attachment relationships in later life. However, the review also reveals a gap in IPARTheory literature about the influences of perceived parental acceptance-rejection and psychological adjustment on the adult intimate relationships. Attachment theory deals with some of these issues. As such relevant attachment literature is reviewed in the following section.

Attachment Research Literature

Although attachment researchers were originally involved in studying emotional bonds between infants and their caregivers, Bowlby (1994, p. 29) considered attachment an important element of experience "from the cradle to grave." Hence, attachment research gradually developed across the lifespan including (Bretherton, 1995; Fraley & Shaver, 2000) (1) infant attachment, (2) childhood attachment, (3) adolescent attachment, and (4) adult attachment. The major focus here is on adult attachment research.

Review of Adult Attachment Research

Although numerous studies have been conducted on various aspects of attachment theory during the last 25 years, empirical research on adult attachment made little progress until the mid-1980s. Since then, researchers have concentrated mainly on the following areas of adult attachment (Simpson & Rholes, 1998): (1) early attachment and later development, (2) attachment and intimate adult relationships, (3) adult attachment measurement issues, and (4) adult attachment and psychological adjustment.

Early Attachment and Later Development

Ainsworth (1973) and Bowlby (1973) suggested that differences in the security of infant-mother attachment might have significant long-term implications for later intimate relationships and psychological adjustment. Reviewing empirical studies on this topic during the past two decades, Thompson (1998) indicated that sometimes attachment in infancy predicts later psychological functioning, and sometimes it does not. For example, there is evidence that securely attached infants are more popular with their peers and socialize more competently as preschoolers than insecurely attached infants (Sroufe, 1983; Troy & Sroufe, 1987; Vandell et al., 1988). Teti and Abalard (1989) found that securely attached children displayed more harmonious interactions with their siblings than did insecurely attached children. However, long-term follow-up studies showed weak relationships between attachment security and peer interactions at age 4 (Howes, Hamilton, & Matheson, 1994), interactions with close friends at age 5 (Youngblade & Belsky, 1992), and friendships at age 9 (Lewis & Feiring, 1989). On the other hand, several studies reported greater social competence and stronger friendship among adolescents with a secure attachment history in childhood (Elicker, Englund, & Sroufe, 1992; Grossmann & Grossmann, 1991; Shulman, Elicker, & Sroufe, 1994; Sroufe, Carlson, & Shulman, 1993). In another study, Cohen (1990) found that teachers and peers liked securely attached boys better than insecurely attached boys. Feiring and Lewis (1996), however, failed to find any relation between early attachment and later psychological maladjustment. Although some studies found associations between early attachment and later romantic relationships (e.g., Kalmuss, 1984), others found no such relationships (e.g., DeMaris, 1990). As an explanation of inconsistent empirical findings, Thompson (1998, p. 275) argued: "Though attachment security in infancy may reliably inaugurate short-term continuity in the harmony of parent-child relations, the evidence concerning long-term consistency is mixed, with continuity probably depending on important mediating conditions in the ecology of family life."

Attachment and Intimate Adult Relationships

This subsection reviews studies on attachment as they relate to intimate adult relationships, including close relationships and romantic relationships. Research efforts to explore adult intimate relationships from an attachment perspective draw extensively from attachment theory. Although attachment has been studied mostly in infants and children, Bowlby (1969/1982) made it clear that attachment is a lifelong process.

Despite similarities between infant attachment and adult attachment, adult romantic attachment received little attention before Hazan and Shaver's (1987) seminal study. Shaver and colleagues (Shaver & Hazan, 1988) presented a theoretical analysis of the relation between attachment and adults' romantic love. They found close similarities between infant attachment and adults' romantic love. For example, both children and adults tend to seek proximity and a secure base in attachment relationships. However, the authors noted two distinct differences: (1) infant-caregiver bonds have highly asymmetrical patterns of caregiving, but romantic love usually involves reciprocal caregiving; and (2) unlike infant attachment, romantic love almost always has a sexual component.

Hazan and Shaver (1987) showed that secure attachment with one's partner is associated with higher quality relationships (happier, closer, and more trusting). In their review, Feeney, Noller, and Roberts (2000) cited several studies that supported this finding (e.g., Collins & Read, 1990; Kirkpatrick & Davis, 1994; Simpson, 1990). Studies on romantic attachment were gradually extended to include marital relationships. Senchak and Leonard (1992) found that couples had more intimate marital relationships when both partners were secure than when one or both partners were insecure. In another study, Feeney (1994) reported a significant relation between secure attachment and marital satisfaction over all stages of the marital life cycle (Feeney, 1999). However, reviewing recent studies on romantic attachment, Feeney, Noller, and Roberts (2000) indicated that secure attachment does not necessarily lead to enduring intimate adult relationships because of the interaction of a wide variety of related factors.

Following an early study of Hazan and Shaver (1987), several other researchers became interested in exploring a wide range of issues related to adult romantic attachment. For example, Ainsworth (1989) identified six criteria for lifespan attachment typically characterizing adult romantic relationships: (1) stability, (2) specificity to the individual, (3) emotional significance, (4) desire for proximity, (5) distress at separation, and (6) security and comfort. Cassidy (2000) has indicated that individual differences in adult romantic attachment may emerge, in part, from individual differences in childhood attachments characterized by continuity or discontinuity across development. Although several attachment theorists and researchers have predicted that continuity or discontinuity in childhood attachment are likely to influence adult romantic relationships (Bowlby, 1973, 1980; Fraley & Shaver, 2000), very few empirical studies have so far been conducted to examine this prediction. A study conducted by Collins and Read (1990) showed that adults' descriptions of their childhood relationship with opposite-sex parents were related to their partners' descriptions of their attachment relationships. For example, women who described their fathers as responsive and warm were more likely to date men who described themselves as dependable and comfortable in getting close. On the other hand, men who described their mother as cold or inconsistent were more inclined to date women who considered themselves anxious about being abandoned. There are some other studies that provide evidence that individuals' earlier attachment history significantly influences their later attachment relationships (Elicker, Englund, & Sroufe, 1992; Sroufe & Fleeson, 1986). In this connection Cassidy (2000) suggested that individuals' attachment relationships can be influenced by variety of factors including (1) current attachment environment, (2) early experiences, (3) variations in personality characteristics, and (4) stability and change in values and expectations.

Adult Attachment and Psychological Adjustment

In a recent review of adult attachment research literature, Cassidy and Shaver (1999) indicated that intimate adult relationships have significant impact on the psychological well-being of partners. Psychological consequences of intimacy problems are found in couples and in single adults who have difficulty in forming and maintaining intimate relationships (Hendrick & Hendrick, 2000). Individuals often experience the human limitations of their partners and develop fear of hurtful consequences of disrupted intimate relationships (Roberts & Prager, 1997). Results of some empirical studies show that fear of intimacy is negatively related to comfort with emotional closeness and with relationship satisfaction. On the other hand, fear of intimacy is positively related to loneliness and trait anxiety (Descutner & Thelen, 1991; Greenfield & Thelen, 1997). Because intimacy fulfills certain psychological needs, individuals who avoid intimate relationships are likely to feel lonely, anxious, or depressed (Solano, 1986). Several empirical studies show that disrupted intimate adult relationships make individuals susceptible to many psychological problems including stress, anxiety, substance abuse, suicide, and other forms of psychopathology (Bloom, Asher, & White, 1978; Goodwin et al., 1987; Lynch, 1977; Uchino, Cacioppo, & Kiecolt-Glaser, 1996).

It is interesting to note that a number of empirical studies have found connections between childhood attachment and adult psychological adjustment. For example, several longitudinal studies provide consistent evidence that disruption in early childhood attachment due to death of a parent increases risk for depression in later life (e.g., Harris, Brown, & Bifulco, 1990). Warren and colleagues (1997) found that infants with insecure attachment were significantly more prone than infants with secure attachment to develop anxiety disorders as adolescents. In addition, several researchers (see Dozier, Stovall, & Albus, 1999) have found links between childhood attachment-related experiences and some forms of adult psychological maladjustment including eating disorders, borderline personality disorder, and antisocial personality disorders. This brief review indicates that attachment in early life is likely to have important implications for psychological adjustment and attachment relationships in later life.

Adult Attachment Measurement Issues

Over the last two decades two independent traditions of research have emerged about the conceptualization and assessment of adult attachment (Cassidy & Shaver, 1999; Shaver, Belsky, & Brennan, 2000). The first tradition is pursued by developmental psychologists, who use mostly observational techniques to study child-parent relationships (Ainsworth et al., 1978), along with interview methods to study parents' psychological conditions about attachment (George, Kaplan, & Main, 1985). The first and probably most widely used measure of adult attachment in this tradition—the Adult Attachment Interview (AAI)—was developed by George, Kaplan, and Main (1985) to assess and predict the strange situation behavior of respondents' infants. The AAI classifies adults into four attachment categories: (1) secure/autonomous, (2) preoccupied, (3) dismissing/avoidant, and (4) disorganized/disoriented. Several studies showed that adults whose scores on the AAI fall in the secure category have infants who are rated as secure in the strange situation; adults whose scores fall in the preoccupied categories have infants who are rated as ambivalent; and adults whose scores fall in the disorganized category have infants who are rated as disoriented (Main, 1995; Main & Goldwyn, 1984).

The second tradition of research was initiated in the mid-1980s by social psychologists (Hazan & Shaver, 1987) who applied attachment concepts to the study of romantic relationships. Hazan and Shaver developed a simple self-report questionnaire to measure adult romantic attachment, based on Ainsworth's three patterns of childhood attachment: secure, avoidant, and anxious (Simpson & Rholes, 1998). The questionnaire asks respondents to think back about their most important romantic relationship and indicate which of the three types (secure, avoidant, or anxious) is most self-descriptive. Although few studies have correlated this measure with the AAI, it is generally assumed that the two measures are highly related because both place respondents into similar categories (see Crowell, Fraley, & Shaver, 1999; Hasse, 1999).

However, Bartholomew and Shaver (1998) contended that some authors who compared attachment measures overlooked or misinterpreted the domain differences between the AAI—which focuses on adults' childhood attachment relationships with parents, and the Hazan-Shaver measure—which focuses on adults' romantic relationships.

In addition to the AAI and the Hazan-Shaver questionnaire, a number of other instruments for measuring adult attachment were developed around the mid-1980s and the early 1990s. For example, Pottharst and

Kessler (reported in Pottharst, 1990) developed an Attachment History Questionnaire (AHQ) to assess adults' memories of attachment-related experiences in childhood. Armsden and Greenberg (1987) developed the Inventory of Parent and Peer Attachment (IPPA) to assess adolescents' perceived quality of current attachment with parents and peers. West and Sheldon-Keller (1992) developed the Reciprocal Attachment Questionnaire for Adults (RAQA) to measure secure relationships with primary attachment figures (parents, peers, or partners) in adulthood. Attachment researchers also developed a number of other scales including the Adult Attachment Questionnaire (AAQ; Simpson, 1990), the Adult Attachment Scale (AAS; Collins & Read, 1990), and the Attachment Style Questionnaire (ASQ; Feeney, Noller, & Hanrahan, 1994).

Accordingly, Crowell, Fraley, and Shaver (1999) argued that there is a great deal of confusion about what different measures of adult attachment do really measure, and how they are related to each other. On the other hand, Bartholomew and Shaver (1998) argued that despite differences in method, domain, dimension, and categorization, different assessment measures are likely to converge to varying degrees—particularly when the reliability and statistical power of these measures are high. However, considering substantial differences among adult attachment measures, Crowell, Fraley, and Shaver (1999) have suggested that researchers should evaluate underlying assumptions for each measure and its connection with attachment theory. In addition, they stressed the need to evaluate the relationship domain, whether it is parent-child, close friendships, or romantic partners.

It is apparent that there is still lack of convergence on a common reliable measure for assessing intimate adult relationships. Further works seem to be needed to develop a psychometrically robust measure, if researchers are to assess and communicate clearly with each other about the same constructs of adult attachment, especially intimate adult relationships.

Contributions of IPARTheory and Attachment Theory Research

Despite differences in concepts and measures, both IPARTheory and attachment theory research have made significant contributions to the understanding of the nature, characteristics, and dynamics of childhood attachment and adult intimate relationships. Research on both these theoretical traditions have provided empirical evidence of influences of childhood attachment on adult attachment, psychological adjustment, and personality and behavioral development. An important empirical contribution of attachment research on adult partnerships is the identification of forms of relationships depending on the characteristics and affective history of individuals (Cassidy, 2000). These forms of relationships indicate two pathways leading to positive psychosocial outcomes, such as healthy and adaptive relationships and behavior; or negative psychosocial outcomes, such as unhealthy and maladaptive relationships and behavior (Lopez & Brennan, 2000). IPARTheory research has also advanced existing knowledge about the effects of childhood parental love on adults' romantic and nonromantic relationships and psychological adjustment (Ahmed, Rohner & Carrasco, 2012; Rohner, 2008).

Attachment research has been increasingly focusing on clinical interventions for childhood attachment problems as well as intimate relationship problems in adulthood. Several authors have conducted studies on attachment correlates of different psychopathologies in adulthood, such as depression, anxiety, and posttraumatic disorders (Dozier et al., 2008). These works contributed to the development of strategies for effective psychotherapy and empirical validation of these strategies (Slade, 2008). Similarly, IPARTheory research on adult intimate relationships has also made significant contributions to the development of knowledge and skill for clinical interventions with couples who are experiencing adjustment and behavior problems resulting from perceived rejection within their intimate relationships (Donoghue, 2010; Rigazio-DiGilio & Rohner, 2008). Finally, attachment theory and IPARTheory researchers and practitioners could benefit through collaboration and exchange of knowledge and experiences in dealing with attachment-related developmental problems of children and adults globally.

CHAPTER SUMMARY

Chapter 6 contains reviews of IPARTheory research literature on consequences of parental rejection including depression, behavior problems, substance abuse, psychological maladjustment, personality development, significance of *paternal versus maternal* acceptance-rejection, parental control, and developmental outcomes of children and adults. The chapter also discusses IPARTheory measures of adult intimate relationships. In addition, the chapter explores attachment research literature on early attachment and later development, attachment and intimate adult relationship, adult attachment and psychological adjustment, and adult attachment measurement issues. The chapter also examines contributions of IPARTheory and attachment theory research on intimate relationships.

Consequences of parental acceptance-rejection. Research on parent-child relations consistently indicates that perceived parental rejection typically has serious consequences for the psychological development and personality functioning of children and adults across culture, gender, ethnicity, and geographical boundaries.

Significance of paternal versus maternal acceptance-rejection. Cross-cultural research findings support the IPARTheory's postulate that perceived *paternal* acceptance or love is likely to have as strong or even stronger effects on children's and adult offspring's psychological adjustment and emotional and behavioral development than does perceived maternal acceptance or love.

Outcomes of perceived parental and partner acceptance-rejection and control. Global research findings show that parental and partner control have no independent effects on the psychological adjustment of adults, and much of the influence of control on the developmental outcomes is mediated to a large degree by perceived parental and partner acceptance and rejection.

Adult intimate relationships, quality of life, and psychological adjustment. Global research findings confirm that positive romantic relationships and resilience are important for people's quality of life, happiness, and psychological adjustment.

IPARTheory measures of adult intimate relationships. IPARTheory researchers have been using two standardized questionnaires for measuring adult intimate mate relationships. These questionnaires are (1) the Intimate Partner Acceptance-Rejection/Control Questionnaire (IPAR/CQ), and (2) the Intimate Adult Relationship Questionnaire (IARQ).

Early attachment and later development. Reviews of empirical studies on this topic during the past two decades indicate that sometimes attachment in infancy predicts later psychological functioning, and sometimes it does not—because individuals' attachment relationships can be influenced by a variety of factors including current attachment environment, early experiences, variations in personality characteristics, and stability and change in values and expectations.

Adult attachment and psychological adjustment. Reviews of adult attachment research literature indicate that intimate adult relationships have a significant impact on the psychological well-being of partners. Disrupted intimate adult relationships make individuals susceptible to many psychological problems including stress, anxiety, substance abuse, suicide, and other forms of psychopathology.

REFLECTIVE QUESTIONS

1. Discuss correlations between parental acceptance-rejection and other mental health issues including depression and depressed affect; behavior problems—conduct disorders, externalizing behaviors, and delinquency; substance abuse; and psychological maladjustment on the basis of worldwide evidence.

2. Discuss the significance of paternal versus maternal acceptance-rejection on children's and adult offspring's personality development and psychological adjustment.

3. Discuss with research evidence the developmental outcomes of perceived parental control on children and adults.

4. Discuss with cross-cultural research evidence how childhood attachment influences intimate adult relationships.

5. Discuss and compare contributions of interpersonal acceptance-rejection theory and attachment theory, specifically on three areas of intimate relationships: development of empirical knowledge, assessment, and clinical applications with research evidence.

Communication in Intimate Relationships

Communication refers to a process of two-way exchange of thoughts, opinions, and information by speech or writing through a common language, or using some other modes, such as symbols, signs, body postures, etc. Since communication is a two-way process, a message should be prepared and conveyed in a way that the recipient understands it exactly the way it is intended. Moreover, the recipient should be open, attentive, and willing to understand the full meaning of the message to make the sender feel heard and understood.

Different Categories of Communication

Three major categories of communication frequently used by intimate partners are:

- *Verbal or spoken communication.* Face-to-face, telephone, wireless, etc.
- *Nonverbal communication.* Facial expression, body language, gesture, gaze, touch, etc.
- *Digital communication.* E-mail, text message, Skype, MySpace, Facebook, Twitter, and other modes of Internet communication.

The categories of communication just mentioned are not necessarily mutually exclusive. For instance, some subcategories of verbal communication can also be digital or Internet based such as Skype. However, verbal, nonverbal, and online communications are the most common and frequently used categories of communication in intimate relationships.

Verbal Communication

Verbal communication plays a very vital role in the development of close relationships, especially at the initial stage of intimacy (Miller, 2015; Solomon & Theiss, 2013). Verbal communication is more than words and grammar (Wiley, 2007).

Topics of Verbal Communication

Topics of verbal communication among intimate partners may vary by gender and age. For instance, women, more often than men, tend to focus their discussion on personal matters, such as experiences, expectations, feeling, and emotions related to their own lives, and different aspects of intimate relationships. Women want greater depth of communication (Barth & Kinder, 1988), more emotional involvement (Barth & Kinder, 1988), and closeness (Markiewicz & Doyle, 2012) in their friendships than do men. While men, more often than women, tend to focus their conversation on impersonal matters such as jobs, sports, cars, celebrities, politics, and economics instead of friends (McHugh & Hambaugh, 2010).

Generally, friendship networks tend to become smaller in middle adulthood and late adulthood than young adulthood. Middle-aged adults and older adults generally talk more about real life issues with friends than young adults who tend to focus their discussion more on emotional and love-related matters (Antonucci, Akiyama, & Merline, 2001).

Style of Verbal Communication

Research has shown that the quality of intimate relationship is related to the quality and style of communication (Knapp & Vangelisti, 2009). It means that in an intimate relationship, it matters what partners say and how they say it. Partners are likely to be more attracted to each other when they use language more skillfully and appropriately (Ireland et al., 2011).

Gender Differences in Verbal Communication

Women and men often vary in their style of conversation. Women tend to speak somewhat less forcefully and less directly than do men (Leaper & Robnett, 2011). Women are generally more tentative, less assertive, more feeling oriented, and less profane than men in conversation with other-sex friends (McHugh & Hambaugh, 2010; Palomares, 2009). Moreover, men and women differ in self-disclosure. Women self-disclose more than men in conversation with other-sex intimate friends. But men self-disclose much less to same-sex friends than they do to the other-sex friends (Dindia, 2002).

Personality and Conversation Style

Another factor that has been found to influence individuals' social interactions and conversation style is masculinity and femininity characteristics in their personality (Aube & Koestner, 1995). According to Bem (1985), people of both sexes have a mixture of masculinity and femininity. Bem places people in one of the four categories in terms of personality characteristics:

- *Masculine.* Predominantly manly characteristics.
- *Feminine.* Predominantly womanly characteristics.
- *Androgynous.* High in both masculinity and femininity.
- *Undifferentiated.* Low in both masculinity and femininity.

An androgynous individual is likely to be assertive, dominant, compassionate, and understanding; and such a person tends to have meaningful social interactions with both men and women (Aube et al., 1995).

Nonverbal Communication

People communicate verbally as well as nonverbally. Nonverbal communication is speaking without words, especially expressing meaning and feeling without any spoken language. Major components of nonverbal communication include facial expressions, body posture or body language, proximity, eye contact, and touching. Some people are better able to understand nonverbal cues than others (Myers, 2010). Some researchers have viewed that nonverbal communication accounts for the majority of information transmitted in interpersonal interactions (Onsager, 2014).

Similarities and Differences in Communication across Cultures and Gender

Although there are some similarities in expressing human emotions throughout the world, there are also distinct cultural differences in expressing emotions, such as happiness, fear, and sadness nonverbally. People all over the world understand that when children cry they reflect a feeling of sadness, and when smile they indicate a feeling of happiness (Myers, 2010). There are, however, differences in nonverbal communications across cultures. In some cultures, such as the Arab and Iranian cultures, people express grief openly, while in other cultures (e.g., China and Japan) people are more subdued as they believe that it is not acceptable to show emotion openly (whether sadness or happiness). People of different cultures differ in nonverbal expressions of emotion about love and intimacy. Feelings of love and intimacy exist everywhere in the world, but expressions of such feelings vary widely in different cultures. For instance, it is acceptable in some cultures for men to kiss, hug, or embrace openly—the women they love, while in other cultures public display of such emotions are discouraged as not usual or acceptable.

As in nonverbal communication, what is considered usual or acceptable behavioral practice in one culture may be seen as unusual or impolite in another culture. For example, in one culture snapping fingers to call a waiter may be appropriate, whereas in another culture it may be considered an indecent or rude gesture. The following section describes cultural similarities and differences in transmitting information, meaning, and feeling through a number of components of nonverbal communication.

Facial Expression

There is a common proverb that the face is the index of the mind. For example, people across cultures can easily understand the facial expression of happiness, surprise, fear, sadness, anger, and disgust. Peoples' facial expressions indicate their moods and emotions that can be recognized by others more or less similarly (Matsumoto & Hwang, 2013a). Despite cultural differences, the facial expressions of basic human emotions speak a universal language, which can be easily understood by people across cultures (Myers, 2010). The universality of facial expressions is supported by the fact that people who are born blind display the same facial expressions to express their emotions as the rest of others with normal eye sight (Matsumoto & Hwang, 2013a).

Do facial expressions have different meanings in different cultures? Findings of several studies reveal that despite cultural differences, people show a great deal of agreement in categorizing facial expressions as indicators of basic emotions—happiness, surprise, fear, sadness, anger, and disgust (e.g., Ekman & Friesen, 1994; Galati, Scherer, & Ricci-Bitti, 1997). But it is also true that facial expressions may carry different meanings in different cultures. For example, in American culture the smile is typically an expression of pleasure. But its meaning may vary in the same culture depending on situations and relationships, such as a woman's smile at an intimate partner does not carry the same meaning as the smile she gives to a young child. A smile may reflect affection, or love, or disguise of true feelings. For example, typically people in Russia consider smiling at strangers in public to be unusual. Yet Americans in general smile freely at strangers in public places. In Southeast Asian cultures, a smile is frequently used to cover unpleasant feelings or embarrassment. Thus the degree of facial expression one exhibits may vary among individuals within the same culture and between cultures.

People generally can better recognize the emotional expressions, including facial expressions, of individuals from their own culture than individuals from other cultures (Elfenbein, 2013). That is why it is difficult to generalize about Americans' facial expressions because of interethnic differences in the United States. People of one ethnic group in the United States may be more facially expressive than other ethnic groups. The bottom line is not to try to judge people whose ways of expressing emotions are culturally different on the basis of our own cultural norms; if we do, we may read other people's facial expressions incorrectly.

Because of social desirability, people often try to cover up their true nonverbal emotional expressions deliberately. There are at least four ways people try to mask their true nonverbal emotional expressions (Matsumoto & Hwang, 2013b; Miller, 2015):

1. *Exaggerating expressions.* To be consistent with the demand of a situation, people may try to maximize or intensify their expressions so that they appear to be experiencing stronger feelings than they are really experiencing.

2. *Minimizing expressions.* People sometimes try to downplay their emotional expressions to appear less emotionally affected than they really are. For instance, because of social desirability, a man may try to minimize his emotional expressions not to look too affected by a sad event.

3. *Neutralizing expressions.* People may try to cover up or downplay their true feelings by masking their emotional expressions. For example, people usually try to control and minimize overt expression of their feelings of frustration and anger against seniors and higher authority openly in public.

4. *Replacing expressions.* People may try to mask their negative emotional expressions by replacing them with apparent positive emotional expressions. For example, a person who expected to win a beauty contest may show apparent excitement when another contestant is declared the winner, masking her true feeling of frustration.

However, it is possible to mask real emotional expressions only partially and temporarily, and not completely for a long time. Several research findings show that despite people's efforts to control their emotional expressions, real emotion can be visible either during momentary lapses of control or during longer interactions (e.g., Gunnery, Hall, & Ruben, 2013; Yan et al., 2013).

Eye Contact

Eye contact is one of the most effective nonverbal communication tools, which is essential for communicating positive involvement (Manusov & Patterson, 2006). Eye contact is another important nonverbal communication because insufficient or excessive eye contact can create barriers to effective communication. While talking with a person, direct and frequent eye contact reflects interest, likability, and attraction for that person rather than talking with little or no eye contact (Mason, Tatkow, & Macrae, 2005; Wirth et al., 2010). Intimate partners usually make more eye contact in their communication than friends do, and friends make more eye contact than acquaintances or strangers do (Kleinke, 1986).

Patterns and meanings of eye contact vary across cultures. For example, it is quite usual in the United States for two strangers walking toward each other to make eye contact, smile, and say "Hi" when they are walking on the road or meeting for a short time. This type of eye contact doesn't mean much, except acknowledging another person's presence and exchange of courtesy. Talking with little or no eye contact is considered a lack of interest, inattention, or even mistrust in Western cultures (Wirth et al., 2010). In contrast, in Oriental cultures (especially in Asian cultures) a person's lack of eye contact toward an authority figure signifies respect.

Body Posture

Body posture or body language can convey either positive feelings or negative feelings. For example, in a job interview, an individual can show positive body language to signal confidence by entering the interview room with a smiling face, head up, giving a firm handshake, exchanging warm greetings, and maintaining eye contact—instead of entering the room with head down, eyes averted, and sliding into a chair with a gloomy face.

Gesture and posture of different parts of the body (e.g., head, hands, and fingers) may convey different meanings in different cultures (Matsumoto & Hwang, 2013c). For example, nodding the head up and down indicates "yes," "agreement," or "approval," and shaking the head from side to side indicates "no" or "disagreement" in many cultures including Indian subcontinent, Southeast Asia. Although in some other countries and cultures, such as Greece, Macedonia, Bulgaria, Albania, Turkey, and Syria, nodding of the head indicates refusal or disagreement. The handshake is another form of nonverbal communication, which is a common ritual for expressing feelings of warmth and friendliness, and offering welcome and greetings in many cultures (Kurien, 2010). There are different styles of handshake, such as the bone crusher (shaking hands too strongly) and the limp fish (shaking hands too weakly). Handshakes are popular in Western cultures and are appropriate forms of greetings between men and women. However, in Muslim cultures handshakes between men and women are not considered appropriate. Likewise, in Hindu customs, men generally don't shake hands with women (Black, 2011). Finger gestures are also commonly used for nonverbal communication worldwide. However, in certain cultures, pointing one's index finger is considered appropriate, whereas in some other cultures (e. g., Hindu culture) finger pointing is considered offensive. Instead, people point with their thumbs (Black, 2011). Similarly, the thumbs-up gesture indicates "OK" or "good" in many countries such as the United States, France, and Germany. But the same gesture is considered insulting in other countries such as Iran, Bangladesh, and Thailand (Black, 2011).

Touching

Interpersonal feelings of warmth, love, affection, care, sympathy, and concern are often expressed physically through touching, which includes hugging, kissing, fondling, caressing, and comforting (Rohner & Khaleque, 2005). Two persons who are involved in an intimate relationship are more likely to touch each other than people who are not involved in such a relationship (Debrot et al., 2013). Meanings, feelings and emotions conveyed by touches are often clearly understood by the giver and the recipient (Hertenstein, 2011). Loving touches have many beneficial effects on health. For instance, frequent loving touches, such as kissing, from a partner can reduce one's cholesterol, stress, and depression (Burleson et al., 2013; Hertenstein, 2011).

Interpersonal Proximity

Physical proximity often affects spontaneity and comfort in communication. Physical distance between two persons in interpersonal communication often depends on the nature of the relationship. For example, people usually feel more comfortable standing closer to family members or to close friends and intimate partners than to strangers. Distances people keep during interpersonal communication also vary by culture. In some cultures people tend to interact with others from a closer physical distance than in other cultures (Matsumoto & Hwang, 2013a). Physical distance in interpersonal communication is also influenced by an individual's gender and social status. Physical distance during communication between an unknown or less known man and woman is likely to be larger than between intimate partners; and individuals usually keep a larger distance while communicating with people of higher social status than with people of lower social status (Holland et al., 2004).

Gender Differences in Nonverbal Communication

Men and women tend to differ in using nonverbal communication. Gender difference is evident in their skill in interpreting communication for understanding its meaning (Carnes, 2015). Research findings consistently showed that women are better than men at reading people's emotional cues (e.g., Grossman & Wood, 1993; Sprecher & Sedikides, 1993). Understanding gender differences in nonverbal communication is especially important when communicating with the other sex. One of the reasons for gender differences in nonverbal communication is that men and women have different reasons for communication. According to Gray (2012), men generally communicate to transmit information and solve specific problems, whereas women usually communicate to express feelings and achieve emotional intimacy. That is why women tend to use nonverbal communication more often than do men. Moreover, women are generally better able than men in interpreting nonverbal signals. Since women often use communication to establish an emotional connection, they make more eye contact during communication than do men. In addition, women are more likely to use facial expressions to convey their meaning and the intensity of their feelings (Gray, 2012). If culture permits, women tend to be more tolerant of physical proximity than men in communicating with friends of the same sex or of the opposite sex. Since women consider touching an expression of sympathy or friendship or love, they are far less reticent than men in touching the same sex or their opposite-sex friends during conversation (Carnes, 2015).

Digital Communication

Young adults are among the most frequent users of digital communication technologies, including e-mails, texting, instant messaging (IM), audiovisual chat, Internet sites such as blogs, social networking sites such as MySpace and Facebook, and photo and video sharing sites such as YouTube (Duggan & Brenner, 2013; Lenhart et al., 2011). Millions of young adults all over the world have been extensively using these networks for communication with peers (Subrahmanyam et al., 2008). One study showed that texting is the most frequently used digital communication among young adults in the United States today (Lenhart, 2012). Today's young adults are often described as "digital natives" because they have been excessively using digital technologies to develop and maintain friendships from adolescence through adulthood (Baird, 2010; Valkenburg & Peter, 2009). Some researchers have suggested that adolescents and young adults generally use digital communication mainly to maintain existing connections with acquaintances, friends, and family members (e.g., Reich, Subrahmanyam, & Espinoza, 2012; Subrahmanyam et al., 2008). Research evidence also showed that young adults can attain more or less the same level of connectedness with friends and intimate partners through digital communication as they can achieve through in-person communication (Sherman, Michikyan, & Greenfield, 2013).

Communication and Relational Interaction

An individual can realize through communication whether a partner's response is compatible with her/his expectations. Communication allows partners to test and be tested of mutual expectations in the friendship relationship. According to Knapp and Vangelisti (2009), there are 10 stages of interaction that explain how relationships are formed and come apart. These stages are presented in Table 7.1 and discussed in more detail in the following section. Note also that relational partners do not always follow through the stages sequentially, and some partners may not go through all the stages in their relationships (Knapp & Vangelisti, 2009). However, the 10 stages of relationship development, discussed as follows, provide some insights into the complicated nature of communication that affects processes of formation, development, deterioration, and termination of a relationship.

Initiating. Initiating is the introductory stage in which people try to present themselves favorably and impressively. The nature of introduction may vary from person to person in different situations. For example, an individual's introduction may vary depending on familiarity with a person (e.g., meeting a known or an unknown person, an acquaintance, or a friend), and setting (e.g., quick passing, a short encounter in an airplane, or a formal meeting).

Table 7.1   Relationship Stages

Processes	Stages	Communication Patterns
Coming together and formation	Initiating	"I am Nicole. It's good to meet you."
	Experimenting	"I like to visit friends in my spare time. What about you?"
	Intensifying	"I feel we are getting closer day by day."
	Integrating	(To friend) "How do you think about living together as intimate partners?"
	Bonding	"I am seriously thinking about getting married!"
Breaking apart	Differentiating	"Sometimes I'd like to spend my spare time in my own ways."
	Circumscribing	"Don't worry I can deal with my problems alone."
	Stagnating	(To self) "I don't know how long we can go along."
	Avoiding	"Sorry, I won't be able to go to the party together because I have an important program in my office."
	Terminating	"I am seriously thinking about living apart as I find it difficult to stay together."

Source: Adapted from Knapp & Vangelisti, 2009.

Experimenting. Experimenting is the stage where people begin to exchange information and try to move from strangers to acquaintances. The main purpose of experimenting is to find interesting people to establish friendly relationships. At this stage people begin with small talk politely and cheerfully just to find an entry point that can lead to conversation about topics of common interests (Knapp & Vangelisti, 2009).

Intensifying. In the intensifying stage, people indicate that they are ready and open to intimacy, and try to develop a level of intimacy gradually. This gradual intensification of intimacy can occur over a short period such as weeks or months, or over a long period such as years depending on several factors (e.g., personality, interest, motivation, gender, and level of interaction). Although processes of intensification may vary from person to person, people usually start meeting a new friend informally at a convenient time and place then may invite a friend to join a party or dinner and at certain point of further intimacy may invite to vacation together. As intimacy grows, people may start sharing personal information and asking for mutual favors. However, if one person asks for too many favors but fails to reciprocate favors granted, the relationship can be adversely affected and can result in differentiation and distancing.

In addition to sharing more intense personal time, requests for favors and granting favors may also play in the process of intensification of a relationship. For example, one friend helping the other prepare for a big party on their birthday can increase closeness. Maintaining a balance in mutual expectations and managing increasing closeness effectively are necessary for relational integration (Knapp & Vangelisti, 2009).

Integrating. In the integrating stage, two friends develop a sense of interdependence and identification with each other. Although this stage is most evident in romantic relationships, some elements of integration are also present in nonromantic relationships. However, when two people integrate, they are also likely to maintain some sense of self-identity by keeping contact with other friends and family separately, which helps them balance their needs for independence and connection.

Bonding. The bonding stage includes a public ritual of announcing a formal commitment of establishing a relationship between two couples, especially between romantic couples. These types of rituals are common in weddings or in civil unions. Although a formal announcement of bonding is a symbolic act, it has important social significance and can have positive effects on developing, maintaining, and integrating a romantic relationship, if and when conflict threatens it (Knapp & Vangelisti, 2009).

Differentiating. Differentiating may occur at any point in relational interactions due to individual differences in opinions, expectations, and behaviors about decision making and setting limits or boundaries for the handling of family matters and possessions. Differentiating may also begin with unpleasant discoveries about the other person's past history and personality characteristics during experimenting and integrating stages. Differentiating leads to disintegration of the relationship. Differentiating decision may be communicated to the partner directly through conversation or indirectly through behavior. Differentiating is likely to occur in a relationship that was bonded before the individuals knew each other sufficiently thoroughly.

Circumscribing. In the circumscribing stage, communication between partners decreases on a certain issue that is considered by one or both partners as unpleasant. They may not like to talk about that anymore. If this issue can't be settled amicably, a decrease in communication may occur in more areas. Eventually, if one partner becomes more interested in differentiating and terminating the relationship, the positive attitude and behavior of the other partner may not elicit any favorable response. A gradual decrease in communication may lead to further deterioration and stagnation of the relationship.

Stagnating. During the stagnating stage, the relationship may reach almost to a dead stop, and finally it comes to an end. In some cases this stage may continue for a short period, while in some other cases it may continue for a long duration. For example, couples in a dysfunctional marriage may wait for a short or a long time to repair or restore the relationship before they finally go for a divorce. Although people usually don't like to linger in this unpleasant stage, some may do so because they are unwilling to terminate the relationship, and may still hope somehow to restore and rebuild it.

Avoiding. As stagnation may lead to termination of the relationship, people in such a situation tend to avoid communication with partners because of awkwardness. Avoidance of communication may be direct—no talk with the partner anymore, or indirect—communicating through a third person. These situations may occur between friends who are living as roommates where a lease agreement prevents them from leaving immediately, or between two spouses who are living in the same house while they are fighting a legal battle to settle their marriage and property rights. In such situations, individuals may not like to communicate with each other even though they still temporarily share the same physical space.

Terminating. The termination of a relationship can occur shortly after initiation or after a long history of establishing the relationship. Termination can result from external factors such as conflicts over material possessions or geographical separation, or from internal factors such as changing expectations, values, or personalities that may lead to a weakening of the relationship bond. Communication to terminate may be direct (e.g., "Due to some ups and downs, our relationship has deteriorated so much that I find no way to rebuild it") or indirect (e.g., "We should rethink if we should continue such a dysfunctional relationship or better terminate it").

Effective Communication

Effective communication helps building and maintaining a healthy and solid foundation for an intimate relationship. It deepens connections and relationships between friends and intimate partners. It enables one to communicate even negative or difficult messages without causing misunderstanding, distrust, and conflict, and damaging or destroying relationships. Effective communication is a learned skill. It requires experience and training to develop spontaneous skills for good communication. It also takes time and effort to develop necessary skills to become an effective communicator.

Characteristics of Effective Communication

Effective communication refers to a clear and unambiguous delivery of the content of a message, so that the recipient can understand it correctly and respond to it appropriately. Several researchers have identified a number of essential characteristics of effective communication (e.g., Broom, 2012; Porges, 2011; Sollier, 2005). According these investigators, to be effective, communication should be (1) clear, (2) concise, (3) comprehensive, (3) concrete, (4) complete, (5) correct, (6) constructive, (7) realistic, (8) genuine, and (9) courteous.

Barriers to Effective Communication

Interpersonal communication may become problematic and dysfunctional for many different reasons. Several researchers have identified a host of reasons for dysfunctional communications in intimate relationships, including unwilling to listen and accept different viewpoints, being defensive and belligerent, lack of tolerance, unwilling to pay attention and share ideas and thoughts with partners, unwilling to compromise and agree, lack of mutual respect, lack of correct focus, inappropriate body language, miscommunication, lack of humor, using harsh words, hurting partners' feelings, interrupting partners' expressions of genuine feelings, and insincerity and dishonesty in communication (Bloch, Haase, & Levenson, 2014; Gottman, 2011; Kellas, Willer, & Trees, 2013).

Techniques for Removing Barriers to Effective Communication

According to researchers (e.g., Broom, 2012; Robinson, Segal, & Smith, 2015), techniques for removing barriers to effective communication combine a set of skills including:

- *Developing understanding.* Paying attention to partner's feelings, sharing ideas and thoughts with the partner, and caring for partner's values and beliefs—even if those are different from one's own values and beliefs—can improve communication.
- *Expressing intimacy.* Intimacy can be communicated through pleasant words, gestures, facial expressions, and touching.

- *Active listening.* To make communication effective, listening is as important and sometime more important than talking. Being a good listener can help make a conducive and congenial atmosphere for communication. An engaged listener can better understand the other person and can make that person feel heard and understood, which can help build a stronger and deeper connection with the other person.

- *Sincere self-disclosure.* Frank and honest self-disclosure may enhance trustworthiness of communication and increase emotional warmth and intimacy between partners.

- *Making partner a priority.* The focus of intimate communication should be to make a partner happy and feel loved. Focusing more on giving to the partner and less on getting from the partner can improve the intimate relationship.

- *Being respectful and supportive.* Being courteous, avoiding interruption, showing interest in what the partner is telling, and showing support by nodding and smiling can make intimate communication effective.

- *Appropriate humor.* Appropriate humor can be a good way to relieve stress and tension when communicating. When communication becomes too serious, humor can lighten the mood by sharing a joke or a funny story.

- *Providing positive feedback.* Positive feedback is important for constructive conversation. But feedback is effective only when it is authentic.

- *Authentic praise.* Praising is more effective when it is linked directly to a specific activity or attribute of a person, and when it is done publicly and genuinely. When one conveys negative information or criticism, one should begin with a praise and end with a positive statement.

- *Managing conflict.* Controlling anger, staying calm under pressure or provocation, being tolerant and willing to accept different views and feelings, and focusing more on positive than on negative aspects of partners' behavior can resolve conflict.

Finally, effective communication is more than an exchange of information. It is more about understanding the feeling, emotion, intention, and the overall meaning underlying the communication. Effective communication is critically important for building and maintaining strong intimate relationships (Wiley, 2007).

CHAPTER SUMMARY

Chapter 7 deals with major categories of communication, similarities and differences in communication patterns across cultures and gender, communication and relational interactions, characteristics of effective communications, and techniques for removing barriers to effective communication.

Communication in intimate relationships. Intimate communication is a process of two-way exchange of thoughts, opinions, and information between partners.

Categories of communication. Three major categories of communication that are frequently used by intimate partners are verbal or spoken communication, nonverbal communication, and digital communication.

Similarities and differences in communication across cultures and gender. Despite some similarities in expressing human emotions throughout the world, there are also distinct cultural differences in expressing emotions, such as happiness, fear, and sadness nonverbally.

Communication and relational interaction. Communication allows partners to test and be tested of mutual expectations in the intimate relationship. Partners can understand through communication whether their responses are compatible or not with one another's expectations.

Effective communication. Effective communication between partners helps building and maintaining a healthy and solid foundation for an intimate relationship.

Characteristics of effective communication. Effective communication should be clear, concise, comprehensive, concrete, complete, correct, constructive, realistic, genuine, and courteous.

Removing barriers to effective communication. Techniques for removing barriers to effective communication combine a set of skills including developing understanding, expressing intimacy, active listening, sincere self-disclosure, being respectful and supportive, appropriate humor, positive feedback, authentic praise, and effectively managing conflict.

REFLECTIVE QUESTIONS

1. What are the different categories of communication? Discuss similarities and differences in communication across cultures and gender.

2. Because of social desirability, people often try to cover up their true nonverbal emotional expressions deliberately. Discuss how people try to mask their true nonverbal emotional expressions.

3. Discuss the complicated nature of communication and relational interaction that affect processes of formation, development, deterioration, and termination of an intimate relationship.

4. What are the characteristics of effective communication and barriers to effective communication?

5. How can barriers to effective communication be removed?

Attraction and Intimate Relationships

As defined in the *Oxford English Dictionary,* "attraction is an action or a power of evoking interest in or liking for someone or something." Attraction may work as a motivating force that influences individuals to move toward one another, get closer, and develop interest, liking, and intimacy.

Foundation of Attraction

The foundation of interpersonal attraction is based on a number of elements including common interests, values, needs, desires, and preferences; mutual likability—good looks and appealing personality; beneficial interactions; and rewarding experiences (Braxton-Davis, 2010; Buss, 2012; Eastwick, 2013).

Types of Attraction

There are different types of attraction. They are not necessarily mutually exclusive but rather partially overlapping. Some of the major types of attraction are physical, psychological—personality, sexual, romantic, emotional, aesthetic, sensual, and intellectual attractions. Each type of these attractions is briefly discussed in the following section.

Physical Attraction

Physically attractive people are generally more likable than those who are physically unattractive (Brewer & Archer, 2007). Physical appearance is almost always the basis of a first impression people tend to form about one another. Although forming an impression about an individual on the basis of her/his physical attractiveness is just like judging the quality of a car by looking at its color, physical attractiveness still does matter. However, an important factor in physical attractiveness is matching. People usually prefer physically attractive to unattractive individuals as intimate partners, but they also tend to establish romantic relations with individuals who match their own physical attractiveness (Taylor et al., 2011). Generally, good-looking people want to pair with good-looking partners (Lee et al., 2008). Thus, similarity in physical attractiveness is often used as a criterion for finding an attractive romantic partner (Montoya, 2008). That is why husbands and wives tend to have matching physical attractiveness (Little, Burt, & Perrett, 2006). Different aspects of physical attraction are briefly discussed as follows:

Biological and evolutionary determinants of physical attraction. Despite cultural differences, people worldwide tend to agree on some criteria for attraction (Jones, 1995). For example, decisions of judges for international beauty contests on certain agreed criteria is an indication that there are some common determinants of attraction (e.g., biological and evolutionary aspects), which transcend cultural differences. Several researchers have found physical traits to be major determinants of attractiveness, dating, and intimate relationship development (e.g., Luo & Zhang, 2009; Simon, Aikins, & Prinstein, 2008). Attraction seems to be partially inherited because after birth infants tend to show preferences for attractive faces like adults (Perilloux, Webster, & Gaulin, 2010). Moreover, the biological basis of attraction is evident from variability in attractions of women toward men before and after their period of ovulation and fertility. For example, during their period of fertility women find some characteristics of men (such as manliness—dominance, bold, strong, and assertive) more attractive than during the period when they are not fertile (Gildersleeve, Haseltone, & Fales, 2014). Women also find scents of men with high testosterone than scents of men with low testosterone to be more attractive (Thornhill, Chapmen, Gangestad, 2013). During the fertile period women also tend to use more cosmetics and wear more sexy dress than during the period when they are not fertile (Gueguen, 2012; Schwarz & Hassebrauck, 2008).

People's preferences for physical attraction may also have an evolutionary basis. According to evolutionary views, human beings have acquired through the process of evolutionary adaptiveness a propensity to develop enduring preferences for physical and psychological attractions that serve adaptive functions (Little, Jones, & DeBruine, 2011).

Bias for physical attraction. Both males and females tend to be biased in favor of physically attractive persons. People generally presume without objective basis that physically attractive individuals are likely to have positive personality dispositions such as sociability, friendliness, warmth, nurturance, kindness, conscientiousness, and responsiveness (Lemay & Neal, 2014; Segal-Caspi, Roccas, & Sagiv, 2012).

Dating and physical attraction. Many researchers have found that physical attraction is a major determinant in potential mate selection process such as dating and marriage (Simon, Aikins, & Prinstein, 2008; Toma & Hancock, 2010). Compared to a young man's physical attractiveness, a young woman's physical attractiveness is a better predictor of frequency of dating (Toma & Hancock, 2010).

Gender and physical attraction. Importance of physical attraction in intimacy varies by gender. For example, men tend to give more importance to women's physical beauty, but women tend to give more importance to men's financial stability and pleasing personality than their physical appearance (Braxton-Davis, 2010). Despite individual and cultural differences, there is overall agreement among men about physical attractiveness of women, and among women about physical attractiveness of men (Jones, 1995). For example, women are generally considered attractive if they have baby-faced features combined with a slim body, large eyes, narrow waist, long hair, proportionately large breasts (proportionate to body size), average height and weight, and feminine and youthful appearance (Cunningham, Barbee, & Philhower, 2002; Faries & Bartholomew, 2012; Furnham, Swami, & Shah, 2006; Voracek & Fisher, 2006). Unlike women's attractiveness, men's attractiveness is somewhat more complex. Men are generally considered physically attractive to women if they (men) are tall and have broad shoulders and foreheads and a well-built body—giving a strong, energetic, and masculine look (Hughes & Gallup, 2003; Stulp, Buunk, & Pollet, 2013). However, a handsome physical feature does not attract a woman to man unless it is combined with an attractive personality and other resources including wealth, power, position, influence, and social status (Li, Valentine, & Patel, 2011; Singh, 1995).

Culture and physical attraction. Preference for physical attractiveness in an ideal intimate partner varies across cultures. Moreover, the definition of physical attractiveness also varies across cultures. For example, heavier women were considered more attractive in cultures in which the food supply was insufficient (Anderson et al., 1992). Similar findings were reported in another study in which respondents from Uganda, a relatively poor country, rated heavier women as more attractive than respondents in the United Kingdom (Furnham, Moutafi, & Baguma, 2002). Buss et al. (1990) reported substantial cultural variability in attraction for mate preferences in different societies globally. Some studies reported that the preference for physical attractiveness tended to be higher in

Western societies than Oriental societies, perhaps because of mass media influences in Western cultures (e.g., Gangestad, Haselton, & Buss, 2006). Moreover, criteria for judging physical attractiveness can vary between different ethnic groups in the same country. For example, different ethnic groups within the United States adhere to different standards of feminine beauty. Black and Hispanic men and women consider bulgy women to be more attractive than Whites do, because obesity is less stigmatized in Black and Hispanic subcultures than in White subculture (Glaser, Robnett, & Feliciano, 2009; Hebl & Heatherton, 1998). In addition, criteria for judging physical attractiveness can change in the same culture over a certain period of time. For example, attraction for slender women, especially in Western culture, increased as more and more women entered the workforce leaving their traditional homemaking and child care roles, perhaps because a slim body better reflects fitness and competence in occupational success (Barber,1998). Although research findings on ratings of facial attraction, especially of women, revealed substantial cultural agreement (e.g., large eyes), still there are some cultural differences for some specific facial features (Langlois et al., 2000). For example, Asian, Hispanic, and White males reported women's youthful facial features to be attractive, but Asian men reported a large chin to be less attractive than did Hispanic and White men (Cunningham et al., 1995). Finally, the attraction process is continuously changing, and cultural forces significantly determine the shape of our judgment about who is attractive and who is not (Eastwick, 2013). Moreover, regardless of cultural differences, people tend to agree on the importance of some physical features of both men and women to look attractive or not (Gangestad, Haselton, & Buss, 2006).

Age and physical attraction. Physical attractiveness has a strong impact on intimacy and love of people over their lifespan. Physical attractiveness of both women and men usually diminishes with aging. Research findings showed that husbands generally become less attracted to their wives as their beauty fades with aging, which often negatively affects the husband's sexual and marital satisfaction (Braxton-Davis, 2010). Research results further showed that although physical attractiveness is valued by both men and women, men typically show a higher preference for beauty than do women (Buss & Shackelford, 2008; Feingold, 1990).

Sexual Attraction

Sexual attraction can originate from different qualities of a person such as physical beauty, appealing personality, intellectual abilities, social status, wealth, power, position, fame, etc. Sexual attraction can be classified in different subtypes such as heterosexual attraction—sexual attraction to a person of the opposite sex; homosexual attraction—sexual attraction to a person of the same sex; bisexual attraction—sexual attraction to both sexes; pansexual attraction—sexual traction to male, female, and transgender; and asexual—people who lack sexual attraction. Sexual attraction is often experienced along with other forms of attraction such as romantic or emotional attractions. But sometimes sexual attraction can be experienced quite independently of other forms of attractions.

Romantic Attraction

Romantic attraction refers to an emotional response based on an individual's feeling or desire for a romantic relationship with another person. Romantic attraction can be experienced with or without any sexual attraction and interaction. For example, an asexual person can experience romantic attraction without any feeling of sexual attraction. Romantic actions can include a wide range of activities of an individual with a romantic partner such as taking dinners, watching movies, taking a long walk, sharing hobbies, and so on. There is no clear-cut boundary between the end of a romantic attraction and the beginning of a sexual attraction. Like sexual attractions, there can be different combinations of romantic attractions such as heteroromantic attraction—a romantic attraction to a person of different sex; homoromantic attraction—a romantic attraction to a person of the same sex; and biromantic or panromantic attraction—romantic attractions to persons of the same or opposite sex or transgender; and aromantic attraction—lack of any romantic attraction.

Emotional Attraction

Emotional attraction is a deep and intense feeling of attraction for someone. It is an enduring feeling of interconnectedness in which the partner is considered an important and a unique individual who is interchangeable with none. Emotional attraction makes one feel being accepted by the partner. When individuals are emotionally attracted to each other, they feel comfortable in the presence of each other and enjoy spending time together, and feel distressed when separated. Emotional attraction is present in most romantic and sexual relationships. Emotional attraction is much more deep and enduring than physical and sexual attraction. When a man is emotionally attracted to a women, he feels an exclusively possessive romantic drive to share life with her. On the other hand, a man can feel a physical or sexual attraction toward a woman without feeling a need to possess her exclusively. Emotional attraction may be considered an intensely possessive desire for shared oneness. It is characterized by a heart to heart relationship where two persons feel enmeshed. Emotional attraction gives a sense of security, comfort, safety, and a feeling of happiness in the relationship with the partner.

Aesthetic Attraction

Aesthetic attraction of an individual is connected with the liking and appreciation of appearance or beauty or charming personality of another individual. Aesthetic attraction can also include other components of an individual's image such as figure, hair style, body color, dress pattern, etc. Aesthetic attraction is not directly connected with sexual attraction or romantic attraction. This type of attraction is called aesthetic attraction because it is just like other aesthetic desires such as liking and appreciation for a good painting, a good song, beautiful architecture, a charming natural scene, and so on.

Sensual Attraction

Sensual attraction is a desire to express attraction and intimacy by interacting with others in a tactile way such as through shaking or holding hands, touching, kissing, hugging, and cuddling. Sensual attraction may or may not include romantic attraction or sexual attraction. But sexual attraction almost always includes sensual attraction. Some asexual and aromantic individuals may not experience any sensual attraction.

Intellectual Attraction

Intellectual attraction refers to the attraction to engage with people in an intellectual manner, such as participating in thought-provoking conversations with famous intellectuals and interacting with distinguished persons in creative, inquisitive, insightful, and problem-solving activities. Intellectual attraction may have little or no relation with other types of attraction. For example, a person can be physically repulsive but intellectually attractive. In intellectual attraction, the main focus is on intellect and cognition, and not on emotion or body. However, in some cases intellectual attraction can lead to romantic attraction and/or sexual attraction.

Attraction and Personality

Like physical attraction, personality also plays an important role in shaping our judgment about attraction and forming relations with others (Braxton-Davis, 2010). Part of perception of physical attraction is subjective.

Furthermore, the subjective perception of physical attraction is significantly influenced by our personality. Research on personality and physical attractiveness supports this view. For example, Swami and others (2010) conducted a study on the influence of personality on perceptions of physical attractiveness. They showed photographs of various female figures to male participants and asked them to rate the attractiveness of those pictures. One group of participants received information about positive personality characteristics (e.g., extraverted, agreeable, conscientious, open, and stable) about the women in the pictures, while another group received information about negative personality characteristics (e.g., introverted, rigid, and unstable), and the third group received no personality information. Results showed that the participants who were given positive personality information rated a significantly wider range of body sizes physically attractive, compared to the group who received no information. The group who received negative personality information rated a significantly narrower range of body sizes attractive than the group who received no personality information. Another study on both male and female participants showed that pictures paired with positive personality traits were rated as more attractive, and those paired with negative traits were rated as less attractive by both men and women, but women were more sensitive to negative personality information than men (Lewandowski, Aron, & Gee, 2007). Some other studies found that judgments of physical attractiveness of both men and women are influenced by perceived honesty, self-esteem, and intellectual ability (Kniffin & Wilson, 2004; Paunonen, 2006). Finally, physical features undoubtedly influence attractiveness, but personality counts too and goes a long way as well.

Attraction among Gays and Lesbians

Like heterosexual women and men, gays and lesbians tend to make close relations with people having similar personality traits, beliefs, and values like them (Jepsen & Jepsen, 2002). Both gays and lesbians want their romantic partners to be warm, loving, caring, affectionate, kind, and compassionate (Felmlee, Orzechowicz, & Fortes, 2010). They also give importance to shared values, mutual trust, confidence, agreeableness, and interdependence in long-term mating relationships (Peplau & Fingerhut, 2007).

Attraction in Heterosexual, Gay, and Lesbian Relationships

In a study, Felmlee, Hilton, and Orzechowicz (2012) reported that the top four partner qualities rated by heterosexual women and men are intelligent, caring, friendly, and nice; whereas the top four partner qualities rated by gays and lesbians are fun, humor, intelligent, and kind. The same study also revealed that although there was significant mean difference between the ratings of heterosexual women and men, there was no significant mean difference between the ratings of gays and lesbians. The findings further showed that heterosexual men rated physical attraction more highly than heterosexual women; and heterosexual women rated caring, nice, and humor more highly than heterosexual men. Finally, the study showed that regardless of genders and sexual orientations, there is overall agreement among heterosexuals, gays, and lesbians about some perceived attractive qualities (such as intelligent, extraversion, agreeableness, and kind) for women and men in long-term close relationships.

Attraction and Gender Stereotypes

Gender stereotypes refer to persistent and pervasive social beliefs that men and women possess opposite physical attributes, personality traits, and behavioral dispositions (Howard & Hollander, 1996). Therefore, masculine and feminine identities are not only different but also contrary in nature. In a review of studies on gender stereotypes, Lueptow, Garovich-Szabo, and Lueptow (2001) found little change in gender stereotyping over a period of about 40 years. There are two different categories of gender stereotypes: (1) heterosexual—opposite-gender stereotypes, and (2) same-gender stereotypes—gay and lesbian stereotypes.

Heterosexual stereotypes. Common gender stereotypic traits for heterosexual men, which are called masculine traits, include adventurous, aggressive, authoritative, competitive, firm, and independent (Seem & Clark, 2006). On the other hand, common gender stereotypic traits for heterosexual women, which are called feminine traits, include affectionate, empathetic, sympathetic, compassionate, gentle, beauty conscious, and worldly (Seem & Clark, 2006).

Gay and lesbian stereotypes. Gender stereotypes for gays and lesbians are different from and more complex than the gender stereotypes for heterosexuals. Several studies show that Americans perceive gays as gentle, passive, and effeminate (Glick et al., 2007; Taywaditep, 2001), while lesbians are perceived as women with masculine characteristics, who are disinterested in feminine appearance (Geiger, Harwood, & Hummert, 2006). Moreover, both gays and lesbians are perceived as promiscuous who tend to be sexually predatory and having unstable and conflicting expectations about attraction in romantic relationship (Geiger, Harwood, & Hummert, 2006; Glick et al., 2007). In addition, gay and lesbian relationships are stereotypically perceived as a sort of heterosexual relationship—because in both gay and lesbian relationships one partner assumes the masculine role and the other partner assumes the feminine role in every aspect of life from domestic activities to sexual intercourse (Ivory, Gibson, & Ivory, 2009).

Attraction and Gender-Atypical Traits

Women and men who follow gender stereotypes more closely are perceived more positively by others in society than those who deviate from gender stereotypes (Felmlee, Hilton, & Orzechowicz, 2012). People who fail to adhere to the traditional gender schemas may often experience negative social consequences for not living up to traditional social beliefs and expectations. Felmlee, Hilton, and Orzechowicz (2012) argued that gender-atypical traits may affect intimate relationship negatively. They reported that men who reflected submissive behavior were rated by women as less attractive than men who reflected dominance in their behavior. On the other hand, women who reflected assertiveness in their behavior were rated by men as less attractive than women who reflected submissiveness in their behavior. Research indicates that the effect of gender stereotypes on attraction can be moderated by individuals' acceptance or rejection of traditional gender ideology (Koyama, McGain, & Hill, 2004). For example, individuals with egalitarian (i.e., gender equality) belief gave little or no importance to gender stereotypic traits in finding attractive romantic partners, compared to individuals who endorsed traditional gender stereotypic traits (Koyama, McGain, & Hill, 2004).

Predictors of Attraction

An overview of the literature on attraction reveals that researchers have identified some important predictors of attraction. Some of the extensively studied predictors include proximity, similarity, familiarity, and reciprocity (Eastwick, 2013; Orbuch & Sprecher, 2003).

Proximity

Geographical proximity is a powerful predictor of attraction. Intimacy often originates from proximity. People who are geographically close have greater possibility of frequent exposure and contact than people who are geographically far away. Repeated encounters and frequent contact provide opportunity to know one another more closely and develop liking and friendship. People often fall in love and marry someone who is a classmate or who lives in the same neighborhood or who works together in the same company. A study on the effect of proximity on the formation of friendships showed that social foci (e.g., attending the same school or living in the same neighborhood) that provide opportunity for constant and continual interactions among individuals resulted in a strong effect on friendship formation. But this effect was not found among individuals going to separate schools and living in different neighborhoods (Preciado et al., 2011). Researchers indicated two probable reasons why individuals tend to form interpersonal relations with those who are close by (Sacerdote & Marmaros, 2005): first, human beings have a tendency to like people who are familiar to them; and second, the more individuals come in contact with one another, the more likely the interaction will grow into a relationship.

Similarity

A basic principle of attraction—like attracts like is quite consistent with the popular saying that "birds of same feather flock together." People, generally, like and are attracted to others who are similar to them (Watson, Beer, & McDade-Montez, 2014). Similarity seems to have considerable importance in the initial process of attraction (Dryer & Horowitz, 1997). A meta-analysis on a large body of research suggests that people are most attracted to others who share similar attitudes, beliefs, values, ethnicity, and culture (Montoya & Horton, 2013). Another study shows that people who share similar important attitudes are more likely to be attracted to each other than those who share less important attitudes (Byrne, 1971). Moreover, people tend to be more attracted to those who share similar personality characteristics (e.g., optimism, self-esteem, and conscientiousness) than dissimilar personality characteristics (Watson, Beer, & McDade-Montez, 2014). But the relation between similarity and attraction is stronger for similar attitudes than for similar personality characteristics (Watson et al., 2004). In addition, the relation between similarity and attraction varies from culture to culture (Gebauer, Leary, Neberich, 2012). For example, personality characteristics of marital couples are more similar in China than in the United States (Chen et al., 2009). Furthermore, people are attracted to intimate partners who have similar physical characteristics, such as tall people are more likely to marry tall partners than short ones (Montoya, 2008; Taylor et al., 2011). People's preference for similarity in intimate partners is not limited to physical and psychological characteristics only. Research evidence (Li, Valentine, & Patel, 2011) shows that people report greater liking for and attraction to other people who are like them in the social aspects of life such as education, income, socioeconomic status, and social habits.

There may be several reasons why similarity is an important predictor of an intimate partner's attraction. One important reason may be that sharing similar attitudes with a partner provides support and boosts confidence that the individual is not alone in his or her beliefs (Montoya, Horton, & Kirchner, 2008). On the basis of the findings of a meta-analysis on over 300 studies, Montoya and Horton (2013) reported that similarity produces a positive effect on attraction. The authors tried to explain their findings from two perspectives: the reinforcement perspective (Byrne, 1971) and the information-processing perspective (Ajzen & Fishbein, 1980). According to the reinforcement perspective, individuals have a fundamental need (called *effectance motive*) for a logical and consistent view of the world. Individuals favor those people who agree and support their views. This support acts as a reinforcement to induce positive feelings, which in turn leads to attraction for people providing support. According to the information-processing perspective, one individual's attraction to another individual is determined by the similar or dissimilar information one has about the other. The available similar information has a positive effect on attraction or liking, and dissimilar information, on the other hand, has a negative effect on attraction or liking.

If and When Opposites Attract?

There has been an ongoing debate on the question of whether opposites attract, or likes attract likes. This debate comes down to the issue of whether the couple's similarity or complementarity leads to more attraction and better relational outcomes. There is no denying that people are attracted to partners who are similar than dissimilar to them in attitudes, values, beliefs, and personality, but similarity does not mean that one partner should be a true copy of the other. A study found that when it comes to partner preference, people desired partners who resembled them and also desired partners who are complementary instead of similar to them (Dijkstra & Barelds, 2008). Although similar lifestyles are much more valuable when seeking a long-term than a short-term relationship, it is almost inevitable that there are and will be, more or less, individual differences between partners in any type of intimate relationship, whether it is long term or short term. People often get attracted to others who are good looking, and they also tend to expect that people to whom they are attracted have attitudes and values that are similar to their own (Morry, Kito, & Ortiz, 2011). But later on they may discover striking dissimilarities that may be damaging to attraction (Rick, Small, & Finkel, 2011). But partners often find it difficult to reconcile with major differences in core values of life. For example, a shared belief may be important in an intimate relationship if both the partners are highly religious, but similarity or dissimilarity in faiths has little effect on the relationship, if faith is not important to them or they don't believe in any religion (Lutz-Zois et al., 2006). Thus, opposites don't attract and also don't disturb intimacy unless partners attribute much importance to them (Miller, 2015). Moreover, minor differences in attitudes and values between partners may change or fade away in the course of time as they try to seek compatibility and satisfaction in their relationships (Becker & Lois, 2010). Finally, partners need to make a right balance between similarities and differences for attaining compatibility in relationships.

Familiarity

Research literature on familiarity and attraction consistently indicates that familiarity is a strong predictor of attraction. A study by Heine and Renshaw (2002) examined relations between familiarity and liking among Japanese and American students who knew each other through interactions in small groups at their respective universities. The findings revealed that frequency of interaction with each group member was positively associated with liking for the Japanese as well as for the American students. However, the positive relations between perceived familiarity and liking was much stronger for Americans than for Japanese (Heine, Foster, & Spina, 2009). But familiarity depends on exposure, which is linked with proximity. Through exposure people gain recognition and familiarity. Although people believe that familiarity breeds contempt and more familiarity breeds more contempt, research evidence shows that familiarity tends to breed liking rather than contempt (Bartlett, 2013). Another study reported that more interactions and more chatting lead to higher levels of liking among newly acquainted peers (Reis et al., 2011). Fiske (2010) suggested a familiar and a similar individual is more appealing to a person than an unfamiliar and a dissimilar individual mainly because familiarity and similarity interact to create an affinity among interacting individuals that ultimately leads to attractions. In addition, a familiar person is considered more safe, understandable, and trustworthy for making a relationship than an unfamiliar person.

Reciprocity

Reciprocal liking is one of the important predictors of attraction, along with proximity, similarity, and familiarity. People tend to like others who reciprocate their liking. Reciprocity can be of two types: sharing likes and sharing dislikes. For example, people not only tend to like those who like them but also tend to like those who share their dislikes—sharing negative attitudes about others (Bosson et al., 2006). Based on reward theory, Brown (2006) perceived that individuals develop attraction and form relationships with persons who reward and reciprocate them. Brown (2006) argued that familiarity, similarity, and reciprocity jointly create attraction between individuals. He also viewed that individuals may develop a liking for persons who initially disliked them but gradually changed their mind due to some positive experiences. Contrarily, individuals may develop a disliking for persons who initially liked them but gradually changed their mind due to some negative experiences. Ultimately, individuals like people whom they perceive as willing to understand and reaffirm them. People not only tend to like similar but also like those who reciprocate their likings, partly because the reciprocity confirms their likable qualities and promotes positive feelings about themselves (Bradbury & Karney, 2010). Individuals tend to exhibit an intense desire for reciprocal liking in developing romantic relationships (Fisher, 2016). Individuals' attitudes and feelings of reciprocal liking can fluctuate dramatically, especially during the early stage of a potential romantic relationship (Finkel, Eastwick, & Matthews, 2007). Dyadic reciprocal liking becomes stronger with the increase of a relationship length, and couples that reciprocate positive affect are more likely to experience a successful and enduring relationship than do couples who reciprocate negative affect (Eastwick et al., 2007).

Theories of Attraction

A close look into the research literature on attraction reveals that most of the studies on attraction have been conducted on the basis of certain theoretical perspectives. The major theories of attraction briefly discussed in this chapter include evolutionary theory, similarity theory, social exchange theory, complementary needs theory, ideal mate theory, equity theory, and propinquity theory.

Evolutionary Theory

The evolutionary theory is based on Darwin's theory of sexual selection (Wood & Brumbaugh, 2009). The theory of sexual selection emphasizes adaptive characteristics including the ability to choose a mate capable of effective reproduction, and ensuring the survival of offspring to continue the cycle of reproduction and thus passing of the genotype from one generation to the next generation, and so on (Buss & Barnes, 1986). The theory assumes that opposite-sex attraction is most often linked to fertility because the primary purpose of conjugal/romantic relationships is reproduction. One major criticism against the evolutionary theory is that the theory cannot explain relationships between same-sex couples or couples who do not want to have children.

Similarity Theory

One of the basic assumptions of similarity theory is that like attracts like (Buss, 1994). This theory is also called social homogamy theory. According to this theory people prefer to choose partners who are more alike than different from themselves. In other words, individuals are attracted to those who have similar socioeconomic backgrounds including race, ethnicity, culture, income, education, social status, role, and expectations. In addition, people also tend to be attracted by partners who have similar physical features, age, personality dispositions, faith, beliefs, and values. An important criticism against this theory is that people are not necessarily always attracted by similarities. For example, young women sometimes marry wealthy older men instead of marrying young men of the same age. In addition, people may not like that their intimate partners should share negative personality traits like them; rather they want that, unlike them, their partners should have positive personality traits. Thus, in some cases, dissimilar attitudes may have a stronger influence on interpersonal attraction than similar attitudes (Singh & Ho, 2000). So the theoretical postulate that "like attracts like" may not be true in all social conditions. For this reason, some scholars have suggested that people may more likely be attracted to partners who complement rather than replicate some of their attributes (Dijkstra & Barelds, 2008).

Social Exchange Theory

Social exchange theory was initially formulated by the sociologist George Homans (1958). Later on several other scholars made significant contributions to further develop the theory (e.g., Blau, 1964; Emerson, 1976). One of the basic postulates of the theory is that human relationships are formed on the basis of a subjective cost-benefit analysis and comparisons of viable alternatives. According to this theory, people may consider the desirable qualities they want in a partner in exchange of what they have to offer in return. These qualities may include physical attributes, personality characteristics, cognitive abilities, social skills, promising career, etc. A partner becomes attractive to an individual if she/he brings the best of these qualities at the minimum cost. Thus, the fundamental assumption of the theory is that any decision for a social relation has two elements: rewards (e.g., support, approval, acceptance, and companionship) and costs (e.g., effort, time, and money). The theory contends that people calculate the overall worth of a particular relationship by subtracting its costs from the rewards it accrues. The simple equation for calculating worth is: Worth=rewards—costs. In addition, the worth of a relationship determines its outcomes, such as satisfaction and continuity of the relationship (West & Turner, 2007). The theory also postulates that in making relationships individuals choose those alternatives that provide maximum long-term rewards in the shortest time with maximum freedom, autonomy, and security in the relationship (McDonell et al., 2006).

Homans developed a set of five key propositions to explain the conceptual basis of the social exchange theory. These propositions represent the core theoretical structure of Homans's version of social exchange theory (Emerson, 1976). The propositions are as follows:

- *The first proposition (success proposition).* This proposition is based on the assumption that behavior that results in positive outcomes is likely to be repeated. When individuals are rewarded for their actions, they tend to repeat those actions.

- *The second proposition (stimulus proposition).* This proposition assumes that if an individual's behavior was rewarded in the past, the individual will repeat the same behavior in the future. The more often a particular stimulus has led to a reward in the past, the more likely a person will respond to it in the future.

- *The third proposition (value proposition).* This proposition postulates that if the outcome of an action was valuable to the individual, it is likely that the individual will repeat that action in the future.

- *The fourth proposition (deprivation-satiation proposition).* This proposition assumes that if an individual has previously received the same reward several times, the value of that reward will diminish. The more often an individual has received a particular reward in the recent past, the less attractive the reward becomes.

- *The fifth proposition (expectation proposition).* This proposition states that if the outcome of an action exceeds an individual's expectation, the individual will be happy and will act approvingly.

Several researchers (Katherine, 2005; Walczak, 2015) have outlined some major limitations of the social exchange theory including:

- The theory has reduced a rational process to an economic process by focusing only on cost-benefit analysis of loss and gain.

- The theory assumes that the ultimate goal of a relationship is intimacy, but all social relationships are not necessarily always intimate relationships.
- The theory places relationships in a linear structure, when some relationships might not follow the linear structure.

Complementary Needs Theory

The complementary needs theory assumes that people choose a partner who they think can complement or enhance their own personal needs. People tend to make up their deficiency by balancing it with their partners' strength. For example, a shy person may be attracted to an outgoing person. Similarly, a submissive person may be attracted to an assertive person. This theoretical view of mate selection contends that needs can be complementary, if they are different such as introvert and extrovert, or if the partners have the same need at different levels of intensity such as more innovative and less innovative (Winch, Ktsanes, & Ktsanes, 1955). Thus, as the complementary needs theory construed that people tend to choose partners who they believe will bring the qualities they lack and help supplement their deficiencies.

Ideal Mate Theory

The ideal mate theory is a psychodynamic theory mainly based on early life experiences of an individual. According to this theory, most people have a preconceived image of how their ideal partner should be like. This image may be based on expected physical attributes, personality characteristics, cognitive abilities, social skills, and other desired qualities. People search for someone as an ideal partner who approximates these desired qualities. This image is shaped by perceived images of one's ideal persons, such as parents, teachers, or any other role models. For example, a woman may like a man who is like her father or a man may like a women who is like her mother. Past experiences of an individual in dating, media exposures, and interactions with others in various social settings may also play important roles in forming an image for an ideal partner. However, when this ideal mate does not live up to the expectations of an individual after marriage, it can cause a lot of problems in the relationship.

Equity Theory

The equity theory was first developed to ensure equity between inputs and outcomes in work performance (Adams, 1965). Later on the concept of equity was extended to interpersonal relationship to understand the perception of equity among relational partners (Guerrero, Trost, & Yoshimura, 2005). The equity theory postulates that individuals not only want most rewards with least costs, but also want equity in their relationships, wherein their costs and rewards in the relationship are roughly equal to the costs and rewards of their partners (Snell & Belk, 2002).

The theory focuses on determining equitable ratios of contributions and benefits for each partner in the relationship. The equity is calculated by the following equation (Adams, 1965):

$$\frac{\text{Individual's outcomes}}{\text{Individual's inputs}} = \frac{\text{partner's outcomes}}{\text{partner's inputs}}$$

According to equity theory the relationship is happiest and most stable if it is based on equity principle. On the other hand, an inequitable relationship, where one person is overbenefited and the other is underbenefited, results in unhappiness and instability.

Propinquity Theory

The propinquity theory states that people are more likely to meet and know others who are geographically nearby (Piercy & Piercy, 1972). People have greater opportunity to know, interact, and develop relationships with those who live in the same neighborhood, same town, study in the same educational institution, work in the same organization, share the same religious institution, and so on. However, long-distance relationships are becoming increasingly easier and less costly to establish and sustain with Internet accessibility, global travel, and long-distance telephone services.

CHAPTER SUMMARY

Chapter 8 focuses on the foundation and types of attraction; differences in age, culture, gender, and personality in attraction; biological and evolutionary determinants of attraction; sexual attraction among heterosexual, gay, and lesbian couples; attraction and gender stereotypes; predictors of attraction; and theories of attraction.

Foundation of attraction. The foundation of interpersonal attraction is based on a number of elements including common interests, values, needs, desires, preferences, and mutual likability.

Types of attraction. Two major types of attraction are physical and psychological attractions. Psychological attraction has several subtypes including personality, sexual, romantic, emotional, aesthetic, sensual, and intellectual attractions.

Sexual attraction. Human sexual attraction is based on a combination of physical, psychological, and social factors including physical beauty, appealing personality, intellectual abilities, social status, wealth, power, position, fame, etc.

Attraction in heterosexual, gay, and lesbian relationships. Regardless of genders and sexual orientations, there is overall agreement among heterosexuals, gays, and lesbians about some perceived attractive qualities (such as intelligent, extraversion, agreeableness, and kindness) for women and men in long-term close relationships.

Theories of attraction. Some of the major theories of attraction discussed in this chapter are evolutionary theory, similarity theory, social exchange theory, complementary needs theory, ideal mate theory, equity theory, and propinquity theory.

REFLECTIVE QUESTIONS

1. What are the foundations and types of attraction?
2. Discuss the biological and evolutionary determinants of physical attraction.
3. Discuss gender and cultural differences in physical attraction with relevant research evidence.
4. Discuss how attraction is related to personality.
5. Discuss attraction in heterosexual, gay, and lesbian relationships with research evidence.
6. Discuss different theories of attraction in intimate relationships.

CHAPTER NINE

Friendship

> In poverty and other misfortunes of life, true friends are a sure refuge. They keep the young out of mischief, they comfort and aid the old in their weakness, and they incite those in the prime of life to noble deeds.
>
> —Aristotle

In his effort to understand and explain the essence of friendship, Vernon (2006) explored a variety of definitions from well-known personalities including Aristotle. Supporting Aristotle's viewpoints, Vernon observed that friendship is vital for an individual's well-being, but it takes time to develop. It develops spontaneously and can't be artificially created. He thought that a close friend is a mirror of our own self, and someone with whom we can share our views. A true friendship gives us a feeling that we are not alone. He also viewed that by cultivating true friendship, we can reduce some of the burden from our isolated and unhappy selves. Friendship typically refers to a relationship between two individuals who like each other and enjoy each other's company. Fehr (1996, p. 7) defines friendship as "a voluntary personal relationship, typically providing intimacy and assistance, in which the two parties like one another and seek each other's company." Friendship relationships are a means to fulfill an individual's social needs throughout his/her life (Bubaš & Bratko, 2008). Unlike relationships with family members or colleagues at work, friendship relationships are formed, maintained, and terminated mainly by the free will of the participants. The level of intimacy in friendship relationships differs from friendly behavior between colleagues or acquaintances (Van Lear, Koerner, & Allen, 2006).

Friendship is one of the three major foundations of intimate relationships. The other two major foundations of intimate relationships are love and sexuality. This chapter focuses on different aspects of friendship, including its relationship with love and sexuality.

Basis of Friendships

Friendship usually develops among people of the same age group or at the same stage of life who perceive themselves as equals and who share common interests and values (Davis, 2004). Friendship often develops, for example, through frequent contacts among classmates in the same educational institution, colleagues in the same organization, members of the same voluntary organizations, or people living in the same neighborhood. Friendship provides companionship, sharing of activities, emotional support during difficult times, feelings of enjoyment, and a sense of well-being (Myers, 2000a). The meaning of friendship changes little over the lifespan, although its context and content may change. Adults, especially older adults, having an active circle of friends, tend to be healthier and happier than older adults who don't have such a friend circle (Rowe & Kahn, 1998). Although a friend cannot completely fulfill the vacuum of a missing spouse or a partner, a friend can partially compensate for the lack of a spouse or a partner (Hartup & Stevens, 1999). Friends are a powerful sense of immediate enjoyment, but family members provide long-term emotional support and security.

Components of Friendship

There are eight important components of a successful friendship (Davis, 2004):

- *Companionship and enjoyment.* Friends like each other and enjoy each other's company. Though they may have occasional differences of views, most of the time they tend to get along very well.
- *Acceptance.* Good friends are willing to accept each other as who they really are, without trying to change each other's identity.
- *Trust.* Friends are dependable and trustworthy to each other, especially in difficult times. It takes time to build up trust and confidence among friends. Trust develops with positive experiences of help and support from friends (Simpson, 2007a). Lack or loss of trust has corrosive effects on any close relationship including friendship (Miller & Rempel, 2004).

- **Respect.** True friends are respectful to each other's opinions, judgments, beliefs, values, likes, and dislikes. Mutual respect for friends is usually associated with admiration, high esteem, and acceptance of one another (Hendrick, Hendrick, & Logue, 2010).
- **Mutual assistance.** Friends are always willing to help each other when called upon and are ready to support each other, especially in difficult times.
- **Mutual confidence.** Friends feel confident and comfortable in expressing and sharing each other's experiences and feelings.
- **Mutual understanding.** Friends try to understand each other's values, beliefs, feelings, and behaviors, which may or may be not identical with that of their own. They are open to each other, which leads to mutual understanding.
- **Spontaneity.** Friends' attitudes and behaviors toward each other are spontaneous and real, and there is no artificiality in it.

Different Aspects of Friendship

According to de Vries (1996) there are three general aspects of friendship:

Affective aspect. Common affective aspects of true friendship include sharing personal thoughts and feelings, self-disclosure, intimacy, appreciation, and affection. They also include mutual encouragement, emotional support, and empathy with a sense of trust, loyalty, and commitment.

Communal aspect. The communal aspect is reflected in participating with a friend in common activities, and giving and receiving assistance to each other's needs.

Sociable aspect. The sociable aspect of friendship is characterized by the feeling that a friend is a source of amusement, fun, and recreation.

Characteristics of a Good Friend

Researchers have tried to identify the characteristics of a good friend. Sapadin (1988) has identified the following important characteristics of a good friend:

- Someone who is trustworthy.
- Someone who is dependable.
- Someone with whom one can share life experiences, ideas, and values.
- Someone who is accepting.
- Someone with similar characteristics.

- Someone with whom one has a close relationship.
- Someone who is enjoyable.

Difference between Friendship and Love

According to Davis (2004) both friendship and love have the above mentioned eight components in common, but love has two extra elements or components—passion and caring. These two extra components are explained in the next chapter on love. However, both friendship and love involve warmth and closeness but love, especially romantic love, is based on an emotionally more intense and exclusive relationship than friendship (Balzarini, Aron, & Chelberg, 2014). Love is based on a more stringent relationship than friendship, and romantic partners are more loyal to each other than friends (Fuhrman, Flannagan, & Matamoros, 2009). Friendship is less confining and entails fewer obligations than love. Moreover, friendship is less passionate than love and typically does not involve sexual intimacy like romantic love (Fehr, 1996).

The basic differences between attributes of friendship and love are as follows:

- Friendship involves less strict standards of conduct than love.
- Friends are less involved with each other's affairs than lovers and tend to spend less time with one another than do lovers.
- Friendship is emotionally less intense and includes fewer obligations than a love relationship.

Rules of Friendship

Rules of friendship are shared beliefs of people in a particular culture about appropriate and inappropriate behaviors in a friendship relationship. Although our interactions with other people begin in infancy, we learn about particular rules of friendship in childhood with the development of language, comprehension, and expression. However, our attitudes, feelings, beliefs, and behaviors about friendship rules keep changing with maturity throughout the lifespan (Bigelow, Tesson, & Lewko, 1996). Argyle and Henderson (1984) have extensively investigated detailed rules of friendship. They emphasize that the use of informal rules is important for achieving satisfaction in a friendship relationship and for minimizing the level of conflict. They showed that highly endorsed rules for friendships were related to:

- Volunteering help in time of need.
- Respecting a friend's privacy.
- Standing up for a friend in his/her absence.
- Not to criticize each other in public.
- Showing emotional support.
- Keeping trust and confidence in each other.
- Striving to make friend happy.
- Not to be jealous or critical of each other's relationships.
- Be tolerant of each other's friends.
- Sharing news of success with each other.
- Asking for personal advice and help.
- Avoid nagging.
- Engage in joking with the friend.
- Disclosing personal problems and feelings to the friend.

Argyle and Henderson (1984) also found that these rules are related to the type of friendship (current, lapsed) and the quality of the friendship relationship. Argyle and Henderson (1984) conducted investigations of friendship rules in multiple societies, including Great Britain, Italy, Hong Kong, and Japan. They found that different cultures endorse different rules of friendship. People do not always follow rules. It is estimated that about 50 percent of people follow friendship rules (Gambrill, Florian, & Thomas, 1999). Argyle, Henderson, & Furnham (1985) also found, despite cultural differences, several rules of friendship such as giving help in time of need, respecting privacy, keeping confidences, and self-disclosure were universally endorsed across various cultures.

Quality of Friendship

Research results show that positive and negative behaviors of partners in a friendship relationship have a significant influence on relationship quality and satisfaction with the friendship at different stages of life (Brendgen et al., 2001). Prosocial behavior, a lower level of aggressiveness, and emotional stability, for example, are some of the factors that contribute to the development of friendship relationships in childhood and adolescence (Cillessen et al., 2005; Mensini, 1997). The application of positive rules is connected with the degree of closeness in the relationship between friends for children as well as for adults (Kline & Stafford, 2004).

Qualities of friendship relationships are associated with reliance on the basic rules of social interaction (Kline & Stafford, 2004). Friendship rules are important for the initiation of interpersonal relations, achievement of cohesion and harmony, maintenance of the relationship, and for the preservation of relationship quality (Metts, 1994).

Several studies have shown the effects of the friendship quality on the psychological adjustment of children, adolescents, and adults. For instance, the relationship quality of friendships between adolescents has been found related to their self-esteem (Keefe & Berndt, 1996) and psychosocial adjustment (Bagwell et al., 2005; Burk & Laursen, 2005). Children with a low level of relationship quality in friendship relationships are less accepted by their peers (Brendgen et al., 2001). Friendships are important for individuals' well-being both in childhood and adulthood, and lack of friends may result in problems in school in childhood; and substance abuse, antisocial behavior, anxiety, and depression in adolescence (Samter, 2003). The quality of friendship relationships at work can influence job satisfaction in adulthood (Winstead et al., 1995), and worsening of friendship relationship at work can cause emotional stress and a decrease in job performance (Sias et al., 2004). On the other hand, friendly relations among team members in organizational settings may have positive effects on job satisfaction and performance (Francis & Sandberg, 2000).

Friendship Expectations

In the course of formation and maintenance of friendships, individuals develop certain expectations about how their friends should be and should behave (La Gaipa, 1987; Wiseman, 1986). Friendship expectations refer to an individual's cognitive conceptualizations about desired attributes and behaviors of a friend (Hall, 2011). Collectively, these expectations form a standard for judging a current and a new friend (Fehr, 1996; Hall, Larson, & Watts, 2011). Friendship satisfaction largely depends on meeting or exceeding these expectations (Hall, Larson, & Watts, 2009). Violations of friendship norms (Felmlee, 1999) and rules (Argyle & Henderson, 1984) can lower the quality of friendship and may negatively affect its continuation (Clark & Ayers, 1993). Although many studies of friendship expectations have examined the relational and socioemotional qualities of friendships (e.g., Bigelow & La Gaipa, 1980), some studies have also explored friends' fitness and resource-based aspects, such as attractiveness, wealth, and business connections (e.g., Lusk, MacDonald, & Newman, 1998; Vigil, 2007).

Friendship expectations are cultivated through experiences with past and present friends. These experiences create a cycle that changes and strengthens individuals' expectations (Elkins & Peterson, 1993). Moreover, cognitive representations of friendship can be regarded as a series of if-then contingencies. For example: "If I need help, my friend will provide it" (Fehr, 2004). These "built-up expectations" may work as implicit cognitive constructs of an ideal friend—a friend that individuals may never have but nonetheless desire and prefer (Wiseman, 1986). Friendship expectations can influence all stages of friendship, including formation (La Gaipa, 1987), maintenance (Oswald, Clark, & Kelly, 2004), and dissolution (Clark & Ayers, 1993). This influence continues throughout an individual's life course. For example, children who can meet the expectations of their peers are more likely to be accepted and included in peer groups by other children (Bigelow & La Gaipa, 1980; La Gaipa, 1987). Similarly, the degree to which friends can meet expectations is an excellent predictor of friendship satisfaction for young adults (Hall, Larson, & Watts, 2011). Expectations of support from friends are also highly valued by older adults (Weiss & Lowenthal, 1975), and fulfilment of these expectations play an important role in successful aging (Mancini & Simon, 1984).

Dimensions of Friendship Expectations

Hall (2012) proposed a four-dimensional model of friendship expectations. These dimensions are symmetrical reciprocity, communion, solidarity, and agency. Symmetrical reciprocity includes loyalty, mutual regard, trustworthiness, and support in the friendship relationship. According to Wright (2006), the essence of friendship can be distinguished by the degree to which each friend considers the other as genuine and trustworthy. The importance of symmetrical reciprocity to friendship is reinforced by loyalty, trust, and support as they are the most important characteristics of friendship (Sapadin, 1988). Loyalty, trust, and support are also the basic elements in producing intimacy (Fehr, 2004) and can differentiate a close friend from an acquaintance (Newcomb & Bagwell, 1995). The second dimension is communion, which includes emotional availability and self-disclosure given and received (Hall, 2012). Emotional self-disclosure is an important and critical factor in developing intimacy in friendship (Fehr, 2004). The third dimension is solidarity, which refers to mutual sharing of common activities (Wright, 2006) and friendship inclusion and maintenance (Oswald, Clark, & Kelly, 2004). According to Hall (2012), expectations of attitude, disposition, and activity similarity all are categorized as solidarity expectations. The fourth dimension is agency, which refers to friendship as a means to ends or as a resource to obtain help and benefits (Hall, 2012). In other words, agency pertains to what a friend can do, has access to, and is able to offer. Although Hall (2011) proposed these four dimensions on a theoretical basis, the factor structures of these dimensions were not tested empirically.

Differences in Friendship

Individual differences. Individuals may differ in friendship due to differences in personal needs, personality, and psychological problems. Individuals who need a high level of intimacy tend to have friendships that involve a high level of self-disclosure, common beliefs and value, loyalty, and a desire to avoid separation (McAdams, 1985). Individuals' psychological problems may contribute to difficulties in establishing and maintaining friendships. For example, people who are depressed often have fewer friends and other supportive social networks (Gotlib & Whiffen, 1991).

Gender differences. Men and women differ in several areas of friendship relationships. Women want greater depth of communication (Barth & Kinder, 1988), more emotional involvement (Barth & Kinder, 1988), closeness and security (Markiewicz & Doyle, 2012) in their friendships than do men. Women typically have more close friends than men. Women find friendship with other women more satisfying than friendship with men. Women often place more emphasis on intimacy in their friendships than do men, and they are prone to have relatively higher expectations of their social relationships (Felmlee & Muraco, 2009). Unlike women, men are more likely to share information and activities but not confidential matters with friends (Rosenbluth & Steil, 1995). Another gender-related area that makes a difference in the friendship relationship is sexual orientations. Few heterosexual men and women have friendships with gay, lesbian, and bisexual individuals, but many gay, lesbian, and bisexual individuals have friendships with individuals who are heterosexual (Galupo, 2009). Friendship between individuals with different sexual orientations can be as close and enjoyable as friendship between individuals with similar sexual orientations (Ueno et al., 2009), and the more contact heterosexual individuals have with gay, lesbian, and bisexual individuals, the more they like them (Merino, 2013).

Cross-Sex Friendship

Cross-sex heterosexual friendships are common among individuals of different ages and occupations (Wright, 1998). Although cross-sex heterosexual friendships have many benefits, there are some challenges in such relationships, including lack of social support, presumptions of sexual involvement, and lack of cultural models to follow (West, Anderson, & Duck, 1996). In some cases, older women perceive cross-gender ties as preludes to romance and courtship among older adults (Blieszner, 1995). However, cross-sex friendships flourish in aging life because of the diminishing focus on the possibility of sexuality in old age in such relationships (Matthews, 1986). There are clear differences in social norms between cross-sex friendships and same-sex friendships among older adults and young adults (Felmlee, 1999). Gender often continues to play an important role in shaping the normative expectations in cross-gender friendship over the individual's lifespan. The effects of gender are often stronger than that of other structural factors, such as age, ethnicity, and marital status (Felmlee, 1999). The social and cultural constructions of gender and the influences of these factors continue from childhood through adulthood and persist over the individual's lifespan. In addition, gender inequality also has ramifications, which is why women often place somewhat more stake in friendship intimacy than do men (Felmlee & Muraco, 2009). However, differences between men and women about the norms and expectations in cross-sex friendships tend to be of degree and not of kind (Felmlee, 1999).

Challenges of Sexual Attraction in Cross-Sex Friendship

According to Felmlee and Muraco (2009), sexual attraction is really a challenge for cross-sex friendship. Nonetheless, if and when sexual attraction is expressed, the friendship prevails in the majority of the cases (Halatsis & Christakis, 2009). Despite some social constraints, friendship between heterosexual men and women has continued to grow. For example, in the 1950s the percentage of men reporting having a friendly relationship with women was negligible. However, during the last 30 years, cross-sex friendship has emerged as a reality, which is evident from the fact that approximately 40 percent of men and 30percent of women were found to have been involved in such a relationship (Maisonneuve & Lamy, 1993). Some people, moreover, have more than one cross-sex friend (Bleske & Buss, 2000). Over the past several decades an increasing number of women with higher education have entered in the public services leading to an increase in the functional coexistence of men and women, and to an increase in cross-sex friendship (Maisonneuve & Lamy, 1993; Monsour, 2000/2002). Several studies showed that through cross-sex friendships, men and women gain a greater understanding of how members of the other sex think, feel, and behave (Sapadin, 1988; Swain, 1992). Moreover, in cross-sex friendship, men often find greater intimacy and emotional depth, which are typically not available in their same-sex friendship (Reeder, 2003).

As women and men enter into cross-sex friendship, they are to deal with the challenges of sexual and/or romantic attractions, even though such attractions may or may not actually exist (O'Meara, 1994; Rubin, 1985). Although sexual attraction is generally not the starting point and foundation of a cross-sex friendship, we cannot rule out the possibility that sexual attraction may emerge as a result of the intimacy that might develop between cross-sex friends. There may occur a unilateral or mutual sexual attraction. However, in some cases the emergence of sexual attraction may jeopardize the friendship as it threatens its integrity (Bell, 1981; Rubin, 1985). Nonetheless, in some cases the friendship may continue to be the primary relational focus, with the sexual dimension playing a secondary role (Rubin, 1985). But nonromantic friendship does not necessarily mean that sexuality or passion is totally absent or forbidden in the relationship (O'Meara, 1994). Reeder (2000) showed that 90 percent of respondents who felt some kind of romantic attraction for their cross-sex friends also felt sexual attraction. Contrarily, only 46 percent of those who reported sexual attraction also reported a feeling of romantic attraction. Although sexual attraction is not a fundamental element of friendship, the presence of romantic or sexual attraction does not necessarily nullify a friendship relationship (Felmlee & Muraco, 2009). The sexual dimension, however, should be managed in a way that is acceptable to both partners involved in a friendship relationship (O'Meara, 1994).

Existence of Sexual Attraction

Several studies provided evidence of the existence of sexual attraction in cross-sex friendships. Sapadin (1988), for instance, reported that 66 percent of men and 46 percent of women responded affirmatively to the statement, "Friends can become my sexual partners." Bell (1981) found that 25 percent of women wanted to have sexual dimension in their friendships with males. In addition, Reeder (2000) found that 30 percent of the participants in a study reported that they have experienced sexual attraction for other-sex friends. Fuiman, Yarab, and Sensibaugh (1997) showed that 14 percent of their participants reported having engaged in sexual activity, including sexual caressing, oral sex, and sexual intercourse with cross-sex friends. Afifi and Faulkner (2000) reported that 51 percent of participants were involved in sexual contact with a cross-sex friend at least once, and 33 percent reported repeated sexual activity with a cross-sex friend. These findings support the view that sexual attraction poses a challenge in cross-sex friendship, although it does not trouble cross-sex friendship (Monsour, Harris, & Kurzweil, 1994).

Managing Sexual Attraction in Friendship

Although research evidence clearly indicates the existence of sexual interaction in cross-sex friendship, it is also evident that the findings vary dramatically. Some researchers have viewed that this diversity is due to individual differences in gender, social, and cultural values. For example, Monsour (2000/2002) and Rubin (1985) viewed that one's stance toward the sexual dimension of the friendship depends on one's sex and general worldview. In support of this view, they reported that men appear to be more focused on, and are more likely to seek the sexual dimension of friendship than women (Monsour, 2000/2002; Rubin, 1985). However, an individual's level of conventionality, in addition to one's sex, determines whether an individual will manage sexual attraction in a cross-sex friendship in a satisfactory manner (Halatsis & Christakis, 2009). In this connection, Bell (1981) showed that over 50 percent of men possessing traditional values and attitudes consider the sexual component as threatening for friendship. Contrarily, men with less conventional belief think that sexual attractions in cross-sex friendship may have positive relational outcomes. These findings suggest that people approach sexual attraction in cross-sex friendship in many different ways (O'Meara, 1994; Sapadin, 1988). Several researchers have suggested that how sexual attraction in cross-sex friendship is managed depends on interactions of multiple psychological, social, and other contingent factors including (1) how one perceives a particular cross-sex friendship; (2) the perceived quality of this relationship; and (3) sexual values—the mental models by which each friend defines sexual attraction and behavior as acceptable or unacceptable within the friendship relationship (e.g., Afifi & Faulkner, 2000; Fletcher & Thomas, 1996).

Obstacles to Friendship

Several researchers have identified some common barriers to making friends, and building and maintaining friendships (e.g., Busboom et al., 2002; Monsour, 2000/2002; Terrell, 2014):

Temperament. People who feel shy and uncomfortable to meet and interact with less known or unknown individuals tend to make fewer friends.

Insecurity. People who can't trust others, and feel anxious and insecure to interact with other people, and want to keep a distance from people around may find it difficult to make new friends and maintain existing friendships.

Preference. Some people may prefer being alone rather than spending time with friends, or may prefer to make friend with a few people who fulfill their expectations and specifications.

Psychological problems. Some people have psychological problems due to a history of childhood abuse by parents or other attachment figures. They may feel uncomfortable to share life experiences, opinions, beliefs, values, and feelings with friends. These may create barriers and distance between friends.

Personality characteristics. People who are introverted—inward focused, and tend to be preoccupied with their own thoughts and feelings, minimize their contact with other people and like to stay alone. They are poor in making friends and maintaining friendships. Contrarily, people who are extroverted—outgoing, humorous, gregarious, and extraordinarily social—enjoy the company of others. They are good in making and maintaining friendships.

Developmental disabilities. People with psychological and/or physical disabilities have less scope to interact with many people and have limited opportunity to make friends. Moreover, due to social stereotype and stigma, some people may not like to make friends with disabled people.

Lack of experience. Some people, regardless of age and gender, may lack the knowledge, skills, and experience of making friends and maintaining friendships.

Communication problems. Some people may have language deficiency or lack of facilities to keep contact with friends, using friends' preferred modes of communication (e.g., Internet, Skype, Facebook, and Twitter).

Occupational and situational obstacles. Some people may have an abnormal work schedule, such as a night shift, and sleep during the daytime or work during the weekend and get days off during weekdays. For them it may be difficult to participate in social activities and interact with friends. Furthermore, some people may live in remote geographical areas, where it is difficult to be connected with people.

Culture, gender, and ethnicity. Some people may have a preference to make friends with individuals from a particular race, ethnicity, and culture. For cultural reasons, some people may like to make friends only with an individual of the same sex.

Family responsibilities and workload. Some people may find it difficult to spend time with friends because of caregiving responsibilities to young children or aging parents or grandparents after work. Some people may feel tired after overtime work and prefer to take rest at home instead of spending time with friends.

Unrealistic expectations. Some people may have unrealistic expectations for friendships. For example, they may expect all friendships to be perfect, for them always to be supportive, agreeable, and available when they need, and for friendship to last forever.

Friendship across the Lifespan

As people grow and change from infancy through old age, so do their friendships. Variations in friendships exist not only between individuals but also within the same individual over the lifespan. Friendship relationships differ at different stages of individuals' lives depending on social context, degree of closeness, age, and sex.

Friendship in Childhood

Children have different concepts of friendship at different stages of their lives (Slee, 2002). Children begin to develop friendship with playmates of the same age. Initially, their concept of friendship is quite simple, which gradually becomes more complex as they grow cognitively (Howes, 2011). Good relationships in childhood pave the way for good relationships in adolescence and adulthood. Children who experienced secured attachment from their primary caregivers tend to develop secured childhood friendships and secured intimate relationships during young adulthood (Orina et al., 2011).

Sullivan (1953) and Selman (1980) proposed two important models for explaining children's friendship development. Sullivan (1953) proposed the following three-stage model at which friendship concepts of children undergo remarkable changes:

Stage 1 (2–5-year-olds). At this stage, relationships with adults are very important. Children rely on the adults to fulfill their physical, social, and emotional
needs.

Stage 2 (4–8-year-olds). During this stage, children increasingly turn to their
playmates as friends.

Stage 3 (8–11-year-olds). This is the stage when chumship develops and children
learn how to help other children grow and develop.

Selman (1980, 2007) developed a five-stage model of children's friendship development, which is consistent with the model of Jean Piaget and
the theoretical approach of Kenneth Rubin (Rubin & Andrea, 2003).
According to Selman, children's and adolescents' social awareness and
concepts of friendship develop in a series of five stages, and each of these
stages involves reorganization of their mental elements. Selman thought
that children's social understanding and concepts of friendship depend on
their level of intellectual and social experiences and not on their chronological age. Selman's five stages are:

Stage 1 (3–6-year-olds). In this stage, a child generally does not develop a clear
conception of an enduring friendship relationship, except some specific
encounters. The child perceives a close friend as one who lives nearby and is
playing with him/her at that moment. A child's focus is on momentary play-
mate and proximity.

Stage 2 (5–9-year-olds). In this stage, a child thinks that a friend is someone who
does something that pleases her/him, and who is known to her/him better
than other people. Children can differentiate between their own views and
wishes from those of their friends.

Stage 3 (7–12-year-olds). An awareness of interpersonal relationships develops
at this stage. Although friendship becomes reciprocal, still the focus is on
specific incidents rather than enduring relationships. At this stage children
begin to develop self-reflective and reciprocal perspectives.

Stage 4 (10–15-year-olds). In this stage children and adolescents start reflecting
and focusing on intimacy and mutual sharing of opinions and interests within
a continuing relationship. In addition, children and adolescents can take an
objective perspective of friendship.

Stage 5 (14 years–adulthood). This stage is mainly characterized by sharing of
common interests with friends and developing deeper feelings for friends.
Adolescents and adults develop a sense of autonomy and interdependence. At this stage more complex friendship patterns emerge as adolescents and adults can realize that their friends need other independent
relationships.

As children become mature, they realize that different people can react differently to the same situation. In addition, they develop the ability to analyze objectively the perspectives of other people involved in a situation from the viewpoints of cultural and social differences in beliefs, attitudes, and values (Rubin & Andrea, 2003).

Friendship in Adolescence

Adolescence is a period of transition from late childhood to the beginning of the adult stage. This transition is accompanied by developmental challenges; relationship-building tasks are especially critical during this period (Arnett, 2010). This stage is characterized by the growing importance of peer relationships. Adolescents gradually decrease conformity to parents and increase conformity to peers. Compared with children, adolescents spent significantly more time with friends than with family members. In a study, Larson et al. (1996) found that fifth grade children spent 30 percent of their time with family members, whereas twelfth grade teens spent only 14 percent of their time with family members. Peer relationships play an important role in adolescents' identity formation and self-esteem development (Turner & Welch, 2012). Moreover, adolescents turn to their friends for emotional support (Furman, 2002) and satisfaction of attachment needs (Fraley & Davis, 1997). A study showed that about 30 percent of teens identified peers, not parents, as their primary attachment figures (Rosenthal & Kobak, 2010).

Berndt (1996) has identified three important features of adolescents' peer relationships:

- *Support.* Supporting each other in difficult times, especially during emotional problems.
- *Peer pressure.* Influences on adolescent's choice of dress patterns, drinking behavior, smoking, romantic relationships, sexual behavior, etc.
- *Conflict.* Disagreements and arguments over differences of opinions, interests, attitudes, values, and beliefs, which may lead to an end of the friendship, if such differences can't be settled amicably.

Young Adulthood

Intimacy is an essential component of friendship relationships in young adulthood (Berndt, 1996; Erikson, 1950/1963). Erikson thought that a central task during late teens and early twenties is the development of

intimacy versus isolation. He believed that during young adulthood individuals learn how to develop enduring and committed intimate relationships. When young adults enter college, their friendships developed in
high school tend to be eroded and replaced by new friendships on campus
(Roberts & Dunbar, 2011). Their interactions and intimacy levels with
new friends gradually increase and become deeper (Miller, 2015). Young
adults try to adjust to new environments and enter in new social networks
by making new friends and forgetting some old friends, especially in the
first year of college (Shaver, Furman & Buhrmester, 1985). Time spent by
young adults with opposite-sex partners tends to increase, while time
spent with same-sex partners tends to decrease. One study found that
young adults' level of interactions and depth of relationships with friends
increased after college, although the number of friends decreased (Reis
et al., 1993). Young adults who are involved in carrier building and caring
for babies have little time to interact with friends. Nonetheless, they consider it important to have friends to make life easy and enjoyable, and feel
good (Hartup & Stevens, 1999; Myers, 2000a).

Middle Adulthood

Researchers exploring issues about midlife friendships have focused on
three components of friendships (Adams & Blieszner, 1994):

- **Structure.** Power, prestige, or status of each partner; similarity or dissimilarity between partners; liking or disliking for each other; and connection of
  friendships with networks of relationships.
- **Process.** Partners' behavior toward each other, and attitudes and feelings of
  friends toward each other.
- **Phases.** Formation, maintenance, and discontinuation of friendships.

Research on the structure, process, and phases of midlife friendships
show that younger middle-aged individuals, especially men, tend to be
more concerned about personality factors in forming friendships, while
older middle-aged men tend to be more concerned about lack of time for
friends (Hruschka, 2010). Life events and roles may also influence midlife
friendships. For example, some major life events such as romantic relationships, marriage, parenthood, and adult offspring departing from home
can have effect on midlife friendships (Fehr, 1999). Middle-aged adults
often turn to friends for emotional support, guidance, comfort, and companionship at the time of any crisis in life such as divorce or death of a
spouse, losing a job, life-threatening disease, and so on (Hartup & Stevens,

1999). Married middle-aged couples tend to shift their relationships from personal friends to common friends they share with their spouses.

Generally, friendship networks tend to become smaller and more intimate in middle adulthood as compared with young adulthood. The friendship circle tends to become limited to colleagues, neighbors, and members of voluntary organizations with whom individuals have frequent contacts (Antonucci, Akiyama, & Merline, 2001; Hartup & Stevens, 1999). Most middle-aged people have little time to spend with friends as they are too busy with family and work. Nonetheless, friendship continues to be a strong source of emotional support and well-being during middle age, especially for women (Antonucci, Akiyama, & Merline, 2001).

Late Adulthood

Many older adults, especially women, lose their spouse either due to death or divorce, and consequently start feeling the need for close ties with acquaintances and friends (Lopata, 1988, 2010). But due to a variety of reasons, aging people become more selective in choosing friends as their social networks and friendship circle become limited (Wrzus et al., 2013). For instance, after retirement interaction opportunities for some aging people may decrease, some may have minimal income and reduced transportation facilities, and some may be at risk of serious health problems, which can limit their mobility and participation in social activities (Carstensen, Isaacowitz, & Charles 1999; Carstensen et al., 2015). Consequently, older adults may choose to maintain relatively fewer, but high-quality, close friends by discontinuing relationship with casual friends and retaining more meaningful ones (Lang et al., 2013). Some researchers argue that change in friend selection in old age occurs because older adults have different interpersonal goals than younger adults (Löckenhoff & Carstensen, 2004). While younger adults tend to pursue more future-oriented goals through interpersonal relationships with many people, older adults tend to focus more on present goals than on future goals through interaction with a limited number people in a short time, as their future seems more finite (Fung & Carstensen, 2004). As their time perspective shrinks, older adults emphasize quality rather than quantity in friendship; and they prefer a selected number of good-quality intimate friends instead of large group of casual friends (Fingerman & Charles, 2010). Older women meet their friends more frequently and consider friendship more important than do older men (Felmlee & Muraco, 2009; Field & Minkler, 1988). Older adults consider self-disclosure, sociability, mutual assistance, shared activities, loyalty, and trust as important and desirable characteristics of a good friend (Adams, Blieszner, & De Vries, 2000). Older adults, regardless of gender, often try to compensate for the absence or lack of spouse or partners by spending time with friends (Hartup & Stevens, 1999).

Developmental Outcomes of Friendship

A large number of empirical studies have shown the significance of friendship for positive developmental outcomes of friendships in childhood and adolescence (Rubin, Bukowski, & Parker, 1998). The children feel the need to be accepted by other children when they enter into elementary school. Those who are not accepted by their classmates feel isolated (Buhrmester & Furman, 1986). Children who experience parental rejection, teacher rejection, and peer rejection tend to develop a variety of developmental difficulties, such as psychological maladjustment, poor school achievement, behavior problems, drug addiction, and delinquency (Ali, Khaleque, & Rohner, 2013; Wong & Schonlau, 2013).

From the viewpoints of childhood peer acceptance-rejection and later well-being, some researchers have described three categories of children (Bukowski & Cillessen, 1998):

- Children who are popular.
- Children who are neglected.
- Children who are rejected.

In a study on 266 Italian preschool children about the behavior of pre-schoolers belonging to different sociometric status groups (e.g., popular, average, neglected, and rejected), Hart et al. (2010) found that sociometrically popular children were highest in sociability and lowest in physical and relational aggression and victimization. The opposite pattern emerged for rejected-status children, and the neglected-status children were not distinguished from the average-status group. Several studies have predicted that children with poor peer adjustment are at risk for problems in later life. More specifically, children who are rejected by their peers are at risk for school dropout, criminal behavior, and poor psychological adjustment (Kupersmidt et al., 1990; Parker & Asher, 1987). In a longitudinal study on 579 children with ADHD, Mrug et al. (2012) reported that peer rejection is an important predictor of long-term impairments in children with ADHD that persist despite treatment. Childhood peer rejection was also found uniquely predictive of smoking, delinquency, and anxiety in middle adolescence.

In adolescence, relationships with friends are important for social supports like relationships with the family members. Positive relationships with friends influence the development of social competence of an individual, and such relationships also have effects on the formation of relationships with other people during adulthood (Collins & Madsen, 2006). For example, the experiences in friendship relationships during adolescence are connected with the display of intimacy and support toward others in later life (Fullerton & Ursano, 1994). Moreover, the experiences in friendship relationships during childhood and adolescence help the development of interpersonal competence that is essential for the development of effective romantic relationships in adult life (Furman, 1999). Friendship quality predicts well-being among children and adolescents, especially across periods of transition (Berndt, Hawkins, & Jiao, 1999).

A study by Bagwell et al. (2005) indicated that perceived negative changes in friendships (i.e., weakened relationships over time) were associated with interpersonal negative sensitivity symptoms (e.g., discomfort in interpersonal interactions, self-doubt, and feelings of inferiority) in young adulthood. The study also showed that negative friendship features were associated with clinical symptoms; and positive features, social support, and satisfaction in the friendship were associated with less depression and high self-esteem. In addition, supportive interpersonal relationships, such as close friendships, can minimize depression episodes by providing a buffer for stressful events (Bagwell et al., 2005).

Although most middle-aged people have little time to spend with friends and have a limited friendship network as they are too busy with family and work, still friendship continues to be a strong source of emotional support and well-being during middle age, especially for women (Antonucci, Akiyama, & Merline, 2001). Aging people who have a network of good friends have happier, healthier, and longer lives than those who are relatively isolated and less connect with good friends (Sabin, 1993). Research has shown that close friendships tend to decrease the risk of developing disabilities and increase the probability of recovering from health problems in old age (Mendes de Leon, Glass, & Berkman, 2003). Good friendship has many health benefits for aging people. For example, a good marital relationship as well as good relations with friends were found related to increased survival rates of aging people (Rasulo, Christensen, & Tomassini, 2005). Extended social networks and higher levels of social engagement were found significantly correlated with higher cognitive functioning, and a lower rate of cognitive decline, among older African Americans and Whites (Barnes et al., 2004). A socially active lifestyle and social support in old age were found to have protective effects against the development of dementia and Alzheimer's disease (Fratiglioni, Paillard-Borg, & Winblad, 2004), and subsequent physical disability after a stroke (Clarke, 2003). This is evident from the research findings discussed previously as well as from several other research findings that despite individual differences in age, gender, ethnicity, and culture, people having good friends tend to be happy and healthy across the lifespan (e.g., Felmlee & Muraco, 2009; Mendes de Leon & Glass, 2004; Myers, 2000b).

CHAPTER SUMMARY

Chapter 9 contains discussion about the basis of friendship; components of friendship; characteristics of a good friend; difference between friendship and love; rules of friendship; quality of friendship; friendship expectations; dimensions of friendship expectations; differences in culture, gender, and personality in friendship; cross-sex friendship; managing sexual attraction in cross-sex friendship; obstacles to friendship; friendship across the lifespan; and developmental outcomes of friendship.

Friendship. Friendship is a voluntary personal relationship based on individuals' liking for one another, and seeking and enjoying each other's company.

Basis of friendship. Friendship usually develops among people of the same age group who perceive them as equals and share common interests and values.

Characteristics of a good friend. Researchers have identified some common characteristics of a good friend such as trustworthy, dependable, accepting, caring, enjoyable, and so on.

Difference between friendship and love. Both friendship and love involve warmth and closeness, but love is based on an emotionally more intense and exclusive relationship than friendship, and romantic partners are more loyal to each other than friends.

Managing sexual attraction in friendship. Several researchers have suggested that how sexual attraction in cross-sex friendship is managed depends on interactions of multiple psychological, social, and other contingent factors.

Obstacles to friendship. Several researchers have identified some common barriers to making friends such as temperament, insecurity, preference, psychological problems, personality characteristics, communication problems, and occupational and situational obstacles.

Friendship across the lifespan. As people grow and change from childhood through old age, so do their friendships. Friendship relationships differ at different stages of individuals' lives depending on social context, degree of closeness, age, and sex.

REFLECTIVE QUESTIONS

1. Discuss the different components of friendship. What are the characteristics of a good friend?

2. Explain how a friendship is formed and maintained.

3. Discuss the differences between friendship and love.

4. Discuss the quality of friendship and satisfaction with friendship at different stages of life.

5. Explain differences in social norms between cross-sex friendship and same-sex friendship among young adults and older adults.

6. What are the challenges of sexual attraction in cross-sex friendship? How is sexual attraction managed in friendship?

7. Discuss the developmental outcomes of friendships across people's lifespan.

CHAPTER TEN

Love

Love is an irresistible desire to be irresistibly desired.

—Robert Frost

Love is a human emotional and behavioral experience that varies from culture to culture and individual to individual (even in the same culture) both in how it is experienced and how it is displayed (Martinez, 2005). Love is a complex concept that is very difficult to define. No single definition is sufficient enough to account for all the factors and perspectives connected with the concept of love. Love is a common term that is often used to refer to a variety of love such as parent-child love, romantic love, erotic love, fatuous love, consummate love, self-love, spiritual love, love of God, love of life, love of humanity, and so on. These types of love are distinctly different from one another, and they arouse different emotions and elicit different behaviors in individuals (Martinez, 2005).

Components of Love

According to Sternberg (1988b) there are three components or elements of love. They are:

Intimacy. Intimacy is the emotional element of love that leads to self-disclosure, connection, warmth, and trust between the partners.

Passion. Passion is the motivational element that leads to sexual desire and physiological arousal.

Commitment. Commitment is the cognitive element of love that determines whether to stay in love or quit it.

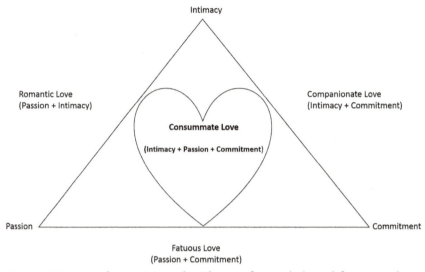

Figure 10.1   Sternberg's Triangular Theory of Love (Adapted from Sternberg, 1988b)

Sternberg (1988a) argues that what kind love people will feel depends on the degree to which these three elements are present in love. Figure 10.1 displays Sternberg's triangular concept of love and how different combinations of these three elements can change the patterns of love.

Patterns of Love

Figure 10.1 shows different patterns of love as construed in the triangular theory of love. Different concepts displayed in the figure are briefly described in the following section.

Liking. Intimacy is the only component present in liking; neither passion nor commitment is present. Liking reflects a feeling of true friendship that is characterized by understanding, closeness, support, affection, and warmth without intense feeling of passion or a long-term commitment.

Infatuation. Passion is the only component present in infatuated love. This can be characterized as "love at the first sight" with strong physical attraction and sexual desire without intimacy and commitment. Infatuated love can appear suddenly and disappear as fast.

Empty love. This is love with commitment but without intimacy and passion. Empty love is often found in a long-term marital relationship, such as an arranged marriage, which continues for some social and practical reasons, even though there are no passion and intimacy in the relationship.

Romantic love. Two elements—intimacy and passion—are present in romantic love. Romantic lovers are attracted to each other physically and bonded emotionally without any sustaining commitment for enduring relationship. This kind of love is more common among younger adults than middle adults or older adults.

Companionate love. This type of love is characterized by the presence of intimacy and commitment without passion or physical attraction. Companionate love has stronger feelings of affection and attachment than romantic love or passionate love (Fisher, 2004). It is characterized by intimacy, warmth, affection, commitment, care, and concern for the well-being of the partner (Frijda, 2006; Hatfield, Rapson, & Martel, 2007). This type of love is found in long-lasting marriages, especially among older adults, where physical attraction has died down but a deep feeling of affection and a strong sense of commitment have remained alive.

Fatuous love. In this kind of love two elements—passion and commitment—are present without the third element—intimacy. Fatuous love is also called passionate love or "obsessive love" because it is characterized by an intense desire for union and sexuality with the loved one (Hatfield & Rapson, 2016). Fatuous love often leads to a whirlwind courtship and marriage, in which partners make a commitment on the basis of passion before developing intimacy. Fatuous love usually does not last long, despite the initial commitment of the partners.

Consummate love. This is an ideal type of love in which all three components—intimacy, passion, and commitment—are present. Consummate love is also called "complete" love. Many people strive for this ideal love but only few can achieve it, and it is harder to maintain than to achieve it (Sternberg, 1987). Thus, consummate love is not necessarily permanent because it can die if and when all three components are not present.

Love, regardless of the type, doesn't last permanently. This is more true for younger adults than for older adults. A study showed that college students who could explain satisfactorily why they fell in and out of love with their previous partners were more satisfied with their present partners than those whose earlier relationships were unresolved (Clark & Collins, 1993).

Individual Differences in Love

Personality

Love has different meanings for people with different personalities (Fehr & Broughton, 2001). In a review, Dion and Dion (1985) indicated that personality and gender are important for understanding love because they are systematically associated with subjectively different experiences of love. Research evidence shows that there is association between individuals' personality traits and compatibility in romantic relationships (Ahmetoglu, Swami, & Chamorro-Premuzic, 2010). More detailed information regarding relationships between different personality traits and individuals' conception of love is reported in a study by Fehr and Broughton (2001). The researchers found that people tend to hold different views about love, depending on their personality traits. For example, people with high-nurturance traits (e.g., warm and agreeable) tend to conceptualize love in terms of its companionate characteristics including emotional stability, interdependence, commitment, trust, support, and nurturance. On the other hand, people with low-nurturance traits (e.g., low in warmth and agreeability) tend to conceptualize love in terms of its passionate characteristics including excitement, arousal, sexuality, fantasy, and emotional instability. Furthermore, people who are high in dominance tend to conceptualize love in terms of its romantic, passionate, and sexual characteristics. Whereas people who are submissive tend to conceptualize love in terms of its infatuation and commitment characteristics.

Findings of a number of studies indicate a positive relationship between extraversion and various dimensions of love (intimacy, passion, and commitment), because extroverts are better able to communicate love than introverts (e.g., Donnellan, Conger, & Bryant, 2004; Taraban, Hendrick, & Hendrick, 1998; Watson, Hubbard, & Wiese, 2000). Several studies have reported a negative relation between neuroticism and marital love quality, and a positive association between neuroticism and dissolution of the marital love relationship (e.g., Barelds, 2005; Davila et al., 2003; Heaven et al., 2006). In addition, two other personality traits—agreeableness and conscientiousness—are found to be related to different dimensions of love. For example, agreeableness is found to have a positive relationship with all three dimensions of love (intimacy, passion, and commitment); whereas conscientiousness is found to have a positive relationship associated only with intimacy and commitment (Ahmetoglu, Swami, & Chamorro-Premuzic, 2010). Moreover, agreeableness is found to have positive relations with marital satisfaction, partner interactions, and conflict resolution in romantic relationships (Donnellan, Conger, & Bryant, 2004).

Age

Does age matter in love? Yes it does. As people's attitudes and behaviors change with age, so do their patterns of love. Although love does not die in old age, its excitement, euphoria, and obsession diminish with aging.

Findings of a study, for example, show that as couples grow old, intimacy and commitment in love become more important for them than passion (Shallcross et al., 2013). The nature and characteristics of love change with aging, especially the psychological aspects of love—warmth, affection, care, and concern—become more important than the physical aspects of love—excitement, arousal, and sexual pleasure (Kalra, Subramanyam, & Pinto, 2011). A study by Tucker and Aaron (1993) reveals that satisfaction in marital love is typically highest in new marriages, especially in young age, followed by a downward trend during midlife, and improving again later in aging life. However, changes in attitudes and behaviors toward love and sex are not the same for every aging person. For some individuals, unlike others, age is nothing more than a number and has little effect on love and sex. Finally, in love: "Age is an issue of mind over matter. If you don't mind, it does not matter."—Mark Twain

Gender

Research evidence indicates that the way people experience love partially depends on their gender (Durik et al., 2006; Schmitt et al., 2009; Sprecher & Toro-Morn, 2002). For example, women tend to experience attraction and love for men who are intelligent, charming, and dominant; whereas men are more likely to experience attraction and love for women who are physically attractive (Fletcher et al., 2004; Lucas, Wendorf, & Ima-moglu, 2004). Women are more likely to perceive love in terms of emotional commitment and security, but men tend to think of love in terms of sexual commitment and the physical pleasure of intercourse (Buss, 2000).

Similarities and differences between men's and women's attitudes and perceptions of love depend on the gender as well on the type of love (Fehr & Broughton, 2001). These researchers, for example, found that men consistently assigned higher ratings to passionate love than did women, but both men and women agreed that companionate love is more important than passionate love. Moreover, women more often than not tend to endorse friendship-based love style than do men (Hendrick & Hendrick, 1995). Thus gender difference is evident in passionate love, where men hold stronger romantic and sexual views of love than do women. Findings of a study showed that passion is the best predictor of men's satisfaction in love, and commitment is the best predictor of women's satisfaction in love (Sternberg, 2006, 2013). The difference between men and women in attitude toward love becomes more evident as women tend to give importance to love with or without sex, and men tend to give importance to sex with or without love. Similarly, women tend to have sex for love and men tend to have love for sex (Sukel, 2013). Women intend to experience love before consenting to sexual intercourse (Schmitt, 2005), whereas men are more likely to consent to sex without love, such as sex with a friend or with a stranger (Voracek, Hofhansl, & Fisher, 2005). Women, on average, are likely to experience more intense emotional feelings in love than do men (Brody & Hall, 2010). Men often fall in love "at first sight" as they tend to enter into a romantic relationship more quickly than women (Galperin & Haselton, 2010). Unlike men, women do not like to rush in love. They are slow, cautious, and selective about picking an intimate partner, and they feel passion more slowly and steadily than do men (Li, Sing, & Jonason, 2012). Another area where men and women differ in intimate partner selection is the social status of partners. According to the sociocultural model, compared to men, women prefer partners with high social status, because of traditionally lower social status of women in many societies globally (Eagly & Wood, 2013).

Thus based on the previous discussion, it seems clear that there are similarities as well as differences between men's and women's perceptions of love. However, contrary to stereotyped belief, differences between men and women about the perception of love is rather small (Schmitt, 2008, 2016). It seems an overstatement that men and women perceive love completely differently (Fehr & Broughton, 2001).

Different Perspectives on Love

Although human love is universally based on individuals' biological and emotional needs, as well as on evolutionary heritage of mate selection and survival, attitudes, feelings, and behaviors related to love are different in different cultures, and in different historical periods. Reviewing research literature on different perspectives on love, Karandashev (2015) viewed love as a universal emotion that has existed throughout human history and has been experienced by people regardless of differences in culture, gender, and geographical boundary. Moreover, people's conceptions of love, and way they feel, think, and behave in romantic relationships are impacted by their historical, biological, psychological, and social contexts (Hatfield & Rapson, 2016). The following section focuses on different perspectives on love.

Historical Perspectives

For centuries, love, especially romantic love, has been explored by philosophers, anthropologists, psychologists, and sociologists, who have described its various aspects in different ways. For examples, Aristotle described love as "Love is composed of a single soul inhabiting two bodies," and Robert Heinlein described it as "Love is that condition in which the happiness of another person is essential to your own." The term *romantic love* was first coined by Gaston Paris, a 19th-century literary critic, to describe a specific constellation of attitudes and behavior patterns to characterize a body of literature on courtly love (Paris, 1883). Although romantic love was originally considered a uniquely European affair, researchers have found its existence in other world cultures, including Arabian, Chinese, Greek, and Indian cultures, and literatures (Hsu, 1985; Karandashev, 2015; Stone, 1989). History reveals that romantic love has always existed regardless of times, cultures, and geographical boundaries. Yet attitudes and behaviors related to romantic love varied dramatically from culture to culture and place to place throughout human history (Hatfield & Rapson, 2005).

For examples, people in ancient China would consider love and sexual pleasure positively as they would think love and sex two great joys of life (Ruan, 1991). But at the time of the Neo-Confucianists (approximately 1,000 years ago), Chinese attitudes toward love and sexuality gradually changed and became more repressive. Erotic literature and art were banned. Their primary goal of marriage was to procreate. But a husband could seek sexual satisfaction with a variety of women. Extramarital sex was typically allowed for wealthy married men but not for women. A woman's major function was to give birth to children, and she was expected to be faithful to her husband (Murstein, 1974, p. 469). The Chinese considered sex to be a natural biological need, so if a husband would feel the need, he could take a concubine. But it was unacceptable for a wife to have sex with any male other than her husband. The status of concubines would vary. A concubine would typically be a maidservant, who would do most of the menial works of the family and would fulfill the husband's sexual needs when he would desire. However, public displays of nonmarital love were restricted (Murstein, 1974). Later on during 1950s and 1960s, the government of communist China considered love and sexual activity beyond marriage as "inappropriate" and imposed strict controls on premarital and extramarital love and sexual activity. In keeping with communist ideology, China gives more importance to collective welfare than individual pleasure and happiness. So romantic love has not been a major focus in people's life in China during 1950s and 1960s. In an official booklet of the Chinese government, love was described as "psychosomatic activity that consumes energy and wastes time" (as quoted in Murstein, 1974, p. 482). In the 1990s, when China opened its door to Western countries for political and economic interests, a rapid change occurred in attitudes of the Chinese government and the people, especially young people, toward love and sexuality. Due to the effects of globalization of mass media, availability of international cinema, and accessibility of the Internet, romantic love is no longer a taboo in modern China. Nowadays, Chinese young people are enjoying increasingly more freedom in choosing their romantic partners and expressing their sexual desire without any restriction from their government and society (Hatfield, Rapson, & Martel, 2007).

Europe is another example of variations in the patterns of love at different historical eras. In medieval England, love was greatly influenced by Christianity. In 12th-century England, love was mainly perceived as a self-sacrificing, compassionate, and benevolent relationship between individuals rather than passionate relationships. Sexual attraction was not necessarily considered a part of love, but rather friendship was considered to be closely related to love (Kalyuga, 2012). The meaning of love started changing in England during the 13th century, when the meaning of love was gradually expanding to include passion and sexual attraction toward the opposite sex. During the 13th and 14th centuries, English literature was gradually shifting its focus from religious topics to courtly love. The concept of courtly love came to English literature from French literature in which courtly love was depicted as a sort of idealization of women as an object of devotional and romantic love (Lewis, 2013). Love was described, during the 16th and 17th centuries (Shakespeare's era), as a consuming passion and irresistible force. In the Victorian era (the period of Queen Victoria's reign from 1837 to 1901), romantic love was considered to be a delicate spiritual feeling—a puritan view of love, which does not encourage a crude lust. The concept of courtly love gradually gained ground in many parts of Northern and Western Europe. This concept, however, was unfamiliar to some other parts of Europe including Russia. The concept of love in Russia, until the 18th century, was strongly influenced by Christianity. The concept of romantic love was not a focus of Russian literature during that time. The topic of romantic love gained popularity in Russian literature after the reforms of Peter the Great in the 18th and 19th centuries (Kalyuga, 2012). A major factor that influenced the understanding of romantic love in Europe during the 20th century was the liberalization of sexual values and the sexual revolution in 1960s and 1970s.

Scientific research on romantic love began in the mid-20th century when scholars from various disciplines including anthropology, sociology, and psychology started exploring romantic love from different perspectives (Karandashev, 2015). Around the same time scholars started developing major constructs and theories of love.

Thus, throughout human history, people have perceived and interpreted love conceptually, attitudinally, and behaviorally from different perspectives including anthropological, evolutionary, biogenetic, cultural, and psychosocial perspectives. Historically, the crucial question was whether romantic love was only a Western cultural construct, or if it also existed in other world cultures including ancient Greek, Indian, and the Islamic cultures. Scholars agreed that love is a universal emotion experienced by most humans in all cultures throughout various historical eras, although due to cultural differences people's conceptions of love and the way they feel, think, and behave in romantic relationships have never been the same. In a review of the literature on love, Karandashev (2015) has extensively documented contributions of a large number of anthropologists, sociologists, and psychologists in expanding our understanding of cross-cultural variations of love worldwide.

Anthropological and Evolutionary Perspectives

Several anthropologists and social psychologists reported that despite cultural differences, love is universal and not limited to certain cultures (de Munck et al., 2011; Vangelisti & Perlman, 2006). Evolutionary psychologists think that passionate love is based on human biological processes and is innate and universal, which existed in most people of all cultures globally during all historical eras (Hatfield & Rapson, 2016). Since Darwin, evolutionary psychologists have argued that mate selection for fulfillment of biological and emotional needs including love and sexual activity is crucially important for human evolution and development (Hatfield, Rapson, & Martel, 2007). The evolutionary psychologists also suggested that passionate and companionate love evolved to solve different problems in human pair bonding (Fisher, 2004). Passionate love is characterized by an intense desire for union and sexuality with the loved one, which helps the continuation of the human reproductive process. Companionate love is characterized by intimacy, warmth, affection, commitment, care, and concern for the well-being of loved ones, which helps make the mating relationship endure so that children can be nurtured until they are able to survive on their own.

In a global study, Jankowiak and Fischer (1992) explored romantic love in 166 cultures all over the world. They found that romantic love was present in about 89 percent of cultures in the world. Thus the findings showed that romantic love is almost universal, except for having some cultural differences. The researchers observed that despite the universal nature of love, people's love-related attitudes and behaviors are substantially influenced by their cultural values and beliefs. For instance, people fall in love less frequently in societies where romantic love, particularly premarital and extramarital romantic love, is not approved. In a review of anthropological research on love, Jankowiak (1995) has shown that anthropologists have studied folk conceptions of love in many diverse cultures including China, Indonesia, Morocco, Nigeria, Trinidad, Turkey, the Fulbe of North Cameroun, the Mangaia in the Cook Islands, the Mangrove (an aboriginal Australian community), Palau in Micronesia, and the Taita of Kenya. Results showed that in all these studies, people's conceptions of passionate love are surprisingly similar. There is also clear evidence that culture has a profound impact on people's perceptions, attitudes, and behaviors concerning romantic love (Hatfield, Rapson, & Martel, 2007). The authors have concluded that passion is universal because it is based on biogenetic and evolutionary basics of mate selection, which is important for human survival; whereas romance is culture specific as it is based on historical traditions and cultural norms.

Genetic and Biological Perspectives

Neuroscience research indicates that passionate love has a strong biological basis (Hatfield & Rapson, 2016). Bartels and Zeki (2000, 2004), for instance, conducted functional magnetic resonance imaging (fMRI) to explore the neural basis of passionate love. They found that passionate love leads to increased levels of activity in the brain areas connected with euphoria and reward, and decreased levels of activity in the brain areas connected with distress and depression. They also found that passionate love suppresses the activity in the areas of the brain associated with critical thinking. Evidence of deactivations were also found in other parts of the brain including posterior, prefrontal, parietal, and middle temporal cortices. An analysis of the chemistry of passionate love reveals that a variety of neurochemical elements stimulate passionate love and sexual desire. In a study, for example, Fisher (2004) found that passionate love is connected with the natural stimulant dopamine and serotonin. The author also indicated that the lust for sexual activity is mainly stimulated by the hormone testosterone, and the feeling of emotion connected with love and sexual activity is produced by the hormones oxytocin and vasopressin. In addition, companionate love also has physiological and neurochemical bases.

Carter (2014), for example, indicated that since the presence of neuropeptide oxytocin in the bloodstream reduces stress and tension and promotes relaxation and a soothing sense of well-being, it may have effects on companionate love because there is less euphoria and excitement, and strong feelings of relaxation, stability, and long-term commitment and well-being in companionate love. People with higher levels of oxytocin in their blood have been found to have a tendency to behave more warmly with their spouses, and behave more pleasantly during disagreement with partners (Floyd, 2006).

Psychological Perspectives

Love can't be comprehensively understood without understanding its psychological perspectives (Sternberg & Weis, 2006). In any definition or description of love a number of important psychological concepts, including emotion, attachment, feeling, attitudes, motivation, behavior, personality, etc., are frequently used. Although love is an abstract concept, a large number of psychologists from different countries have been doing empirical research on love, and eventually several theories have been developed to explain emotion, feeling, experience, and behaviors related with love in the contexts of personality, gender, and culture. Four important theories in connection with the psychology of love are Sigmund Freud's psychoanalytic theory, Abraham Maslow's need hierarchy theory, John Bowlby's attachment theory, and Ronald Rohner's interpersonal acceptance-rejection theory. One can't discuss psychological perspectives on love without discussing these theories. As these theories are discussed in more detail in Chapters 4 and 5, only the relevant portions of these theories are discussed here.

Freud viewed that how people pick up their mates largely depends on their childhood experiences and relationships with their parents. He argued that many aspects of an individual's personality development originate in response to childhood sexual instincts. He also proposed that as individuals attain puberty and maturation of sex organs, they seek gratification of psychosexual pleasure through actual sexual activities. Freud believed that sexual urges and pleasures are the primary determinants of behavior. He suggested that during the phallic stage, boys develop the Oedipus complex (sexual attraction for the mother and envy against the father), and girls develop the Electra complex (sexual attraction for the father and envy against the mother). These complexes are resolved by boys through the identification with their fathers and by girls through the identification with their mothers, thus developing their beliefs, values, and behaviors in socially desirable ways.

Maslow (1967) proposed that people are innately motivated to satisfy their needs in a hierarchical order. Physiological needs are at the bottom of the hierarchical order, followed by safety needs and psychological needs such as belonging and love needs, esteem needs, and self-actualization needs. Maslow considered belonging and love needs (i.e., the need to love and to be loved, and to share one's life with attachment figures and significant others) as very important psychological needs. Maslow suggested that physiological needs are more basic and more similar with the needs of animals, and that the psychological needs are more distinctly human. Once the physiological needs are reasonably fulfilled, feelings about the psychological needs and efforts to realize them increase in intensity.

Attachment theory focuses on intimate relationships over an individual's lifespan (Ainsworth & Bowlby, 1991; Bowlby, 1969/1982; Cassidy & Shaver, 1999; Colin, 1996). The theory provides important concepts and constructs for explaining intimate relationships in childhood, adolescence, and adulthood. Ainsworth and Bowlby (1991) defined attachment as an enduring tie with a partner who is an important and unique person, and interchangeable with no other person. Although attachment researchers were originally involved in studying emotional bonds between infants and their caregivers, Bowlby (1994) considered attachment an important element of experience extending over the individual lifespan—childhood through aging life. Ainsworth and Bowlby (1991) classified attachment into different types such as secure attachment, insecure attachment, avoidant attachment, anxious attachment, and ambivalent attachment. They suggested that children and adults with secure attachment tend to develop positive psychosocial characteristics, and they tend to develop negative psychological characteristics with insecure attachment. Research evidence shows that people with secure attachment enjoy greater intimacy with their partners than do people with insecure attachment (Mikluincer & Shave, 2013). On the other hand, people with avoidant attachment tend to be suspicious with their partners (Sprecher & Fehr, 2011), and people with anxious attachment tend to be apprehensive and nervous in intimate relationships more than people with secure attachment (Davila & Kashy, 2009).

Interpersonal acceptance and rejection theory (IPARTheory) postulates that acceptance or love by attachment figures has consistent positive effects, and rejection or lack of love by them has consistent negative effects, on the psychological adjustment and behavioral functioning of both children and adults worldwide (Rohner & Khaleque, 2015a). IPARTheory's personality subtheory assumes that the emotional need for positive response from attachment figures is a powerful motivator in children and adults. The personality subtheory postulates that when this need is adequately met by attachment figures, children and adults have the phylogenetically acquired tendency to develop positive personality dispositions. When this need is not adequately met by attachment figures, children and adults tend to develop negative personality dispositions. In addition, two other psychologists, Skinner (1953) and Watson (1913), have explained how people's love-related behaviors are influenced by reward and reinforcement.

Social and Cultural Perspectives

The concept of love can be different in different social contexts. Cohen (2016), reviewing findings of several cross-cultural studies, suggested that there are clear conceptual differences in love between collectivistic and individualistic societies. In collectivistic societies, such as socialist countries including China and Russia, love is expected to grow with marriage over time. In such societies, more emphasis is on practical aspects of love such as income, relationship with extended family members, and less emphasis is on romantic aspect of love. On the other hand, people in individualistic societies, for example, Western European and North American countries, emphasize passionate aspects of love such as emotion, feelings, attraction, and excitement. Some scholars view romantic love as a Western phenomenon not found in non-Western countries, except for the elite of those countries who have the time and money to cultivate romantic love (e.g., de Munck et al., 2011; Karandashev, 2015). Several authors indicated a different perspective with a belief that romantic love is a universal phenomenon as they found the evidence of its occurrences in many cultures (Kitayama, Markus, & Kurokawa, 2000; Scollon et al., 2005). As noted earlier, in a global study, Jankowiak and Fischer (1992) found that romantic love was present in about 89 percent of cultures (in 147 out of 166 cultures) in the world. Thus the findings showed that romantic love is almost universal, except having some cultural differences.

However, there is enough evidence of influences of cultural values and beliefs on individuals' attitudes, experiences, and behaviors in romantic love globally (Kitayama, Markus, & Kurokawa, 2000; Scollon et al., 2005; Shiota et. al., 2010). Culture accounts for about 38 to 59 percent of variability in love (Buss, 1994). Culture may have a powerful influence on how people link passionate love and sexual desire. Many men, for example, are taught to separate sex and love, while many women are taught not to separate the two (Hatfield & Rapson, 2005). In a study on cultural aspects of intimacy, passion and commitment on 90 Chinese and 77 American couples showed that ratings on passion were higher among American than Chinese couples, but there were no differences in ratings of intimacy and commitment between these two groups (Gao, 2001). In another study in China, India, Indonesia, Iran, Israel, and Taiwan, young people were found to insist that their mate should be "chaste," while young adults in Finland,

France, Germany, Norway, the Netherlands, and Sweden did not consider chastity as an important factor in mate selection (Wallen, 1989). To explore some cultural differences in love in individualistic and collectivistic societies, de Munck and colleagues (2011) conducted a study in the United States, Lithuania, and Russia. They found that people from all three countries agreed on the following characteristics as the "core" concepts of romantic love, and there was agreement across all cultures that love is a strong feeling that unites the partners in close relationships. But altruism was considered more important in the United States than in Lithuania and Russia. Several differences between individualism (United States) and collectivism (Lithuania and Russia) were found. However, as expected, there were more similarities between Lithuanian and Russian samples than between the U.S. sample and the Russian or Lithuanian samples. In another study, cross-cultural differences were found in the experience of love progression over the years. Ingersoll-Dayton and colleagues (1996), for example, compared progression of marriage in the United States versus Japan. They found that the U.S. marriages start with a relatively high level of intimacy, and in Japan the intimacy develops later in life after marriage. In another cross-cultural study, it was found that young adults in the United States make their marital decisions independently of their parents, but young adults in China ask advice and support from their parents in making marital decisions (Zhang & Kline, 2009). Thus it appears that the cultural influences are very powerful in mate selection and love (Karandashev, 2015).

How Long Does Love Last?

There are several factors that are related to the durability and stability of love. An important factor associated with the durability of love is the type of love. For example, some researchers argued that in general passionate love is less stable than companionate love (Hatfield & Rapson, 2016), because time has different impacts on passionate versus companionate love. Passionate love fades with time more quickly than does companionate love. A study shows that within two years of marriage couples in romantic love express 50 percent less affection for each other than they would do when they were newly married (Huston & Chorost, 1994). Researchers suggest that romantic love diminishes fairly quickly with time because fantasy, novelty, and "idealized glorifications" of partners in romantic love decline and passion slowly subsides with the harsh reality of life as the relationship continues (Ahmetoglu, Swami, & Chamorro-Premuzic, 2010). So enduring passion or romance in a long-term relationship is quite uncommon (Mitchell, 2002). Nonetheless, romantic love is increasingly viewed as an essential component of a marriage. A study reported that 91 percent of American women and 86 percent of men would not marry someone with whom they were not in a romantic relationship (Gregoire, 2014). In a long-term intimate relationship, however, passion and preoccupation with romantic love tend to fade into companionship love (Acevedo & Aron, 2009). Several researchers, however, reported that corrosive effects of time are almost equally strong for all types of love including passionate love as well as companionate love (O'Leary et al., 2012). Contrarily, a number of studies have shown that people married for several years can still enjoy passionate and companionate love with their partners. For example, O'Leary et al. (2012) found that 40 percent of couples who had been married for a decade said that they were very intensely in love with their partners, and 40 percent of women and 35 percent of men who had been married over three decades or more said that they were very intensely in love. To find the answer to the question concerning why some couples enjoy enduring romantic love and others don't, Zentner (2005) reviewed about 500 studies on love but couldn't identify any combination of two personality traits in a love relationship that predicted long-term romantic love, except for one—the ability to idealize and maintain positive illusions about the partner.

CHAPTER SUMMARY

Chapter 10 focuses on components of love; patterns of love; individual differences in love; different perspectives on love, including historical, genetic, biological, anthropological, evolutionary, psychological, social, and cultural perspectives; and how long love lasts.

Love. Love is an emotional feeling and a behavioral experience that varies from culture to culture and individual to individual even in the same culture.

Components of love. Love has three components: intimacy—emotional component, passion—motivational component, and commitment—cognitive component.

Patterns of love. Patterns of love people experience depend on the combinations of these three components.

Infatuation. Passion is the only component present in infatuated love. This kind of love is characterized by strong physical attraction and sexual desire without intimacy and commitment. Infatuated love can appear suddenly and disappear as fast.

Empty love. This is love with commitment but without intimacy and passion. Empty love is often found in a long-term marital relationship.

Romantic love. Intimacy and passion are present in romantic love. Romantic love is without any sustaining commitment for enduring relationship. This kind of love is more common among younger adults than in middle adults or older adults.

Companionate love. This type of love is characterized by the presence of intimacy and commitment without passion or physical attraction.

Consummate love. This is an ideal type of love in which all three components—intimacy, passion, and commitment—are present.

Differences in love. Love has different meanings for people of different gender, personality, and culture.

Different perspectives on love. Although love is universal, attitudes, feelings, and behaviors related to love are different in different cultures, and in different historical periods.

How long does love last? The durability of love depends on the type of love. In general, romantic love is less stable than companionate love.

REFLECTIVE QUESTIONS

1. What is love? What are the components of love?
2. Discuss Sternberg's triangular concept of love. How can different combinations of elements of love change the patterns of love?
3. Discuss personality, gender, and cultural differences in love.
4. Briefly discuss different perspectives on love.
5. How long does love last? Discuss different factors that are related to the stability of love.

CHAPTER ELEVEN

Sexuality

Sexuality is the key to the problem of the psychoneuroses and of the neuroses in general. No one who disdains the key will ever be able to unlock the door.

—Sigmund Freud

Freud proposed a pansexual view of human development assuming that sexual urges and pleasures are the primary determinants of all kinds of human behavior, and the resolution of psychosexual conflicts is the key to a healthy life. Few psychologists endorse his views because of his exaggerated importance on the biological aspect of sexuality, ignoring the social and moral aspects of human sexuality. Although many psychologists find it difficult to accept his proposition that any kind of pleasure is related to sex, nobody denies his view that a healthy sexual relationship is an important determinant of a healthy adult intimate relationship and psychological adjustment.

Thus sexuality is considered an important component of intimate relationships or close personal relationships. Today there is more openness in expressing sexuality than at any time in the past, especially in Western countries including the United States. Moreover, sexual activity is accepted as a pleasurable, healthy, normal, and positive human behavior. One major change in attitude toward sexuality in Western societies is marked by the greater acceptance of premarital and nonmarital sex in a loving relationship, and more openness, less opposition, and more acceptance of homosexual and bisexual relationships. Another significant change in sexual attitude in Western societies is the decline in the double standard on sex—more sexual freedom for men than women.

Sexual Attitudes and Behavior

A survey on sexual attitudes and behavior shows that Americans have different types of views about sexuality. Laumann and Michael (2000), for example, found that about 30 percent of Americans have a traditional or reproductive attitude toward sex. They think that sexual activity should be permissible within the marital relationship for reproductive purposes. Approximately 25 percent of Americans (more men than women) hold a recreational view about sex. This group thinks that sex is for enjoyment, and as long as people enjoy sex and it does not hurt anyone, it should be okay. About 45 percent of Americans have a relational view about sex. They think that sex should be in loving relationships, but not necessarily in the marital relationship only.

Since the 1950s a great deal of change has occurred in the sexual attitude and behavior of adults in Western countries, especially in the United States. Sex outside of marriage was regarded as taboo for Americans born before the 1950s. If such sexual activity happened, people would rarely discuss it publicly during those days. At that time unmarried men and women in the United States would rarely live together. Unmarried women who bore children would be shunned, and homosexuality was considered shameful and unacceptable during and before the 1950s. Recently, Americans, especially younger generations, are more accepting and willing to participate in sexual activity outside of marriage than ever before (Twenge, Sherman, & Wells, 2015). Americans are increasingly becoming more permissive about premarital sex as long as it occurs in a loving and caring relationship (Sprecher, Schmeeckle, & Felmlee, 2006).

A survey on 33,380 American adults between the years 2000–2012 showed that compared to the 1970s and 1980s Americans were increasingly more willing to have had casual sex with multiple partners, and were more accepting to various types of nonmarital sex including premarital sex, teen sex, and sex with people of the same gender, but less willing to accept extramarital sex (Twenge, Sherman, & Wells, 2015). The study also showed that these changes were more evident among White males (especially among the baby boomer generation but less so among ethnic minority males) than females in general. The findings of the study show that the percentages of American adults who believed that premarital sex was not at all wrong gradually increased from 29 percent in the 1970s to 42 percent in the 1980s. The level of increase is highest for the acceptance of premarital sex, followed by teen sex, and the same sex, and lowest for extramarital sex. In addition, several studies reported that attitudes toward premarital sex changed substantially between the 1960s and 1970s but remained fairly steady during the 1980s and 1990s (Harding & Jencks, 2003; Treas, 2002; Wells & Twenge, 2005). On the other hand, attitudes toward sex with same-sex partners were steady until the 1990s and thereafter became significantly more accepting (Harding & Jencks, 2003; Percell, Green, & Gurevich, 2001). A meta-analysis by Petersen and Hyde (2010) found a decreasing trend in gender difference over time in behaviors and attitudes toward premarital sex with multiple partners.

Americans are becoming increasingly more ambivalent about casual sex or hookup—temporary sexual interactions with nonromantic partners without any expectation of a lasting intimate relationship (Lewis et al., 2013). Although more men than women prefer premarital and casual sex while dating with someone (Hyde, 2014), overall casual sex is not very popular among women and men (Reiber & Garcia, 2010). Research findings show that most women tend to regret their past actions about casual sex, while some men regret their past inactions about it (Galperin, Haselton, & Frederick, 2013).

A number of researchers (e.g., Markus & Kitayama, 2010; Twenge, 2014; Yang, 2008) have indicated that sexual attitudes and behavior might have undergone significant changes for different reasons including time period (changes over time that affects people of all ages), generation/birth cohort (variations in sexual attitudes and behavior among people of different generations), and aging (people are living longer than before). Mixed effects analyses separating time period, generation/birth cohort, and aging revealed that generational changes are the strongest predictor of sexual permissiveness than changes due to time period and aging (Twenge, Sherman, & Wells, 2015). A generation gap in sexual attitudes and behavior suggests that in the future, older generations may not practice as much abstinence as the current generation of aging people do; rather they are likely to be more active in sexual behavior in old age (Burgess, 2004).

Sexual Attitudes and Behavior of Older Adults

Sexual attitudes and behavior, especially about premarital and extramarital sex, vary by age and gender. One report showed that about 61 percent of men and only 12 percent of women born before 1910 admitted to have had premarital sexual experiences, but by the 1980s an almost equal percentage of women and men reported premarital sexual experiences (Papalia, 2012). Several cross-sectional surveys reported that frequency of sexual intercourse gradually declines in old age (DeLamater & Moorman, 2007; Kontula, 2002). A study on 6,785 married adults showed that 96 percent of young adults (aged 19 to 24 years) had sexual intercourse at least once in a month, whereas 83 percent of middle adults (aged 50 to 54 years), and only 27 percent of older adults (aged 75 or older) had sexual intercourse at least once in a month (Call, Sprecher, & Schwartz, 1995). Yucel and Eroglu (2013) found that there was consistent decline in sexual activity with increasing age. They reported that while sexual activity of couples in the 40–49 years age group decreased about 50 percent, the rate of decrease in the 50–59 years age group was 71 percent, and the rate of decrease in the 60–69 years age group was 83 percent. Findings of another study on influences of age, biological, and psychosocial factors on sexual attitudes and functions in later life showed that although the nature of sexual expression in later life reflects the interactions of body, mind, and social context, the effect of age remains significant after controlling other factors (DeLamater & Moorman, 2007).

On the basis of a review of literature, Burgess (2004) concluded that age has a strong effect on sexual frequency. Moreover, several authors suggested that changes in sexual attitude and decline in sexual activity for both aging women and men occur due to a variety of reasons including biochemical changes in the body, health problems, loss of partners, psychological changes, and sociocultual influences (e.g., Burgess, 2004; DeLamater & Moorman, 2007). As far as bodily changes are concerned, women and men undergo different types of bodily changes (i.e., biochemical changes) with aging. Women's estrogen production level goes down with aging and menopause. Due to menopause the uterus shrinks, the vagina becomes drier, and the vaginal tissues become thinner. These hormonal changes result in inadequate lubrication and vaginal atrophy, and consequently many women experience pain during intercourse (Dennerstein, Dudley, & Burger, 2001). As a result they lose interest in sexual activity. Yucel and Eroglu (2013) reported that during menopause about 22 to 66 percent of women experience sexual problems. On the other hand, men's testosterone levels decrease slowly with aging, and their sperm count goes down although they remain fertile until very old age. But men often experience erectile dysfunction with aging as the erection may not be firm or not easy to achieve. Consequently, many aging men lose desire for sexual intercourse. Another problem for men is prostate gland enlargement, which happens in about 80 percent of the male population over 60 years of age, causing the urinary canal to become compressed. This is called prostatic hypertrophy, which often requires surgical removal. The surgical procedure usually does not make a person sexually disabled, but it can damage some nerves and consequently may lead to impotence.

Some researchers have indicated that decreasing frequency of sexual activity in aging life may be due to cohort effects as well as age effects.

Reviews of the literature on this topic have provided evidence showing that both factors are at work (Burgess, 2004). Although sexual activity becomes less frequent with age for all cohorts, the future older cohorts are likely to be more sexually active than are current older cohorts (Edwards & Booth, 1994).

Psychological factors that affect sexual behavior in old age include monotony and boredom—habituation to sex with a long-term partner— that may lead to a decline in interest and frequency of sexual behavior (Burgess, 2004). Some researchers have reported significant effects of psychosocial factors such as self-image, religious values, psychological well-being, social connectedness, and relationship satisfaction on sexual behavior in aging life (Matthias et al., 1997).

Aging is associated with increasing health problems. A substantial amount of research suggests that chronic illnesses and effects of medications interfere with sexual function in old age (e.g., Burgess, 2004; Marumo & Murai, 2001; Trudel, Turgeon, & Piche, 2000). Chronic physical and mental illness, such as cardiovascular disease, diabetes, arthritis, prostate cancer, cancers of the reproductive organs, and depression are commonly associated with sexual problems in old age (Schover et al., 2004; Thors, Broeckel, & Jacobsen, 2001). Findings of a study on diabetes, for instance, showed that women with diabetes report significantly more sexual dysfunction than nondiabetic women (Enzlin et al., 2002). In the same study, diabetes was found associated with pain during sex, decreased sexual desire, and low arousal level. On the other hand, the diabetic men reported decreased penile sensitivity and ejaculatory and orgasmic difficulties (Veves et al., 1995).

Medications used to treat chronic illnesses in old age also have negative effects on sexual functioning. Many medications have side effects resulting in slowing the autonomic nervous system, reducing its responsiveness and sensitivity to stimulation. Anti-androgen treatment for prostate cancer, for example, can reduce sexual drive and can cause erectile dysfunction (Marumo & Murai, 2001). Antihypertensive drugs often cause difficulties in attaining orgasm for both women and men (Masters, Johnson, & Kolodny, 1994).

Despite age-related physical and psychological changes and health problems, some aging women and men enjoy sex as much as or even more than they enjoyed sex during their young and middle adulthoods. Some of the reasons are (1) more freedom and privacy as children left home; (2) couples know and understand one another's emotion, feeling, liking, and expectation about sex from a long period of experience and intimacy; and (3) the female partners have no fear of pregnancy after menopause.

Importance of Sexual Attitudes and Behavior

Sexual attitudes and behaviors are critically important for a variety of outcomes, such as sexually transmitted diseases (Scott-Sheldon et al., 2011), prevention of sexual abuse and assault (Santos-Iglesias, Sierra, Vallejo-Medina, 2013), and mental health (Vrangalova, 2014).

Research on gender differences on attitudes and behavior related to casual sex shows that women experience more shame and guilt for pre-marital sexual behavior than do men (Fielder & Carey, 2010; Sprecher, 2014; Townsend & Wasserman, 2011). However, there are cultural differences in sexual conservatism and liberalism including sexual attitudes toward premarital sex and same-sex sexual activity (Meston & Ahrold, 2010). Regardless of gender and cultural differences, sexual attitudes are strong predictors of sexual behaviors, including risky sexual behavior (Lam & Lefkowitz, 2013), being involved in casual sex (Katz & Schneider, 2013), and sex with multiple partners (Townsend & Wasserman, 2011).

Sexual Double Standard

The double standard in sexual behavior refers to a worldwide traditional social practice in which men enjoy greater sexual freedom than do women. Historically, women have been treated more harshly for sexual permissiveness than men. But this gender asymmetry in sexual attitude and behavior is gradually decreasing, as Western societies are becoming more tolerant of premarital sex and less accepting of extramarital sex for both women and men (Allison & Risman, 2013). But the sexual double standard still exists to some extent in many societies, especially among men (Rudman, Fetterolf, & Sanchez, 2013), where women (and not men) who get involved in casual sex with multiple partners are still perceived negatively (Conley et al., 2013). Research evidence shows that compared to men, women with sexually transmitted diseases are perceived more unfavorably and judged more harshly in many societies (Smith, Mysak, & Michael, 2008).

Sexual Orientation

Sexual orientation refers to the pattern of an individual's sexual attractions based on gender. There are four major categories of sexual orientation:

1. **Heterosexual orientation.** Sexual attraction for people of the opposite sex. Heterosexual orientation is also called *strait sexual orientation* because this is the most common form of sexual orientation.

2. *Homosexual orientation.* Sexual attraction for people of the same sex. Homosexual orientations are of two subtypes:

   a. *Gay.* Males' sexual attraction for males; and

   b. *Lesbian.* Females' sexual attraction for females.

3. *Bisexual orientation.* Sexual attraction for both men and women.

4. *Asexual orientation.* Sexually not attracted to anyone, regardless of gender.

Researchers have suggested that individuals' sexual orientations can't be divided in such definable and distinct categories, because sexual orientations are not always static and discrete but can be mixed and are changeable over time (Diamond, 2007; Peplau & Garnets, 2000).

Sexual Orientation and Gender Identity

Gender identity refers to an individual's sense of being a male, female, or transgender, regardless of one's biological sex characteristics, such as reproductive organs and external genitals. It is how one feels about and expresses one's gender. In short, it refers to the meaning of being a woman or a man. It is an individual's subjective perception about himself or herself as a male or female in relation to the values, beliefs, behavior, roles, and responsibilities associated with gender identity. An individual's gender identity may or may not be always congruent with his/her biological sex. When biological sex and gender identity are congruent, the individual is categorized as heterosexual, and when incongruent, the individual is categorized as transsexual (Gainor, 2000). Gender identity is a social construction based on different norms, values, roles, and responsibilities assigned by the society to males and females.

In almost every society there exists gender stereotype—widely held and long-standing beliefs about different physical and psychological characteristics of women and men. Stereotyped characteristics for women and men are called femininity and masculinity, respectively. Stereotypes for femininity include beliefs that women are physically weak, passive, dependent, emotional, warm, pretty, submissive, and so on. By contrast, stereotypes for masculinity include beliefs that men are physically strong, independent, active, unemotional, dominant, aggressive, and so on. Different stereotypes about gender can cause unequal and unfair treatment because of an individual's gender, which is called sexism.

Biological Aspects of Sexual Orientation and Identity

Freudian views seem pertinent to explain the biological basis of an individual's sexual orientation and identity. Freud believed that every individual is inherently bisexual. That is why each person is attracted to members of the same sex as well to the members of the opposite sex. He thought that each person has a constitutional basis for homosexuality, although the homosexual impulses remain dormant for most people.

Later research evidence supports Freudian views as it shows that people's sexual orientations are mainly the outcomes of interaction between nature and nurture (Diamant & McAnulty, 1995). A review of a large number of studies indicates that a complex process including biology—brain, genes, and hormones—and environmental events are involved in determining an individual's sexual orientation (Gladue, 1994).

There are basic physiological differences between men and women in reproductive and sexual mechanisms that have significant influences on their sexual activities and orientations. Some of the most obvious distinctions include differences in:

Arousal. An indication of male arousal is erection of the penis, and for female it is vaginal lubrication.

Orgasm. A climax of sexual excitement, ejaculation is a common feature of male orgasm, but there is a wide variation in female orgasm ranging from no orgasm to a single orgasm or multiple orgasms.

Fertility. Men's sperm production declines with aging but does not stop suddenly. But women's production of ova begins to decline in the late thirties or forties and stops with menopause. Although men's sperm production begins to decline in the late forties or fifties, unlike a woman, a man can continue to remain fertile until late life. Despite differences in fertility, some men and women can stay sexually active throughout adulthood depending on the condition of health, interest, drive in sexual activity.

Hormones. Hormone that is connected with male sexual arousal and activation is called testosterone and that for female is called estrogen. Although the male and female reproductive glands produce both testosterone and estrogen, typically the male reproductive gland produces more testosterone than estrogen and the female reproductive gland produces more estrogen than testosterone. Low testosterone can result in a drop in men's sex drive, low sperm counts, and poor erection. A decrease in estrogen level can result in a drop in women's sex drive, vaginal dryness, decrease in breast size, decreased functioning of the ovaries, a drop in ova production, and climacteric culminating with menopause. Men's hormone production declines with aging, but women undergo a sudden drop in hormone production at midlife.

Effects of hormones on sexual orientation. Several studies have provided substantial evidence supporting that exposure to atypical hormonal conditions during the embryonic stage have a link with sexual orientation, especially with homosexuality (e.g., Balthazart, 2011a; LeVay, 2010). Some studies have suggested that embryonic sex steroids affect sexual orientation in humans; and homosexuals were found to be more exposed than heterosexuals to atypical embryonic sex steroids, including testosterone during the prenatal stage of development (Balthazart, 2011b; Hines, 2011).

Brain structure and sexual orientation. Research findings indicate that sexual orientations—heterosexuality, bisexuality, and homosexuality—are determined by the differences of brain structure and brain chemistry (Bao & Swaab, 2011). Cultural or societal factors and upbringing do not determine sexual orientations as much as neural mechanisms do (Balthazart, 2011a). Scientists have identified several areas of the brain including the hypothalamus, the amygdala, and interhemispheric neural connectivity that they believe largely determine human sexual orientations (Becker et al., 2008). A study by Savic and Lindström (2008), for example, indicates that there are differences between heterosexual and homosexual individuals in brain anatomy, brain functions, and neurological connections. Their study specifically shows cerebral differences between homosexual and heterosexual individuals.

Genetic and Environmental Contributions to Gender Identity Development

To assess the relative contributions of genetic and environmental factors to the development of gender identity, several studies have been conducted on concordant or discordant for gender identity of male and female monozygotic and dizygotic twins (e.g., Diamond, 2011; Segal, 2012). In one study 33 percent of monozygotic male pairs and 22 percent of monozygotic female pairs were found concordant for transsexual identity; in comparison, concordance between either male or female dizygotic twins was as low as about 3 percent (Diamond, 2013). Based on the responses of the twins, the researcher concluded that gender identity tends to be more influenced by genetic than environmental factors. In another study, Heylens et al. (2012) found that among 23 monozygotic female and male twins 39 percent were concordant for gender identity, and none among the 21 dizygotic twins were found concordant for gender identity. A number of studies reported the influence of child rearing on children gender identity development. For example, boys were found to develop more feminine and less masculine gender identity in father-absent families (e.g., De Lange, 2011; Stevens et al., 2002).

Cultural Aspects of Sexuality

Another important factor that influences individuals' sexual attitudes and behavior is culture (variations in individualistic and collectivistic cultural norms). A lot of work on cultural changes has focused on increases in individualism in Western countries including the United States (e.g., Myers, 2000a; Twenge, 2014). Individualism promotes the idea that social values, norms, and rules are less important than individuals' freedom, needs, and desires (Welzel, 2013). Thus individualism encourages more sexual freedom outside of traditional marital sex, and increased acceptance of premarital sex and sexual permissiveness (Ven-hwei, So, & Guoliang, 2010). On the other hand, a review of a large body of research on this topic from 1985 to 2007 showed that stronger connectedness to friends, family, and communities, as encouraged in collectivism, is associated with reduced sexual permissiveness including premarital and extramarital sex (Markham et al., 2010).

Sexual attitudes and behavior of the people of the United States in general are less permissive than that of the people of most of the West European countries (Pew Research Center, 2014b). For example, unlike the United States, gay and lesbian marriages became legal in Denmark and Norway since 1990s. A large cross-cultural research shows that in comparison to Australia, Germany, Great Britain, Russia, Spain, and Sweden, the United States is more conservative and less permissive about premarital sex, extramarital sex, and same-sex relationships (Widmer, Treas, & Newcomb, 1998). Even neighboring Canadians hold more liberal sexual attitudes than Americans (Pew Research Center, 2014a). Ethnically, African Americans hold sexually more permissive attitudes than European Americans, Hispanic Americans, and Asian Americans (Fugère et al., 2008). However, African Americans hold stronger negative attitudes about same-sex marriage than European Americans (Vincent, Peterson, & Parrott, 2009). In addition, more Republicans than Democrats, more fundamentalist than nonreligious Americans, and more aging than young Americans are opposed to same-sex marriage (Pew Research Center, 2013).

Sexual Desire and Gender

Men and women in general differ in sexual desire, motivation, and drive. Men have stronger sexual impulse and drive, and less control over sexual temptation than women (Tidwell & Eastwick, 2013). Typically, men feel more frequent need and higher motivation for sexual activity than do women (Das, Waite, & Laumann, 2011; Lippa, 2009). A study on young adults shows that young men felt sexual desire on average for 37 times per week, whereas young women felt it only 9 times per week (Regan, 2015). In another study it was found that on average young men think about sex 34 times a day, and young women think only 19 times a day (Fisher, Moore, & Pittenger, 2012).

Despite having regular sex partners, about 50 percent of men and only 16 percent of women get involved in masturbation more than once in a week (Klusmann, 2002). Men are more likely than women to feel dissatisfied if they get sex less frequently than they desire (Sprecher, 2002). In a romantic relationship, men typically show readiness for sex earlier than do women, and when women give indication of readiness for sex, men rarely say no (Sprecher, Barbee, & Schwartz, 1995). Men spend more money on buying sexy books, magazines, and porn than do women (Pitts et al., 2004). More men than women are willing to have casual sex more often with multiple partners (Sprecher, Treger & Sakaluk, 2013). The gap in sexual desire becomes increasingly wider between middle and aging men and women, especially with a significant drop in sexual desire in women after menopause (McCabe & Goldhammer, 2012).

Sex in Marital and Nonmarital Relationships

The frequency of adults' sexual intercourse largely depends on the nature and duration of relationships with partners. Marital and cohabiting partners are involved in sexual intercourse more often than singles because single individuals are less likely to have consistent access to sexual partners in comparison to marital and cohabiting adults (Smith, 2006). Married and cohabiting young partners have little or no difference in their frequency of sexual intercourse. In one study, for example, married and cohabiting partners were found to have sex on average two to three times per week (Willetts, Sprecher, & Beck, 2004). Regardless of marriage and cohabitation, age is an important factor in sexual frequency. Younger adults, regardless of gender, generally have more frequent sex than middle and older adults (Karraker & DeLamater, 2013). Physical changes and health problems, especially in old age, have negative effects on the frequency of sex of aging people (DeLamater, 2012).

Research in the United States and other Western countries shows that some married adults (26 to 50 percent of men and 21 to 38 percent of women) are involved in extramarital or nonmarital sex. One study, for example, showed that about 20 to 25 percent of Americans had sex with someone other than their spouse (Atkins, Baucom, & Jacobson, 2001). A survey in the United States showed that about 16 percent of married adults of whom nearly twice as many men as women have had extramarital sex (ABC News, 2004). In most cases, nonmarital and extramarital sex relationships are likely to be short termed and casual. The frequency and duration of extramarital or nonmarital sex, however, may vary depending on the stability of such relationships.

Same-Sex Sexuality

Types of same-sex sexuality vary from couple to couple. Like heterosexual relationships, gay and lesbian sex relationships can be temporary, casual, or anonymous. In some cases, same-sex sexuality can be more permanent, like that in most committed heterosexual relationships between two persons, and not having sexual relationships with multiple partners. Some same-sex couples continue their relationship openly, while other couples continue it secretly for fear of social discrimination, stigma, and pressure from family and friends. The legal recognitions of same-sex relationships may vary depending on the laws of the land. For example, same-sex relationships may be legally recognized in the forms of marriage, civil unions, domestic partnerships, or registered partnerships, and so on. Homosexual marriages are legal in many countries of the world including Australia, most of the European countries, the United States, a number of Latin American countries, and a few Asian countries. Although some states of the United States have constitutional restrictions on same-sex marriages, following the U.S. Supreme Court's verdict in 2015, all states of the United States are required to issue marriage licenses to same-sex couples and to recognize same-sex marriages as valid as heterosexual marriages.

Although same-sex relationships can take many forms, most homosexual couples (like most heterosexual couples) tend to seek love and sexual fulfillment through a relationship with one partner only, but lesbian women tend to have more stable and monogamous sex relationships than gay men (Papalia, 2012). Same-sex couples often have better sex than heterosexual couples; because of being the same gender the homosexual couples can understand and communicate each other's sexual needs and desires better than do the heterosexual couples (Miller, 2015).

Safe and Healthy Sex

For protection of health, safer sex and/or abstinence are necessary to prevent the transmission of HIV and other sexually transmitted infectious diseases, especially among late adolescents and emerging adults

(Lefkowitz et al., 2003; Lefkowitz & Vasilenko, 2014). Boone and Lefkowitz (2005) observed that those in late adolescence and emerging adulthood are sexually riskiest during the college years. College students' health risks include, among others, sexually transmitted infectious diseases, unplanned pregnancies, and drug/alcohol abuse (National Institute on Alcohol Abuse and Alcoholism, 2002). To identify predictors of safer sexual behavior, Boone and Lefkowitz (2004) proposed a model called the Health Belief Model (HBM). The authors tested their model on a sample of 154 sexually active late adolescent college students (mean age 21 years, 62 percent female, and 76 percent European Americans). Predictors included perceived vulnerability, attitudes toward condoms, peer norms for condom use, condom use self-efficacy, general sexual attitudes, and sexual double standard. Results showed that attitudes toward condoms, condom use self-efficacy, perceived vulnerability, and the sexual double standard emerged as significant correlates of condom use. In addition, general sexual attitudes and the sexual double standard were significantly correlated with alcohol use before or during sexual activity.

A report of the Centers for Disease Control and Prevention (CDC, 2016) reveals that every year nearly 20 million new sexually transmitted diseases (STDs) are diagnosed in the United States, and about half of these are among the young people aged 15–24 years. About 1 in 4 (25 percent) of all new HIV infections is among youth aged 13 to 24 years, and about 4 in 5 of these infections occur in late adolescent and emerging adult males, and the majority of them are college students. Many college students in the United States are involved in casual sex. One study shows that about three-fourths of sexually active college students are engaged in hookups (LaBrie et al., 2014). About half of the hookups involves sexual intercourse and in which condoms are not used about 50 percent of the time, especially if individuals were drinking before or during sexual activity (Lewis et al., 2012). Many young adults don't use condoms when they have casual sex with new or temporary partners. There are several reasons why they ignore or forget to use condoms: (1) many people don't use condoms because they underestimate the risk of unprotected sex (Purdie et al., 2011); (2) when people are sexually aroused they often lose patience to use condoms (Skakoon-Sparling & Cramer, 2014); (3) when people get drunk and intoxicated they ignore the risk or forget to use condoms (Zawacki, 2011); (4) young women often agree to have sex without condoms due the pressure of male partners or to please the male partners; (5) if two partners involved in sex have different levels of power and positions and if the more powerful partner is unwilling to use a condom, they are unlikely to use a condom (O'Sullivan et al., 2010); and (6) people are less likely to use condoms, if and when they believe that the use of condoms will make sex less enjoyable (Lefkowitz et al., 2014).

Sexual Ethics, Morality, and Religion

Although consensual nonmarital and extramarital sex and homosexuality among adults are not legally wrong in many Western countries, such kinds of sex are not legally allowed and considered ethically and morally unacceptable in most Oriental countries (Judd & Sajn, 2008; Nguyen, 2016), and prohibited in most religions—regardless of geographical boundary (Parrinder, 1996). However, as noted earlier in this chapter, Americans are increasingly more willing to accept various types of nonmarital sex including premarital sex, teen sex, and sex with people of the same gender, but less willing to accept extramarital sex. According to a Gallup poll (Gallup, 2003), despite the sexual revolution in recent decades, about 93 percent of Americans consider extramarital sex morally wrong. This is also true globally, as most people around the world consider extramarital sex morally wrong (Pew Research Center, 2014a). Despite this overall global trend, there are some people everywhere around the globe who commit sexual infidelity. A review of 47 studies involving 58,000 married respondents revealed that although a majority of husbands and wives never have had sex with people other than their spouses, about 33 percent of husbands and 20 percent of wives were unfaithful to their spouses (Tafoya & Spitzberg, 2007). Men, generally, are more likely than women to commit sexual infidelity (Impett, Muise, & Peragine, 2014). Similarly, gay men are involved in more extradyadic sex than lesbian women (Peplau & Fingerhut, 2007). People who are unfaithful to their partners have been found to be low in agreeableness and conscientiousness (Schmitt & Shackelford, 2008), and high in anxiety about abandonment (Russell, Baker, & McNult, 2013).

Sex with minors and incest are disapproved in most cultures of the world. Incest is defined in Webster's dictionary as sexual intercourse between persons so closely related that they are forbidden by law to marry. Although marriage and sexual relation between mother and son, father and daughter, and between siblings are disapproved almost universally, marriage between cousins is allowed in some religions, while not approved in others. There is a consensus in almost every society and culture that sexual intercourse below a certain age is inappropriate and likely to be harmful. But there is no universal agreement, however, of just what age is too young for sex. Children in some societies can marry even before puberty, although the marriage may not be consummated until puberty is attained.

But in some societies marriage with and between minors is prohibited. In the United States, for example, marriage is not legally permitted with and between minors who are under 18 years of age.

Sexual Satisfaction

In a review of sexual satisfaction research, several factors have been found to play important roles in people's sexual satisfaction including good health, free of sexual dysfunctions, and having a steady partner (Sanchez-Fuentas, Santos-Iglosias, & Sierra, 2014). People who are deeply committed to a single partner and faithful to the partner are likely to have more sexual satisfaction than people who are involved in extradyadic sex with multiple partners (Waite & Joyner, 2001). Studies on adult males in multiple countries including Brazil, Germany, Japan, Spain, and the United States show that men with the history of having sex with a few sexual partners are sexually more satisfied than men having sex with many partners (Heiman et al., 2011). The frequency of having sex is also associated with sexual satisfaction. In one study, it was found that couples who had sex more frequently reported more sexual satisfaction than did couples who had sex less frequently (Harvey, Wenzel, & Sprecher, 2004). It was also found that more newlywed men than women are happy when sex is more frequent and unhappy when sex is less frequent (Heiman et al., 2011). But it is difficult to predict clearly if people are sexually more satisfied because they have more frequent sex or they have more frequent sex because they are sexually more satisfied. However, a Chinese study found interest in sex as the strongest predictor for both sexual frequency and satisfaction of both husbands and wives (Cheung et al., 2008). Sexual interactions, regardless of frequency, are more rewarding when they fulfill the basic human needs including autonomy, confidence, and close connections (Deci & Ryan, 2014). Individuals who believe in traditional gender roles that men should be dominant and women should be submissive in directing sexual interactions are likely to have less exciting sex because such a belief decreases women's initiative and desire in sex and makes them less active, and lowers their level of arousal and chances of orgasm (Kiefer & Sanchez, 2007). Sex becomes more enjoyable and gratifying when both couples are actively involved in sexual interactions (Sanchez et al., 2012). Motivations and purposes of sexual interactions also have influence on individuals' sexual satisfaction (Stephenson, Ahrold, & Meston, 2011). Sex is more satisfying when people are motivated to have sex for positive reasons such as getting and giving pleasure, and deepening love and intimacy (Muise et al., 2013); in contrast, sex becomes less satisfying when people get involved in it for negative reasons such as to prevent a partner's displeasure, not to lose a partner's interest and attraction, and to avoid any other unpleasant consequences (Pascoal, Narciso, & Pereira, 2014).

Sexual Satisfaction and Communication

Many people, especially women, feel shy and awkward in communicating sexual desire to the partner directly, verbally, and openly. They mostly signal sexual desire through intimate touching, kissing, or not resisting (Vannier & O'Sullivan, 2011). But clear and candid communication between partners about each other's sexual desires significantly contributes to high sexual satisfaction (MacNeil & Byers, 2009). Couples who are more sexually assertive and open with dyadic sexual communication reported increased relational satisfaction (Greene & Faulkner, 2005). Open sexual communication has been found to account for a unique variance in sexual satisfaction and overall relationship satisfaction. The relationship between open sexual communication and sexual satisfaction was stronger for couples who had been together for longer than shorter duration, and the relationship between open sexual communication and overall relationship satisfaction was stronger for males than for females (Montesi et al., 2011). Although homosexual couples are more open than heterosexual couples in discussing their sexual desires, likes, and dislikes with partners, heterosexual couples can have more sexual satisfaction if they are engaged in free and frank sexual communication (MacNeil & Byers, 2009).

As noted earlier, men tend to have stronger sexual desires and think more often about sex than do women. Men often misunderstand women's friendly feelings and behavior as expressions of sexual intentions (Haselton & Galperin, 2013), and such misjudgments can be avoided through unambiguous and assertive communication (Yagil et al., 2006).

Sexual Satisfaction and Relationship Quality

Relationship quality has significant effects on individuals' sexual satisfaction. Regardless of being married or not, heterosexual or homosexual, people enjoy sex when they have positive and committed relationships with their partners (Holmberg, Blair, & Phillips, 2010). Married couples tend to have satisfactory sex when they have similar sexual histories. The larger the difference between the spouses in number of their past sexual partners, the less satisfied they tend to be in marital relationship and sexual interaction (Garcia & Markey, 2007). Stress at home and work and health problems also affect people's relationship quality and sexual satisfaction

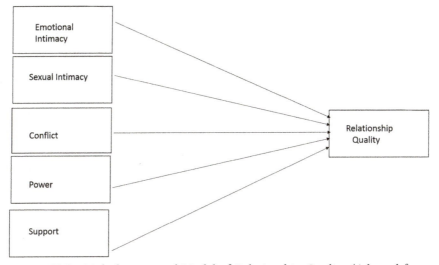

Figure 11.1 Multidimensional Model of Relationship Quality (Adapted from Lawrence et al., 2011)

(Bodenmann et al., 2010). Relationship quality is a strong predictor of people's quality of life, including the quality of dyadic relationships and sexual satisfaction (Ripoll-Núñez, 2016). A multidimensional model of relationship quality, proposed by Lawrence et al. (2011) and reported by Ripoll-Núñez (2016), shows that individuals' intimate relationship quality is influenced by several factors including support, power, conflict, sexual intimacy, and emotional intimacy. The model is presented in Figure 11.1.

Several researchers, however, found that good sex improves the quality of an intimate relationship, and in turn a good-quality intimate relationship makes sex more rewarding and enjoyable (e.g., Yucel & Gassanov, 2010). Thus sexual satisfaction seems to enhance relationship quality and relationship quality in turn increases sexual satisfaction (Burleson, Trevathan, & Todd, 2007). The interactions between the quality of intimate relationship and sex tend to continue throughout adulthood. A study, for example, on elderly couples married over 40 years, found that even though their frequency of sexual intercourse decreased with age, sex continued to be an important factor for their marital satisfaction (Hinchliff & Gott, 2004).

Sexual Coercion and Aggression in Intimate Relationships

Sexual coercion and aggression commonly happen in all forms of intimate relationships including marital, nomarital, and dating relationships.

Sexual coercion is a pressure from one partner to the other to engage in sexual behavior. Sexual coercion may or may not necessarily lead to aggressive behavior against partners. Coercive sexual behavior may range from fondling to sexual intercourse. Sexual pressure may take many forms, such as verbal pressure (e.g., threat to end the relationship), use of physical force (e.g., hitting or beating), intoxication (e.g., making a partner drunk with alcohol or drugs), or by more subtle manipulation instead of explicit threats and the use of physical force (Shackelford & Goetz, 2004). Three subtle manipulation tactics used by men are (1) resource manipulation in which men give or withhold gifts and benefits to women partners for agreeing or not agreeing to sexual interactions, (2) commitment manipulation in which men manipulate their partners by telling them that the couple's relationship status obligates sexual access, and (3) defection threat in which men threaten to pursue casual or long-term affairs with other women (Buss, 2004).

To explain the nature and dynamics of different types of sexual pressures and coercive sexual behavior, a two-dimensional model of sexual misconduct has been proposed by DeGue & DiLillo (2005). An adapted version of the model is shown in Figure 11.2.

This model explains sexually coercive acts in the context of male sexual misconduct with a nonconsenting partner. The first dimension of the

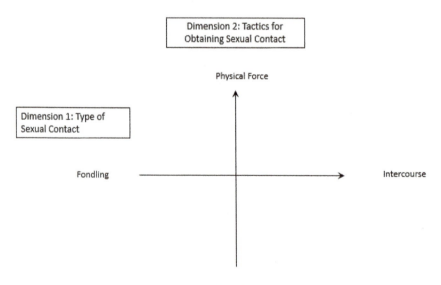

Figure 11.2   A Two-Dimensional Model of Sexual Misconduct (Adapted from DeGue & DiLillo, 2005)

model, represented along the *X* axis, shows different *types of sexual contact* that may take place between partners. The sexual contact may range from a relatively low level of sexual activity, such as fondling, at one end of the spectrum, to a more intense level of sexual activity, such as sexual intercourse, at the other end. The second dimension, shown along the *Y* axis, represents specific *tactics* used by a perpetrator for sexual contact with an unwilling participant. These tactics may vary from a mildly coercive verbal behavior at one end of this continuum to a more extremely coercive physical force at the other end. A range of behaviors can take place between the two ends of each dimension. For example, behaviors such as touching, kissing, undressing, genital fondling, and sexual intercourse may take place in the sexual contact continuum, whereas tactics such as mild verbal warning, threats of harm, and from a low to high level of physical force may take place along the tactics continuum.

Although sexual coercions in any forms are unacceptable and distressing, many young people don't consider mild form of sexual violations as coercions; rather they take these as a part of expression of romantic behavior, especially in any dating relationships (Oswald & Russel, 2006). Some men believe that most women secretly like to have forced sex (Hoyt & Yeater, 2011). Characteristics that predispose individuals to sexual coercion and aggression include belief in rape myths, sexual promiscuity, aggressive tendencies, and empathic deficits (DeGue, DiLillo, & Scalora, 2010). Most men and women, however, never indulge in any form of sexual coercions against their partners (Spitzberg, 1999). Nonetheless, about 10 to 17 percent of married women experience sexual coercion and aggression in a marital relationship (Shackelford & Goetz, 2004), and 1 in every 6 college women encounters some form of sexual coercion in every two months (Gidycz, Van Wynsberghe, & Edwards, 2008). Moreover, about 56 percent of college women experience coercive sexual behavior during their college careers (Crown & Roberts, 2007). A study on youth's risk behavior in the United Stated found that about 10 percent of students who had dated someone in the last one year reported that they experienced kissing, touching, and physically forced sexual intercourse against their will by a dating partner (CDC, 2013). The National Longitudinal Study of Adolescent Health in the United States showed that about 30 percent of youth, aged 12 to 21, reported experiencing psychological abuse in sexual interactions in the past 18 months in heterosexual relationships (Halpern et al., 2001).

Researchers have suggested several steps for minimizing the frequency of sexual coercion and aggression (Miller, 2015). First, alertness about intoxication of the self and the partner, because most incidents of sexual coercion occur under intoxication with alcohol or drug abuse (Cleere & Lynn, 2013). Second, not to passively submit but to actively and boldly resist unwanted sexual advances (Gidycz, Van Wynsberghe, & Edwards, 2008). Third, there should be clear communication (an understanding in advance) about the ground rules and limits of romantic interaction between partners (Winslett & Gross, 2008). Fourth, respect for a partner's expectations, likes, and dislikes can reduce the frequency of sexual coercion and increase sexual satisfaction (Rudman & Phelan, 2007). Finally, people should be careful to avoid dating and developing romantic relationships with individuals having a history of committing sexual coercion and aggression (DeGue, DiLillo, & Scalora, 2010).

CHAPTER SUMMARY

Chapter 11 discusses sexual attitudes and behavior across cultures, gender, and the lifespan of adults; sexual orientation and gender identity; sexual double standard; biogenetic and environmental aspects of sexual orientation; cultural aspects of sexuality; sexual desire and gender; sex in marital and nonmarital relationships; same-sex sexuality; safe and healthy sex; sexual satisfaction; sexual ethics, morality, and religion; and sexual coercion and aggression in intimate relationships.

Sexual attitudes. Americans have different types of views about sexuality. A survey revealed that about 30 percent of Americans have a traditional reproductive attitude toward sex, approximately 25 percent of Americans hold a recreational view about sex, and about 45 percent of Americans have a relational view about sex.

Biological, psychological, and sociocultural aspects of sexuality. Individuals' sexual attitudes and behaviors are influenced by their biological (such as reproductive system), and psychological aspects (such as personality and emotion), and culture (such as variations in individualistic and collectivistic cultural norms).

Importance of sexual attitudes and behaviors. Sexual attitudes and behaviors are critically important for a variety of outcomes including sexually transmitted diseases, prevention of sexual abuse, and mental health.

Sexual double standard. This refers to a worldwide traditional social practice in which men enjoy greater sexual freedom than do women.

Sexual orientation. Sexual orientation refers to the variation in sexual attractions based on gender. There are four major categories of sexual orientations: heterosexual, homosexual, bisexual, and asexual.

Gender identity. Gender identity refers to an individual's sense of being a male, or female, or transgender, regardless of one's biological sex characteristics.

Environmental influences of gender identity development. Research findings show that boys develop more feminine and less masculine gender identity in father-absent families.

Sexual desire and gender. Men and women generally differ in sexual desire, motivation, and drive. Men tend to have stronger sexual impulse and drive, and less control over sexual temptation than do women.

Sex in marital and nonmarital relationships. The frequency of adults' sexual intercourse largely depends on the nature and duration of relationships with partners. Marital and cohabiting partners are involved in sexual intercourse more often than do singles or never married because of the lack of consistent access to sexual partners in comparison to marital and cohabiting adults.

Same-sex sexuality. Like heterosexual relationships, gay and lesbian sex relationships can be temporary, casual, or long lasting.

Sexual satisfaction. Several factors have been found to be related with people's sexual satisfaction including good health, free of sexual dysfunctions, and having a steady partner.

REFLECTIVE QUESTIONS

1. Explain how sexual attitudes and behaviors are critically important for a variety of outcomes such as sexually transmitted diseases, prevention of sexual abuse, and mental health.

2. What is sexual orientation? What are the different types of sexual orientation? How does sexual orientation differ from gender identity?

3. Discuss the biological aspects of sexual orientation and identity.

4. Discuss differences in sexual desire, motivation, and drive between men and women.

5. Discuss similarities and differences in sex in marital and nonmarital relationships.

6. Discuss how sexual ethics and morality differ in different cultures.

7. Discuss how a couple's relationship quality depends on sexual satisfaction.

8. Discuss sexual coercion and aggression in intimate relationships including marital, nonmarital, and dating relationships.

CHAPTER TWELVE

Intimate Relationships in Married Life

Since marriage is basically a long-term union between a man and a woman, this chapter focuses on intimate relationships in heterosexual marriages, which is the most common marital relationship. Marriage is a socially, religiously, and legally recognized contract between spouses that establishes rights and obligations between them, and between them and their children. Traditionally, marriage is considered an exclusive and relatively permanent bond between a man and a woman. The central elements of marital bonds include sexual rights of each partner and parental responsibility for the children born of the union. Despite cultural variations, most common rights a marriage provides include the exclusive right to have sex with the spouse, the right to have children, the right to be a legal father or mother of children, and the right of each partner over property belonging to the other according to the laws of the land. Marriage is considered by anthropologists to be a cultural universal, because despite cultural differences, marriage is an institution that is common in all human cultures worldwide. People may marry for a variety of reasons, including emotional, libidinal, social, religious, legal, and financial purposes.

Types of Marriage

The types of marriage have varied at different periods of history and in different cultures across the world. Two major types, regardless of history and culture, are monogamy and polygamy.

Monogamy. Monogamy is a type of marriage in which one man marries one woman. It is the most common and acceptable type of marriage globally.

Polygamy. Polygamy involves marriage with more than one spouse at a given time. It has two subtypes: polygyny and polyandry. Polygamy is less common than monogamy.

Polygyny. Polygyny is a type of marriage in which one man marries more than one woman at a given time.

Polyandry. Polyandry is the marriage of one woman with more than one man simultaneously. Polyandry is much less common than monogamy and polygyny. In polyandry children are designated by the mother's last name or family name.

In addition, there is another very uncommon type of marriage called group marriage. In *group marriage* two or more women marry two or more men concurrently. In group marriage the husbands are common husbands and the wives are common wives for all the group members, and children belong to the entire group as a whole.

Marital Partner Selection

There are wide cultural variations in the social rules about the selection of a partner for marriage. In some cultures, especially in individualistic societies, partner selection is an individual decision by the partners. But in some other cultures, especially collectivistic societies, partner selection is a collective decision by the partners' family and close relatives.

Performing Marriage

In the United States and in most of the European countries marriage is required to be performed by civil authorities according to legal rules. Marriage in the United States is still mainly regulated by state laws. All states (and the District of Columbia) require a marriage license to be issued by local civil authorities after performing the marriage. Following the civil marriage ceremony, couples are free to marry in a religious ceremony. In many other countries, especially in Muslim countries, all marriages are conducted by religious authorities and are registered by civil authorities at the same time or after the religious marriage.

Effects of Social Changes on Marriage

Historically, in most cultures, married women had been enjoying fewer rights and less power than married men. Still most societies in the world are patriarchal with male dominance and female submission in married life. Beginning in the late 19th century, marriage systems have undergone gradual social and legal changes all over the world, especially in Western countries, aimed at improving the rights of married women. These changes include abolishing the right of husbands to physically discipline their wives, giving property rights to women, liberalizing divorce laws, providing reproductive rights to women, and husbands requiring wives' consent when sexual relations occur. Moreover, there has been an increasing trend, especially in Western countries, to legally and socially recognize interfaith, interracial, and same-sex marriages (Vucheva, 2013). Since the late 20th century, major social changes in Western countries have led to changes in people's attitudes and behaviors about marriage, such as the age of first marriage is increasing, fewer people are marrying, and more people are choosing to stay single or cohabit rather than marry.

Changing Lifestyles in the United States

Since the 1950s enormous changes have occurred in the lifestyles of American adults. Current lifestyles have become more elastic and diverse than they were during the first half of 20th century. Currently, the number of adults staying single and childless has increased, the marriage age has gone up and the marriage rate has dropped, the divorce rate has increased, an increasing number of adults are cohabiting with partners of either sex, and the number of unmarried mothers and single-parent families has increased (Papalia, 2012). A report by Elliott et al. (2012), based on decennial data of the U.S. Census Bureau, shows that the 1950s has been the "golden age" of marriage in the United States and that the marriage rate has declined since the 1960s. A recent survey by Wang and Parker (2014), based on data of the Pew Research Center, shows that in 1960, only 9 percent of adults age 25 and older had been never married, but the percentage has increased to 20 percent in 2012 for the same age group, and men are more likely than women to be never married (23 percent vs. 17 percent in 2012). The survey also found that this trend has been more pronounced among Black than White ethnic groups, where 36 percent of Blacks had never been married in 2012, up from 9 percent in 1960, and 16 percent of Whites had never been married in 2012, up from 8 percent in 1960. Despite this trend, marriage is still an important part of American life (Fields, 2004). Most Americans (68 percent) still continue to believe that marriage is an important part of life, and among them about 47 percent believe that marriage is very important, and 21 percent consider it somewhat important (Wang & Parker, 2014).

Intimacy in Marriage

Married couples are often so overwhelmed with the demands of domestic and occupational works and child care responsibilities that they simply can't create any space to share intimate moments with their partner. The result can be a host of relational and behavioral problems including an increasing sense of disconnectedness, poor communication, disagreements and conflicts about child care responsibilities, sharing domestic works, making decisions about family finances, or insufficient sex. Marital intimacy is a continuous process that grows and changes over time and is never fully accomplished. It needs constant nurturing, warmth, affection, support, and continuous care. Intimacy can be nurtured through mutual trust and respect, acceptance, open communication, and respecting boundaries (Heller, 2015). Couples can work jointly to enhance their marital intimacy in each area as they build their marital life through the years. If the couples neglect intimacy in their marriage, the marriage may eventually become dysfunctional and fall apart.

Marriage and Happiness

A number of national surveys have shown that marriage is one of the most important factors in happiness. For instance, a survey by the United Kingdom's Office for National Statistics in 2013 on 165,000 British people found that being married is 20 times more important to individuals' happiness than their earnings and 13 times more important than owing a home. The same survey found that marriage is the third most important factor after health and job. Married people reported being happier than those who are single, cohabitating, divorced, or widowed (Lee & Ono, 2012). Marriage has also been found to protect people against age-related declines in happiness (Kennelly, 2012). Another study (Siegler, 2013) on an American sample showed that individuals who were never married were twice more likely to die early than people who were married or in some sort of long-term relationship.

Marital Quality, Satisfaction, and Happiness

Marital quality, marital satisfaction, and marital happiness are closely related but not synonymous terms. Marital quality is a blanket term that includes marital adjustment, happiness, and satisfaction. Marital quality largely depends on marital adjustment—the greater the marital adjustment, the better the marital quality. Marital adjustment is an aspect of the relationship between spouses that affects marital quality. Marital satisfaction is a positive feeling about the marital relationship based on the perceived ratio of costs and benefits of the marriage. The greater the perceived benefits than costs of the marriage, the higher the marital satisfaction. Contrarily, the greater the perceived costs than the benefits of the marriage, the lower the marital satisfaction. Marital happiness is a subjective evaluation made by a spouse about the sense of well-being or satisfaction she/he experiences in the marital relationship. Thus both marital satisfaction and marital happiness are subjective evaluations about the outcomes of marriage by one or both of the spouses. Both marital satisfaction and happiness refer to positive feelings that married couples derive from a marriage, and both satisfaction and happiness have broader and more global meanings than such terms as marital enjoyment or pleasure. Both marital satisfaction and happiness are highly correlated to one another and to other similar variables. However, marital satisfaction seems to have a more cognitive basis involving a relation of one's circumstances to some criteria, whereas marital happiness is based on an affective evaluation about the feeling of well-being of one or both spouses.

Relations between Marital Quality, Adjustment, and Happiness

Intimacy is a core and unique issue in marriage with its important implications for quality of life, especially life at home (Bradbury & Karney, 2010). Married couples' quality of life largely depends on how they perceive and handle intimacy conflicts (Rehman et al., 2011). Intimacy conflicts, if not handled properly, are likely to be recurrent with long-term importance to the marital relationship (Papp, Goeke-Morey, & Cummings, 2013). Moreover, constructive marital conflict was found related to warm parenting, and destructive conflict was linked to the use of inconsistent paternal discipline (McCoy et al., 2013). Married couples generally fall into three marital quality profiles: positive, positive-negative, and negative. Both women and men think marital satisfaction important for quality of life, but it is more important to women than men (Cohen, Geron, & Farchi, 2009). A couple of studies have shown that positive aspects of marriages do not have as much of an impact as do negative aspects, and the combinations of these characteristics can have a large impact on satisfaction (Boerner et al., 2014; Proulx, Helms, & Buehler, 2007).

Research findings reveal that marriage offers many benefits. According to Olson and Olson (2000), married people tend to be healthier, happier, live longer, have more satisfying sexual relationships, and have more wealth and economic assets than single or cohabiting individuals. In addition, children of happily married parents generally do better emotionally and academically. A study on the relation between partner acceptance and psychological adjustment of married people, involving 354 Bangladeshi married adults (178 men and 176 women), showed that spousal acceptance or love is a significant predictor of married adults' psychological adjustment (Khaleque, Shirin, & Uddin, 2013). The same study also showed that about 20 percent of variability in adults' psychological adjustment is accounted for only by spousal love. Another study on the relation between perceived intimate-partner acceptance and the psycho-logical adjustment of 389 married individuals in Kuwait showed that the more accepting and loving both men and women perceived their spouses to be, the better was their psychological adjustment (Parmar, Ibrahim, & Rohner, 2008).

The beneficial effects of marriage for physical and psychological well-being are widely documented (Carr & Springer, 2010). However, several researchers have found that these effects are conditional upon the quality of the marriage; high-quality marriages provide benefits, whereas problematic marriages can have emotional toll, especially for women (Proulx, Helms, & Buehler, 2007) and older adults (Umberson et al., 2006). A number of studies reported positive correlation between marital quality and subjective well-being, and this correlation is stronger for women than men (Bookwala, 2012; Jackson et al., 2014). Some research suggested that marriage and intimate relationships are more central to women's identities, and more important for their overall well-being relative to men (Loscocco & Walzer, 2013). Some scholars argued that women traditionally enjoy less power and status in marriage than men, and thus they have a greater emotional investment than men in maintaining a healthy marital relationship (Bulanda, 2011). Some researchers, however, found no significant gender difference for association between marital quality and well-being, especially for older couples (Carr et al., 2014; Jackson et al., 2014).

Happy and Stable Marriage

A variety of factors contribute to a happy and stable marriage. Some of these factors are briefly described as follows:

- *Commitment to marriage.* Couples who have a strong commitment to marriage have greater marital satisfaction. Couples who believe that marriage is a lifetime relationship and should never be ended except in extreme circumstances report, on average, higher levels of marital satisfaction than couples who don't believe that marriage is a lifetime relationship (Wilcox & Nock, 2006).

- *Premarital education.* Couples who received premarital education services had, on average, higher levels of satisfaction with their marriages, less conflict with their spouses, more commitment to their marriages, and strong and stable marital relations than couples who did not receive premarital education (Stanley et al., 2006).

- *Family background.* Marriages tend to be enduring and stable if both spouses come from two-parent intact families. Marriages in which one spouse experienced a parental divorce were nearly twice as likely to end in divorce, compared to marriages in which neither spouse experienced parental divorce while growing up. Moreover, marriages in which both spouses experienced a parental divorce were more than three times as likely to end in divorce, compared to marriages in which neither spouse experienced parental divorce (Wolfinger, 2003).

- *Divorce proneness.* Couples who tend to perceive their marriages to be less stable and frequently think about divorce are more likely to divorce. Divorce proneness significantly increases the chances of divorce (Previti & Amato, 2003).

- *Cohabitation.* Individuals who cohabited prior to their marriage reported lower levels of marital satisfaction and happiness and higher levels of marital conflict than individuals who did not cohabit prior to their marriage (Dush, Cohan, & Amato, 2003). Cohabitation prior to marriage is related to a greater likelihood of divorce. Women who cohabited with the men they married were more likely to divorce, compared to women who had not cohabited prior to their first marriage. Those who had cohabited with more than one partner were even more likely to divorce. Premarital cohabitation was found associated with a 29 percent increase in the likelihood of divorce (Teachman, 2003). In addition, the likelihood of divorce was 44 percent greater for women who cohabited with two or more men than for women who cohabited only with their eventual husbands (Teachman, 2003).

- *Previous divorce.* Previous divorce(s) may adversely impact the quality of subsequent marriages. Although previously divorced individuals initially tend to report higher levels of positive marital experiences in their subsequent marriages, they later on report an accelerated rate of decrease in positive marital qualities and an increase in negative marital experiences (Umberson, 2005).

- *Parenthood.* Older married couples who have children tended to experience better marital quality and more stable marriage than those without children. Older married couples without children tended to experience significant declines in marital quality over a period of 8 to 10 years (Umberson et al., 2005).

- *Leisure time.* New parents who spend more time together before the birth of their first child reported less marital conflicts and greater closeness with the spouse after the birth of the child (Claxton & Perry-Jenkins, 2008).

- **Religious attendance.** Women who regularly attended church with their husbands reported higher levels of marital love, affection, and happiness than women who neither alone nor with their husbands attended services weekly (Wilcox & Nock, 2006).

Theories of Marital Satisfaction and Happiness

This section discusses theories that are directly and indirectly related to marital satisfaction and happiness. Some important theories that directly or indirectly focus on marital satisfaction and happiness are discussed in the following pages.

Dynamic Goal Theory of Marital Satisfaction

The dynamic goal theory of marital satisfaction argues that individuals have multiple goals to achieve through their marriage (Li & Fung, 2011). According to Li and Fung, there are three different categories of marital goals, such as personal growth goals, companionship goals, and instrumental goals. These three types of marital goals keep changing over an individual's lifespan according to perceived priority of these goals. The priority of marital goals differs with the stages of development. For example, young couples tend to prioritize the personal growth goals, whereas middle-aged couples and aging couples tend to prioritize the instrumental goals and the companionship goals, respectively. According to Li and Fung, marital satisfaction depends on how much the prioritized marital goals are achieved in a marriage. They suggested that different factors influencing marital satisfaction can be linked with marital goals in two ways: (1) Some factors such as cultural values and life transitions are likely to affect the priority of different marital goals; (2) while some other factors, such as communication pattern and problem solving, can facilitate the achievement of the prioritized marital goals.

Core elements of the dynamic goal theory of marital satisfaction are the goals people want to attain in their marriage. According to this theory, the most important determinant of marital satisfaction is the achievement of marital goals that have priority to an individual. The four central elements of the theory as proposed by Li and Fung (2011) are described here. First, people intend to achieve multiple goals through their marriage. Second, these goals have different priorities, and the priority of different marital goals keeps changing across adulthood. Third, marital satisfaction at a certain developmental stage depends on whether and how much the prioritized marital goals in a particular developmental stage are fulfilled in the marriage. Fourth, interactions between different factors can also influence marital satisfaction mainly in two ways—either by changing the priority of different marital goals or by facilitating the achievement of the prioritized goals.

As noted earlier, marital happiness is an enduring positive emotional state that includes satisfaction with marriage as well as with one's life. Since marital satisfaction is strongly correlated with life satisfaction, theories of life satisfaction are likely to be relevant to marital satisfaction as well. Some theories that focus on life satisfaction and happiness are discussed briefly in the following pages.

Ratio Theory of Happiness

William James (James, 1890, 2000) offered a formula for achieving happiness in life. Happiness, according to James, is the ratio of one's accomplishments to one's aspirations:

$$\text{Happiness} = \frac{\text{Accomplishments}}{\text{Aspirations}}$$

The closer the individuals' accomplishments to their aspirations, the happier they are likely to be. Thus there are two ways to be happy: working hard for a high degree of accomplishment or lowering expectations. However, how hard an individual may try to achieve expected goals, there is a reasonable limit for achievement, depending on a number of factors, such as physical, psychological, and social factors. To be happy in marital life couples should be realistic in their expectations from their partners.

Social Comparison Theory

Social comparison theory was initially proposed by the social psychologist Leon Festinger in 1954. Following the initial theory, several researchers began to focus on social comparison in relation to life satisfaction and self-enhancement, and introduced new concepts of downward and upward comparisons (e.g., Gruder, 1971; Suls & Wheeler, 2012; Wills, 1981). As much as it relates to life satisfaction, the theory basically proposed that individuals evaluate their own conditions of life by comparing themselves to others. The theory contends that like other domains of life happiness is relative. People tend to feel happy or unhappy by comparing their lives with others living around them or known to them. People tend to ask: "Am I better off than most people I know?" Individuals are likely to feel happy when they think that they are doing better than most other people known to them including their neighbors, friends, and relatives. They are likely to feel unhappy when they think that they are not doing as well as others around them are doing.

According to this theory, there are two kinds of social comparisons: (1) upward social comparison—comparing with the more fortunate, and (2) downward social comparison—comparing with the less fortunate. Generally, upward social comparison leads to unhappiness and downward social comparison leads to happiness.

In addition, people also use their own past as a standard for comparison. People tend to ask: "Am I better off today than I was before?" Here the central point is that the degree of satisfaction people experience depends not so much on the absolute value of their current conditions, but on how their situation compares to those of their friends, peers, neighbors, and relatives; and also on how their present compares with their past. A major criticism against this theory is why people who are extremely fortunate in relation to others sometimes feel unhappy.

Adaptation Theory

This theory argues that when something positive or pleasant happens, people quickly get adapted to it and the thrill comes to an end within a short time. This is called habituation effect. That is why pleasure and happiness depend on continuous change. According to this theory, happiness is unlikely to be permanent unless circumstances are constantly improving. Although people tend to get adapted to comfort quickly, it takes more time to get adapted to uncomfortable situations. According to Myers (2015), in the pursuit of happiness, human beings are also influenced by a tendency to judge various situations in relation to those previously experienced. However, this theory fails to explain adequately why some individuals live more or less happily without much favorable change in their life conditions.

Personality Theory

Personality theory posits that certain personality traits foster happiness (Albuquerque, Matos, & Figueiredo, 2013). An individual who is high in extroversion traits (sociability, warmth, friendliness, and involvement with others) and low in neurotic traits (tendency to worry, be irritable and anxious) tend to be happier than an individual who is low in extroversion and high in neuroticism (Kirkpatrick, 2015; Salami, 2011).

Happiness Skills Theory

Happiness skills theory (HST) was proposed by George Ortega (2006). According to this theory, the state of happiness is achieved by the sequential exercise of five separate skills: (1) experience, (2) valuation, (3) anticipation, (4) hedonic acquisition, and (5) habit formation. The theory also contends that the desire for happiness is an integral element of each of the five skills. An individual's happiness, infancy through old age, depends on the implementation of the aforementioned five distinct sequential skills. Additionally, the theory proposes that the most basic element of happiness is hedonic cognitions—reward-related cognitions. According to hedonic principles, one will continually seek to increase one's level of happiness by seeking increased levels of pleasure and satisfaction. The hedonic cognitions are characterized by four components: (1) presence of pleasant affect, (2) absence of unpleasant affect, (3) domain satisfaction, and (4) global satisfaction. According to HST, people learn to value happiness by recognizing the benefits it brings. For example, based on experience most people learn that happiness enhances their relationships, work, health, and quality of life.

Money and Marital Happiness

Does money lead to life happiness, especially happiness in marital life? Research results show no necessary relation between money and happiness (Quiñones, 2006). This indicates that the wealthy people are not necessarily happier than nonwealthy people. Recent research suggests that wealth alone doesn't provide any guarantee of happiness. What matters in happiness is not the amount of money people have but how they spend it. For instance, giving money to needy and distressed people makes individuals a lot happier than lavishly spending it on themselves (Blackman, 2014). Although more money provides more material benefits, money does not necessarily guarantee life happiness in general and marital happiness in particular. However, money provides opportunities that can contribute to happiness in life, including marital happiness. Researchers found no significant differences between more wealthy and less wealthy couples in their overall life satisfaction and marital satisfaction (Dakin & Wampler, 2008). However, several researchers have suggested that although wealth does not contribute much to marital happiness, poverty does contribute a lot to marital unhappiness (Amato et al., 2007; Dakin & Wampler, 2008; Rauer et al., 2008). Although there are not enough research findings that provide strong evidence for consistent positive relation between money and marital happiness, there are studies that strongly suggest that financial disagreements between couples are among the consistent top predictors of marital conflict and unhappiness leading to divorce (Dew, 2009; Dew & Dakin, 2011). A study based on longitudinal data from the National Survey of Families and Households involving 4,574 couples showed that both wives' and husbands' financial disagreements were the strongest predictors of divorce compared to other common marital disagreements (Dew, Britt, & Huston, 2012).

Predictors of Happiness

Different researchers have proposed different predictors of happiness in life including marital life. For example, Compton (2005) has identified the following six important predictors of happiness:

- Positive self-esteem
- Sense of perceived control of life circumstances
- Extroversion
- Optimism
- Positive social relationships
- Sense of purpose and meaning in life

According to a number of researchers (e.g., Diener & Diener, 2009; Haidt, 2006; Lyubomirsky, 2008; Myers, 2007), the most important life circumstances predicting happiness are:

- Good health
- Happy marriage
- Healthy family life
- Positive religious belief

However, after reviewing several studies, Aron and associates concluded that the single biggest predictor of human happiness is the quality of intimate relationships (Aron, Fisher, & Strong, 2007).

Steps to Happiness

After reviewing happiness research, psychologist Michael Fordyce (2000) has suggested the following steps to enhance overall happiness and marital happiness:

- Spending time with loved one
- Being appreciative, affectionate, and accepting
- Sharing joy and fun with loved one
- Thinking positively
- Making time for activities one enjoys
- Expressing emotions and feelings in positive ways
- Finding better ways to express emotional needs
- Keeping fit
- Being organized but flexible
- Making compromise and adjustment

Divorce

The divorce rate has risen in many Western countries. According to a recent report of the UN's Demographics and Social Statistics Division (UNDSSD, 2015), the top 10 countries with the highest divorce rates (based on divorce to marriage ratio) are:

1. Belgium: 71 percent
2. Portugal: 68 percent
3. Hungary: 67 percent
4. Czech Republic: 66 percent
5. Spain: 61 percent
6. Luxembourg: 60 percent
7. Estonia: 58 percent
8. Cuba: 56 percent
9. France: 55 percent
10. United States: 53 percent

Although more than half of the marriages (53 percent) in the United States currently end in divorce, its position is at the bottom (10th) among the top 10 countries with the highest divorce rate in the world. It is interesting to note that among the 10 countries with the highest divorce rate, 8 countries are from Europe, and the country with the top most divorce rate (71 percent) is Belgium, a European country.

Both marriage rates and divorce rates in the United States were quite high in 1990s, and then the rates slowly declined and leveled off since 2000 through 2007 (Statistical Abstract, 2009). A recent study found that divorce rates in the United States have been dropping during the last few decades, indicating that marriages have lasted longer in the 21st century than they did in the 1990s. But still about 40 to 50 percent of all first marriages and 60 percent of second marriages end in divorce, and the rates of divorce are even higher for subsequent marriages. In the United States, a marriage lasts on average only about 10 to 11 years (Bindley, 2011).

In the United States, divorce rates also vary by race and ethnicity. A report by the U.S. Bureau of Labor Statistics (2013) on marriage and divorce patterns in the United States shows the variation in the duration of first-time marriages for women of different races and ethnic groups. Black women have the least chance of long-lasting marriages followed by White women and Hispanic women, and Asian women have the best chance of longest-lasting marriage than do other ethnic groups.

Blacks are less likely to get married and more likely to get divorced than Whites (Sweeney & Phillips, 2004). The marriage and divorce rates of Hispanics are closer to that of Whites than Blacks (Bulanda & Brown, 2004). Hispanics, especially Mexican Americans, have a higher rate of marriage and a lower rate of divorce than do Blacks (Raley, Durden, & Wildsmith, 2004). Although Hispanic Americans and Black Americans are similar in their experiences of economic disadvantages in the United States, Hispanic Americans, especially Mexican Americans, more closely resemble Whites than Blacks in their marriage and divorce rates. This phenomenon has been termed "the paradox of Mexican American nuptiality" (Bulanda & Brown, 2004). According to several researchers (e.g., Bulanda & Brown, 2004; Raley, Durden, & Wildsmith, 2004), a more likely explanation of this paradox is the fact that Mexican American culture may play a role in preserving the marital quality and stability of this ethnic group, despite their precarious economic condition in the United States.

Causes and Correlates of Divorce

A number of researchers (Amato & Previti, 2003; Hawkins, Willoughby, & Doherty, 2012; Teachman, 2003) have identified several factors as probable causes or correlates of divorce including premarital cohabitation, premarital pregnancy and child bearing, less education, low income, having no children after marriage, stepchildren in the home, experience of parental divorce, ethnicity and gender (e.g., being an African American woman), feeling of insecurity, personality problems (such as low self-esteem, self-inadequacy, emotional instability, etc.), religious affiliation (people without a religious affiliation have a higher divorce rate), greater financial independence of women, lack of tolerance and trust between couples, and decreased expectation about permanence of marriage.

A U.S. national survey (National Fatherhood Initiative, 2005) found that the most common reasons people give for divorce in terms of percentages were lack of commitment in marriage (73 percent), too many arguments between spouses (56 percent), lack of trust and infidelity (55 percent), too young at marriage (46 percent), too high expectations (45 percent), unequality in the relationship (44 percent), unprepared marriage (41 percent), and partner abuse (29 percent). Some people gave more than one reason.

Another study (Hawkins, Willoughby, & Doherty, 2012), based on a sample of 886 divorcing parents, showed that common reasons cited for seeking a divorce in terms of percentages were growing apart (55 percent), not being able to talk together (53 percent), money problems (40 percent), personal problems of spouse (37 percent), infidelity (37 percent), not getting enough attention from the spouse (34 percent), spouse's personal habits (29 percent), sexual problems (24 percent), differences in tastes and preferences (23 percent), alcohol or drug problems (22 percent), dividing household responsibilities (21 percent), conflicts over raising children (20 percent), in-law problems (18 percent), spouse's leisure activities (18 percent), dividing child care responsibilities (17 percent), physical violence (13 percent), spouse's friends (11 percent), spouse worked too much (9 percent), and religious differences (9 percent). The percentages add up to more than 100 because most respondents mentioned more than one category.

Cultural differences in marital discord and divorce. Causes and correlates of divorce may vary by sociocultural differences. A report on the causes and consequences of divorce in Bangladesh, a South Asian country, shows that the common causes of divorce in the South Asian culture include marital discord due to conflict between the spouses and with the in-laws over domestic works and family responsibilities, physical oppression and psychological abuse of the wife by the husband and in-laws, poverty, illiteracy, lack of independent income of the wife and financial dependence on the husband for livelihood, dowry—marriage gift (cash or in kind) demanded by the groom from the bride's family, polygamy, early age at marriage, infertility of the wife, and lack of physical attractiveness of the wife to the husband (Khaleque, 2011).

Gender differences in marital discord and divorce. In happy marriages, there are little differences between husbands and wives in behavioral and emotional expressions, but all possible gender differences emerge in unhappy marriages (Gottman & Levenson, 2002). Husbands and wives can have very different grievances in different domains of marital lives. Men often focus on the practical importance of a family issue, downplaying or failing to recognize its emotional consequences. Unlike men, women often emphasize the emotional importance of a family issue. Women often complain about their husbands being emotionally cold and unresponsive. But husbands often tend to ignore it, and wives are likely to interpret their husbands' lack of response as rejection, which may lead to divorce (Birditt et al., 2010a). Although gender differences can lead to a variety of marital conflicts, two major areas of marital discord are housework and sex (Anderson & Sabatelli, 2011). Housework may be considered as a minor issue by a man, but to a woman it may be a major issue affecting the quality of the marital relationship. If and when a husband does little or no domestic work, the wife is likely to think that her husband cares little for her comfort, health, and happiness, and this is likely to be a big issue when the couples have children and the wife is employed.

Men and women usually differ in sexual attitude and behavior. Men generally want more sex than do women because of differences in biological characteristics and socialization. Men tend to consider sex as a source of pleasure with little or no emotional involvement. Men often tend to have sex even during marital discord, whereas women want emotional attachment with their husbands in and out of sex. These differences can make marriage more strained and vulnerable.

Consequences of Divorce

Effects of divorce on children. Economic and psychosocial impacts of divorce are more likely to be negative for children and women than men. One major effect of divorce and of parental conflicts that precede the divorce is the significant decline in parent-child relationships. The stress of divorce damages the parent-child relationship for as many as 50 percent of divorced parents (Amato & Afifi, 2006). Another study reported that divorce leads to a decline in the frequency of parent-child contact and quality of parent-child relationships, as it becomes difficult for nonresidential parents (90 percent of whom are fathers) to keep close ties with their children (Peters & Ehrenberg, 2008). A report of the APA's Public Policy Office (2004) based on an overview of the psychological literature on the effects of divorce on children showed that children of divorced families are at a higher risk for adjustment problems than children from intact families. Although it is difficult to isolate a lot of different factors that impact children of divorced families, researchers have found that children of divorced families experience some common problems including smoking, alcohol abuse, drug addiction, less financial security, lower academic achievement, lower social skills, poor interpersonal relationships, and lower rates of employment as young adults (Sigle-Rushton & McLanahan, 2004).

Compared with children of two-parent intact families, children of divorced mothers are likely to live in poorer and less stimulating home environments. Moreover, divorced mothers, despite their best intentions and efforts, are less able than married mothers to provide emotional support to their children. In addition, divorce often lowers children's trust of their mothers and fathers (King, 2002). Divorced mothers are likely to be less affectionate and less communicative with their children than married mothers. Compared with married mothers, divorced mothers tend to discipline their children more harshly and inconsistently during the first year after the divorce.

After reviewing a large number of studies conducted in the United Kingdom, reviewers concluded that although children of divorced parents are at increased risk of negative outcomes, the difference between children from intact and nonintact families is not big enough to adversely affect the majority of children in the long term (Mooney, Oliver, & Smith, 2009). Similarly, some researchers suggested that despite many problems experienced by the children of divorce, some children adjust fairly quickly and others show long-term deficits in adjustment, but the majority of them fall within the normal range of adjustment (Amato, 2000). Moreover, whether the long-term consequences for most children of divorce will be of resilience or dysfunctionality depend on several factors such as the age of the child, time since the divorce, financial security, and postdivorce parenting style and adjustment (Amato, 2000; Furstenberg & Kiernan, 2001). For instance, economic problems faced by divorced households contribute to almost half of the adjustment problems of children from divorced families (McLanahan, 1999). The report of the APA (2004) also revealed that children's repeated exposure to violence in a high-conflict parental marriage is a stronger predictor of their adjustment problems than parental divorce. For example, children in high-conflict marriages tend to experience a host of behavioral problems including disobedience, aggression, delinquency, poor self-esteem, antisocial behaviors, and depression. Young adults, who experienced a high level of parental marital conflict during childhood, are more likely to experience depression and psychological disorders than young adults from low-conflict families. Moreover, parents in high-conflict marriages tend to be less loving, more rejecting and controlling, and more harsh and punitive in disciplining children. Buffers that can protect children in high-conflict marriages include good relations with one parent or other caregivers, and support of peers, siblings, grandparents, and other attachment figures (Soboleswki, 2007).

Effects of divorce on adults. Effects of divorce on adults vary by gender. Women are more negatively affected by divorce than men at any age

(Papalia, 2012). Women are more likely than men to live in poverty after divorce (Kredeir & Fields, 2002). An American National Survey of Families and Households (NSFH, 2005) found that household income for mothers and children generally fell by almost 50 percent or more after divorce. Additionally, their standard of living went down significantly after divorce. However, the negative effects of divorce on women's income depend on the relative earning capacity of the husband and wife. Women who experience the largest income losses are typically the less educated women married to highly educated men. Conversely, highly educated women married to less educated men experience the smallest effect of divorce on their household income.

A study (Khaleque, 2011) shows that divorced women in South Asian countries experience psychological, social, financial, and health and well-being related problems. Psychologically, women in South Asian countries often experience emotional shock, tension, anxiety, and a feeling of helplessness after divorce. Women with little or no education usually become financially vulnerable after divorce. Socially, divorced women tend to be stigmatized, and divorce often lowers a woman's prestige in her social circle. Divorce often lowers the chance of remarriage of a woman, and the possibility of remarriage is much less for a divorced woman who has children. Chances of remarriage after divorce are generally higher for men than women.

The summary results of a 25-year landmark longitudinal study by Wallerstein and Lewis (2000) on 60 families presented in Table 12.1 provide evidence of detrimental effects of divorce on the husband, wife, and children.

Remarriage

Although remarriages are more likely to end in divorce than first marriages, an estimated 66 percent of women and a little over three-quarters of men in the United States remarry within 10 years of divorce (Bramlett & Mosher, 2002), and about 50 percent of men and women remarry within about 3 years of divorce (Kreider & Fields, 2002). The chance and stability of remarriage depend on a number of factors including age, gender, and ethnicity.

Age

According to a survey of the Pew Research Center (2014c), the percentages of remarriage of Americans vary widely with age. In the year

Table 12.1   Effects of Divorce on Husbands, Wives, and Children

- Most young fathers don't maintain a relationship with their children because they perceive that they are no longer important to their children after divorce.
- About 50% of women and 33% of men are still very angry at their former spouses 10 years after divorce.
- About 33% of women and 25% of men feel that divorce has made life disappointing and lonely.
- 65% of women and 35% of men actively sought to end the marriage even though the other spouse opposed it.
- Divorced couples become happier after divorce only in 10% of cases.
- The quality of life of about 50% of women and 66% of men is no better off or worse even after 10 years of divorce.
- About 25% of older men feel isolated and lonely after divorce.
- Most women over 40 years of age find it difficult to remarry and stay unmarried.
- 25% of the divorced families reported violence in the marriage.
- Many fathers are not aware that their children feel rejected after parental divorce.
- In about 80% of cases, children live with divorced mothers.
- About 10% to 12% of parents are engaged in bitter litigation over the children's custody.
- About 66% of divorced men and 50% of women get remarried.
- About 10% of men and women cohabit after divorce.
- Approximately 50% of men and 25% of women who remarried end up with second-time divorce.

Source: Adapted from Wallerstein & Lewis, 2000.

2013 the highest percentage (67 percent) of remarriage took place among the divorced older adults in the age group of 55 to 64, as compared to the divorced adults of other age groups. The lowest percentage (29 percent) of divorced younger adults aged 18 to 24 remarried in the same year. The highest remarriage rate among the aging adults may be partially accounted for by two demographic factors such as the rise in divorce, which has made more Americans available for remarriage; and increase in the life expectancy, which gives people more length of life to make, dissolve, and remake marital unions.

Gender Difference in Remarriage

Generally, divorced men are more likely than divorced women to remarry. In 2013, about 64 percent of eligible American men had remarried, compared with 52 percent of women taking into account adults of all age groups. Over a period of five decades, the gender gap in remarriage has closed substantially among younger and middle-aged American adults. Divorced or widowed women aged 25 to 54 years are now as likely to remarry as men in the same age range. But the gap is still substantial among 55 years and older adults.

Race and Ethnicity

Ethnically, White American divorced adults are the most likely to have married again, as compared to previously married Hispanic, Black, and Asian American adults. This trend is more consistent in the first marriage than in the next marriages, where Whites are more likely than Blacks or Hispanics to enter into marriage for the first time (Pew Research Center's report, 2014c). For example, in 2012, about 60 of Whites who had been divorced before had remarried, compared with 51 percent of Hispanics, 48 percent of Blacks, and 46 percent of Asians. This increase in the remarriage rate of White American adults has been partially due to the increase in the remarriage rate of White women than that of White men. For instance, the remarriage rate of White women rose from 47 percent in 1960 to 55 percent by 2012. By contrast, the remarriage rate of White men declined from 69 percent to 66 percent for the same period (Pew Research Center's report, 2014c).

Success in Marriage

A number of researchers (e.g., Amato et al., 2007; Glenn, Uecker, & Love, 2010; Vespa, 2014) have found several important factors in marital success including but not limited to:

1. Positive attitudes and behavior: the more positive the partners are to each other, the more likely they'll be happy in their marital relationships.
2. The way couples react to each other's good news—either with excitement, pride, or indifference—that makes a difference in their marital happiness.
3. Providing constructive support to a partner is generally better for a relationship than detachment.

4. Avoiding conflict, reconciling differences, and making joint decision about spending money.

5. Sharing household chores, family and child care responsibilities, if there are children.

6. Positive, open, and frank communication with understanding and love.

7. Finding better ways to express emotion and feelings through love, warmth, care, concern, affection, appreciation, and empathy, and sharing joy and fun.

8. Sharing common faith, beliefs, and values; and appreciating and respecting differences, when faiths and beliefs are not common.

9. Having commitment for the marital relationship and mutual trust between the partners.

10. Regardless of age and length of marriage, the more sex the couple has, the higher the level of marital satisfaction.

CHAPTER SUMMARY

Chapter 12 focuses on types of marriages; marital partner selection; effects of social changes on marriage; changing lifestyles in the United States; intimacy in marriage; marital quality, satisfaction, and happiness; determinants of stable marriage; divorce—causes, correlates, and consequences of divorce; age, gender, and cultural differences in marital discord and divorce; remarriage—age, gender, and cultural differences.

Marriage. Marriage is a socially, religiously, and legally recognized contract between spouses that establishes rights and obligations between them, and between them and their children.

Types of marriage. Two major types of marriage, regardless of history, geography, and culture, are monogamy and polygamy.

Marriage and social changes. Since the late 19th century, marriage systems have undergone gradual social and legal changes all over the world marked with significant improvement of the rights of married women.

Marital intimacy. Marital intimacy is a continuous process that grows and changes over time and is never fully accomplished. It needs constant nurturing, warmth, affection, support, and continuous care.

Marriage and happiness. A number of national surveys have shown that marriage is one of the most important factors in happiness.

Marital quality, satisfaction, and happiness. Marital quality, marital satisfaction, and marital happiness are closely related but not synonymous terms.

Happy and stable marriage. A variety of factors contribute to a happy and stable marriage including commitment, premarital education, family background, previous divorce, cohabitation, and parenthood.

Theories of marital satisfaction and happiness. Some of the important theories relating to marital satisfaction and happiness are dynamic goal theory, ratio theory, social comparison theory, adaptation theory, personality theory, and happiness skills theory.

Money and marital happiness. There is no necessary relation between money and happiness. Recent research suggests that wealth alone doesn't provide any guarantee of happiness.

Predictors of marital happiness. Most important predictors of marital happiness are making compromise and adjustment, sharing, caring, and enjoying life together.

Divorce. About half of the marriages in the United States currently end in divorce.

Causes and correlates of divorce. There are several factors that are related to divorce including premarital cohabitation, premarital pregnancy and child-bearing, low income, having no children after marriage, stepchildren in the home, experience of parental divorce, ethnicity and gender, greater financial independence of women, and lack of tolerance and trust between couples.

Consequences of divorce. Economic and psychosocial impacts of divorce are more likely to be negative for children and women than men.

REFLECTIVE QUESTIONS

1. Define marriage. What are the different types of marriage? Discuss effects of social changes on marriage.
2. Discuss relations between marital quality, satisfaction, and happiness.
3. Discuss factors that contribute to a happy and stable marriage.
4. Does money lead to life happiness? Explain why yes or no.
5. Discuss causes, correlates, and consequences of divorce.
6. Discuss important factors that contribute to marital success.

Intimate Relationships in Alternative Lifestyles

Intimate relationships in alternative lifestyles refer to intimacy between partners whose lifestyles are different from traditional monogamous and heterosexual marital relationships. Because of increasing marital problems and a high divorce rate, over the past four to five decades dramatic changes have occurred in the concepts of marriage and intimate relationships in Western industrialized countries. An increasing number of people in Western societies are seeking intimate relationships through nonmarital or "marriage like" long-term alternative unions such as cohabitation, gay, and lesbian relationships.

Cohabitation

Cohabitation is usually a premarital relationship, which used to be regarded as a prelude to formal marriage. Unlike marriage, it is an informal union of intimate couples who live together and usually get involved in a sexual relationship and can have children like married couples. Cohabitation has become the norm in many European countries, especially Scandinavian countries such as Norway, Sweden, Denmark, and Finland, where cohabiting couples have the same legal rights of married couples (Seltzer, 2000). In the United Kingdom, about 70 percent of the first partnership consist of cohabiting couples and about 60 percent of them eventually marry (Ford, 2002). In recent decades, cohabitation has increased rapidly in the United States, rising from roughly 500,000 couples in 1970 to more than 7.7 million couples in 2010 (Lofquist et al., 2012). Cohabitation has spread widely across the population, regardless of race, ethnicity, education, and age (Leifbroer & Dourleijn, 2006). The trend in cohabitation is changing, as today's cohabiting couples less often plan to marry their partners, and consequently serial cohabitations are rising (Vespa, 2014). Recent cohabiting unions are less likely to culminate in marriage and more likely to end in separation (Kennedy & Bumpass, 2011).

In the United States today, increasingly more cohabiting couples are not only partners but also parents as well. About 20 percent of births are to cohabiting parents, and nearly 50 percent of children spend a part of their lives in cohabiting families (Kennedy & Bumpass, 2011). In the United States, the percentage of births to unmarried women has become almost double over the past 25 years, ranging from 22 percent in 1985 to 41 percent in 2010 (Martin et al., 2012). As of the mid-2000s, 21 percent of all births and 59 percent of nonmarital births in the United States belonged to cohabiting parents (Lichter, 2012).

Relationship Quality in Cohabiting Union

Although studies in the past two to three decades have more or less consistently shown that cohabiting couples tend to report poorer relationship quality than do married couples (Skinner et al., 2002), the differences in the relationship quality between marriage and cohabitation that were documented in the past have diminished now as cohabitation has become more common and socially acceptable in the United States (Manning, 2013; Musick & Bumpass, 2012). Moreover, the negative influence of premarital cohabitation on marital stability has also diminished substantially (Manning & Cohen, 2012; Reinhold, 2010).

However, results of a recent study on the relationship quality among cohabiting versus married couples showed that differences still exist in the relationship quality between married couples and cohabiting couples (Brown, Manning, and Payne, 2014). For example, the study showed that the relationship quality varied by the type of relationship for both women and men. Among women, those who married directly without cohabitation were happiest, followed by married couples who cohabited before marriage, next cohabiting couples with plans to marry, and the last were cohabiting couples without any marriage plans. Similarly, cohabiting men without marriage plans reported the lowest average levels of relationship happiness than the other three groups. Another study, however, demonstrates that the level of emotional intelligence and the sense of coherence displayed by partners are the key psychological factors that determine the quality of intimate relationships in both cohabiting and marital unions (Pokorski & Kuchcewicz, 2012).

Cohabitation among Younger and Older Adults

Although cohabitation is more prevalent among younger adults, it is rapidly increasing among older adults as well. Cohabitation among older adults is likely to increase further as today's cohabiting younger adults become the older adults of tomorrow (King & Scott, 2005). As cohabitation is more prevalent among the previously married than among the never married older adults, the rate of cohabitation among this age cohort is likely to be accelerated by the continuing high rate of divorce (Bumpass & Lu, 2000). Cohabitation in the future is likely to be a common form of union for achieving intimacy among younger and older adults (Cooney & Dunne, 2001). Similarly, some researchers argued that like marriage, cohabitation can be a long-term union in later life (Musick & Michelmore, 2015).

The relationship quality of cohabiting unions among younger and older adults has important implications for their psychological well-being (Bumpass, 2002). Early research on relationship quality in cohabiting versus marital unions showed that cohabiting unions are relatively short-lived than marital unions. Moreover, cohabiting unions are characterized by greater relationship instability and lower levels of relationship quality than marital unions (Brown, 2003). But a couple of later studies reported that these differences are gradually decreasing. Furthermore, these differences partially depend on the age of the cohabitors. For example, compared to younger adults, older adults were found to report on average relatively higher quality and longer duration of cohabiting unions (King & Scott, 2005). Some researchers indicated that cohabiting couples and married couples enjoy similar levels of relationship quality in older adulthood. But over time, the relationship quality among older cohabiting couples and married couples follows a similar linear downward path (Musick & Michelmore, 2015).

Although the rate of cohabitation, as a form of union, is increasing among both younger and older adults, there are differences between these two age cohorts regarding the reasons to cohabit, and the quality and stability of cohabitation. A national survey of the young and older cohabitors in the United States showed that younger adults are more likely to view their cohabiting union as a prelude to marriage, whereas older adults are more likely to view their relationship as an alternative to marriage (King & Scott, 2005). King and Scott also explored other reasons for cohabiting, including compatibility, independence, sexual satisfaction, commitment, and financial autonomy but found no significant differences between these two age groups. In addition, researchers (King & Scott, 2005) found that older adults experience significantly higher levels of relationship quality and stability than do younger adults, although the older adults are less likely to have plans to marry their partners. Previously married older cohabitors are less likely to have remarriage plans. As the older adults are less sanguine about remarriage, they tend to cohabit for longer durations. They also experience lower levels of relationship quality. In fact, many unmarried older adults, especially women, are not interested in marriage, yet they do have the desire for companionship, love, and affection, and many other benefits of marriage in cohabiting relationships without legal hassles and economic and social constraints (Musick & Michelmore, 2015; King & Scott, 2005).

Although cohabitation has gained widespread acceptance regardless of age, the attitudes of older adults toward cohabitation are still less favorable than those of younger adults (Hansen, Moum, & Shapiro, 2007). Because some older adults who came of age during the era when cohabitation was rare and would be stigmatized as "living in sin," many still have some lingering influences of this stigma, and consequently consider cohabitation as a less desirable living arrangement (Musick & Michelmore, 2015).

Effects of Cohabitation

Cohabitation now appears to have similar beneficial effects on psychological well-being, health, and social ties like marriage (Musick & Bumpass, 2012). Close relationships, in cohabiting unions or marital unions, are central to well-being, and the quality of these relationships has significant consequences for health, especially among older adults (Brown & Kawamura, 2010).

Determinants of Stability in Cohabiting Union

A couple of researchers have found a number of factors related to the stability of cohabiting union including but not limited to the following:

Cohabitation and birth of a child (or children). Cohabiting parents are more likely to separate after the birth of a child than married couples. A study, for instance, reported that about 27 percent of couples who were cohabiting when their first child was born have separated by the time the child was 5 years old, compared with only 9 percent of couples who were married when their first child was born and separated when their child was 5 years old (Benson, 2009). But research findings about the relations between stability of cohabitation and having children are not consistent. For example, another study found no significant differences between the separation risks for couples who had a birth in marriage without ever cohabiting, who first cohabited then married and had a birth in marriage, and who had a birth in cohabitation and then married (Musick & Michelmore, 2015). The authors also found that cohabiting unions with children are significantly less stable for divorcee cohabiting couples than for non-divorced couples.

Parental cohabitation. The children born of cohabiting parents have a higher risk of greater instability in their own cohabiting union when they are adults than the children born of married couples (Osborne, Manning, & Smock, 2007). The authors also found that the difference in union instability was greater for White American adult offspring than for Black or Hispanic American adult offspring.

Economic factors. Economic factors are an important predictor of the relationship stability for both married and cohabiting couples. Economic hardship was found to be a significant predictor of conflict and instability in relationships among married and cohabiting couples (Hardie & Lucas, 2010). Several studies have shown that economic well-being is positively related to the possibility that a cohabiting couple will marry (Edin & Reed, 2005; Lichter, Qian, & Mellott, 2006). Many people enter into cohabiting arrangements for financial necessity, but that may ultimately result in fragile partnerships (Sassler, 2004). Unlike cohabitation, marriage often leads to an increase in economic well-being, because married couples typically manage their resources jointly to increase their economic well-being (Sweeney, 2002), whereas cohabiting couples are less likely to pool their income together (Treas & De Ruijter, 2008).

Education. Although there are not many studies on the relationships between education, and quality, and stability of cohabiting unions, there are a few studies that reported positive correlations between couples' educational levels and the quality of cohabiting unions. For example, one study showed that educational attainment promotes positive interactions within cohabiting couples (Brown, 2003). Similarly, another study found that couples' education is positively associated with their relationship quality (Skinner et al., 2002).

Gender. Women who cohabited with men they married were more likely to divorce than women who had not cohabited prior to their first marriage. Premarital cohabitation with two or more partners was found to be associated with an 86 percent increase in the likelihood of dissolution of marital and cohabiting unions (Teachman, 2003). But a meta-analysis shows that premarital cohabitation with the spouse prior to marriage has little or no significant negative effects on the marital quality or stability of the couples (Jose, Daniel O'Leary, & Moyer, 2010).

Sexual relationships. Sexuality has a more prominent role in cohabitation than in marriage, and poor sexuality is more likely to lead to the dissolution of cohabitation than marriage. Sexual frequency and satisfaction are more important in cohabitation than in marriage, because the majority of cohabitors are young people, and they have a strong sexual desire and a high demand for sexual activity. Accordingly, results of a study indicate that low sexual frequency is associated with significantly higher rates of union dissolution in cohabitation than in marriage (Yabiku & Gager, 2009), probably because it is easier to end a cohabiting union than a marital union and cohabitation has lower costs than marriage to ending a union.

Lesbian, Gay, Bisexual, and Transgender Relationships

Because of fear of discrimination, isolation, and social stigma, many lesbian, gay, bisexual, and transgender (LGBT) people don't like to be openly identified as such. Because of sampling problems due to secrecy of identity, there are not many studies on LGBT. According to a report of the Centers for Disease Control and Prevention (CDC, 2013b), approximately 1.50 percent of women and 1.80 percent of men identified as homosexual (lesbian or gay), and about only 1 percent of women and men (0.9 percent of women and 0.4 percent of men) identified as bisexual, and 97.7 percent of women and 97.8 percent of men identified as heterosexual or straight. Although LGBT are still not common forms of union in the United States, polls and surveys show an obvious trend toward tolerance and acceptance of the LGBT community among the mainstream American population. For example, results of Gallup polls (Statista, 2016) from 1996 to 2015 on Americans 18 years and older on the question "Do you think marriages between same-sex couples should be recognized by law as valid?" show that in the year 1996 about 70 percent of adults said that same-sex marriage should not be recognized by law as valid and only about 30 percent said it should be recognized as valid. But in year 2015 about 60 percent said that same-sex marriage should be recognized by law as valid, and about 40 percent said it should not be recognized as valid. Results of another survey among American adults about reasons for opposing same-sex marriage show that 47 percent of respondents stated that they oppose same-sex marriage because their religion says it's wrong (Statista, 2012). The detailed results are as follows:

Why Do You Oppose Same-Sex Marriage?

- Religion says it is wrong (47 percent).
- Marriage should be between a man and a woman (20 percent).
- Morally wrong and/or have traditional beliefs (16 percent).
- Civil unions are sufficient (6 percent).
- Unnatural and against laws of nature (5 percent).
- Undermines traditional family structure (5 percent).
- Other (7 percent).
- No opinion (4 percent).

The total percentage exceeds 100 because some respondents gave more than one reason.

Lesbian Relationships

Lesbian Relationship Quality

Lesbians are female homosexuals who have attraction for love and sex with other females. Although research literature on lesbian couples' relationship quality and stability is quite scanty, a study on this topic shows that lesbian couples report higher relationship satisfaction than do heterosexual couples (Borneskog et al., 2012). The study also showed that lesbian women with children from previous heterosexual relations assessed the relationship quality lower than did lesbian women without children from such previous relations. But overall, lesbian women are more likely to have stable and monogamous relationships than do gay men, and lesbian couples tend to be as committed as married heterosexual couples (Kurdek, 2008). Contrarily, another study based on data from Norway and Sweden indicates that the rate of relationship dissolution within five years of entering a legal union is higher among same-sex couples than among heterosexual married couples, with lesbian couples having the highest rates of union dissolution. Lesbian women with higher education levels rated their relationship satisfaction lower than did lesbian women with lower education levels. But lesbian women with higher education reported more success in conflict resolution in the relationship than did lesbian women with lower education levels (Andersson et al., 2006). Several other studies, however, found no significant differences between lesbian couples and heterosexual couples in relationship quality, psychological well-being, and social adjustment (e.g., Biblarz & Savci, 2010; Patterson, 2000).

Lesbian Parenting

Researchers found little difference between children raised by lesbian couples and heterosexual couples in their psychosocial development (Biblarz & Savci, 2010). Most studies on lesbian parenting focus on three broad types: (1) lesbian mothers who have children from previous heterosexual relationship and later on formed a family with another lesbian woman with or without biological children; (2) lesbian comothers who chose to have a child or children together through donor insemination (DI); and (3) lesbian adoptive parents. In the first case, the parents are often termed as the biological mother and stepmother within lesbian stepfamilies. In the second case they are frequently termed as the biological mother and social mother within lesbian comother families, and in the third case they are termed as adoptive lesbian mothers. A number of studies have shown that lesbian couples tend to be egalitarian in their relationships, as they are willing to share family and parenting responsibilities equitably (Fulcher, Sutfin, & Patterson, 2008; Kurdek, 2006). Lesbian couples have a high satisfaction with their parenting responsibility and activity (Bos & Van Balen, 2008). Lesbian mothers, especially DI mothers, have a strong desire for children and are devoted to parental responsibility. They often exceed heterosexual married couples on time spent with children, parenting skill, and warmth and affection toward children (Bos et al., 2006; MacCallum & Golombok, 2004). Moreover, children raised by lesbian couples and heterosexual couples showed little difference in their psychosocial development (e.g., Biblarz & Savci, 2010; Patterson, 2000). Some researchers, however, indicated that the family dynamics of lesbian couples often change with the arrival of children in their family and keep changing further as children grow (Biblarz & Savci, 2010). For instance, a couple of researchers found that, similar to heterosexual couples, warmth decreases and conflict increases to some extent among lesbian couples after transitioning to parenthood (e.g., Goldberg & Sayer, 2006; Goldberg & Smith, 2011; Schumm, 2016), and children sometimes develop a closer relationship with one or the other lesbian parent during the early stage of life (e.g., Goldberg, Downing, & Sauck, 2008). Another important issue in lesbian parenting is the gender of children. Several studies have found that lesbian mothers prefer to have daughters over sons (Dempsey, 2005; Goldberg, 2009), and more frequently they adopt girls than boys (Shelley-Sireci & Ciano-Boyce, 2002). In addition, lesbian mothers who have daughters rated the quality of their interaction with their children higher than those who have sons. Similarly, sons of lesbian comother families scored lower than daughters in such families in self-rated perceptions of parental acceptance (Vanfraussen, Ponjaert-Kristoffersen, Brewaeys, 2003). A study found that lesbian couples who preferred to adopt girls to boys did so because they believed that boys would encounter more heterosexism than girls as they age (Goldberg, 2009).

Gay Relationship

The term *gay* refers to men and women who are attracted to the same sex. But the term *gay* is more commonly used to describe homosexual men, whereas the term *lesbian* is more commonly used for homosexual women. Research on gay relationships is as scanty as or even more than that of lesbian relationships. According to a report of the Centers for Disease Control and Prevention (CDC, 2013b), approximately 1.80 percent of men expressed their sexual identity as gay. There are many reasons why people become homosexual (gay or lesbian). Some people become homosexual by choice, some for physiological or genetic reasons, and others for environmental reasons. For example, some social settings such as prison can lead heterosexual adults to form sexual relationships with same-sex prison mates.

Since the past one or two decades, however, an increasing number of studies on gay relationships have been conducted. These studies mainly focus on gay relationships, processes of becoming gay fathers, and gay parenting (Biblarz & Savci, 2010). Gay men who don't express their homosexual identity usually go through a prolonged identity confusion, and they are likely to suffer from conflicting relationships with both sexes. Contrarily, those gay men who openly express and accept their homosexual identity have little confusion in developing homosexual relationships. Some of them may move to big cities with large gay populations, where they can seek out and find intimate partners to develop gay relationships.

Gay Relationship Quality and Stability

Like lesbians, most gay men intend to have long-term companionship, love, and sex through a relationship with a partner of the same sex; and the ingredients of long-term relationships are quite similar in gay, lesbian, and heterosexual relationships (Patterson, 2013). But lesbian women are more likely to have a stable and monogamous relationship than gay men. Gay men have more frequent sexual intercourse than lesbian women and heterosexual men. According to some researchers the reasons for these differences in sexual frequencies are mainly due to differences in gender socialization of women and men (Peplau, Fingerhut, & Beals, 2004). In most societies, women don't express their sexual desire overtly like men. They often keep their sexual feelings dormant and prefer to play a somewhat passive role in initiating sex with a partner. Men, on the other hand, are more interested and active in initiating sexual interactions than women. Women generally give more importance to love than sex, but men want to have love through sex. These are some of the reasons for more frequent sexual activity in a couple with at least one male partner.

Gay men also differ from both lesbian and heterosexual couples about their attitudes and behavior on sexual exclusiveness. Unlike lesbian and heterosexual couples, gay men more often get involved in nonmonogamous sexual activity (Gotta et al., 2011). A study found that while few lesbian and heterosexual couples had sex outside their relationships, nonmonogamous sexual activity was reported by about 50 percent of gay men in their gay relationships (Solomon, Rothblum, & Balsam, 2005). Gay men disagree more than lesbian women about sexual monogamy, and they argue and fight more often with their partners about sex outside their relationships than do lesbian women. However, for fear of a high risk of HIV and AIDS, an increasing number of gay men are becoming committed to a long-term monogamous sexual relationship with one homosexual partner (CDC 2013a: Kurdek, 2008). For example, a study found that the percentage of gay men who had ever had sex outside their relationship decreased from 83 percent in 1975 to 59 percent in 2000 (Gotta et al., 2011). A survey on a group of gay and lesbian youth found that 82 percent of gay and 92 percent of lesbian youth expressed desire for long-term relationships with one partner, and many of them were hopeful that someday they would be able to marry their same-sex partners (D'Augelli et al., 2006/2007). Another study reported that the majority of the gay and lesbian couples described their relationship as satisfactory (Kurdek, 2008). Results of a longitudinal study on gay, lesbian, and heterosexual couples showed that at the beginning of the study couples of all three groups described their relationships as happy but after five years all of them perceived a drop in their relationship satisfaction with no significant differences among the three groups (Kurdek, 2004). Research has also identified several correlates of relationship qualities for gay and lesbian couples, including the feeling of sharing equal power in the relationship, perceiving more attractions and fewer arguments and conflicts, shared decision making, and egalitarian attitudes (Kurdek, 2004). Another study found that gay couples are more egalitarian in their relationships, as they share decision making and housework almost equally with their partners than do heterosexual couples (Gotta et al., 2011).

Sexual health of homosexuals, especially nonmonogamous gay men, is an important issue for health researchers. Public health researchers have often expressed concerns and included gay men, especially nonmonogamous ones, in the high risk group for sexually transmitted diseases, but there is not enough research evidence yet to support this concern.

Gay Parenting

Although parenthood is a universal and highly valued human desire, gay couples are less likely than their heterosexual counterparts to be parents (Gates et al., 2007). Low parenting desires may be partly responsible for lower parenthood rates among gay couples (Riskind & Patterson, 2010). The low parting desire might be associated with the fact that gay fathers often experience psychological distress because their traditional gender role socialization as men comes into conflict with their new child care role as major caregivers (Benson, Silverstein, & Auerbach, 2005; Schacher, Auerbach, & Silverstein, 2005).

An overview of the existing research literature on homosexual parenting reveals that more studies have been conducted on lesbian parenting than on gay parenting (Biblarz & Savci, 2010). The research on gay male parenting falls into three broad categories: (1) studies on the process of gay men's conceptualizing and actualizing gay fatherhood, (2) studies of family processes of gay fathers in raising children, and (3) gay fathers' views about sons and daughters. Most of the national surveys in the United States show that gay male couples are disproportionately White and middle class (Johnson & O'Connor, 2002). Gay and lesbian couples, regardless of their ethnic and social class identities, become parents through two major ways, such as birth or adoption (Patterson & Riskind, 2010). In some families, children were born or adopted in couples' previous heterosexual relationships that might have been later dissolved when one or both parents came out as gay or lesbian. In other families, children were adopted by gay or lesbian couples after they affirmed homosexual relationships and entered in a gay or lesbian union. The families of the first type might have experienced a lot of difficulties in their process of transition as parents. Parents and children of the second type, however, are unlikely to have experienced such a difficult process of transition to parenthood (Goldberg, 2009). Gay cofathers who had a child or children within the relationship used the highest levels of positive discipline techniques and were much less likely to spank their children in comparison to heterosexual parents. Several studies reported that when two gay men coparented, they did so in a way that parenting became closer to that of lesbian and heterosexual women than to married heterosexual men (Schacher, Auerbach, & Silverstein, 2005; Stacey, 2006). Most gay parents are ready to undertake the challenges and overcome the difficulties to ensure their children's healthy development (Biblarz & Savci, 2010). A study on gay fathers' views about sons and daughters revealed that many gay fathers considered their daughters as significantly more sympathetic and supportive to them than their sons when their children grew up. Gay fathers believed that being a gay or bisexual male parent was highly beneficial in helping their children to develop tolerance of other people's sexual orientations. Fathers also felt that this effect was stronger for their daughters than for their sons, although being raised by gay male parents was more beneficial to their sons than daughters in developing children's understanding and acceptance of their own sexual diversity (Barrett & Tasker, 2001).

A considerable body of research has indicated that there are no consistent differences between children of homosexual and heterosexual parents in their physical and emotional health, social and moral judgments, and psychological adjustment (Patterson, 2013). Moreover, the children of gay and lesbian parents are no more likely than the children of heterosexual parents to have social and psychological problems (Patterson & Riskind, 2010). Furthermore, Children of gay and lesbian parents are no more likely to be homosexual themselves than the children raised by heterosexual parents (Anderssen, Amlie, & Ytteroy, 2002; Biblarz & Savci, 2010).

Relationships between Bisexual Men and Women

Bisexual individuals are sexually attracted to both men and women. An individual is characterized as a bisexual if his/her lifetime history of sexual attitudes and behavior includes partners of both sexes. According to a longitudinal study, bisexuality is a third type of sexual orientation for individuals with sexual fluidity, who are neither distinctly homosexual nor heterosexual, at least in the early adult life course (Diamond, 2008). One study showed that many teenagers preferred bisexual identities over gay and lesbian identities and rejected categorical conceptions of sexuality (Savin-Williams, 2006).

A national survey in the United States found that only 0.8 percent of adult men self-identified as bisexual, but 4 percent of them said that they had had sex with both male and female partners since age 18 (CDC, 2013b). Similarly, the same survey found that only 0.5 percent of women identified themselves as bisexual, but 3.7 percent had had sex with both male and female partners since age 18. A couple of studies showed that many bisexuals who are in a primary relationship have a partner of the other sex, and many of them are legally married. Some heterosexual individuals tend to view bisexuality as a sign of immaturity, indecisiveness, or promiscuity. A large survey on several thousands of the U.S. adolescents found that 3.9 percent of girls and 6.3 percent of boys reported romantic attractions to both males and females (Diamond, 2008). A couple of longitudinal studies have found *sexual fluidity* among young adults as many of them change their sexual identity and behavior over time (Diamond, 2012).

Although there are many anecdotal records about bisexual relationships, scientific research on this issue is very limited (Biblarz & Savci, 2010). There is not enough research evidence to form a clear understanding about sexual satisfactions, conflicts, and health outcomes of bisexual men and women. Some researchers have indicated that concordance between sexual identity and sexual behavior is good and healthy (Diamond, 2005). In a few studies, negative health outcomes—including substance use, depression, suicide, and sexually transmitted diseases—have been found among those bisexuals whose sexual behavior and sexual identity are discordant (Friedman et al., 2014; Schick et al., 2012). However some researchers have indicated that concordance and discordance between sexual identity and sexual behavior may not be as central to the sexual risk as the other aspects of sexual behavior, such as monogamous or nonmonogamous sexual activities, protected or unprotected sex, etc. (Baldwin et al., 2015).

Transgender Relationships

The term *transgender* refers to individuals who have a gender identity, or gender expression, that differs from their assigned sex. It is an umbrella term that includes people whose gender identity is the *opposite* of their assigned sex, and who are not exclusively masculine or feminine but are bigender or gender variant or gender fluid (Forsyth & Copes, 2014). Transgender people may identify themselves as heterosexual, homosexual, bisexual, asexual, etc. If a transgender individual feels comfortable with her/his bodily appearance and accepts a consistent identity, she/he is called a *transgender congruent person* (Kozee, Tylka, & Bauerband, 2012). According to a recent study, about 0.6 percent of Americans identified themselves as transgender (Katy, 2016). Many transgender individuals experience gender dysphoria, and some seek medical treatments including hormone replacement therapy, sex reassignment surgery, or psychotherapy. But some transgender people do not want these treatments or cannot afford medical treatments for financial reasons (Maizes, 2015). Most transgender people face social discrimination in home, workplace, public accommodations, and health care; and they have little or no legal protection against these discriminations in many places (Lombardi et al., 2008).

Research on transgender individuals and their family relationships is almost nonexistent (Biblarz & Savci, 2010). Transgender youth usually experience a number of unique challenges in their lives and find few formal or informal sources of social support. Their parents often react with alarm when their children engage in gender nonconforming behaviors (Kane, 2006). Transgender youth sometimes try to please parents by gender conforming behaviors at the cost of anxiety, depression, and low self-esteem (Mallon & DeCrescenzo, 2006).

There are a couple of studies about the causes of transsexuality, and most of these studies focused on biological factors. One of the early studies (Zhou et al., 1995) reported that transgender women's brain structure (volume and density of neurons) is similar to that of cisgender (people whose gender identity matches the sex that they were assigned at birth) women but not of men. Another study, however, suggested that significant sexual dimorphism in the bisexual, transgender, and cisgender does not become established until adulthood. The authors also argued that changes in fetal hormone levels produce changes in synaptic density gradually as individuals grow causing observed differences during adolescence and adulthood in the bodily systems of bisexual and transgender individuals, often leading to differences in the formation of a gender identity inconsistent with their assigned sex (Chung, De Vries, & Swaab, 2002). A number of studies confirmed that gender identity is influenced by brain structure (Garcia-Falgueras & Swaab, 2008; Gooren, 2006; Guillamon, Junque, & Gómez-Gil, 2016; Swaab, 2003).

Genderqueer Relationships

Genderqueer people do not identify or express their gender identity within the gender binary—female or male. They are gender fluid. As defined by Ryan Watson (2017), genderqueers are "People who reject static, conventional categories of gender and embrace fluid ideas of gender (and often sexual orientation). They are people whose gender identity can be both male and female, neither male nor female, or a combination of male and female."

As noted earlier, there is insufficient research on LGBTQ; unlike heterosexual individuals, lesbian, gay, bisexual, transgendered, and genderqueer (LGBTQ) individuals receive little support from society when developing their sexual identity and intimate relationships. This societal negative attitude is illustrated by the lack of consistent legal recognition of LGBTQ relationships in American society (Closs, 2010).

CHAPTER SUMMARY

Chapter 13 explores cohabitation including relationship quality in cohabiting union; cohabiting among younger and older adults; determinants of stability in cohabiting union; lesbian, gay, bisexual, and transgender (LGBT) relationships; relationships between bisexual men and women; and gay and lesbian parenting.

Cohabitation. Cohabitation is a premarital relationship, which is characteristically an informal union of intimate couples who live together and usually get involved in a sexual relationship and can have children like married couples.

Relationship quality in cohabiting union. Although cohabiting couples tend to report poorer relationship quality than do married couples, the difference is decreasing now as cohabitation has become more common and socially acceptable in Western countries.

Effects of cohabitation. Like marriage, cohabitation seems to have similar beneficial effects on psychological well-being, health, and social relations.

Determinants of stability in cohabiting union. Some of the factors that have been found to be related to the stability of cohabiting union are birth of a child (or children), parental cohabitation, economic factors, education, gender, and sexual relationships.

Lesbian, gay, bisexual, and transgender relationships. Because of fear of discrimination, isolation, and social stigma, many lesbian, gay, bisexual, and transgender (LGBT) people don't like to be openly identified as such.

Lesbian relationship. Lesbians are female homosexuals who have attraction for love and sex with other females.

Lesbian parenting. Research findings revealed little difference between children raised by lesbian couples and heterosexual couples in their psychosocial development.

Gay relationship. The term *gay* refers to men and women who are attracted to the same sex. But the term *gay* is more commonly used to describe homosexual men.

Gay parenting. Gay couples are less likely than lesbian couples to be parents. The low parting desire might be associated with the fact that gay fathers often experience psychological distress because their traditional gender role socialization as men is traditionally not consistent with their new child care role as major caregivers.

Bisexual relationship. Bisexual individuals are sexually attracted to both men and women. Bisexuality is a third type of sexual orientation for individuals with sexual fluidity, who are neither distinctly homosexual nor heterosexual.

Transgender relationships. Individuals in transgender relationships have a gender identity, or gender expression, that differs from their assigned sex.

REFLECTIVE QUESTIONS

1. Discuss the relationship quality in cohabiting unions among younger and older adults.
2. Discuss determinants of stability in cohabiting unions among adults of different age groups.
3. Discuss the relationship quality, satisfaction, and stability in LGBT relationships.
4. Discuss with research evidence if there are any differences between children of homosexual and heterosexual parents in their physical and emotional health, social and moral judgments, and psychological adjustment.

CHAPTER FOURTEEN

Conflict, Abuse, and Violence in Intimate Relationships

Conflict in Intimate Relationships

The term *conflict* usually refers to antagonistic opinions or actions resulting from opposing ideas, values, beliefs, interests, needs, drives, wishes, or internal and external demands. Although the term *conflict* is often used to mean hostile disputes and dysfunctional relationships, research has shown that the mere existence of conflict does not necessarily lead to negative outcomes in a long-term interpersonal relationship. In fact, sometimes conflict can lead to positive outcomes. Conflict may create an atmosphere in which relational partners can candidly express their pent up emotion and important feelings that may lead to exploring creative solutions to problems. Moreover, successful management of conflicts can strengthen relational bonds and increase relational cohesion and solidarity (Cupach & Canary, 2016).

Frequency and Intensity of Conflicts

It is difficult to determine how much conflict in an intimate relationship is typical or common and how much is too much. Because some couples develop a relational culture of arguing frequently over any major or minor issues; others develop a norm to argue infrequently only when they disagree on any major issues. Researchers have found that various factors are related to the amount of conflict couples are likely to encounter, including but not limited to the following factors (Asadi et al., 2016).

Personality

A couple of researchers have demonstrated that personality is related to exposure and reactivity in interpersonal conflicts as individuals differ in their propensity to avoid, accommodate, compromise, compete, or collaborate with partners in long-term marital or nonmarital relationships (Bono et al., 2002). There are at least three levels in which individual differences in personality can be related to conflict: level 1—traits or characteristics (what a person has); level 2—contextual factors including plans, strategies, and goals (what a person does); and level 3—life narratives (how a person makes sense or meaning of his/her experiences (McAdams, 1995). In addition, the following personality traits have been found to have significant influences on interpersonal conflicts (Bono et al., 2002; Heaven et al., 2006).

Agreeableness. Individuals who are high on agreeableness tend to be altruistic, trusting, cooperative, compliant, and are likely to experience fewer conflicts than those who are low on agreeableness.

Extroversion. Individuals who are extroverts generally tend to be positive, social, energetic, joyful, friendly, and interested in other people. Individuals who score high on extroversion are likely to experience less interpersonal conflicts than those who score low on extroversion.

Neuroticism. People who are high on neuroticism tend to experience negative affect and emotions such as fear, sadness, anger, and hostility; and they are likely to experience more conflict in interpersonal relationships than those who score low on neuroticism.

Attachment Style

People with secure attachment style experience less interpersonal conflict and manage it more effectively if and when it does occur than do people with insecure attachment style (Mikulincer & Shaver, 2013). Moreover, individuals with secure attachment style tend to be more cool and calm, and less angry during conflicts than individuals with insecure attachment style (Overall, Simpson, & Struthers, 2013). People with anxious and avoidant attachment style are likely to have high tensions and exaggerated fear and worries about the outcomes of conflict on the stability of intimate relationships (Overall et al., 2014).

Lifestyle

Life style factors such as alcohol addiction, drug abuse, and sleep deprivation have been found to be associated with interpersonal conflicts. For example, heavy alcohol drinking was reported to be associated with increased problems in intimate relationships including both marital and nonmarital relationships, and these problems further aggravate when one partner drinks heavily and the other fully abstains from drinking (Homish & Leonard, 2008). Poor quantity and quality of sleep make partners short-tempered, irritable, and prone to conflict; if and when either or both partners experience sleep problems—they tend to get involved in more frequent and unexpected conflicts even on minor issues (Gordon & Chen, 2014).

Stage of Life

Some young adults are likely to experience more frequent conflicts with partners at the early stage of an intimate relationship. But this trend changes and the rate of conflict goes down as they establish a stable romantic relationship and settle down with a professional career in their midtwenties (Chen et al., 2006). Older adults, generally, experience fewer partner conflicts than do young and middle adults (Holley, Haase, & Levenson, 2013).

Intensity of Conflicts

However, the mere frequency of conflict has little impact on the quality and stability of intimate relationships. More important factors are the seriousness of conflicts and the manner in which they are resolved (Gottman, 2011). The intensity and seriousness of conflicts can vary largely within and between couples. Mild forms of disagreements and conflicts are likely to have minimal and short-lived effects. But serious and long-term ongoing struggles can produce intense personal anxiety and relational tension among couples. Stable or recurring intense conflicts are most problematic for relational stability. However, relational harm can be partially or fully mitigated through positive communication and mutual understanding (Johnson & Roloff, 2000).

Is Conflict Inevitable in Any Intimate Relationship?

Difference of opinions, disagreements, and conflicts are natural and inevitable in any intimate relationships, no matter how deeply two partners are close to each other and how intensely they feel and care for one another (Canary & Lakey, 2013). No two partners are identical in their personalities, preferences, ideas, and habits. It is inconceivable and undesirable to have partners who match each other on every single human characteristic. These are some of the reasons why disagreements and conflicts in any relationship are a common feature. Thus some forms of conflict are certainly inevitable in any healthy relationships. Whether conflicts are sporadic or frequent, it is quite common to have differences of interests, opinions, approaches, and viewpoints on any relevant issues. The point is how effectively conflict is managed and resolved rather than whether there will be any conflict or no conflict in a relationship. So the fact of the matter is, conflict has its place in any relationship, and it does not get resolved itself automatically. If the parties involved do not control the conflict fairly quickly, the conflict may start controlling them and make their relationship worse.

Sources of Conflicts

Some of the common sources of conflict in a long-term intimate relationship (either marital or nonmarital) are as follows:

Role expectations. Each couple in a dyadic relationship has her/his unique expectations. Similarity and consistency of expectations and finding agreed ways and means of fulfilling expectations of each partner are important for avoiding interpersonal conflicts. Differences in expectations may be a major source of tension and conflict in any long-term marital or nonmarital close relationship (Anderson & Sabatelli, 2011).

Needs for connectedness and separateness. In an intimate relationship, people want to fulfill, among others, two needs—connectedness and separateness. Connectedness refers to needs for intimacy, closeness, belongingness, companionship, and togetherness. Contrarily, separateness refers to needs for privacy, autonomy, individual freedom, and independence. To develop and maintain a harmonious intimate relationship, couples need to devise a right balance between these two competing demands of connectedness and separateness. Misunderstanding, frustration, disappointment, and conflicts in intimate relationships are likely to occur when couples have to sacrifice one for the sake of the other. An intimate relationship usually thrives when both needs can be fulfilled; and couples can stay close without becoming lost, and stay separate without becoming isolated (Busch & Jarosewitsch, 2012).

Fairness and equity. Fair sharing of duties and responsibilities, resources, and benefits is important to assure partners feel that the relationship is just. The behavioral interactions between the couples should also be guided by the principles of fairness and equity. The violation of these norms can lead to conflict in the intimate relationship (Anderson & Sabatelli, 2011). Partners who are overbenefited are likely to feel guilty, and partners who are underbenefited tend to be angry with their privileged peers (Hatfield, Rapson, & Aumer-Ryan, 2007).

Power sharing. Another potential source of conflict in an intimate relationship is unequal power sharing (Conroy, 2014). The power distribution between couples should be equal and balanced, and not uneven like the power distribution between a master and a slave, or a boss and a subordinate employee. Interpersonal power between couples is based on the control of valuable resources and how these resources are used in the relationships. When one partner has more control over important resources (such as income and wealth) of the family, she/he may try to dominate the other partner by exercising more decision-making power and controlling joint activities (Impett & Peplau, 2006). As male partners usually enjoy more power, they often tend to be more controlling and domineering over female partners, and that often leads to conflict and violence among the couples (Vescio, Schlenker, & Lenes, 2010).

Incompatible and conflicting goals and unfair demands. Couples often engage in conflict because their goals are incompatible, and goals of both partners can't be attained at the same time. So the more powerful partner often tries to block the goals of the less powerful partner, and tries to attain his/her own goals at the cost of goals of the weaker partner (Fisher, 2000). Peterson (2007) reported that the four most common factors that often trigger conflicts between couples are:

- *Unfair demands.* Unjust and unexpected demands can upset a partner.
- *Criticism.* Frequent criticism even about trivial matters can provoke conflicts.
- *Cumulative annoyances.* Repeated trivial differences and recurring nuisances can cause cumulative annoyance.
- *Rebuffs.* Ignoring or not responding to a partner's desired expectations, such as having sex, may cause rebuffs.

Peterson (2007) argued that undue criticism can damage a partner's self-esteem, unfair demands can create a feeling of inequality among partners, cumulative annoyances can cause a sense of mutual disrespect between partners, and being rebuffed can create a sense of self-devaluation in a partner.

Attributions. Attribution is another potential source of interpersonal conflict. For example, partners may agree about a wrong action but may disagree about each other's explanations. Attributions can be either internal—assigning the cause of behavior to some internal characteristics, rather than to some outside forces; or external—assigning the cause of behavior to some outside factors, rather than to some internal characteristics. Internal attributions, generally, instigate more anger and trigger more conflicts than do external attributions (Canary & Lakey, 2013).

The role of significant others. The role of significant others, especially mothers-in-law and fathers-in-law, can be a potential source in the development of conflicts between marital couples. Although couples may live far from their in-laws, the in-laws can and often do interfere in married couples' decision-making processes, especially in Oriental societies (Asadi et al., 2016).

In addition, Gary Lewandowski (2016) has identified the following behaviors as potential sources of conflict in intimate relationships:

1. *Condescending.* Treating a partner as stupid or inferior.
2. *Possessive.* Demanding too much attention or time of a partner.
3. *Neglecting.* Ignoring or rejecting a partner's feelings.
4. *Abusive.* Verbally abusing (using insulting language, such as name calling) and behaviorally abusing (such as slapping) a partner.
5. *Unfaithful.* Breach of trust, such as having sex with a person other than a partner.
6. *Inconsiderate.* Unsupportive and noncooperative partner.
7. *Physically self-absorbed.* Worrying and focusing too much about appearance.
8. *Moody.* Emotionally and behaviorally unstable partner.
9. *Sexually withholding.* Frequently refusing to respond to a partner's request for sex.
10. *Attraction for others.* Talking about others as sex partners or showing sexual attraction for others.
11. *Substance abuse.* Being an alcoholic or a drug addict.
12. *Disheveled.* Being careless about dress and appearance.
13. *Lack of respect for partner.* Being rude and discourteous to a partner (such as saying to a partner that he/she looks ugly and unattractive).
14. *Sexually aggressive.* Forcing sex on a partner.
15. *Self-centered.* Thinking and behaving selfishly.

Instigation and Escalation of Conflicts

Researchers have identified two types of behaviors or tactics of partners that frequently incite and ignite interpersonal conflicts directly or indirectly (Canary & Lakey, 2013). Direct tactics include (1) accusation, criticism, and attributions of negative qualities to the partner; (2) threats of physical and emotional harm to the partner; (3) using hurtful, demeaning, sarcastic, and abusive language about the partner's physical appearance, choices, dresses, and lifestyles; and (4) shouting at and putting down the partner.

Indirect tactics include (1) showing a feeling of superiority, arrogance, and snobbish attitudes toward the partner; (2) showing displeasure, dejection, and depression; (3) abrupt and erratic conducts; and (4) tendency to be evasive and elusive. These sorts of obnoxious behavior, whether direct or indirect, tend to instigate and inflame partner conflicts (Birditt et al., 2010a). Surly and rude interactions between partners, especially when such interactions escalate too much and too often, can have damaging effects not only on their relationships but also on their health. A study in England, for instance, on a sample of 9,000 people over a period of 12 years, showed that individuals who encounter frequent surly conflicts with their partners are more likely to have heart attacks (De Vogli, Chandola, & Marmot, 2007).

Areas of Conflicts

Several researchers have identified a couple of common areas of conflicts in intimate relationships, including but not limited to financial issues, sexual issues, issues related to children, sharing housework, etc. (e.g., Cahn, 2009; Thompson, 2015).

Financial matters. Conflicts concerning money are more frequently about how much money is earned and spent. How do the couples make budget? What do they spend it on? Who makes the decisions about what is spent? How do they save? Each one of these topics can be a source of conflict. It is more often about sharing bank accounts, making decisions about buying or selling properties, daily expenses, etc. Parrott and Parrott (2013) indicated that sometimes conflicts arise for fear of (1) not having power and influence in spending money on important matters impacting her/his life, (2) not feeling secure about financial stability in the future, (3) a partner not showing respect for one's choice and values while spending money, (4) not realizing one's dreams, and (5) a partner spending too much on unnecessary things and too little on essential things.

Sexual issues. Most couples do not expect that their sexual relationship will be an issue when they start an intimate relationship. They tend to believe that their sexual relationship will continue to be very enjoyable and fulfilling; yet it is a common area of frustration and conflict for many couples. It is also not uncommon for one or both partners to feel resentful that he/she is not getting his/her sexual needs fulfilled for a long time, because he/she is not having enough sex or satisfactory sex due to a partner's lack of mood, interest, and motivation, or feeling of tiredness, etc. Other sexual issues that often lead to conflicts are being unfaithful to partners, having extradyadic sex with multiple partners, having sex without love for the partner, forcing sex on the partner, sexual pressures, and coercive sexual behavior.

Children. Couples quite often fight about children. The topics of concern about children are when to have a child, how many children the couple should have, how to share responsibilities of caring children, how to educate the children, and how to discipline them. The issue of discipline can become more delicate when a couple have children from other relationships. Moreover, with the birth of a child, one partner (typically male), may begin to feel not getting enough attention and love from the partner, because after the birth a child or children she gives more time and attention to the kid(s).

Household chores. Housework can trigger conflicts when one partner believes that the other partner is not contributing his/her fair share of the domestic duties. Not sharing domestic duties equitably is one of the major predictors of conflict between intimate couples in marital and nonmarital long-term relationships. Couples fight over who does what around the house almost as much as they fight over money. A couple of researchers noted that conflicts sometimes occur because even though many women work outside the home, they have to do most of the household chores because their husbands or partners don't like to share domestic work equitably (Blumstein & Schwartz, 2008; Cardoso et al., 2016). That does not necessarily mean a 50–50 split of domestic work but rather splitting housework in a way that both partners work as a team of a well-organized home, where each partner does the work he/she likes to do (Gregoire, 2013).

Effects of Conflict

The effects of interpersonal conflict can vary from positive to negative. Conflicts can lead to constructive outcomes, such as changing attitudes and behavior, minimizing differences of opinion, making compromises, and improving relationships. On the other hand, conflicts can lead to destructive and damaging outcomes, such as aggression, abuse, and separation. As noted earlier, disagreements and fighting are not uncommon in any partnership, but some fighting styles are destructive and damaging. Couples who use hurtful language during arguments—such as yelling, resorting to personal criticisms or accusation and attributions of negative qualities to the partner—are more likely to break up the relationships than couples who fight constructively—trying to figure out ways of resolving disagreements in a mutually acceptable manner focusing on the partner's feelings, listening to his/her point of view, and trying to make him/her feel happy. Individuals who either withhold conflicts or withdraw from conflicts without resolving them tend to be unhappy in their long-term relationships (Noller, 2012). Keeping concerns or problems to oneself can breed resentment. Trying to sort out disagreements and conflicts by discussing problems more deeply often minimizes resentment and helps one to stay connected to one's partner over the long term (Lavner & Bradbury, 2012). Looking critically at the problem and understanding its nature and the root and making sincere efforts to eliminate the problem before it becomes severe can save the relationship (McNulty & Russell, 2010). Effective handling of conflict, not withdrawing from it, helps intimate relationships to grow and prosper (Fincham, 2003).

The outcomes of conflicts can range from constructive and beneficial to destructive and damaging (Peterson, 2002). Constructive outcomes can occur through *compromise*—settling a dispute by mutual concession, *integrative agreements*—making selective concessions by minimizing and prioritizing goals, and *structural improvement*—making desirable changes in the characteristics and dynamics of the relationship. Whereas destructive and damaging outcomes can occur through *domination*—one partner forcing the other to concede, *separation*—one or both partners withdrawing without resolving the conflict, and *termination*—ending the relationship when the partners feel that nothing will work and little or no hope is left to salvage the relationship.

Conflict Management

Conflict is not necessarily always harmful to intimate relationships; rather it can be helpful if managed constructively. But if not managed properly, it can have corrosive effects on intimate relationships and destructive conflict can erode the basic foundations of intimate relationships. Goals and strategies for conflict management can vary from individual to individual and from couple to couple. However, some of the common goals include maintaining intimacy and minimizing or eliminating conflicts. Minimizing conflicts and maintaining intimacy through compromise and cooperation, patience, self-control, flexibility, and integrative agreements are likely to work better than using power assertive techniques, such as forcing the partner to give up differences and agree (Canary & Lakey, 2013). Differences and disagreements are common in any intimate relationship, but some fighting styles are damaging and destructive. Couples who resort to destructive behaviors during conflicts—such as yelling, personal criticisms, or name calling—are more likely to break up the relationship than do couples who fight constructively (Birditt et al., 2010b). Couples generally differ in their styles and skills of managing conflicts (Zeidner & Kloda, 2013). When a couple develops successful techniques or strategies of managing conflict that tend to last long (Kamp & Taylor, 2012).

Conflict Management Strategies

Couples often try to eliminate their conflicts using positive and/or negative strategies. These two types of strategies are discussed in the following pages.

Positive strategies. Common positive strategies for conflict management include (Birditt et al., 2010a; Lavner & Bradbury, 2012):

- *Maintaining intimacy.* Emphasis on compromise and cooperation.
- *Talking openly.* Discussing deeper or more personal subjects with the partner to stay connected.
- *Finding constructive strategies for resolving disagreements.* Listening to the partner's viewpoints patiently with an open mind and trying to make the partner feel better.
- *Situational adaptability.* Adapting conversational styles and behaviors in a situation appropriate manner.
- *Setting boundaries.* Keeping the argument or fight within the limit of decency and civility.
- *Positive understanding.* Developing awareness that differences are not problems but hurtful behaviors are, and the couples are lovers and not enemies.
- *Win-win approach.* Trying to resolve conflicts in a way that both partners can save face and feel positive about it.
- *Keeping things interesting.* Breaking old routines and trying new things or news ways of doing the same thing.
- *Agree to disagree.* If the couples can't dissolve a conflict, it is better to drop it without escalating it any further.
- *Saying what one means.* Being clear in conveying messages and seeking partner's confirmation and agreement.
- *Being polite and staying cool.* Not to make the situation too tense, taking a break when the discussion becomes too heated, and coming back to the issue later.
- *Asking professional help.* Seeking professional advice when the conflicts are too complex to resolve through mutual discussions.

Negative strategies. Common negative strategies for conflict resolutions include (Spangle & Isenbart, 2003; Wertheim et al., 2006):

- ***Denial.*** Refusing to admit the existence of conflict in the relationship or trying to suppress conflict.
- ***Power assertion.*** Trying to win an argument at any cost, such as by asserting power and dominance over the partner, or forcing the partner to concede.
- ***Fear of retaliation.*** One partner, generally the weaker one, often doesn't protest or fight for fear of personal attack or verbal abuse.
- ***Unfair demand.*** Insisting that the partner apologize publicly for a minor mistake.
- ***Win-lose approach.*** Trying to resolve conflicts in a way that fulfills one partner's interests at the expense of the other partner.
- ***Displaying a negative attitude.*** Mocking or insulting the partner, being defensive, withdrawing from the conversation, and being aggressive or belligerent.

Positive strategies have been found to be more effective than negative strategies for managing conflicts (Deutsch, 2006; Rizkalla, Wertheim, & Hodgson, 2008). Conflicts in intimate relationships often lead to abuse of and violence against the weaker partner by the stronger or more powerful partner.

Partner Abuse

Partner abuse refers to a pattern of offensive and insulting behavior of one partner intended to establish and maintain control over the other partner. A common pattern of partner abuse is that the perpetrator often alternates between abusive behavior and apologetic behavior with apparent promises to change. The abuser may be quite pleasant much of the time, which is why many abused partners don't leave the abusive relationship, hoping that the perpetrating partner will change behavior in course of time. The victim of partner abuse or violence may be a woman or a man. Partner abuse usually occurs in traditional heterosexual marriages, in cohabiting relationships, and in same-sex partnerships. The abuse may happen during a relationship, or while the couple is on the point of breaking up, or after the relationship has ended. Partner abuse can aggravate and escalate from threats and verbal abuse to physical violence ending up in murder. Partner abuse is not a result of unintended losing of control, but trying to control the partner by intentionally abusing her/him verbally, emotionally, or physically. Unfortunately, in many cultures, control of women by men has been an accepted norm with a long history. However, some cultures, especially Western cultures, are gradually moving from male dominance to egalitarian family relationships with decreased subordination of women to increased equality in relationships.

Types of Partner Abuse

The common types of partner abuse, though somewhat overlapping, are (de Benedictis, 2016; Smith & Segal, 2014):

- Physical abuse.
- Emotional or psychological abuse.
- Sexual abuse.
- Stalking.
- Economic abuse or financial abuse.
- Spiritual abuse.

Physical Abuse

Physical abuse is characterized by the use of physical force against the partner ranging from physical injury to murder. In most cultures of the world, physical assault is a criminal offense whether it occurs inside or outside a family.

Patterns of physical abuse. Some common modes of physical abuse include:

- Pushing, throwing, kicking, slapping, hitting, punching, beating, pinching, biting, bruising, choking, etc.
- Restraining or confinement.
- Forcing partner for alcohol and/or drug use.
- Assaulting with a stick or a weapon such as a knife or a firearm.
- Burning.
- Murder and so on.

Emotional or Psychological Abuse

Emotional or psychological abuse can be either verbal or nonverbal or both. Although physical abuse might appear worse, the effects of emotional abuse are more deeply rooted. Research shows that emotional abuse is as damaging or even more damaging than physical abuse.

Some common patterns of emotional abuse may include:

- Intimidation or threat to gain control and compliance.
- Threat to damage or destroy or the actual destruction of the victim's personal property and possessions, or for example, harming a pet, name calling.
- Yelling or screaming.
- Making fun of, or mocking the victim, either alone or in front of family or friends.
- Downplaying the victim's accomplishments or goals.
- Undermining the partner's self-worth and self-esteem.
- Trying to isolate the victim from friends and family.
- Making the victim feel that there is no way out of the relationship, etc.

Sexual Abuse

Some common forms of sexual abuse include:

- Sexual assault: forcing the partner to participate in unsafe or degrading sexual activity.
- Sexual harassment: ridiculing the partner's sexual choices and ability to perform satisfactorily in sexual activity.
- Marital rape, attack on sex organs, forcing sex through physical violence.
- Sexual exploitation: forcing the partner to look at pornography, or to participate in pornographic filmmaking, etc.

Stalking

Stalking can take place in many different ways, such as:

- Repeated phone calls.
- Tracking personal document s and records (possibly even with a global positioning device).
- Online searching.
- Watching with hidden cameras.
- Suddenly showing up where the victim is, such as at home, school, or work.
- Cyberstalking, such as sending e-mails and instant messaging.
- Sending unwanted packages, cards, or gifts.
- Monitoring the victim's phone calls or e-mails.
- Contacting the victim's friends, family, coworkers, or neighbors for his/her personal information.

Economic or Financial Abuse

Some common financial abuse includes:

- Withholding money or credit cards.
- Trying to make the partner financially dependent by controlling her/his financial resources.
- Stealing from or defrauding a partner of money or assets.
- Exploiting the partner's money for personal gain.
- Forcing the partner to share bank account or real estate property.
- Preventing the partner from working or choosing an occupation or not allowing the partner to work outside the home, etc.

Spiritual Abuse

Some common spiritual abuse includes:

- Criticizing the partner's religious rituals.
- Forcing the partner to follow one's own religious values and beliefs against his/her will.
- Ridiculing the partner's religious or spiritual beliefs.
- Forcing the children to be reared with religious faith that the partner does not approve.

Causes of Partner Abuse

Some individuals tend to resort to partner abuse and violence because:

- They have past experience of solving their problems through abusive means.
- They might have effectively exerted control and power over partners through abuse in the past.
- They have encountered no effective opposition from partners to stop abuse.

Some common causes of partner abuse are (CDC, 2014; de Benedictis, 2016):

- Stress.
- Provocation from the partner.
- Economic hardship—prolonged unemployment.
- Depression.

- Anxiety and frustration.
- Alcohol and drug addiction.
- Rejection and isolation.

Characteristics of Partner Abuse

Research literature has revealed some common characteristics of partner abuse worldwide as follows (Itzin, Taket, & Barter-Godfrey, 2010; National Institutes of Justice, 2015; Vagianos, 2015; WHO, 2016):

- Women are generally subjected to partner abuse more often and more severely than are men.
- The most likely victims of partner abuse are women who are young, poor, uneducated, separated, or divorced.
- Men who abuse women tend to have low self-esteem, sexual inadequacy, a feeling of dominance, social isolation, and frustration.
- Intimate partner abuse happens to adults of all ages, regardless of race, ethnicity, and geographical boundaries.
- Partner abuse can take place during a relationship or after a relationship has ended.
- Most often older abuse happens to frail elderly people living with a spouse or an intimate partner, and the abuser is most likely to be a spouse, since more elder people live with spouses.

Outcomes of Partner Abuse

Several studies have indicated that people who are abused by a spouse or by an intimate partner may develop following problems (Archer, 2000; CDC, 2014):

- Sleeping problems.
- Depression.
- Anxiety and tension.
- Low self-esteem.
- Low self-adequacy.
- Lack of trust between partners.
- Feelings of abandonment.
- Rejection sensitivity.
- Diminished mental and physical health.

- Inability to work.
- Poor relationships with children.
- Substance abuse as a way of coping.
- Physical injury and death.
- Termination or end of relationships.
- Financial problems, such as poverty and homelessness.

Prevention of Partner Abuse

Rising political agitation and the women's movement during the 19th century led to increasing awareness of domestic violence against women, and changes in popular opinion and legislation regarding domestic violence in Western Europe and North America (Gordon, 2002). Consequently, some measures for intervention and prevention of domestic violence were adopted by the government and private organizations in Western Europe and North America, especially in the United States. Some of these measures are:

- Enacting laws—Violence Against Women Act, Family Violence Prevention and Services Act.
- Domestic Violence Prevention Enhancement and Leadership Through Alliances (DELTA) program, funded by Centers for Disease Control and Prevention (CDC).
- Domestic Violence Offender Gun Ban. This is a U.S. federal law enacted in 1996 to ban firearms and ammunitions to individuals convicted of misdemeanor domestic violence.
- U.S. asylum for victims of domestic violence.
- Freedom from domestic violence resolution movement. In 2011, 26 local governments in the United States have passed resolutions declaring freedom from domestic violence to be a fundamental human right.
- National Coalition Against Domestic Violence. This is a private organization in the United States, working to develop a culture where domestic violence is not tolerated.
- The National Domestic Violence Hotline. This is a 24-hour confidential and toll-free hotline in the United States, created through the Family Violence Prevention and Services Act to provide help to the domestic violence victims immediately connecting to a service provider in his/her area. This hotline consists of highly trained advocates to provide support, information, referrals, safety planning, and crisis intervention in 170 languages.

However, partner abuse tends to perpetuate in a society where abuse is not considered a crime but a "domestic dispute," the abuser is not ostracized but socially accepted, abuse is considered a normal part of intimate relationships, people don't take it seriously because they tend to think that both partners are more or less responsible for domestic violence, and there is no specific law to try offenders (de Benedictis, 2016).

Violence in Intimate Relationships

Partner violence is an extreme form of partner abuse. Violence refers to behaviors involving intimidation and/or exertion of physical force intended to do physical harm, injury, or damage to others (Spitzberg, 2013). Family violence, especially partner violence, is quite common and happening quite often all over the world (Rakovec-Felser, 2014).

Global Statistics About Partner Violence

Here are some global statistics about partner violence:

- Globally, 10–50 percent of women report of being physically assaulted by an intimate partner at some time in their lives (Itzin, Taket, & Barter-Godfrey, 2010).
- About one-third of all women are victims of domestic violence during their lifetime (Huss, 2009).
- Approximately, 4 million women are assaulted by a domestic partner yearly (Sartin, Hansen, & Huss, 2006).
- About 1 in 4 women and 1 in 8 men, aged 18 to 59, reported experiencing partner abuse and violence from 2008 to 2009 (Rakovec-Felser, 2014).
- A woman's pregnancy is the high-risk period for the escalation of intimate partner violence, and partner violence is one of the leading causes of maternal mortality in the United Kingdom, the United States, and Australia (Itzin, Taket, & Barter-Godfrey, 2010).
- The dangerous type of violence against women often occurs at the ending of an intimate relationship (Huss, 2009).
- About 6 percent of older couples reported partner violence in the past one year, and the rate was much higher (25 percent) for vulnerable (disabled) elders who were abused by their caregiving partners (Itzin, Taket, & Barter-Godfrey, 2010).

In addition, the key facts of a recent report of the World Health Organization on partner violence and sexual violence against women reveal (WHO, 2016):

- About (35 percent) of women worldwide have experienced either physical and/or sexual intimate partner violence in their lifetime.
- Worldwide, almost 1 in 3 women (30 percent), who have been in a relationship report that they have experienced some form of physical and/or sexual violence by their intimate partner.
- Globally, about 38 percent of murders of women are committed by intimate partners.
- About 15percent of women in Japan and 71 percent of women in Ethiopia reported physical and/or sexual violence by an intimate partner in their lifetime.
- Between 0.3 and 12 percent of women reported sexual violence by someone other than a partner since the age of 15 years.
- About 17 percent of women in Tanzania, 24 percent in Peru, and 30 percent in Bangladesh, all of them from rural areas, reported that their first sexual experience was forced.

The WHO report also showed that factors associated with increased risk of physical and sexual violence against women by male partners include low education, exposure to violence in the family, financial dependence of women, harmful use of alcohol, attitudes of accepting violence, and gender inequality.

U.S. Statistics About Intimate Partner Violence

According to a report of the National Coalition Against Domestic Violence in the United States (NCADV, 2012):

- On average, about 24 persons per minute are victims of rape, physical violence, or stalking by an intimate partner in the United States.
- More than 12 million women and men over the course of a year are abused by intimate partners.
- Nearly 29 percent of women and 10 percent of men in the United States have experienced rape, physical violence, and/or stalking by a partner in a year.
- Nearly 15 percent of women and 4 percent of men have been injured as a result of intimate partner violence including rape, physical violence, and/or stalking by an intimate partner in their lifetime.
- 24.3 percent of women and 13.8 percent of men aged 18 and older have been the victim of severe physical violence by an intimate partner in their lifetime in the United States.

- Nearly half (48.4 percent) of all women in the United States have experienced psychological aggression by an intimate partner in their lifetime.
- Women aged 18 to 24 and 25 to 34 generally experienced the highest rates of intimate partner violence.
- From 1994 to 2010, about 80 percent of victims of partner violence were women.
- About 77 percent of females aged 18 to 34 and 81 percent aged 35 to 49 were victimized more than once by the same offenders.

Power Inequality and Partner Violence

Power inequality between partners, especially between male and female partners, is one of the major causes of partner violence. Interpersonal power in an intimate relationship depends on the control of valuable resources. The partner who has control over more resources is likely to exercise more power on the partner who has control over less resources. Although the balance of power generally tends to be heavier for a male partner than for a female partner, the balance of power may change when a female partner enters the workforce and gains economic independence (Lennon, Stewart, & Ledermann, 2013). In most societies throughout the ages, there has been power inequality between men and women, and men have enjoyed more power than did women in most heterosexual relationships (Impett & Peplau, 2006). Globally, most societies are still governed by male dominant and patriarchal norms and beliefs (Carli, 2001). Educational, economic, and technological development do not seem to have made many significant changes in the power inequality between women and men. For example, many Americans still tend to prefer their political leaders, lawyers, surgeons, and airline pilots to be men rather than women (Morin & Cohen, 2008). A report of the National Center on Domestic and Sexual Violence (2016) about power and control inequality between men and women reveals that male partners generally use their greater economic power and privileges as tools for intimidation, coercion, threats, and emotional abuse against female partners.

Correlates of Intimate Partner Violence

Intimate partner violence may be related to a variety of factors, such as gender, age, ethnicity, education, income, substance abuse, history of family violence, history of criminal activity, peoples' attitudes and beliefs, sexual orientations, etc. A number of organizations in the United States and worldwide (e.g., the Bureau of Justice Statistics, 2013; the National Center for Injury Prevention and Control, 2010; the National Institutes of Justice, 2015; and the World Health Organization, 2016) have conducted several surveys on different aspects of partner violence and found that the following factors are associated with intimate partner violence:

Gender. About 85 percent of domestic violence victims in the United States are women (Bureau of Justice Statistics, 2013). Globally, about 38 percent of murders of women are committed by intimate male partners (World Health Organization, 2016).

Age. The age ranges and frequencies of women's intimate partner violence experiences are age 11–17 (22 percent), followed by age 18–24 (38.6 percent), age 35–44 (7 percent), and age 45+(3 percent). Whereas that for men are age 11–17 (15.0 percent), followed by age 18–24 (47 percent), age 25–34 (31 percent), age 35–44 (10 percent), and age 45+(5 percent) (National Center for Injury Prevention and Control, 2010).

Ethnicity. Approximately 44 percent of Black women and 46 percent of Native Americans have been the victim of rape, physical violence, and/or stalking by an intimate partner in their lifetime. These rates are 30–50 percent higher than those experienced by Hispanic, White, and Asian women in the United States (National Center for Injury Prevention and Control, 2010). On the other hand, about 45 percent of Native American men and about 39 percent of Black men in the United States reported experiencing rape, physical violence, and/or stalking by their intimate partners during their lifetime. These rates are nearly twice the rate experienced by Hispanic and White men (National Center for Injury Prevention and Control, 2010).

Sexual orientations. Approximately 44 percent of lesbian women, 61 percent of bisexual women, and 35 percent of heterosexual women experienced rape, physical violence, and/or stalking by an intimate partner in their lifetime. On the other hand, about 26 percent of gay men, 37 percent of bisexual men, and 29 percent of heterosexual men experienced rape, physical violence, and/or stalking by an intimate partner during their lifetime (National Center for Injury Prevention and Control, 2010).

Criminal history. Most studies found that the majority of domestic violence perpetrators have a prior criminal history for a variety of nonviolent and violent, and domestic or nondomestic offenses against males and females (National Institutes of Justice, 2015).

Other factors. The high rates of intimate partner violence in the United States cannot be explained by any single factor, but seems to be related to many risk factors including but not limited to substance abuse, unemployment, low education, cohabitation of unmarried partners, pregnancy, and low income (National Center for Injury Prevention and Control, 2010).

Health Consequences of Partner Violence

Intimate partner and sexual violence have serious short-term and long-term physical, mental, sexual, and reproductive health problems for the victims and for their children; and such violence often leads to serious social and economic sufferings for them including (WHO, 2013):

- Violence against women can have fatal consequences, such as homicide or suicide.
- About 42 percent of women who experienced intimate partner violence reported an injury as a consequence of this violence.
- Sexual violence of an intimate partner can lead to unintended pregnancies, induced abortions, gynecological problems, and sexually transmitted infections and diseases. Women who had been physically or sexually abused were found about twice as likely to have a sexually transmitted disease and HIV, compared with women who had not experienced partner violence.
- The women victims are also twice as likely to have an abortion.
- Pregnancy due to intimate partner sexual violence also increases the likelihood of stillbirth, premature delivery, and low birth weight babies.
- The women who experienced intimate partner violence were almost twice as likely to experience depression, posttraumatic stress disorder, sleep difficulties, eating disorders, emotional distress, problem drinking, and suicidal tendency. The rates were even higher for women who had experienced nonpartner aggressions.
- Children who grow up in families where there is violence tend to suffer a range of behavioral and emotional disturbances throughout the lifespan.
- Intimate partner violence has also been found to be associated with higher rates of infant and child morbidity (e.g., diarrhoeal disease and malnutrition) and mortality.

CHAPTER SUMMARY

Chapter 14 addresses issues about conflict in intimate relationships including frequency and intensity of conflict; sources of conflict; instigation and escalation of conflict; areas of conflict; effects of conflict; conflict management strategies; partner abuse; types of partner abuse; causes of partner abuse; characteristics of partner abuse; outcomes of partner abuse; prevention of partner abuse; violence in intimate relationships; global statistics about partner violence; power inequality and partner violence; correlates of intimate partner violence; and health consequences of partner violence.

Conflict in intimate relationships. Conflict usually means hostile disputes and dysfunctional relationships, but the mere existence of conflict does not necessarily lead to negative outcomes in a long-term interpersonal relationship. In fact, sometimes conflict can lead to positive outcomes. Moreover, successful management of conflicts can strengthen relational bonds and increase relational cohesion and solidarity.

Frequency and intensity of conflicts. Numerous factors are related with the frequency and intensity of conflict couples are likely to encounter, including personality, attachment style, lifestyle, stage of life, etc.

Sources of conflicts. Some of the common sources of conflict in a long-term intimate relationship include role expectations, fairness and equity, power sharing, incompatible goals, and unfair demands.

Instigation and escalation of conflicts. Several factors have been found to incite and ignite interpersonal conflicts such as accusation, criticism, attributions of negative qualities to the partner, threats of physical and emotional harms to the partner, using hurtful, demeaning, sarcastic and abusive language about the partner's physical appearance, choices, dresses, and lifestyles, and shouting at and putting down the partner.

Areas of conflicts. Common areas of conflicts in intimate relationships include financial issues, sexual issues, issues related to children, sharing housework, etc.

Conflict management. Effective management can minimize or eliminate conflicts. Strategies such as compromise, cooperation, patience, self-control, and flexibility are likely to work better than using power assertive techniques, such as forcing the partner to give up differences and agree.

Partner abuse. Partner abuse is a pattern of offensive and insulting behavior of a partner intended to establish and maintain control over the other partner.

Types of partner abuse. The common types of partner abuse are physical abuse, emotional or psychological abuse, sexual abuse, stalking, economic abuse or financial abuse, and spiritual abuse.

Characteristics of partner abuse. The most likely victims of partner abuse are women who are young, poor, uneducated, separated, or divorced. Men who abuse women tend to have low self-esteem, sexual inadequacy, a feeling of dominance, social isolation, and frustration.

Violence in intimate relationships. Partner violence is an extreme form of partner abuse, involving intimidation and/or exertion of physical force intended to do physical harm, injury, or damage to a partner.

Correlates of partner violence. Partner violence is likely to be related to a variety of factors, such as gender, age, ethnicity, education, income, substance abuse, history of family violence, history of criminal activity, peoples' attitudes and beliefs, sexual orientations, etc.

Health consequences of partner violence. Partner violence has serious short-term and long-term physical, mental, sexual, and reproductive health problems for the victims and for their children.

REFLECTIVE QUESTIONS

1. Discuss important factors that are related to frequency and intensity of conflict in intimate relationships.

2. Is conflict inevitable in an intimate relationship? Give reasons for your answer.

3. Discuss different sources and areas of conflict in intimate relationships.

4. Discuss different types of behaviors or tactics of partners that frequently incite and ignite interpersonal conflicts directly or indirectly.

5. Explain why conflict is not necessarily harmful to intimate relationships. How can it be helpful if managed constructively?

6. Discuss different types of conflict management strategies.

7. Discuss different types, causes, and consequences of partner abuse. How can partner abuse be prevented?

8. Discuss the effects of partner violence on physical, mental, sexual, and reproductive health for the victims and for their children.

Deterioration and Loss of Intimate Relationships

There are occasional ups and downs in all varieties of intimate relationships—marital or nonmarital and heterosexual or homosexual. No intimate relationship is completely free of problems, and all intimate relationships are not permanent or everlasting. About 85 percent of adult Americans have experienced at least one breakup of a romantic relationship during their lifetime (Gardyn, 2003; Langlais, 2012). There are multiple reasons why intimate partners may experience problems in the relationship. If any problem in an intimate relationship is not handled properly before it goes too far and becomes severe, the relationship may gradually deteriorate and ultimately fail.

Deterioration of Intimate Relationships

The deterioration of a relationship prior to breakup is a common characteristic of any romantic relationship (Carver, Joyner, & Udry, 2003). Deterioration of a relationship is usually connected with commitment. Commitment is a central component of relationship deterioration (Reed, 2007). Deterioration generally begins when commitments between partners start declining (Langlais, 2012). It is a period of changing commitment or instability of commitment.

Characteristics of Relationship Deterioration

The process of relationship deterioration is related to decreasing levels of commitment. The decreasing levels of commitment are influenced by the four characteristics of relationship deterioration, such as decreased interactions with a romantic partner, relational uncertainty, self- involvement with a romantic alternative partner, and/or a partner's involvement with a romantic alternative partner (Langlais, 2012). According to a number of authors, at the beginning of the relationship deterioration process couples tend to reduce intimacy levels by withdrawing psychologically and questioning the worth of their relationship (Perlman & Duck, 2006; Reed, 2007). Furthermore, they argue that when couples are less committed to their intimate relationships, they tend to find alternative partners and enter into new relationships. How decreased interaction with a romantic partner, relational uncertainty, and alternative partners lead to decreasing commitment and the relationship deterioration process are discussed in the following section.

Decreased interaction with a partner. As individuals experience dissatisfaction with their intimate relationships, they tend to reduce the amount of time spent and frequency of interactions with their partners (Perlman & Duck, 2006). They often avoid going together to attend parties and visiting friends, and make excuses for not going out together. Decreased interactions with declining commitment are clear indications of intimacy deterioration. Moreover, decreases in interactions may occur because of conflict or dysfunctional communication with the partner, which are likely to be associated with declines in commitment levels to the relationship (Welch & Rubin, 2002). In addition, the amount of decreased interactions may be a signal for a relationship breakdown (Langlais, 2012). Couples who do not spend as much time together as they used to do are more likely to break up than those who see each other regularly; and when couples spend less time interacting, there are fewer opportunities to repair their relationship problems and maintain the relationship (Vander-Drift, Agnew, & Wilson, 2009).

Relational uncertainty. Certainty or uncertainty in intimate relationships largely depends on the degree of confidence people have about their involvement in the relationship (Knobloch, 2008). Uncertainty about relationships is likely to occur when individuals lack clear information about themselves and their partners, resulting in confusion and inability to understand and predict thoughts, feelings, and behaviors of each other (Knobloch & Solomon, 2002). Relational uncertainty often originates from three sources: self, partner, and the relationship itself (Knobloch, 2008). Self-uncertainty is related to the individual's own confusion and hesitation about participation in the relationship. Partner uncertainty involves doubts about the partner's feelings and commitment to the relationship.

Finally, relationship uncertainty includes questions an individual may have about the relationship itself, including its benefits, desirability, and worth.

Research findings reveal that relational uncertainty is associated with decreased commitment (Solomon & Theiss, 2008). For example, people who do not communicate with their partner frequently are likely to become uncertain about their intimate relationships, and they tend to report decreases in commitment (Guerrero, Anderson, & Afifi, 2007). Relational uncertainty can also negatively impact a couple's commitment in such a way that leads to breakup of the relationship (Arriaga, 2001). Couples who experience a considerable degree of certainty in their relationships are more likely to stay together than those who are uncertain about their relationships (Arriaga et al., 2006). Taken together, this body of empirical evidence suggests that relational uncertainty is a key factor for relationship deterioration, and that high levels of relational uncertainty may lead to breaking up the intimate relationship.

Alternative partners. An alternative partner is described as an acceptable and attractive option individuals perceive to have, if their current relationships fail. An alternative partner may include a new partner or reuniting with an old partner. Attractive alternative partners are typically viewed as threats to existing intimate relationships, which are commonly associated with declines in relational commitment (Vander-Drift, Agnew, & Wilson, 2009). When individuals perceive that the benefits of an alternative partner outweigh the costs of staying in the existing relationship their commitment levels in the relationship are likely to decrease. When individuals are less committed to their relationship, they are more likely to seek out an alternative partner than to stay with the current partner (Reed, 2007). Individuals who paid more attention to an alternative partner after the experiencing dissatisfaction with the current partner were more likely to report decreased commitment to their existing relationships (Simeon & Miller, 2005). Another study reported that not paying attention to alternative partners increases commitment and stability in the existing intimate relationships (Maner, Rouby, & Gonzaga, 2008). Increasing attention to alternative partners is associated with relationship deterioration (Langlais, 2012).

Loss of Intimate Relationships

In most cases, romantic relationships deteriorate prior to breakup (Carver, Joyner, & Udry, 2003). Findings of a study revealed that participants who reported a relationship breakup were more likely to experience relationship deterioration, especially for couples where both partners perceived deterioration (Langlais, 2012). The literature on relationship breaking up indicates that breakup is a process and not an event, because it encompasses the event of breaking up as well as the process of deterioration of the relationship (Langlais, 2012). Although all four deterioration characteristics discussed previously were found to predict a relationship breakup, the strongest predictor for ending a romantic relationship was connection with alternative partners (Connolly & McIsaac, 2009).

Gottman (2010) identified four major "toxic behaviors" that contribute to deterioration and loss of an intimate relationship. These toxic behaviors are:

Criticism. Complaining, blaming, and/or attacking the partner.
Defensiveness. Each partner tries to defend herself/himself by denying or counter blaming.
Contempt. Contempt may include a wide range of behaviors such as facial expressions, body language, or unpleasant verbal exchanges.
Stonewalling. Stonewalling may include withdrawing, shutting down, and stopping communication.

According to Gottman (2016), women are more likely to criticize their partners than do men, and men are more likely to stonewall and withdraw than do women. The author also suggests that when couples experience a high frequency of these toxic behaviors, their feelings of isolation and loneliness increase, which may lead to gradual meltdown and ultimate breakdown of a marital or a nonmarital intimacy. Gottman's model about deterioration and loss of intimate relationships are discussed in more detail along with a couple of other models in the following pages.

Models for Explanation of Deterioration and Loss of Intimate Relationships

Several authors have proposed diverse models for explaining the causes of deterioration and loss of intimate relationships, including marital and nonmarital relationships. Some of these models are discussed in the following sections.

Two-Factor Model

The two-factor model proposes that there are at least two factors that determine if and when a couple will divorce (Gottman & Levenson, 2002). The first factor is called "unregulated volatile positive and negative affect."

The model proposes that the amount of unregulated volatile positive and negative affect in the marriage predicts a short marriage length for the divorcing couples. The second factor is called "neutral affective style." According to the two-factor model, the second factor predicts a long marriage length for the divorcing couples. Research evidence supporting the two-factor model shows that there are two high-risk critical periods for divorce in the divorcing couple's life course. The first seven years of marriage is the first critical period for divorcing couples. Approximately 50 percent of all divorces often occur in the first seven years of marriage (Ellis & Kreider, 2011). The first seven years of marriage are often characterized as a highly emotional and volatile period of marriage. The midlife is the second critical period for divorce. Several researchers have found that midlife is the lowest point in marital satisfaction in the life course (Brown & Lin, 2012; Montenegro, 2004).

Barrier Model

Over the past few decades, numerous researchers have used the constructs of rewards, barriers, and alternatives to explore and explain marital cohesion. Rewards refer to the positive outcomes (such as satisfaction with the spouse as a companion or as a sexual partner) connected with staying in a relationship, barriers refer to factors (such as obligation to children, moral or religious values, a fear of social stigma, legal restrictions, and financial dependence on one's spouse) that obstruct people from quitting a relationship, and alternatives refer to the attractiveness of potential partners other than one's spouse. Several researchers have suggested that people's perceptions of rewards, barriers, and alternatives determine whether a marriage is likely or not to end in divorce (Levinger, 1976; Previti & Amato, 2003). In the light of these three concepts, George Levinger (1976) proposed a model, which is called the barrier model. According to Levinger, rewards, barriers, and alternatives are three central constructs in marital cohesion frameworks. Drawing from exchange theory, he tried to explain why some marriages stay intact and other marriages end in divorce. Levinger also argued that attraction to a spouse is proportional to the rewards she/he receives from the relationship, excluding the costs involved in the relationship. Rewards reflect the pleasant aspects of the relationship, including warmth, affection, companionship, emotional support, sexual satisfaction, etc. On the other hand, costs reflect unpleasant aspects of the relationship, such as sexual dissatisfaction, distrust, marital conflicts, criticism, neglect, hostility, verbal and physical aggressions, etc. Levinger concludes that couples in general are motivated to stay in marriages when they perceive that the amount of reward in the relationship is higher than that of the cost.

Levinger suggests that unhappy partners who intend to break up the relationship may not do so because it would cost them too much. He also thinks that many barriers to divorce are psychological rather than physical or material. For example, couples may stay together because they psychologically feel distressed, thinking about the potential negative effects of divorce on their children (Poortman & Sheltzer, 2007). Several studies identified a number of factors that work as effective barriers that inhibit divorce, such as anxiety about the risk of losing children, suffering of children, religious beliefs, financial dependence on the spouse, and so on (Knoester & Booth, 2000; Previti & Amato, 2003). Although these barriers can inhibit or delay effecting a divorce for a short term, they can't ultimately stop a divorce if there is a genuine feeling of dissatisfaction among the couples about their marital relationships (Knoester & Booth, 2000). According to Levinger, barriers primarily affect the marital cohesion of couples who are unhappy in their marital relationships and are thinking about leaving their marriages.

In addition, Levinger suggested that the presence or absence of alternatives to the marriage can undermine or strengthen marital cohesion, regardless of people's level of marital satisfaction. According to his view, even happily married persons may be tempted to leave their spouses if they believe that other relationships would be more rewarding. On the other hand, even unhappily married individuals may stay with their spouses, if they believe that no viable alternatives to the marriage are available. However, some spouses may consider living alone as a better alternative to living in a dysfunctional and unhappy marital relationship.

Levinger's barrier model has been found useful in understanding and predicting marital stability and instability. Several studies have shown that barriers inhibit divorce, if the couples strongly believe that marriage is a lifelong commitment, the sexual relationship should be within the marital bond; and divorce will negatively affect family relations, income, and children's healthy development (Amato & Maynard, 2007; Brown, 2010; Kreider, 2007). In a study, Previti and Amato (2003) analyzed the main components of Levinger's model using an open-ended question: "What are the most important factors keeping your marriage together?" The results are presented in Table 15.1.

Results of the study showed that in general, respondents perceived that the cohesiveness of their marriage depends more on rewards and less on barriers or alternatives to marriage, with love, respect, friendship, and good communication being cited as important components of marital

Table 15.1 People's Reasons for Staying Married

Category	Description	Example
Love	Feelings of love and affection	I believe we deeply love each other.
Respect	Showing respect to the spouse	We have respect for each other's feelings, beliefs, and privacy.
Trust	Trusting the spouse and having faith and confidence	We are faithful to each other.
Sharing	Shared and joint lives	We don't hide anything from each other.
Communication	Exchange of information	We talk freely and listen patiently.
Friendship	Liking and enjoying together	We enjoy our time and life together.
Happiness	Life satisfaction	We are living happily.
Compatibility	Common goals	We have similar goals, beliefs, and values.
Emotional security	Dependable relationships	We feel safe and secure in our marriage.
Commitment	Devotion and loyalty	We are truly dedicated and loyal to each other.
Sexuality	Sexual attraction and satisfaction	Our physical relationship is going great.
Family, faith, and children	Beliefs that children are precious and marriage is sacred	Kids and religious faith have enriched our marital bond.
Financial problems	Low income and financial insecurity	We need to earn more and be financially independent of each other.
Lack of better alternatives	Finding no better alternative to marriage	I find no better alternative, and life could be worse alone with children.

Source: Adapted from Previti and Amato, 2003.

cohesiveness. In addition to rewards, some respondents cited barriers as factors that keep their marriages together. Staying married for the sake of the children was the most frequently mentioned barrier. Some other barriers mentioned were financial dependence on the spouse, religious beliefs (such as marriage is sacred), and commitment to the norm of lifelong marriage.

Vulnerability-Stress-Adaptation Model

The vulnerability-stress-adaptation model (also called the trait-context-process model) was developed by Benjamin Karney and Thomas Bradbury (1995) as a framework for understanding and explaining how satisfaction in intimate relationships may remain stable or change over time influencing stability or instability, deterioration, and loss of the intimate relationship. In the light of cognitive-behavioral approaches, the model assumes that partners' interactions with each other are largely determined by the perceptions of their relationships. Their perceptions, in turn, depend on each partner's personality, developmental history, past experiences, education, beliefs, and values; and the demanding or supportive circumstances that they confront in the intimate relationship, and the stressful conditions they encounter outside the relationship. Figure 15.1 shows different elements of the model and their interrelations leading to instability, deterioration, and loss of the intimate relationship.

Consistent with the assumptions of the vulnerability-stress-adaptation model, several studies showed that no intimate relationship is perfect and leads to permanent satisfaction. There are ups and downs in every relationship, but some individuals enter into an intimate relationship with dysfunctional attitudes, maladaptive personality dispositions, and others with enduring vulnerabilities that increase the risk of desertion and breakdown or divorce (Maisel & Karney, 2012; Totenhagen, Butler, & Ridley, 2012).

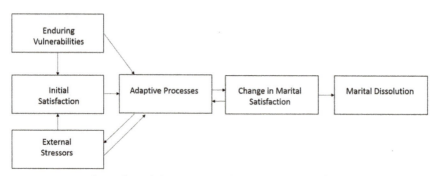

Figure 15.1   The Vulnerability-Stress-Adaptation Model of Marriage (Adapted from Karney & Bradbury, 1995)

Topographical Model

Steve Duck (1982) developed a topographical model of relationship disengagement and dissolution for marital or nonmarital relationships. He identified three broad categories of relationship breakups:

- *Pre-existing doom.* For couples who are badly matched from the beginning and can't dissolve incompatibility, their relationship breakup is almost predestined.
- *Mechanical failure.* The relationship may not work because of poor communication and interactions.
- *Sudden death.* The discovery of betrayal, breach of trust, or infidelity can lead to immediate termination of the relationship.

Duck identified some other factors that could also contribute to relationship loss including:

- *Personal factors.* Such as individual bad habits or emotional instabilities.
- *Precipitating factors.* Such as exterior influences, alternative partners, incompatible working hours. etc.
- *Lack of skills.* Such as being sexually inexperienced or inadequate.
- *Lack of motivation.* Such as loss of interest and attraction in the partner.
- *Lack of maintenance.* For example, staying away from the partner for long time.

Stages of Dissolution

Duck believed that the psychology of relationship breakup occurs through stages in which people look at how they will be perceived by their friends, family, and social circles. He proposed four distinctly different stages of relationship dissolution:

Intrapsychic stage. This stage begins with one partner who is dissatisfied and starts secretly searching for a way to "fix" the relationship or a way of getting out of the relationship.

Dyadic stage. This stage begins when the dissatisfied partner decides to fix the problem by confronting the other partner. If that fails, the unhappy partner may initially withdraw from the relationship and finally decide to depart.

Social stage. This stage begins when the partners decide to disclose to their social circles why and how the breakup happened.

Grave-dressing stage. In this stage the partners try to rationalize and create an acceptable story about their love and loss of love in order to get over the deceased relationship. This is a postrelationship review of the breakup for protecting self-esteem and rebuilding life for new relationships.

Duck's view of breakdown as a process rather than an event is widely accepted. The model takes into account the social context of breakup. Breakup involves the psychological sense of integrity of the individuals involved in it (Rollie & Duck, 2006). However, the model is criticized for not taking into account why the dissatisfaction occurs in the first place. So the model can't give a complete explanation of breakups. The model does not take into account cultural differences in relationship dissolution. Several researchers have criticized the model for not paying attention to gender differences. For examples, some studies showed that women are more likely to attribute unhappiness, lack of emotional support, and incompatibility as reasons for breakup, while men tend to blame lack of attraction and fun (Kalmijn & Poortman, 2006; Rosenfeld, Thomas, & Falcon, 2015; Rudder, 2014).

The models, discussed previously, suggest that deterioration leads to breakup. However, deterioration may not always lead to breakup. In many cases, deterioration may lead to the decision to repair and maintain the relationship or to breakup in extreme circumstances (Langlais, 2012). In addition, some of the models do not explain why or how individuals experience deterioration of relationships that may lead to repair and maintenance or breakup.

Postbreakup Relationships

When couples break up an enduring intimate relationship, whether marital or nonmarital, it is likely to have tremendous effects on their lives (Simon & Barrett, 2010). In some cases, breakup is not necessarily the end of the relationship. It may be temporary, as partners try to forgive each other, and repair and maintain the relationship. But when the breakup is final (permanent), still the couples may continue having a workable contact, especially if they have children from their broken relationship. But their communication may not be as smooth and spontaneous, and interactions may be awkward and uncomfortable (Kellas et al., 2008). Some may become jealous about the other's new romantic partner, while some may think it is good to avoid each other, forget the past, and move forward (Miller, 2015). One study showed that gay and lesbian couples are more likely than heterosexual couples to keep contact with their former partners after the breakup of a relationship (Harkless & Fowers, 2005).

Coping with Relationship Breakups

Different people react differently after the breakup of romantic relationships. In most cases, individuals feel emotionally upset as they experience sadness and pain immediately after a breakup, but the intensity of negative emotional feelings decreases with time (Sbarra & Emery, 2005). Although time heals the effects of relationship loss, for some individuals it may not heal completely. Occasional feelings of grief may occur even after a decade (Meir, Carr, & Currier, 2013). The partner who is unwilling to break up suffers more than the partner who wants to terminate the relationship, especially when the intimacy was very deep (Perilloux & Buss, 2008). Repetitive thinking or rumination about the various aspects of the relationship loss prolongs distress, whereas being optimistic for the future and looking forward to a better life can help recovery effort and positive adjustment (Saffrey & Ehrenberg, 2007). Individuals who remain preoccupied with the ex-partner stay sadder for longer period than those who decide to forget the failed relationship, put it behind them, and start dating to find a new partner (Sbarra, 2006). People who frequently open and go through the ex-partner's Facebook Page take a longer time to forget and move on (Marshall, 2012). People who get out of miserable long-term relationships leaving hostile and abusive partners tend to feel better (Amato & Hohmann-Marriott, 2007).

CHAPTER SUMMARY

Chapter 15 explores characteristics of relationship deterioration; loss of intimate relationships; different models for explanation of deterioration and loss of intimate relationships; stages of dissolution; postbreakup relationships; and coping with relationship breakups.

Deterioration of intimate relationships. The deterioration of a relationship prior to breakup is a common characteristic of any romantic relationship. If any problem in an intimate relationship is not handled properly before it becomes severe, the relationship may gradually deteriorate and ultimately fail.

Characteristics of relationship deterioration. The characteristics of relationship deterioration are generally reflected through decreased interactions with a romantic partner, relational uncertainty, self-involvement with a romantic alternative partner, and/or a partner's involvement with a romantic alternative partner.

Loss of intimate relationship. Most romantic relationships deteriorate prior to breakup. Relationship breakup is a process and not an event because it rarely happens for one single event.

Models for explanation of deterioration and loss of intimate relationships. Several authors have proposed diverse models for explaining the causes of deterioration and loss of intimate relationships including the two-factor model, barrier model, vulnerability-stress-adaptation model, and topographical model.

Coping with relationship breakups. People react differently after the breakup of romantic relationships. In most cases, individuals feel emotionally upset as they experience sadness and pain immediately after a breakup, but the intensity of negative emotional feelings decreases as time passes.

REFLECTIVE QUESTIONS

1. Is intimate relationship breakup an event or a process? Explain with research evidence.

2. Discuss the major characteristics of marital and nonmarital intimate relationship deterioration.

3. What are the "toxic behaviors" that contribute to a relationship breakup or loss? What is the strongest predictor for ending a romantic relationship?

4. What are the important models for explanation of deterioration and loss of intimate relationships?

5. Explain how satisfaction in intimate relationships may remain stable or change over time influencing stability or instability, deterioration, and loss of the intimate relationship?

6. Discuss the topographical model of relationship disengagement and dissolution for marital and nonmarital relationships.

CHAPTER SIXTEEN

Reconstruction and Enhancement of Intimate Relationships

This chapter focuses on repairing, reconstructing, maintaining, and enhancing intimate relationships. A number of authors have suggested different steps for repairing damaged or dysfunctional intimate relationships. For example, Brown and Amatea (2013) have proposed the following techniques for resolving conflicts and repairing intimate relationships.

Techniques for Repairing Intimate Relationships

Selecting a right time. It is more likely that your partner will be willing to cooperate if you have chosen a mutually agreeable time to discuss a grievance. Selecting a time to discuss a grievance when your partner is tired, sick, or under stress may minimize the chance of having a productive discussion.

Being specific and expecting a reasonable change. Convey your grievance to your partner clearly and specifically without being judgmental, and expect a reasonable (not a radical) change in your partner's feelings and behavior gradually and not suddenly.

Dealing with one issue at a time. To be effective, focus on a single grievance at a time and avoid "gunnysacking"—raising too many complaints at a time.

Listening empathetically. Good listening is an effective conflict management skill. Try to understand your partner's feelings by putting yourself in your partner's position.

Brown and Amatea (2013) have identified the following principles for finding effective solutions:

Reflecting and exploring in-depth. Each partner should reflect seriously about the views and feelings of the other partner vis-à-vis his/her own views and feelings.

Exploring options. There may be more than one option to solve a problem in a mutually beneficial way. The partners should try to find the best alternative that is acceptable to them.

Using objective criteria. There should be some mutually acceptable standards or criteria for evaluating the merits and benefits of conflict resolutions, such as fairness, mutual gain, life-changing issues like childbearing, mental health, life satisfaction, and so on.

What should be done when the previously discussed techniques and principles do not work? In such a situation one should think about the following three points (Brown & Amatea, 2013):

1. No human is perfect. We all make mistakes and have limitations. People have different personality dispositions, emotions, feelings, attitudes, values, and life experiences. For a better relationship, we should acknowledge and respect differences, and learn to live with differences (Gottman, 2010).

2. If you sincerely feel that you hurt the feelings of your partner, you should apologize for it, because genuine apology makes you and your partner feel great.

3. A long-term intimate relationship is an enduring process in which couples sometimes make mistakes. The couples who are compassionate, who focus more on the positive than the negative aspects of the relationship, and who are flexible enough to forget and forgive each other's shortcomings are more likely to be successful in fixing their relational problems than couples who are rigid, obstinate, and arrogant (Goetz, Keltner, & Thomas, 2010).

A couple of researchers have suggested that a richer understanding of couple relationships might be gained by focusing on the deeper meanings and motivations about intimate relationships, the positive constructs underlying attitudes, and the behaviors that help to strengthen and repair a relationship (Fincham, Stanley, & Beach, 2007). Some researchers thought that a relationship should be perceived in terms of strengths and well-being rather than deficits and distress (Ooms & Wilson, 2004). Such positive focuses may have significant effects in the repair of relationship discord and enrichment and maintenance of intimate relationships without professional intervention or other external help (Karney, 2007).

Enrichment of Intimate Relationships

Intimate relationship enrichment is also called relationship enhancement. This refers to a process of improving the quality of an intimate relationship to make it enjoyable, healthy, and stable (Markman & Rhoades, 2012). The terms *relationship enhancement* and *enrichment* are often used interchangeably for principles and programs that provide knowledge and skills for assisting individuals and couples to increase their level of satisfaction for healthy and stable relationships (Markman & Rhoades, 2012). For a clear understanding of the fundamental principles and behavioral skills for relationship enrichment, it is necessary to discuss some important theoretical models and programs that have emerged as an educational approach for the purpose of enhancing couples' relationships (Bowling, Hill, & Jencius, 2005).

Theories and Models of Relationship Enrichment

Relationship enrichment is an integrative approach that is drawn from a number of theoretical perspectives including psychodynamic, interpersonal, client-centered, behavioral, and social learning systems perspectives. To explain the principles and process of relationship enhancement, a couple of researchers have proposed a number of theoretical models including, but not limited to, the relational development model (Knapp, 1984), learning models (Bowling, Hill, & Jencius, 2005), and the systems model (Galvin & Brommel, 2000) of relationship enrichment. These models are discussed briefly in the following pages.

Knapp's Relational Development Model

Knapp's relational development model consists of a 10-stage process, divided into two phases. In the first phase, Knapp has outlined 5 stages connected with building up and enhancing intimate relationships. These stages are collectively called escalation stages. The second phase consists of another 5 stages connected with the breaking down of relationships. These stages are called termination stages. The stages can be compared to an elevator ride as it can go either up to higher levels of intimacy or down to lower levels of intimacy ending in termination. The central focus of discussion in this section is the first 5 stages of Knapp's model because these stages are quite relevant to the formation and enhancement of intimate relationships. Each of the 5 stages are briefly discussed in the following sections.

Initiation. As the name indicates, initiation is the first stage of forming impressions about each other. Physical appearance such as bodily features, clothing, conversational styles, and general presentation often play a big role in this stage.

Experimentation. This is the second stage in which individuals begin to engage in self-disclosure to explore and learn about one other. This is usually a decision-making stage in which individuals decide whether to move on with the relationship or not.

Intensifying. At this stage the level of self-disclosure deepens. The topics of discussion are broadened, and the depth in which each individual feels more comfortable in intimate discussions and disclosures increases. This stage is characterized by increased expressions of emotions and feelings with physical touches. In addition, verbal expressions of emotion such as "I love you" and one on one contact through more frequent communication such as face-to-face encounters, text, e-mails, or phone calls are likely to increase.

Integration. At this stage, the relationship becomes very close and intimate. Individuals start thinking of each other as partner, introducing one another as boyfriend and girlfriend, and may start living in shared housing.

Bonding. This is the last stage of the escalation phase. This is a stage in which couples make a declaration of their status formally and legally. They become exclusively bonded to each other either through marriage or other forms of public contracts. The relationship can only be broken through death or formal agreements. However, formal and/or legal bonding may not necessarily guarantee that the relationship will remain bonded for lifelong, though many intimate relationships are enduring and stay until death, and others end in separation or divorce.

Learning Theories

The basic tenets of some learning theories (e.g., classical conditioning, operant conditioning, cognitive theories, and social learning theories) are used for modification of dysfunctional behavior and unhealthy skills used by distressed couples. The enrichment programs using learning theories for enhancing a relationship often include some learning theory based techniques for behavior modification and improvement such as repeated paired associations, prompting, reinforcement, rewards, and consequences.

The cognitive approach is also used to change couples' cognitions, interpretations, and ways of understanding their relationships—how couples perceive their relationship satisfaction (Zimmerman, 2000). Thus couples are provided with relationship education and are then asked to examine how these techniques work to enrich and enhance their relationships. Social learning has been found to be a good predictor of couple relationship enrichment (Chance, 2003).

Systems Theory

According to systems theory, when two individuals come together to establish an enduring relationship, they form some patterns or systems that are more complex than the two individuals apart. Communication is the most important feature of such a relationship, because a relationship is formed, changed, and maintained through communication and interaction among members (Duncan & Rock, 1993). Systems theory proposes that communication is a transactional process, which focuses more on relationships rather than on individuals (Galvin & Brommel, 2000). Components of a relationship systems are mutually dependent upon one another, and that is why each individual in a relationship impacts the other, which subsequently impacts the relationship as a whole. If the communication patterns become problematic, they can cause relationship distress (Gottman, 2014). Rules governing communication between couples are often used to prescribe and limit couples' behavior (Galvin & Brommel, 2000). Relationships are not static but dynamic. Therefore the communication system should also be dynamic to influence a relationship in a positive way (Davis, 2015).

Programs for Relationship Enrichment

Though initially relationship enrichment programs focused on premarital couples, gradually relationship enrichments have evolved and expanded to provide assistance to both premarital and married couples who need and seek relationship enrichment (Halford et al., 2003). Researchers have identified a number of common objectives of different relationship enhancement programs (Hawkins et al., 2008).

Objectives of Enrichment Programs

As reported by Davis (2015), some of the common objectives of relationship enrichment programs include:

- A positive growth for each partner in a relationship.
- A dynamic relationship between the partners who are willing to change as needed for healthy relationships.
- Enabling partners to have a willing companionship.
- An educational approach that teaches partners to develop attitudes and skills in a structured and orderly fashion.
- A preventive approach that supports couples by reducing their interpersonal dysfunctional behaviors.
- Helping couples to achieve a balance between relational and personal growth.
- Developing intimacy through nurturance.
- Developing enrichment programs as a lifespan relational growth process.
- Mutual support between couples through interpersonal and intergroup experiences.

Types of Relationship Enrichment Programs

Relationship enrichment programs first emerged in the early 1950s. Since that time different types of such programs have been developed. Some of the currently available programs in the United States are (Davis, 2015): Relationship Enhancement, Better Marriages, the Couple Communication Program, Celebrating Marriage, Getting the Love You Want, Marriage Encounter, Practical Application of Intimate Relationship Skills, Prevention and Relationship Enhancement Program, Prepare/Enrich-Growing Together Workshop, Training in Marriage Enrichment, Couple Relationship Education Program, Faith-Based Enrichment Program, and the Weekend to Remember. Among these, two major types of programs are the Couple Relationship Education Program (Halford, Markman, & Stanley, 2008) and the Faith-Based Enrichment Program (Jakubowski et al., 2004). These two programs are briefly discussed in the following sections.

Couple relationship education program. The couple relationship education program is designed to provide individuals and couples with the necessary knowledge and skills for increasing their chances of having healthy and stable relationships (Halford, Markman, & Stanley, 2008).

According to Halford and colleagues (2003), a good couple relationship education program has the following seven key features:

1. Measurement of variables related to risk for distress or divorce.
2. Encouraging high-risk couples to participate.

3. Education about relationship aggression.
4. Providing relationship education at transition points (for example, at the time of the birth of the first baby).
5. Providing relationship education before the couple relationship aggravates.
6. Adaptation of programs for couples with diverse populations.
7. Increased accessibility of couples to evidence-based relationship education.

Traditionally, relationship education services were generally limited to couples who are engaged or newly married. But relationship education should be extended to individuals and couples earlier in their relationships for helping couples build enduring and enjoyable relationships (Markman & Rhoades, 2012). Research findings suggested that almost every group that had an opportunity to participate in relationship education programs expressed high levels of interest, though there were barriers unique to each group. But the most common barrier for all couples was the participation of both partners in the program. Despite some limitations, the couple relationship education program has made substantial progress by increasing its access to high-risk and diverse populations (Stanley, 2001)

Faith-based enrichment program. Two widely used faith-based programs are Marriage Encounter and SANCTUS. Marriage Encounter is a weekend retreat program with 44 hours of structured content. In it, couples are taught these structured contents through didactic presentation, and then are provided with time alone with their spouse to reflect about these materials (Jakubowski et al., 2004). Research findings showed that Marriage Encounter effectively increased trust and overall relationship satisfaction in couples. In addition, this faith-based program significantly improved affectional expression among couples and their dyadic consensus, satisfaction, cohesion, sense of commitment, and relationship satisfaction (Jakubowski et al., 2004).

SANCTUS, another faith-based marriage enrichment program, is of Latin origin which means holly. The word is used as the beginning of a Christian hymn. This is a 48-hour weekend retreat program in which couples receive teachings and exercises to build awareness about self, spouse, and spirituality (Sager & Sager, 2005). Participation in the weekend is usually followed by couple group sessions (about five to seven) and about 40 to 50 days of couple meditations and daily exercises. Sager and Sager (2005) evaluated the success of the SANCTUS program by comparing ratings given by participants at the beginning and end of the intervention. Findings revealed that after about 12 retreats there were significant positive changes in participants' relationships with themselves, their spouse, and God, and also positive changes in their level of intimacy and commitment. In a couple studies, religiosity has been found positively associated with attendance at relationship enrichment programs (Busby et al., 2015; McAllister, Duncan, & Busby, 2013). In fact, religiosity was found to be the most predictive factor in participation in relationship enrichment than any other factors such as length of relationship, age, children, education, or minority status (Doss et al., 2009). In addition, religiosity has been found to be associated with several relationship variables, including relationship satisfaction, communication, conflict resolution, forgiveness (Ahmadi & Hossein-abadi, 2009), improved communication within the relationship (Mahoney et al., 1999), and reduced relationship conflict (Fincham et al., 2008). Some researchers suggested that a sense of purpose and value of caring are cultivated through religious teachings, which may promote relationship enhancement among those who are engaged with religion (Lambert & Dollahite, 2006). Religiosity has also been found to be associated with greater capacity for forgiveness toward one's partner (Fincham et al., 2008).

Maintenance of Intimate Relationships

Relationship maintenance is often described as behavioral dynamics that help preserve a relationship (Dindia, 2003). Maintenance behaviors are classified into two types: routine maintenance and strategic maintenance (Ogolsky & Bowers, 2013). Routine maintenance behaviors consist of everyday interactions between partners without any specific goals and strategies to maintain a relationship. Strategic maintenance behaviors, on the other hand, consist of specific goals and strategies to preserve a relationship.

Different Strategies for Relationship Maintenance

Some scholars have proposed different strategies for relationship maintenance (e.g., Ruppel & Curran, 2012; Rusbult, Agnew, & Arriaga, 2012). Some of the frequently used strategies are commitment, sacrifice, forgiveness, trust, attachment, contentment, accommodation, self-control, and professional help. These strategies have two aspects: behavioral aspect and cognitive aspect. The behavioral aspect involves changes or modifications of people's behaviors, whereas the cognitive aspect involves changes in people's attitudes, beliefs, perceptions, and judgments about themselves, their partners, and their relationships. These maintenance strategies are briefly discussed in the following pages.

Commitment

Commitment refers to a desire for the relationship to continue and the motivation to work for its maintenance (Schoebi, Karney, & Bradbury, 2012). Amato (2007) reported that commitment is an important factor contributing to intimate relationship satisfaction and maintenance. Rusbult and colleagues (2006) have proposed an important model of commitment, which is known as the *investment model*. According to this model, people tend to stay with their present partners, if they are happy, find no better alternative, and if the present relationship does not cost too much. Research evidence supports the assumptions of the investment model (Le et al., 2010). The model has been found to be equally applicable to heterosexual and homosexual couples in Eastern as well as Western cultures (Kurdek, 2008). Some researchers argue that based on different sources, commitment can take three different forms, such as *personal commitment, constraint commitment,* and *moral commitment* (Rhoades, Stanley, & Markman, 2010). In personal commitment people tend to continue the relationship because their partner is attractive to them and they are happy with the relationship. Contrarily, in constraint commitment people feel that they should continue with the relationship because leaving it will be too costly for them. In moral commitment people feel that they have a moral obligation to keep their promise of staying with the relationship, and breaking the promise will be improper. People who believe in committed marital relationship feel that marriage is a solemn social relationship and couples have a religious responsibility to stay married under any circumstances (Stafford, David, & McPherson, 2014). Although personal commitment often has the strongest influence on relationship maintenance, the other two types of commitments may also be equally or even more influential depending on certain conditions (Rhoades, Stanley, & Markman, 2012). Despite differences in the nature and forms, commitments significantly affect the satisfaction and maintenance of intimate relationships (Rusbult, Agnew, & Arriaga, 2012). Although commitment has positive correlations with relationship maintenance and happiness, staying in an unhappy relationship does not necessarily imply commitment to it (Amato, 2007).

Sacrifice

Sacrifice serves a positive function as it indicates commitment in relationships. Generally, sacrifices are made for loved ones and not for strangers. Sacrificing one's interest when it is in conflict with the partner's interest is considered an important step in resolving conflict in an intimate relationship (Parker & Pattenden, 2009). Acts of sacrifice can vary in forms and magnitudes, such as a minor sacrifice (for example, watching a movie that your partner likes but you don't like) or a major sacrifice (for example, agreeing to buy a house that you don't like but your partner likes). An act of sacrifice may apparently seem to be unpleasant, but in reality it may help make the relationship pleasant. It can also be a way of understanding and dedication for love (Alley, 2015). The willingness to make sacrifices for the partner have been found to impact the quality of couple relationships in many different ways, including a higher level of commitment to the relationship, higher relationship satisfaction, and greater investment in the relationship (Impett et al., 2013; Parker & Pattenden, 2009).

Although sacrifice has some beneficial effects on intimate relationships, its downside has also been noted, particularly for women in relation to depression (Impett, Gable, & Peplau, 2005). In some cases, sacrificing too much for the partner or the relationship is likely to be harmful both for the individual as well as for the relationship (Gere et al., 2011). Research evidence suggests that there is a point beyond which sacrifice has little or no positive effects, but rather has negative consequences. The relationship between sacrifice and relationship functioning tends to be curvilinear, generating positive effects at a moderate level and negative effects at a very high level (Whitton, Stanley, & Markman, 2002). According to Whitton, Stanley, and Markman (2007), sacrifice might be good or bad for an individual or for the relationship depending on the individual's perception of it. If a sacrifice is seen as an act that benefits the couple's relationship, its effects are likely to be positive. But if it is perceived as a loss to the individual with no benefit to the relationship, its effects are likely to be negative (Whitton, Stanley, & Markman, 2007). Furthermore, dissatisfaction is likely to occur, if sacrifices are not reciprocated, and when one partner perceives that she/he is making unfair sacrifices—more than her/his fair share (Whitton, Stanley, & Markman, 2002).

People who are committed to repair and maintain their intimate relationships tend to display readiness to sacrifice their self-interests for their partners' satisfaction and healthy relationships (Totenhagen et al., 2013). However, sacrifice per se does not help relationships without specific goals that people pursue to improve the quality of their intimate relationships (Impett et al., 2013). Research exploring approach and avoidance perspectives has shown that the highest benefit of sacrifice is obtained when individuals sacrifice their interests for approach goals, such as to please their partners or to improve intimacy in their relationships; than for avoidance goals, such as to avoid disappointment of their partners or to avoid conflict in their relationships (Impett, Gable, & Peplau, 2005). Impett et al. (2013) also found that when people sacrifice in pursuit of approach goals, both the giver and the receiver experience more positive emotions—more joy and delight that contribute to increase relationship satisfaction. Contrarily, when people sacrifice in pursuit of avoidance goals, both partners experience more negative emotions—more anger, frustration, and resentment that contribute to lower the quality of relationships.

Trust

Trust is a useful strategy to reduce uncertainty and increase stability in romantic relationships (Dainton & Aylor, 2001). But it takes time to build trust in an intimate relationship. It can be built gradually through interactions. Deception and infidelity can lower the level of trust between partners (Shuang Xia, 2013). An individual can know whether his/her partner is trustworthy, honest, and reliable from the past experiences with the partner in a romantic relationship. Some researchers proposed a model of building trust in intimate relationships (Rempel, Holmes, & Zanna, 1985). According to these and some other authors, the foundation of trust depends on three components: predictability, dependability, and faith (Simpson, 2007b). In order to rebuild trust in relationships, people have to find ways to reduce distrust. Lewicki and Wiethoff (2000) proposed five steps to rebuild trust after it is damaged by deception. These steps are (1) addressing the behaviors that created distrust, (2) the partner who violated the trust should apologize, (3) they should negotiate the expectations of each other and agree to the terms, (4) establish evaluation procedures acceptable to both partners, and (5) find alternative ways to get needs met. Researchers have suggested that trust and commitment are essential for repairing and maintaining intimate relationships (Ostrom & Walker, 2003).

Forgiveness

Research findings indicate that forgiveness is a critical element for repairing a damaged relationship and enriching marital satisfaction and stability (Harris & Thoreson, 2005). Without forgiveness, grievances of prior hurtful behaviors may impact negatively on couples' efforts to resolve subsequent problems (Fincham, Beach, & Davila, 2004). Forgiveness does not mean acceptance of a transgression because the hurtful behavior is still seen as wrong (Fincham, Hall, & Beach, 2006). It is also not the same as forgetting or denying the transgression (Fincham, Hall, & Beach, 2006). The main purpose of forgiveness is reconciliation for continuing a relationship. But forgiveness of a hurtful behavior does not always prevent the ultimate termination of a relationship (Fincham, Hall, & Beach, 2006).

Researchers increasingly view forgiveness as a process in which an individual becomes less motivated and more inhibited to think, feel, and act negatively about someone who has inflicted an interpersonal injury (Fincham, Hall, & Beach, 2006). Some researchers suggest that forgiveness helps to overcome distrust among partners and strengthen the relationship (Gordon, Baucom, & Snyder, 2005). Findings of research by Fincham, Beach, and Davila (2004) revealed that forgiveness has three dimensions: (1) benevolence (goodwill toward the partner), (2) avoidance of retaliation (revenge or harm to the partner), and (3) avoidance of contact (avoiding physical and/or psychological contact with the partner). All three dimensions were found associated with conflict resolution in couples in both relatively new and more established marital relationships (Parker & Pattenden, 2009).

Infidelity and Forgiveness

Among all the problems that affect intimate relationships, deception is a common problem. Guthrie and Kunkel (2013) found that the discovery of deception, especially infidelity, could cause severe damage to a relationship resulting in ultimate termination of it. Another study showed that infidelity is the most hurtful and has the strongest negative effect on close relationships (Feeney, 2004). The more severe the infidelity, the more difficult it is for the betrayed partner to forgive it (Bachman & Guerrero, 2006; Malachowski & Frisby, 2015). The worst part of infidelity is whether betrayed partners are willing to forgive their unfaithful partners. If a partner does not forgive his or her partner, the damage is likely to be permanent and harder to repair. When deceived partners forgive their infidel partners, the relationship may survive and they are more likely to move on in their relationships. Nonetheless, in most cases, the quality of the relationships may not be the same. Bachman and Guerrero (2006) found that hurt partners were more likely to forgive their deceiver partners when they apologize sincerely and accept responsibility for their mistake.

Attachment

People's attachment styles have profound impacts on their interpersonal relationships and maintenance strategies (Simpson et al., 2007). Stackert and Bursik (2003) found associations between people's differences in attachment styles and irrational beliefs in romantic relationships. For example, insecure romantic partners have significantly more irrational beliefs about relationship-specific issues than secure partners (Stackert & Bursik, 2003). Jang, Sandi, and Timothy (2002) viewed that people's attachment styles are critically important to understand why some people terminate their relationships and some do not when they find their partners deceived them. Jang (2008) indicated attachment tendency had an impact on the way people interacted in relationships after discovering deception from their partners. Moreover, people with different attachment styles like to use different maintenance strategies in their intimate relationships (Shuang Xia, 2013). For example, people with secure attachment are more able than the people with insecure attachment to trust, accept, and support their partners, despite the partners' mistakes (Fraley & Shaver, 2000). Furthermore, unlike insecure partners, secure partners' positive attitudes toward the relationship help them deal with hurtful events more confidently and successfully, and their relationships tend to last longer and are less likely to end in separation or divorce (Shuang Xia, 2013).

Contentment

Contentment is a powerful predictor of stability in intimate relationships (Canary, Stafford, & Semic, 2002). Contented partners are likely to foster positive valence in the relationship, such as assurances, understanding, and feelings of sharing, caring, inclusiveness, and empathy between the partners (Canary & Dainton, 2006). However, the beneficial effects of positive behaviors of contented partners for relationship maintenance can be short-lived unless such behaviors are routinely continued by both partners (Kammrath & Peetz, 2011).

Accommodation and Self-Control

In intimate relationships, accommodation refers to a process of self-control in which an individual tries to inhibit tendencies to react destructively, and instead tends to behave constructively in response to a partner's provocative and aggressive behavior (Finkel & Campbell, 2001). According to Finkel and Campbell (2001), accommodation is a two-stage process through which individuals first inhibit their destructive tendencies and then get involved in constructive behavior. Studies found an association between dispositional self-control and accommodative tendencies in ongoing intimate relationships (Englert, Bertrams, & Dickhäuser, 2011; Finkel & Campbell, 2001). Accommodation minimizes the chances of recurring conflict, bitterness, and quarrels among intimate partners through conscious efforts to protect and preserve intimate relationships (Hafner & Ijzerman, 2011).

Other Strategies

In addition to the strategies discussed previously, Canary, Stafford, and Semic (2002) identified a few other maintenance strategies. These strategies are positivity, openness, assurances, social networks, and sharing tasks. According to those strategies, positivity means optimism, cheerfulness, and avoidance of criticism. Openness refers to direct communication and sharing of feelings about the relationship. Assurance includes expressions of love and commitment. Social networks and sharing refer to the expansion of interconnection through involvement of friends and family members in activities. These strategies have been found to have positive effects on relationship protection and maintenance (Stafford, 2003). Furthermore, Canary and Stafford (2001) reported several strategies for relationship maintenance including communication, prosocial behavior, togetherness, autonomy seeking or granting, and seeking outside assistance. Research also indicated that couples who have been married for a long time reported the use of fewer maintenance and repair strategies than do couples who have been married for a relatively shorter duration (Dindia & Emmers-Sommer, 2006). As time goes by, the relationship between couples becomes more stable and partners know more about each other and learn about the right strategy for maintaining their relationship (Dainton, 2008; Dainton & Aylor, 2002).

Professional Assistance

Finally, if and when the relationship maintenance strategies discussed previously do not work, couples should seek professional help, including expert counseling, marital and nonmarital couple therapies, such as behavioral couple therapy, cognitive-behavioral couple therapy, integrative-behavioral couple therapy, emotionally focused couple therapy, insight-oriented couple therapy, and so on. Decisions about the right type of therapy should be taken by the therapeutic professionals in consultation with the concerned couples. Again, the decision of seeking professional assistance will depend on the willingness and agreement of the partners.

CHAPTER SUMMARY

Chapter 16 explains techniques for repairing intimate relationships; enrichment of intimate relationships; theories and models of relationship enrichment; programs for relationship enrichment; objectives of relationship enrichment programs; different types of relationship enrichment programs; effectiveness of these programs; strategies for maintaining intimate relationships including commitment, sacrifice, trust, forgiveness, accommodation, and self-control; and professional assistance.

Repairing intimate relationships. Techniques for repairing intimate relationships include selecting a right time, specific and reasonable change, dealing with one issue at a time, listening empathetically, reflecting and exploring in-depth, exploring options, and using objective criteria.

Enrichment of intimate relationships. This enrichment refers to a process of improving the quality of intimate relationships to make them enjoyable, healthy, and stable.

Theories of relationship enrichment. Relationship enrichment is an integrative approach that is drawn from a number of theoretical perspectives including psychodynamic, interpersonal, client-centered, behavioral, and social learning systems theory.

Types of relationship enrichment programs. Since the early 1950s a variety of enrichment programs have been developed including Relationship Enhancement, Better Marriages, the Couple Communication Program, Celebrating Marriage, Getting the Love You Want, Marriage Encounter, Practical Application of Intimate Relationship Skills, Prevention and Relationship Enhancement Program, Prepare/Enrich-Growing Together Workshop, Training in Marriage Enrichment, Couple Relationship Education Program, Faith-Based Enrichment Program, and the Weekend to Remember.

Maintenance of intimate relationships. Relationship maintenance is often described as behavioral dynamics that help preserve a relationship. Maintenance behaviors are of two types: routine maintenance and strategic maintenance. Routine maintenance behaviors consist of everyday interactions between partners without any specific goals and strategies to maintain a relationship. Strategic maintenance behaviors consist of specific goals and strategies to preserve a relationship.

Different strategies for relationship maintenance. Some of the frequently used strategies are commitment, sacrifice, forgiveness, trust, attachment, contentment, accommodation, self-control, and professional help.

REFLECTIVE QUESTIONS

1. Discuss different techniques or strategies for repairing intimate relationships.

2. How can intimate relationships be enriched? Discuss different models of relationship enrichment.

3. Discuss different types of relationship enrichment programs. What are the common objectives of these programs?

4. How can intimate relationships be maintained? Differentiate between routine maintenance and strategic maintenance.

5. Critically discuss different strategies for intimate relationship maintenance.

References

ABC News (2004). *The American sex survey: A peek beneath the sheets.* ABC News primetime live poll, October 21.

Acevedo, B., & Aron, A. (2009). Does a long-term relationship kill romantic love? *Review of General Psychology, 13,* 59–65.

Adams, J. S. (1965). Inequity in social exchange. In B. Leonard (Ed.), *Advances in experimental social psychology* (Vol. 2, pp. 267–299). New York: Academic Press.

Adams, R. G., & Blieszner, R. (1994). An integrative conceptual framework for friendship research. *Journal of Social and Personal Relationships, 11,* 163–184.

Adams, R. G., Blieszner, R., & De Vries, B. (2000). Definitions of friendship in the third age: Age, gender, and study location effects. *Journal of Aging Studies, 14,* 117–133.

Afifi, W. A., & Faulkner, S. L. (2000). On being 'just friends': The frequency and impact of sexual activity in cross-sex friendships. *Journal of Social and Personal Relationships, 17*(2), 205–222.

Ahmadi, K., & Hossein-abadi, F. H. (2009). Religiosity, marital satisfaction and child rearing. *Pastoral Psychology, 57*(5–6), 211–221. doi:org/10.1007/s11089-008-0176-4

Ahmed, R. A. (2008). Review of Arab research on parental acceptance-rejection. In F. Erkman (Ed.), *Acceptance: The essence of peace. Selected papers from the first international congress on interpersonal acceptance and rejection* (pp. 201–224). Istanbul: Turkish Psychology Association.

Ahmed, R. A., Rohner, R. P., & Carrasco, M. A. (2012). Relations between psychological adjustment and perceived parental, sibling, best friend, and teacher acceptance among Kuwaiti adolescents. In K. J. Ripoll, A. L. Comunian, & C. M. Brown (Eds.), *Expanding horizons: Current research on interpersonal acceptance* (1–10). Boca Raton, FL: Brown Walker Press.

Ahmetoglu, G., Swami, V., & Chamorro-Premuzic, T. (2010). The relationship between dimensions of love, personality, and relationship length. *Archive of Sex Behavior, 39,* 1181–1190. doi:10.1007/s10508-009-9515-5

Ainsworth, M. (1989). Attachment beyond infancy. *American Psychologist, 44*, 709–716.

Ainsworth, M. (1991). Attachment and other affectional bonds across the life cycle. In C. M. Parkes, J. Stevenson-Hinde, & P. Marris (Eds.), *Attachment across the life cycle* (pp. 33–51). New York: Routledge.

Ainsworth, M. D. S. (1973). The development of infant mother attachment. In B. Caldwell & H. Ricciuti (Eds.), *Review of child development research* (Vol. 3, pp. 1–94). Chicago: University of Chicago Press.

Ainsworth, M. D. S. (1990). Some considerations regarding theory and assessment relevant to attachment and beyond. In M. T. Greenberg, D. Ciechetti, & E. M. Cummings (Eds.), *Attachment in the preschool years* (pp. 463–489). Chicago: University of Chicago Press.

Ainsworth, M. D. S., & Bowlby, J. (1991). An ethological approach to personality development. *American Psychologist, 46*, 331–341.

Ainsworth, M. S., Blehar, M. C., Waters, E., & Wall, S. (1978). *Patterns of attachment: Assessed in the strange situation and at home.* Hillsdale, NJ: Erlbaum.

Ajdukovic, M. (1990). Differences in parent's rearing style between female and male predelinquent and delinquent youth (abstract). *Psychologische Beitrage, 32*(1–2), 7–15.

Ajzen, I., & Fishbein, M. (1980). *Understanding attitudes and predicting social behavior.* Englewood Cliffs, NJ: Prentice Hall.

Alan Guttmacher Institute. (1994). *Sex and America's teenagers.* New York: Author.

Alan Guttmacher Institute. (1999). *Facts in brief: Teen sex and pregnancy.* Retrieved from www.agi-usa-org/pubs/1b_teen_sex.html

Albuquerque, I. L., Matos, M., & Figueiredo, C. (2013). The interplay among levels of personality: The mediator effect of personal projects between the big five and subjective well-being. *Journal of Happiness Studies, 14*(1), 235–250. doi:10.1007/s10902-012-9326-6

Al-Falaij, A. (1991). *Family conditions, ego development and socio-moral development in juvenile delinquency: A study of Bahraini adolescents.* Unpublished doctoral dissertation, University of Pittsburgh, PA.

Ali, S., Khaleque, A., & Rohner, R. P. (2013). Influence of perceived teacher acceptance and parental acceptance on youth's psychological adjustment and school conduct: A cross-cultural meta-analysis. *Cross-Cultural Research, 47*, 1–14.

Ali, S., Khaleque, A., & Rohner, R. P. (2015). Pancultural gender differences in the relation between perceived parental acceptance and psychological adjustment of children and adult offspring: A meta-analytic review of worldwide research. *Journal of Cross-Cultural Psychology, 46*, 1059–1080.

Ali, S., Khatun, M. N., Khaleque, A., & Rohner, R. P. (2017). *They love me not: A meta-analysis of pancultural relationship between perceived parental undifferentiated rejection and offspring's psychological maladjustment.* Unpublished manuscript, Ronald and Nancy Rohner Center for the Study of Interpersonal Acceptance and Rejection, University of Connecticut, Storrs.

Alley, L. M. (2015). *Exploring dietary sacrifice in intimate relationships for couples with celiac disease.* Unpublished master's degree thesis in psychology, Portland State University, Portland, OR.

Allison, R., & Risman, R. B. (2013). A double standard for "hooking up": How far have we come toward gender equality? *Social Science Research, 42,* 1191–1206.

Amato, P. (2007). Transformative processes in marriage: Some thoughts from a sociologist. *Journal of Marriage and Family, 69,* 305–309.

Amato, P. R. (2000). The consequences of divorce for adults and children. *Journal of Marriage and the Family, 62,* 1269–1287.

Amato, P. R., & Afifi, T. D. (2006). Feeling caught between parents: Adult children's relations with parents and subjective well-being. *Journal of Marriage and Family, 68*(1), 222–231.

Amato, P. R., Booth, A., Johnson, D. R., & Rogers, S. J. (2007). *Alone together: How marriage in America is changing.* Cambridge, MA: Harvard University Press.

Amato, P. R., & Hohmann-Marriott, B. (2007). A comparison of high and low-distress marriages that end in divorce. *Journal of Marriage and Family, 69,* 621–638.

Amato, P. R., & Maynard, R. A. (2007). Decreasing nonmarital births and strengthening marriage to reduce poverty. *Future of Children, 17,* 117–141.

Amato, P. R., & Previti, D. (2003). People's reasons for divorcing: Gender, social class, the life course, and adjustment. *Journal of Family Issues, 24,* 602–626.

Ambrose, M. L., & Kulik, C. T. (1999). Old friends, new faces: Motivation research in the 1990s. *Journal of Management, 25,* 142–175.

American Association of Retired Persons (AARP). (2004). *The divorce experience: A study of divorce at midlife and beyond.* Washington, DC: Author.

American Psychological Association. (2004). *An overview of the psychological literature on the effects of divorce on children.* Washington DC: Public Policy Office, APA.

Anderson, J. L., Crawford, C. B., Nadeau, J., & Lindberg, T. (1992). Was the Duchess of Winsor right? A cross-cultural review of the socioecology of ideals of female body shape. *Ethology and Sociobiology, 13*(3), 197–227.

Anderson, K. J., & Leaper, C. (1998). Meta-analyses of gender effects on conversational interruption: Who, when, where, and how. *Sex Roles, 39,* 225–252.

Anderson, S. A., & Sabatelli, R. M. (2011). *Family interaction: A multigenerational developmental perspective* (5th ed.). Boston: Allyn & Bacon.

Anderssen, N., Amlie, C., & Ytteroy, E. A. (2002). Outcomes for children with lesbian or gay parents: A review of studies from 1978 to 2000. *Scandinavian Journal of Psychology, 43,* 335–351.

Andersson, G., Noack, T., Seierstad, A., & Weedon-Fekjaer, H. (2006). The demographics of same-sex marriages in Norway and Sweden. *Demography, 43,* 79–98.

Antonucci, T. C. (1994). A life-span view of women's social relations. In B. F. Turner & L. E. Troll (Eds.), Women growing older (pp. 239–269). Thousand Oaks, CA: Sage.

Antonucci, T. C., Ajrouch, K., & Birditt, K. S. (2014). The convoy model: Explaining social relations from a multidisciplinary perspective. *Gerontologist,* 54(1), 82–92. doi:https://doi.org/10.1093/geront/gnt118

Antonucci, T. C., Akiyama, M., & Merline, A. (2001). Dynamics of social relationships in midlife. In M. E. Lachman (Ed.), *Handbook of midlife development* (pp. 571–598). New York: Wiley.

Antonucci, T. C., Akiyama, M., & Takahashi, K. (2004). Attachment and close relationships across the life span. *Attachment & Human Development, 6*(4), 353–370.

Antonucci, T. C., Birditt, K. S., & Ajrouch, K. (2011). Convoys of social relations: Past, present, and future. In K. L. Fingerman, C. A. Berg, J. Smith, & T. C. Antonucci (Eds.), *Handbook of lifespan development* (pp. 161–182). New York: Springer.

Antonucci, T. C., Fiori, K. L., Birditt, K. S., & Jackey, L. M. H. (2010). Convoys of social relations: Integrating life-span and life-course perspectives. In A. F. Freund, M. L. Lamb, & R. M. Lerner (Eds.), *Handbook of lifespan development.* Hoboken, NJ: Wiley.

Antonucci, T. C., Lansford, J. E., & Akiyama, H. (2001). Impact of positive and negative aspects of marital relationships and friendships on well-being of older adults. *Applied Developmental Science, 5,* 68–75.

Archer, J. (2000). Sex differences in aggression between heterosexual partners: A meta-analytic review. *Psychological Bulletin, 126*(5), 651–680.

Argyle, M., & Henderson, M. (1984). Friendship across the life span. *Journal of Social and Personal Relationships,* 1(2), 211–237.

Argyle, M., Henderson, M., & Furnham, A. (1985). The rules of social relationships. *British Journal of Social Psychology,* 24, 125–139.

Armsden, G. C., & Greenberg, M. T. (1987). The Inventory of Parent and Peer Attachment: Relationships to well-being in adolescence. *Journal of Youth and Adolescence,* 16, 427–454.

Arndorfer, C. L., & Stormahak, E. A. (2008). Same-sex versus other-sex best friendship in early adolescence: Longitudinal predictors of antisocial behavior throughout adolescence. *Journal of Youth and Adolescence, 37*(9), 1059–1070.

Arnett, J. J. (2010). *Adolescence and emerging adulthood: A cultural approach.* Boston: Prentice Hall.

Aron, A., Fisher, H., & Strong, G. (2007). Romantic love. In R. Baumeister & K. Vohs (Eds.), *Encyclopedia of social psychology.* Thousand Oaks, CA: Sage.

Arriaga, X. B. (2001). The ups and downs of dating: Fluctuations in satisfaction in newly formed romantic relationships. *Journal of Personality and Social Psychology, 80,* 754–765.

Arriaga, X. B., Reed, J. T., Goodfriend, W., & Agnew, C. R. (2006). Relationship perceptions and persistence: Do fluctuations in perceived partner commitment undermine dating relationships? *Journal of Personality and Social Psychology, 91,* 1045–1065.

Asadi, Z. S., Sadeghi, R., Taghdisi, M. H., Zamani-Alavijeh, F., Shojaeizadeh, D., & Khoshdel, A. R. (2016). Sources, outcomes, and resolution of conflicts in marriage among Iranian women: A qualitative study. *Electronic Physician, 8*(3), 2057–2065.

Atkins, D. C., Baucom, D. H, & Jacobson, N. S. (2001). Understanding infidelity: Correlates in a national random sample. *Journal of Family Psychology, 15*(4), 735–749.

Aube, J., & Koestner, R. (1995). Gender characteristics and relationship adjustment: Another look at similarity complementarity hypothesis. *Journal of Personality, 63*(4), 879–904.

Aube, J., Norcliffe, H., Craig, J., & Koestner, R. (1995). Gender characteristics and adjustment related outcomes. Questioning the masculinity model. *Personality and Social Psychology Bulletin, 21,* 284–295.

Augsburger, D. (1988). *Sustaining love.* Scottsdale, AZ: Regal Publishing.

Bachman, G. F., & Guerrero, L. K. (2006). Relational quality and communicative responses following hurtful events in dating relationships: An expectancy violations analysis. *Journal of Social and Personal Relationships, 23,* 943–963. doi:10.1177/0265407506070476

Bagwell, C. L., Bender, S. E., Andreassi, C. L., Kinoshita, T. L., Montarello, S. A., & Muller, J. G. (2005). Friendship quality and perceived relationship changes predict psychosocial adjustment in early adulthood. *Journal of Social and Personal Relationships, 22*(2), 235–254.

Baird, A. A. (2010). The terrible twelves. In P. D. Zelazo, M. Chandler, & E. Crone (Eds.), *Developmental social cognitive neuroscience* (pp. 191–207). New York: Psychology Press.

Baldwin, A., Dodge, B., Schick, V., Hubach, R. D., Bowling, J., Malebranche, D., Goncalves, G., Schnarrs, P. W., Reece, M., & Fortenberry, J. D. (2015). Sexual self-identification among behaviorally bisexual men in the Midwestern United States. *Archives of Sexual Behavior, 44*(7), 2015–2026.

Baldwin, M. W. (1992). Relational schemas and the processing of social information. *Psychological Bulletin, 112,* 461–484.

Balthazart, J. (2011a). Minireview: Hormones and human sexual orientation. *Endocrinology, 152*(8): 2937–2947.

Balthazart, J. (2011b). *Biology of homosexuality.* New York: Oxford University Press.

Balzarini, R., Aron, A., & Chelberg, M. (2014). *Examining definition of a romantic relationship with a prototype analysis.* Poster presented at the meeting of the Society for Personality and Social Psychology, Austin, TX.

Bancroft, J., Graham, C. A., Janssen, E., & Sanders, S. A. (2009). The dual control model: Current status and future directions. *Journal of Sex Research, 46,* 121–142.

Bao, A. M., & Swaab, D. F. (2011). Sexual differentiation of the human brain: Relation to gender identity, sexual orientation and neuropsychiatric disorders. *Front Neuroendocrinology, 32,* 214–226.

Barber, B. K. (1996). Parental psychological control: Revisiting a neglected construct. *Child Development, 67,* 3296–3319.

Barber, N. (1998). Secular changes in standards of bodily attractiveness in women: Tests of a reproductive model. *International Journal of Eating Disorders, 23,* 449–454.

Barelds, D. P. H. (2005). Self and partner personality in intimate relationships. *European Journal of Personality, 19,* 501–518.

Barnes, L. L., De Leon Carlos, F. M., Wilson, R. S., Bienias, J. L., Bennett, D. A., & Evans, D. A. (2004). Racial differences in perceived discrimination in a community population of older Blacks and Whites. *Journal of Aging and Health, 16,* 315–337.

Bartels, A., & Zeki, S. (2000). The neural basis of romantic love. *Neuro Report: For Rapid Communication of Neuroscience Research, 11*(17), 3829–3834.

Bartels, A., & Zeki, S. (2004). The neural correlates of maternal and romantic love. *Neuro Image, 21*(3), 1155–1166.

Barth, R. J., & Kinder, B. N. (1988). A theoretical analysis of sex differences in the same-sex friendships. *Sex Roles, 19,* 349–364.

Bartholomew, K., & Shaver, P. R. (1998). Methods of assessing adult attachment: Do they converge? In J. A. Simpson & W. S. Rholes (Eds.), *Attachment theory and close relationships* (pp. 25–45). New York: The Guilford Press.

Barrett, H., & Tasker, F. (2001). Growing up with a gay parent: Views of 101 gay fathers on their sons' and daughters' experiences. *Educational and Child Psychology, 18,* 62–77.

Bartlett, T. (2013). Does familiarity breed contempt or fondness? *The Chronicle of Higher Education,* January 9, comments (11).

Basset-Jones, N., & Lloyd, G. C. (2005). Does Herzberg's motivational theory have staying power? *Journal of Management Development, 24,* 57–56.

Batool, S., & Najam, N. (2009). *Relationship between perceived parenting style, perceived parental acceptance-rejection (PAR) and perception of God among young adults.* Quaide-azam University, Islamabad, Pakistan.

Baumeister, R. F., & Leary, M. R. (1995). The need to belong: Desire for interpersonal attachments as a fundamental human motivation. *Psychological Bulletin, 117,* 497–529.

Becker, J. B., Berkley, K. J., Geary, N., Hampson, E., Herman, J. P., & Young, E. A. (2008). *Sex differences in the brain: From genes to behavior.* Oxford, UK: Oxford University Press.

Becker, O. A., & Lois, D. (2010). Selection, alignment, and their interplay: Origins of lifestyle homogamy in couple relationships. *Journal of Marriage and Family, 72,* 1234–1248.

Bell, R. R. (1981). Friendships of women and men. *Psychology of Women Quarterly, 5,* 402–417.

Bell, S. M., & Ainsworth, M. D. (1972). Infant crying and maternal responsiveness. *Child Development, 43,* 1171–1190.

Belsky, J. (2006). Developmental origins of attachment styles. *Attachment and Human Behavior, 4,* 166–170.

Bem, S. L. (1985). Androgyny and gender schema theory: A conceptual and empirical investigation. In T. B. Sondregger (Ed.), *Nebraska Symposium on Motivation, 1985: Psychology and gender.* Lincoln: University of Nebraska Press.

Bem, S. L. (1993). *The lenses of gender: Transforming the debate on sexual inequality.* New Haven, CT: Yale University Press.

Benson, A., Silverstein, L. B., & Auerbach, C. F. (2005). Gay fathers reconstructing the fathering role. *Journal of GLBT Family Studies, 1,* 1–29.

Benson, H. (2009). *Married and unmarried family breakdown: Key statistics explained.* Bristol, UK: Bristol Community Family Trust.

Berg, C. A., Wiebe, D. J., Butner, J., Bloor, L., Bradstreet, C., Upchurch, R., Hayes, J., Stephenson, R., Nail, L., & Patton, G. (2008). Collaborative coping and daily mood in couples dealing with prostate cancer. *Psychology and Aging, 23,* 505–516.

Berk, L., & Roberts, W. (2009). *Child development* (3rd Canadian ed.). Toronto: Pearson Allyn and Bacon.

Berlin, L. J., Cassidy, J., & Appleyard, K. (2008). The influence of early attachment on other relationships. In J. Cassidy & P. Shaver (Eds.), *Handbook of adult attachment: Theory, research and clinical applications* (2nd ed., pp. 333–347). New York: The Guilford Press.

Berndt, T. J. (1996). Transitions in friendship and friends' influence. In J. A. Graber, J. Brooks-Gunn, & A. C. Petersen (Eds.), *Transitions through adolescence: Interpersonal domain and context* (pp. 57–84). Hillsdale, NJ: Erlbaum.

Berndt, T. J., Hawkins, J. A., & Jiao, Z. (1999). Influences of friends and friendships on adjustment to junior high school. *Merrill-Palmer Quarterly, 45,* 13–41.

Berscheid, E., Snyder, M., & Omoto, A. M. (2004). Measuring closeness: The relationship closeness inventory revisited. In D. J. Mashek & A. Aron (Eds.), *Handbook of closeness and intimacy* (pp. 81–101), Mahwah, NJ: Erlbaum.

Biblarz, T. J., & Savci, E. (2010). Lesbian, gay, bisexual, and transgender families. *Journal of Marriage and Family, 72*(3), 480–497.

Bigelow, B. J., & La Gaipa, J. J. (1980). *The development of friendship values and choice.* In H. C. Foot, A. J. Chapman, & J. R. Smith (Eds.), *Friendship and social relations in children* (pp. 15–44). New York: Wiley.

Bigelow, B. J., Tesson, G., & Lewko, J. H. (1996). *Learning the rules: The anatomy of children's relationships.* London: Guilfors Press.

Bindley, K. (2011). Marriage rates: Divorce fears to blame for low rates? *Huffington Post.* Retrieved from http://www.huffingtonpost.com/2011/12/22 /marriage-rates-divorce-fears_n_1163811

Birditt, K. S., Brown, E., Orbuch, T. L., & McIlvane, J. M. (2010a). Marital conflict behaviors and implications for divorce over 16 years. *Journal of Marriage and Family, 72(5),* 1188–1204. doi:10.1111/j.1741-3737.2010.00758.x

Birditt, K. S., Brown, E., Orbuch, T. L., & McIlvane, J. M. (2010b). Marital conflict behaviors and implications for divorce over 10 years. *Research in Human Development, 9,* 126–144.

Birnbaum, G. E., Cohen, O., & Wertheimer, V. (2007). Is it all about sexual intimacy? Age, menopausal status, and women's sexuality. *Personal Relationships, 14,* 167–185.

Black, R. M. (2011). Cultural considerations of hand use. *Journal of Hand Therapy, 24(2),* 104–111. doi:10.1016/j.jht.2010.09.067

Blackman, A. (2014, November 10). Can money buy you happiness? *The Wall Street Journal Reports: Wealth Management.* Reports@wsj.com.

Blackwell, D. L., & Lichter, D. T. (2004). Homogamy among dating, cohabiting, and married couples. *Sociological Quarterly, 45,* 719–737.

Blau, P. (1964). *Exchange and power in social life.* New York: Wiley.

Bleske, A. L., & Buss, D. M. (2000). Can men and women be just friends? *Personal Relationships, 7(2),* 131–151.

Blieszner, R. (1995). Friendship processes and well-being in later years of life: Implications for interventions. *Journal of Geriatric Psychiatry, 28,* 165–183.

Bloch, L., Haase, C. M., & Levenson, R. W. (2014). Emotion regulation predicts marital satisfaction: More than a wife's tale. *Emotion, 14,* 130–144.

Bloom, B. L., Asher, S. J., & White, S. W. (1978). Marital disruption as a stressor: A review and analysis. *Psychological Bulletin, 85,* 867–894.

Blumstein, P., & Schwartz, P. (2008). *American couples: Money, work, sex.* New York: William Morrow.

Bodenmann, G., Atkins, D. C., Schär, M., & Poffet, V. (2010). The association between daily stress and sexual activity. *Journal of Family Psychology, 24(3),* 271–279. doi:10.1037/a0019365

Boerner, K., Jopp, D. S., Carr, D., Sosinsky, L., & Kim, S. (2014). "His" and "her" marriage? The role of positive and negative marital characteristics in global marital satisfaction among older adults. *The Journals of Gerontology Series B: Psychological Sciences and Social Sciences, 69(4),* 579–589. doi:10.1093/geronb/gbu032

Bogart, L., Elliott, M. N., Klein, D. J., Tortolero, S. R., Murg, S., Peskin, M. F., & Schuster, M. A. (2014). Peer victimization in fifth grade and health in tenth grade. *Pediatrics, 133,* 440–447.

Bono, J. E., Boles, T. L., Judge, T. A., & Lauver, K. J. (2002). The role of personality in task and relationship conflict. *Journal of Personality, 70(3),* 311–344.

Bookwala, J. (2005). The role of marital quality in physical health during the mature years. *Journal of Aging and Health, 17(1),* 85–104.

Bookwala, J. (2012). Marriage and other partnered relationships in middle and late adulthood. In R. Blieszner & V. H. Bedford (Eds.), *Handbook of families and aging* (2nd ed., pp. 91–123). Santa Barbara, CA: Praeger.

Bookwala, J., & Franks, M. M. (2005). The moderating role of marital quality in older adults' depressed affect: Beyond the 'main effects' model. *Journal of Gerontology: Psychological Sciences, 60,* 338–441.

Bookwala, J., & Jacobs, J. (2004). Age, marital processes, and depressed affect. The *Gerontologist, 44,* 328–338.

Boone, T. L., & Lefkowitz, E. S. (2004). Safer sex and the health belief model. *Journal of Psychology & Human Sexuality, 16*(1), 51–68. doi:10.1300/J056v16n01_04

Booth, A., Brown, L. S., Landale, N. S., Manning, W. D., & McHale, S. M. (2012). *Early adulthood in a family context.* New York: Springer.

Borneskog, C., Svanberg, A. S., Lampic, C., & Sydsjö, G. (2012). Relationship quality in lesbian and heterosexual couples undergoing treatment with assisted reproduction. *Human Reproduction, 27*(3), 779–786.

Bos, H. M. W., & van Balen, F. (2008). Children in planned lesbian families: Stigmatisation, psychological adjustment and protective factors. *Culture, Health and Sexuality, 10,* 221–236.

Bos, H. M. W., van Balen, F., Sandfort, T. G. M., & van den Boom, D. C. (2006). *Children's psychosocial adjustment and gender development in planned lesbian families.* Working paper, Social and Behavioral Sciences, Department of Education, University of Amsterdam.

Bosson, J. K., Johnson, A. B., Niederhoffer, K., & Swann, W. B., Jr. (2006). Interpersonal chemistry through negativity: Bonding by sharing negative attitudes about others. *Personal Relationships, 13,* 135–150.

Bowlby, J. (1958). The nature of the child's tie to his mother. *Journal of Psychoanalysis, 39,* 350–373.

Bowlby, J. (1969/1982). *Attachment and loss. Vol. 1: Attachment.* New York: Basic Books.

Bowlby, J. (1973). *Attachment and loss. Vol. 2: Separation.* London: Hogarth Press.

Bowlby, J. (1979). *The making and breaking of affectional bonds.* London: Tavisctock/Routledge.

Bowlby, J. (1980). *Attachment and loss. Vol. 3: Loss: Sadness and depression.* New York: Basic Books.

Bowlby, J. (1988). *A secure base.* New York: Basic Books.

Bowlby, J. (1994). *The making and breaking of affectional bonds.* New York: Routledge.

Bowling, T. K., Hill, C. M., & Jencius, M. (2005). An overview of marriage enrichment. *The Family Journal: Counseling and Therapy for Couples and Families, 1*(1), 1–8.

Bradbury, T. N., & Karney, B. R. (2010). *Intimate relationships.* New York: Norton.

Bramlett, M. D., & Mosher, W. D. (2002). Cohabitation, marriage, divorce, and remarriage in the United States. *Vital Health Statistics, 23*(22). Hyattsville, MD: National Center for Health Statistics.

Bratter, J. L., & King, R. B. (2008). "But will it last?": Marital instability among interracial and same-race couples. *Family Relations, 57,* 160–171.

Braxton-Davis, P. (2010). The social psychology of love and attraction. *McNair Scholars Journal, 14,* 5–12.

Brendgen, M., Markievicz, D., Doyle, A. B., & Bukowski, W. (2001). The relations between friendship quality, ranked-friendship preference, and adolescents' behavior with their friends. *Merrill-Palmer Quarterly, 47*(3), 395–415.

Bretherton, I. (1995). The origin of attachment theory: John Bowlby and Mary Ainsworth. In S. Goldberg, J. Kerr, & R. Muir (Eds.), *Attachment theory: Social, developmental, and clinical perspectives* (pp. 45–84). Hillsdale, NJ: Analytic Press.

Bretherton, I., & Munholland, K. A. (2008). Internal working models in attachment relationships: Elaborating a central construct in attachment theory. In J. Cassidy & P. Shaver (Eds.), *Handbook of adult attachment: Theory, research and clinical applications* (2nd ed., pp. 102–127). New York: The Guilford Press.

Bretherton, I., & Waters, E. (1985). Growing points of attachment theory and research. *Monographs of the Society for Research in Child Development, 50*(1–2), Serial No. 209, 3–35.

Brewer, G., & Archer, J. (2007). What do people infer from facial attractiveness? *Journal of Evolutionary Psychology, 5,* 39–49.

Brody, L. R., & Hall, J. A. (2010). Gender, emotion, and socialization. In J. Chrisler & D. McCreary (Eds.), *Handbook of gender research in psychology* (pp. 429–454). New York: Springer.

Bronfenbrenner, U. (1977). Toward an experimental ecology of human development. *American Psychologist, 32,* 513–531.

Bronfenbrenner, U. (1979). *The ecology of human development: Experiments in nature and design.* Cambridge, MA: Harvard University Press.

Bronfenbrenner, U. (1988). Interacting systems in human development. Research paradigms: Present and future. In N. Bolger, A. Caspi, G. Downey, & M. Moorehouse (Eds.), *Persons in context: Developmental processes* (pp. 25–49). Cambridge, UK: Cambridge University Press.

Bronfenbrenner, U. (1999). Environments in developmental perspective: Theoretical and operational models. In S. L. Friedman & T. D. Wachs (Eds.), *Measuring environment across the life span: Emerging methods and concepts* (pp. 3–28). Washington, DC: American Psychological Association.

Bronfenbrenner, U. (2005). The bioecological theory of human development. In U. Bronfenbrenner (Ed.), *Making human beings human: Bioecological perspectives on human development* (pp. 3–15). Thousand Oaks, CA: Sage. (Original work published in 2001.)

Broom, G. M. (2012). *Cutlip and Center's effective public relations.* Upper Saddle River, NJ: Prentice Hall.

Brown, C. (2006). *Social psychology.* London: Sage.

Brown, N. M., & Amatea, E. S. (2013). *Love and intimate relationships: Journeys of the heart.* New York: Routledge.

Brown, S. L. (2003). Relationship quality dynamics of cohabiting unions. *Journal of Family Issues, 24,* 583–601.

Brown, S. L. (2010). Marriage and child well-being: Research and policy perspectives. *Journal of Marriage and Family, 72*(5), 1059–1077.

Brown, S. L., & Kawamura, S. (2010). Relationship quality among cohabitors and marrieds in older adulthood. *Social Science Research, 39*(5), 777–786. doi:10.1016/j.ssresearch.2010.04.010

Brown, S. L., Lee, G. R., & Bulanada, J. R. (2006). Cohabitation among older adults: A national portrait. *Journal of Gerontology: Social Sciences, 61B,* S71–S79.

Brown, S. L., & Lin, I. F. (2012). The gray divorce revolution: Rising divorce among middle-aged and older adults, 1990–2010. *The Journals of Gerontology: Series B: Psychological Sciences and Social Sciences, 67B,* 731–741. doi:10.1093/geronb/gbs089

Brown, S. L., Manning, W. D., & Payne, K. K. (2014). *Relationship quality among cohabiting versus married couples.* National Center for Family & Marriage Research. Working Paper Series WP-14-03.

Brown, S. L., Van Hook, J., & Glick, J. E. (2008). Generational differences in cohabitation and marriage in the U.S. *Population Research and Policy Review, 27,* 531–550.

Bubaš, G., & Bratko, D. (2008). *Factor analysis of rules in friendship: Relations with personality traits and friendship quality.* Paper presented at the 58th annual conference of the International Communication Association, Montreal, Quebec, Canada.

Buhrmester, D., & Furman, W. (1986). The changing functions of friends in childhood: A neo-Sullivan perspective. In V. J. Derlega & B. A. Winstead (Eds.), *Friendship and social interaction* (pp. 41–62). New York: Springer-Verlag.

Bukowski, W. M., & Cillessen, A. H. (1998). *Sociometry then and now: Building on six decades of measuring children's experiences with the peer group.* San Francisco: Jossey-Bass.

Bulanda, J. R. (2011). Gender, marital power, and marital quality in later life. *Journal of Women & Aging, 23,* 2–22. doi:10.1080/08952841.2011.540481

Bulanda, J. R., & Brown, S. L. (2004, April 1–3). *Race-ethnic differences in marital quality and divorce.* Paper presented at the annual meeting of the Population Association of America, Boston.

Bumpass, L. (2002). Family-related attitudes, couple relationships, and union stability. In R. Lesthaeghe (Ed.), *Meaning and choice: Value orientations and life cycle decisions* (pp. 161–184). The Hague, Netherlands: Netherlands Interdisciplinary Demographic Institute.

Bumpass, L., & Lu, H. (2000). Trends in cohabitation and implications for children's family contexts in the United States. *Population Studies, 54,* 29–41.

Bureau of Justice Statistics. (2013). *Intimate partner violence: 1993–2010*. Retrieved October 26, 2016, from www.bjs.gov/index.cfm?ty=tp&tid=315

Burgess, E. (2004). Sexuality in midlife and later life couples. In J. H. Harvey, A. Wenzel, & S. Sprecher (Eds.), *The handbook of sexuality in close relationships* (pp. 437–454). Mahwah, NJ: Erlbaum.

Burk, W. J., & Laursen, B. (2005). Adolescent perceptions of friendship and their associations with individual adjustment. *International Journal of Behavioral Development, 29*(2), 156–164.

Burleson, M. H., Roberts, N. A., Vincelette, T. M., & Guan, X. (2013). Marriage, affectionate touch, and health. In M. Newman & N. Roberts (Eds.), *Health and social relationships: The good, the bad, and the complicated* (pp. 67–93). Washington, DC: American Psychological Association.

Burleson, M. H., Trevathan, W. R., & Todd, M. (2007). In the mood for love or vice versa? Exploring the relations among sexual activity, physical affection, affect, and stress in the daily lives of mid-aged women. *Archives of Sexual Behavior, 36,* 357–368.

Busboom, A. L., Collins, D. M., Givertz, M. D., & Lauren, A. L. (2002). Can we still be friends? Resources and barriers to friendship quality after romantic relationship dissolution. *Personal Relationships, 9,* 215–223.

Busby, D. M., Larson, J. H., Holman, T. B., & Halford, W. K. (2015). Flexible delivery approaches to couple relationship education: Predictors of initial engagement and retention of couples. *Journal of Child and Family Studies,* 1–12. Retrieved from http://dx.doi.org/10.1007/s10826-014-0105-3

Busch, M., & Jarosewitsch, R. (2012). *Healing relationships: Closeness and separateness.* Retrieved from https://waiorahealingwaters.com/2012/12/07/closeness-and-separateness

Buss, D. M. (1994). *The evolution of desire: Strategies of human mating.* New York: Basic Books.

Buss, D. M. (2000). *The dangerous passion: Why jealousy is as necessary as love and sex.* New York: Free Press.

Buss, D. M. (2004). *The evolution of desire* (Rev. ed.). New York: Basic Books.

Buss, D. M. (2012). *Evolutionary psychology: The new science of the mind* (4th ed.). Boston: Pearson.

Buss, D. M., Abbott, M., Angleitner, A., Asherian, A., Biaggio, A., Blanco-Villasenor, A., et al. (1990). International preferences in selecting mates: A study of 37 cultures. *Journal of Cross-Cultural Psychology, 21,* 5–47.

Buss, D. M., & Barnes, M. (1986). Preferences in human mate selection. *Journal of Personality and Social Psychology, 50,* 559–570.

Buss, D. M., & Shackelford, T. K. (2008). Attractive women want it all: Good genes, economic investment, parenting proclivities, and emotional commitment. *Evolutionary Psychology, 6,* 134–146.

Butt, M. M., Malik, F., & Faran, M. (2016, June 7–10). *Remembered parental acceptance-rejection and fear of intimacy in married and unmarried men and women in Pakistan*. Presented in the 6th International Congress on Interpersonal Acceptance-Rejection, Madrid, Spain.

Buunk, B. P., Dijkstra, P., Fetchenhauer, D., & Kenrick, D. T. (2002). Age and gender differences in mate selection criteria for various involvement levels. *Personal Relationships, 9,* 271–278.

Byrne, D. (1971). *The attraction paradigm*. New York: Academic Press.

Cahn, D. D. (2009). *Conflicts in personal relationships*. New York: Routledge.

Cain, V. S., Johannes, C. B., Avis, N. E., Mohr, B., Schocken, M., Skurnick, J., & Ory, M. (2003). Sexual functioning and practices in a multi-ethnic study of midlife women: Baseline results from SWAN. *The Journal of Sex Research, 40,* 266–276.

Call, V., Sprecher, S., & Schwartz, P. (1995). The incidence and frequency of marital sex in a national sample. *Journal of Marriage and Family, 57,* 639–652.

Canary, D. J., & Dainton, M. (2006). Maintaining relationships. In A. Vangelisti & D. Perlman (Eds.), *The Cambridge handbook of personal relationships* (pp. 727–743). Cambridge, UK: Cambridge University Press.

Canary, D. J., & Lakey, S. (2013). *Strategic conflict*. New York: Routledge.

Canary, D. J., & Stafford, L. (2001). Equity in the preservation of personal relationships. In J. H. Harvey & A. E. Wenzel (Eds.), *Close romantic relationships: Maintenance and enhancement* (pp. 133–151). Mahwah, NJ: Erlbaum.

Canary, D. J., Stafford, L., & Semic, B. A. (2002). A panel study of associations between maintenance strategies and relational characteristics. *Journal of Marriage and Family, 64,* 395–406.

Cardoso, L. F., Gupta, J., Shuman, S., Cole, H., Kpebo, D., & Falb, K. L. (2016). What factors contribute to intimate partner violence against women in urban, conflict-affected settings? Qualitative findings from Abidjan, Côte d'Ivoire. *Journal of Urban Health, 93*(2), 364–378. doi:10.1007/s11524-016-0029-x

Carli, L. L. (2001). Gender, interpersonal power, and social influence. *Journal of Social Issues, 55,* 81–98.

Carnes, D. (2015). *Do men & women use nonverbal communication differently?* Livestorng.com (last updated May 17, 2015).

Carr, D. (2004). The desire to date and remarry among older widows and widowers. *Journal of Marriage and Family, 66,*1051–1068.

Carr, D., Freedman, V. A., Cornman, J. C., & Schwarz, N. (2014). Happy marriage, happy life? Marital quality and subjective well-being in later life. *Journal of Marriage and Family, 76*(5), 930–948.

Carr, D., & Springer, K. W. (2010). Advances in families and health research in the 21st century. *Journal of Marriage and Family, 72,* 743–761. doi:10.111 1/j.1741-3737.2010.00728

Carrillo, S., & Ripoll-Nunez, K. J. (2015). *Adult intimate relationships: Linkages between parental acceptance rejection theory and adult attachment theory*. Unpublished manuscript.

Carroll, J., S., Willoughby, B., Badger, S., Nelson, L. J., Barry, C., M., & Madsen, S. D. (2007). So close, yet so far away: The impact of varying marital horizons on emerging adulthood. *Journal of Adolescent Research, 22,* 219–247.

Carstensen, L. L. (1992). Social and emotional patterns in adulthood: Support for socioemotional selectivity theory. *Psychology and Aging, 7*(3), 331–338.

Carstensen, L. L., Isaacowitz, D. M., & Charles, S. T. (1999). Taking time seriously: A theory of socioemotional selectivity. *American Psychologist, 54,* 165–181.

Carstensen, L. L., Rosenberger, M. E., Smith, K., & Modrek, S. (2015). Optimizing health in aging societies. *Public Policy & Aging Report.* Advance online publication. doi:10.1093/ppar/prv004

Carter, C. S. (2014). Oxytocin pathways and the evolution of human behavior. *Annual Review of Psychology, 65,* 1–23.

Carver, K., Joyner, K., & Udry, J. (2003). National estimates of adolescent romantic relationships. In P. Florsheim (Ed.), *Adolescent romantic relations and sexual behavior: Theory, research, and practical implications* (pp. 23–56). Mahwah, NJ: Erlbaum.

Casalanti, T., & Kiecolt, K. J. (2007). Diversity among late-life couples. *Generations, 31,* 10–17.

Cassidy, J. (2000). Adult romantic relationships: A developmental perspective on individual differences. *Review of General Psychology, 4*(2), 111–131.

Cassidy, J., & Shaver, P. R. (1999). *Handbook of attachment: Theory, research, and clinical applications.* New York: The Guilford Press.

Cassidy, J., & Shaver, P. R. (Eds.) (2008). *Handbook of attachment: Theory, research and clinical applications.* New York: The Guilford Press.

Centers for Disease Control and Prevention (CDC). (2000). *Youth risk behavior surveillance—United States, 1999.* Retrieved from www.cdc.gov/mmwr/preview/mmwrhttml/ss4905al.hum

Centers for Disease Control and Prevention (CDC). (2006). *Data highlights—2006: Tracking STDs in the United States.* Retrieved from www.cdc.gov/mmwr/preview/mmwrhttml/ss4905al.hum

Centers for Disease Control and Prevention (CDC). (2010). *Understanding intimate partner violence.* Washington, DC: National Center for Injury Prevention and Control.Retrieved from www.cdc.gov/violenceprevention/pdf/IPV_factsheet2010-a.pdf

Centers for Disease Control and Prevention (CDC). (2013a). *Surveillance summaries: Youth risk behavior surveillance—United States* (pdf, 172 pp.). MMWR (2014); 63 (no. SS-4).

Centers for Disease Control and Prevention (CDC). (2013b). *U.S. homosexuality—Statistics & facts.* U.S. Department of Health & Human Services, Atlanta, GA.

Centers for Disease Control and Prevention (CDC). (2014). *Understanding intimate partner violence. Fact sheet.* Retrieved from https://www.cdc.gov/ViolencePrevention/pdf/IPV-FactSheet.pdf

Centers for Disease Control and Prevention (CDC). (2015). *Reproductive health: Teen pregnancy in the United States*. U.S. Department of Health & Human Services, Atlanta, GA.

Centers for Disease Control and Prevention (CDC). (2016). *College health and safety*. The U.S. Department of Health & Human Services, Atlanta, GA.

Chance, P. (2003). *Learning and behavior* (5th ed.). Toronto: Thomson-Wadsworth.

Chapman, G. (2004). *Five love languages men's edition: The secret to love that lasts*. Bel Air, CA: Northfield Press.

Charles, C. M., & Mertler, C. A. (2002). *Introduction to educational research*. Boston: Allyn and Bacon.

Chen, H., Cohen, P., Kasen, S., Johnson, J. G., Ehrensaft, M., & Gordon, K. (2006). Predicting conflict within romantic relationships during the transition to adulthood. *Personal Relationships, 13,* 411–427.

Chen, H., Luo, S., Yue, G., Xu, D., & Zhaoyang, R. (2009). Do birds of a feather flock together in China? *Personal Relationships, 16,* 167–186.

Chen, X., Rubin, K. H., & Li, B. (1995). Depressed mood in Chinese children: Relations with school performance and family environment. *Journal of Consulting and Clinical Psychology, 63*(6), 938–947.

Chen, X., Rubin, K. H., & Li, B. (1997). Maternal acceptance and social and school adjustment in Chinese children: A four-year longitudinal study. *Merrill-Palmer Quarterly, 43,* 663–681.

Cherlin, A. J. (2004). The deinstitutionalizing of American marriage. *Journal of Marriage and Family, 66,* 848–862.

Cheung, M. W., Wong, P. W., Liu, K.Y., Yip, P. S., Fan, S. Y., & Lam, T. H. (2008). A study of sexual satisfaction and frequency of sex among Hong Kong Chinese couples. *The Journal of Sex Research, 45*(2), 129–139.

Chisholm, J. S. (1999). Steps to an evolutionary ecology of the mind. In A. L. Hinton (Ed.), *Biocultural approaches to the emotions* (pp. 117–149). Cambridge, UK: Cambridge University Press.

Choi, N., Fuqua, D. R., & Newman, J. L. (2007). Hierarchical confirmatory factor analysis of the Ben Sex Role Inventory. *Educational and Psychological Measurement, 67,* 818–832.

Chung, W. C., De Vries, G. J., & Swaab, D. F. (2002). Sexual differentiation of the bed nucleus of the stria terminalis in humans may extend into adulthood. *Journal of Neuroscience, 22,* 1027–1033.

Chyung, Y. J., & Lee, J. (2008). Intimate partner acceptance, remembered parental acceptance in childhood, and psychological adjustment among Korean college students in ongoing intimate relationships. *Cross-Cultural Research, 42*(1), 77–86.

Cillessen, A. H. N., Jiang, X. L., West, T. V., & Laszkowski, D. K. (2005). Predictors of dyadic friendship quality in adolescence. *International Journal of Behavioral Development, 29*(2), 165–172.

Clark, L. E., & Collins, J. E. (1993). Remembering old flames: How the past affects the assessment of the present. *Personality and Social Psychology Bulletin, 19,* 399–408.

Clark, M. L., & Ayers, M. (1993). Friendship expectations and friendship evaluations: Reciprocity and gender effects. *Youth & Society, 24,* 299–313.

Clark, R. D., III, & Hatfield, E. (2003). Love in the afternoon. *Psychological Inquiry, 14,* 227–231.

Clarke, P. (2003). Towards a greater understanding of the experience of stroke: Integrating quantitative and qualitative methods. *Journal of Aging Studies, 17,* 171–187.

Claxton, A., & Perry-Jenkins, M. (2008). No fun anymore: Leisure and marital quality across the transition to parenthood. *Journal of Marriage and Family, 79*(1), 28–43.

Cleere, C., & Lynn, S. J. (2013). Acknowledged versus unacknowledged sexual assault among college women. *Journal of Interpersonal Violence, 28*(12), 2593–2611. doi:10.1177/0886260513479033

Closs, C. (2010). The effects of oppression on queer intimate adolescent attachment. *Doctorate in social work (DSW) dissertations.* University of Pennsylvania. Retrieved from http://repository.upenn.edu/edissertations_sp2/6

Cohen, D. A. (1990). Child-mother attachment of six-year-olds and social competence at school. *Child Development, 61,* 152–162.

Cohen, L. J. (2016). *Psychology today.* New York: Sussex.

Cohen, O., Geron, Y., & Farchi, A. (2009). Marital quality and global well-being among older adult Israeli couples in enduring marriages. *The American Journal of Family Therapy, 37*(4), 299–317. doi:10.1080/01926180802405968

Cohen, S., & Wills, T. A. (1985). Stress, social support, and the buffering hypothesis. *Psychological Bulletin, 98,* 310–357.

Coleman, J. C. (1956). *Abnormal psychology and modern life.* New York: Scott, Foresman.

Coles, R. (1970). *Erik H. Erikson: The growth of his work.* Boston: Little Brown.

Colin, V. L. (1996). *Human attachment.* New York: McGraw-Hill.

Collins, N. L., & Miller, L. C. (1994). Self-disclosure and liking: A meta-analytic review. *Psychological Bulletin, 116,* 457–475.

Collins, N. L., & Read, S. J. (1990). Adult attachment, working models and relationship quality in dating couples. *Journal of Personality and Social Psychology, 58,* 644–663.

Collins, N. L., & Read, S. J. (1994). Cognitive representations of attachment: The structure and function of working models. In K. Bartholomew & D. Perlman (Eds.), *Attachment processes in adulthood* (pp. 53–92). London: Jessica Kingsley.

Collins, A., & Steinberg, L. (2006). Adolescent development in interpersonal context. In N. Eisenberg (Ed.) & W. Damon (Series Ed.), *Handbook of child psychology: Vol. 3. Social, emotional, and personality development* (6th ed.). New York: Wiley.

Collins, W. A. (2003). More than myth: The developmental significance of romantic relationships during adolescence. *Journal of Research on Adolescence, 13,* 1–25.

Collins, W. A., & Madsen, S. D. (2006). Close relationships in adolescence and early adulthood. In D. Perlman & A. Vangelisti (Eds.), *Handbook of personal relationships* (pp. 191–209). New York: Cambridge University Press.

Compton W. C. (2005). *An introduction to positive psychology.* Belmont, CA: Wadsworth.

Conley, T. D., Moors, A. C., Matsick, J. L., & Ziegler, A. (2013). The fewer the merrier: Assessing stigma surrounding non-normative romantic relationships. *Analyses of Social Issues and Public Policy, 13*(1), 1–30.

Connolly, J., Craig, W., Goldberg, A., & Pepler, D. (2004). Mixed-gender groups, dating, and romantic relationships in early adolescence. *Journal of Research on Adolescence, 14*(2), 185–207.

Connolly, J., & McIsaac, C. (2009). Adolescents' explanations for romantic dissolutions: A developmental perspective. *Journal of Adolescence, 32,* 1209–1223.

Connolly, J. A., Craig, W., Goldberg, A., & Pepler, D. (1999). Conceptions of cross-sex friendships and romantic relationships in early adolescence. *Journal of Youth and Adolescence, 28,* 481–494.

Connolly, J. A., Furman, W., & Konarski, R. (2000). The role of peers in the emergence of heterosexual romantic relationships in adolescence. *Child Development, 71,* 1395–1408.

Conroy, A. A. (2014). Gender, power, and intimate partner violence: A study on couples from rural Malawi. *Journal of Interpersonal Violence, 29*(5), 866–888.

Consedine, N. S., & Magai, C. (2003). Attachment and emotion experience in later life: The view from emotions theory. *Attachment and Human Development, 5,* 165–187.

Coombs, R. H., Paulson, M. J., & Richardson, M. A. (1991). Peer vs. parental influence in substance use among Hispanic and Anglo children and adolescents. *Journal of Youth and Adolescence, 20*(1), 73–88.

Cooney, T. M., & Dunne, K. (2001). Intimate relationships in later life: Current realities and future prospects. *Journal of Family Issues, 22,* 838–858.

Costa, P. T., Jr., & McCrae, R. R. (1994). Stability and change in personality from adolescence through adulthood. In C. F. Halverson, G. A. Kohnstamm, & R. P. Martin (Eds.), *The developing structure of temperament and personality from infancy to adulthood.* Hillsdale, NJ: Erlbaum.

Cournoyer, D. E. (2000). Universalist research: Examples drawing from the methods and findings of parental acceptance-rejection theory. In A. L. Comunian & U. Gielen (Eds.), *International perspective on human development* (pp. 213–232). Berlin, Germany: Pabst Science.

Courtois, C. A. (2004). Complex trauma, complex reactions: Assessment and treatment. *Psychotherapy, 41,* 412–425.

Crissey, S. R. (2005). Race/ethnic differences in the marital expectation of adolescents: The role of romantic relationships. *Journal of Marriage and Family, 67,* 297–709.

Crook, T., Raskin, A., & Eliot, J. (1981). Parent-child relationships and adult depression. *Child Development, 52,* 950–957.

Crowell, J. A., Fraley, R. C., & Shaver, P. R. (1999). Measurement of individual differences in adolescent and adult attachment. In J. Cassidy & P. R. Shaver (Eds.), *Handbook of attachment: Theory, research, and clinical applications* (pp. 434–465). New York: The Guilford Press.

Crown, L., & Roberts, L. J. (2007). Against their will: Young women's nonagentic sexual experiences. *Journal of Social and Personal Relationships, 24*(3), 385–405.

Cruz, J. (2013). *Divorce rate in the U.S., 2011.* National Center for Family and Marriage Research. Retrieved from http://ncfmr.bgsu.edu/pdf/family_profiles/file131530.pdf

Cunningham, M. R., Barbee, A. P., & Philhower, C. L. (2002). Dimension of facial physical attractiveness: The intersection of biology and culture. In G. Rhodes & L. A. Zebrowitz (Eds.), *Facial attractiveness: Evolutionary, cognitive, and social perspectives* (pp. 193–238). Westport, CT: Ablex.

Cunningham, M. R., Roberts, A. R., Barbee, A. P., Druen, P. B., & Wu, C. H. (1995). "Their ideas of beauty are, on the whole, the same as ours": Consistency and variability in the cross-cultural perception of female physical attractiveness. *Journal of Personality and Social Psychology, 68,* 261–279.

Cupach, W. R., & Canary, D. J. (2016). *Conflict—Couple relationships—Theory, family, development, partner, and marital.* Retrieved from http://family.jrank.org/pages/312/Conflict-COUPLE-RELATIONSHIPS.html#ixzz4KtpTeVLQ

Cutrona, C. E. (1996). *Social support in couples: Marriage as a resource in times of stress.* Thousand Oaks, CA: Sage.

Dainton, M. (2008). The use of relationship maintenance behaviors as a mechanism to explain the decline in marital satisfaction among parents. *Communication Reports, 20,* 33–45.

Dainton, M., & Aylor, B. (2001). A relational uncertainty analysis of jealousy, trust, and maintenance in long-distance versus geographically close relationships. *Communication Quarterly, 49*(2), 172–188.

Dainton, M., & Aylor, B. (2002). Routine and strategic maintenance efforts: Behavioral patterns, variations associated with relational length, and the prediction of relational characteristics. *Communication Monographs, 66,* 52–66.

Dakin, J., & Wampler, R. (2008). Money doesn't buy happiness, but it helps: Marital satisfaction, psychological distress, and demographic differences between low- and middle-income clinic couples. *The American Journal of Family Therapy, 36*(4), 300–311.

Daly, M., & Wilson, M. (1989). Killing the competition: Female/male and male/female homicide. *Human Nature, 1,* 81–107.

Darling, N., Dowdy B. B., Van Horn, M. L., & Caldwell, L. L. (1999). Mixed-sex settings and the perception of competence. *Journal of Youth and Adolescence, 28*(4), 461–480.

Darroch, J. E., Frost, J. J., & Singh, S. (2001). *Teenage sex and reproductive behavior in developed countries: Can more progress be made?* Occasional report no. 3. New York: Alan Guttmacher Institute.

Das, A., Waite, L. J., & Laumann, E. O. (2011). Sexual expression over the life course: Results from three landmark surveys. In J. DeLamater and L. Carpenter (Eds.), *Sex for life: From virginity to Viagra, how sexuality changes throughout our lives* (pp. 236–259). New York: NYU Press.

D'Augelli, A. R., Rendina, H. J., Grossman, A. H., & Sinclair, K. O. (2006/2007). Lesbian and gay youths' aspirations for marriage and raising children. *Journal of LGBT Issues in Counseling, 1,* 77–98.

Davidson, K. (2001). Late life widowhood, selfishness and new partnership choices: A gendered perspective. *Ageing and Society, 21,* 297–317.

Davila, J., Karney, B. R., Hall, T. W., & Bradbury, T. N. (2003). Depressive symptoms and marital satisfaction: Within-subject associations and the moderating effects of gender and neuroticism. *Journal of Family Psychology, 17,* 557–570.

Davila, J., & Kashy, D. A., (2009). Secure base processes in couples: Daily associations between supports, experiences and attachment security. *Journal of Family Psychology, 23,* 76–88.

Davila, J., Steinberg, S., Kachadourian, L., Cobb, R., & Fincham, F. (2004). Romantic involvement and depressive symptoms in early and late adolescence: The role of a preoccupied relational style. *Personal Relations, 11,* 161–178.

Davis, A. K. (2015). *An evaluation of the impact of a couple enrichment program on relationship satisfaction, communication, conflict resolution, and forgiveness.* Unpublished doctoral dissertation, University of Nebraska–Lincoln. Chelsi.davis@huskers.unl.edu.

Davis, K. E. (2004). *Love's many faces apprehended.* Washington, DC: American Psychological Association.

de Benedictis, T. (2016). *Domestic violence and abuse: Types, signs, symptoms, causes, and effects.* Nationwide Crisis Line and Hotline Directory. Retrieved from www.aaets.org/article144.htm

Debrot, A., Schoebi, D., Perrez, M., & Horn, A. B. (2013). Touch as an interpersonal emotion regulation process in couples' daily lives: The mediating role of psychological intimacy. *Personality and Social Psychological Bulletin, 39,* 1373–1385.

Deci, E. L., & Ryan, R. M. (2014). Autonomy and need satisfaction in close relationships: Relationships motivation theory. In N. Weinstein (Ed.), *Human motivation and interpersonal relationships: Theory, research, and applications* (pp. 53–73). Dordrecht, Netherlands: Springer.

De Gaston, J. F., Weed, L., & Jensen, L. (1996). Understanding gender differences in adolescent sexuality. *Adolescence, 31,* 217–231.

DeGue, S., & DiLillo, D. (2005). "You would if you loved me": Toward an improved conceptual and etiological understanding of male sexual coercion. *Aggression and Violent Behavior, 10,* 513–532.

DeGue, S. A., DiLillo, D., & Scalora, M. J. (2010). Are all perpetrators alike? Comparing risk factors for sexual coercion and aggression. *Sexual Abuse: A Journal of Research and Treatment, 22*, 402–426.

De Jong Gierveld, J., & Peeters, A. (2003). The interweaving of repartnered older adults' lives with their children and siblings. *Ageing & Society, 23*, 187–203.

DeLamater, J. (2012). Sexual expression in later life: A review and synthesis. *Journal of Sex Research, 49*(2–3), 125–141. doi:10.1080/00224499.2011.603168

DeLamater, J., & Moorman, S. M. (2007). Sexual behavior in later life. *Journal of Aging and Health, 19*, 921–945.

De Lange, G. (2011). Gender identity and self-esteem of boys growing up without a father. *Social Cosmos, 2*, 97–103.

DeMaris, A. (1990). The dynamics of generational transfer in courtship violence: A biracial exploration. *Journal of Marriage and the Family, 52*, 219–231.

Demir, M. (2008). Sweetheart, you really make me happy: Romantic relationship quality and personality as predictors of happiness among emerging adults. *Journal of Happiness Studies, 9*, 257–277.

Demir, M. (2010). Close relationships and happiness among emerging adults. *Journal of Happiness Studies, 11*, 293–313.

Dempsey, D. J. (2005). *Beyond choice: Exploring the Australian lesbian and gay baby boom.* Doctoral dissertation, Melbourne: School of Public Health, La Trobe University.

de Munck, V. C., Korotayev, A., de Munck, J., & Khaltourina, D. (2011). Cross-cultural analysis of models of romantic love among U.S. residents, Russians, and Lithuanians. *Cross-Cultural Research, 45*(2), 128–154.

Dennerstein, L., Alexander, J. L., & Kotz, K. (2003). The menopause and sexual functioning: A review of the population-based studies. *Annual Review of Sex Research, 14*, 64–82.

Dennerstein, L., Dudley, E., & Burger, H. (2001). Are changes in sexual functioning during midlife due to aging or menopause? *Fertility and Sterility, 76*, 456–460.

Descutner, C. J., & Thelen, M. H. (1991). Development and validation of a fear of intimacy scale. *Psychological Assessment, 3*, 218–225.

Deutsch, M. (2006). Cooperation and competition. In M. Deutsch, P. Coleman, & E. Marcus (Eds.), *The handbook of conflict resolution: Theory and practice* (pp. 43–68). San Francisco: Jossey-Bass.

De Vogli, R., Chandola, T., & Marmot, M. G. (2007). Negative aspects of close relationships and heart disease. *Archives of Internal Medicine, 167*, 1951–1957.

de Vries, B. (1996). The understanding of friendship: An adult life course perspective. In C. Magai & S. H. McFadden (Eds.), *Handbook of emotion, adult development, and aging* (pp. 249–268). San Diego: Academic Press.

Dew, J. P. (2009). The gendered meanings of assets for divorce. *Journal of Family and Economic Issues, 30*, 20–31.

Dew, J. P., & Dakin, J. (2011). Financial disagreements and marital conflict tactics. *Journal of Financial Therapy, 2*(1), 23–42.

Dew, J. P., Britt, S., & Huston, S. (2012). *Examining the relationship between financial issues and divorce.* Family, Consumer, and Human Development, Utah State University, 670 E. 500 N., Logan, UT 84321.

Diamant, L. M., & McAnulty, R. (1995). *The psychology of sexual orientation, behavior and identity: A handbook* (pp. 45–80). Westport, CT: Greenwood Press.

Diamond, L. M. (2005). What we got wrong about sexual identity development: Unexpected findings from a longitudinal study of young women. In A. M. Omoto & H. S. Kurtzman (Eds.), *Sexual orientation and mental health: Examining identity and development in lesbian, gay, and bisexual people* (pp. 73–94). Washington, DC: American Psychological Association.

Diamond, L. M. (2007). Sexual desire. In R. Baumeister and K. Vohs (Eds.), *Encyclopedia of social psychology.* Newbury Park, CA: Sage.

Diamond, L. M. (2008). *Sexual fluidity: Understanding women's love and desire.* Cambridge, MA: Harvard University Press.

Diamond, L. M. (2012). The desire disorder in research on sexual orientation in women: Contributions of dynamical systems theory. *Archives of Sexual Behavior, 41,* 73–83.

Diamond, L. M. (2013). Transsexuality among twins: Identity concordance, transition, rearing, and orientation. *International Journal of Transgenderism, 14*(1), 24–38.

Diamond, L. M., Fagundes, C. P., & Butterworth, M. R. (2010). Intimate relationships across the life span. *The handbook of life-span development.* Online. doi:10.1002/9780470880166.hlsd002011.

Diamond, M. (2011). *Gender identity concordance among monozygotic and dizygotic twin pairs.* Paper presented at the World Professional Association for Transgender Health Conference, Atlanta, GA.

Diener, E., & Diener, R. B. (2009). *Rethinking happiness: The science of psychological wealth.* Malden, MA: Blackwell/Wiley.

Dijkstra, P., & Barelds, D. P. H. (2008). Do people know what they want: A similar or complementary partner? *Evolutionary Psychology, 6*(4), 595–602.

Dindia, K. (2002). Self-disclosure research: Knowledge through meta-analysis. In M. Allen, R. W. Preiss, B. M. Gale, & N. A. Burrell (Eds.), *Interpersonal communication research: Advances through meta-analysis* (pp. 169–185). Mahwah, NJ: Erlbaum.

Dindia, K. (2003). Definitions and perspectives on relational maintenance communication. In D. Canary & M. Dainton (Eds.), *Maintaining relationships through communication* (pp. 1–28). Mahwah, NJ: Erlbaum.

Dindia, K., & Emmers-Sommer, T. M. (2006). What partners do to maintain their close relationships. In P. Noller & J. A. Feeney (Eds.), *Close relationships: Functions, forms, and processes* (pp. 305–324). New York: Psychology Press.

Dion, K. K., & Dion, K. L. (1985). Personality, gender, and the phenomenology of romantic love. In P. Shaver (Ed.), *Review of personality and social psychology* (Vol. 6, pp. 209–239). Beverly Hills, CA: Sage.

Doherty, R. W., Hatfield, E., Thompson, K., & Choo, P. (1994). Cultural and ethnic influences on love and attachment. *Personal Relationships, 1,* 391–398.

Domenico, D. M., & Jones, K. H. (2007). Adolescent pregnancy in America: Causes and responses. *Journal for Vocational Special Need Education, 30*(1), 4–12.

Donnellan, M. B., Conger, R. D., & Bryant, C. M. (2004). The Big Five and enduring marriages. *Journal of Research in Personality, 38,* 481–504.

Donoghue, J. M. (2010). *Clinical applications of parental acceptance-rejection theory (PARTheory) measures in relational therapy, assessment, and treatment.* Unpublished doctoral dissertation, University of Connecticut at Storrs.

Dorius, G. L., Heaton, T. B., & Steffen, P. (1993). Adolescent life events and their association with the onset of sexual intercourse. *Youth and Society, 25,* 3–23.

Doss, B. D., Rhoades, G. K., Stanley, S. M., & Markman, H. J. (2009). Marital therapy, retreats, and books: The who, what, when, and why of relationship help-seeking. *Journal of Marital and Family Therapy, 35*(1), 18–29. Retrieved from http://dx.doi.org/10.1111/j.1752-0606.2008.00093.x

Douglas, G., & Heer, D. (2013). *The 5-elements of intimacy.* Retrieved from http://www.barsandbodywork.com

Douvan, E., & Adelson, J. (1966). *The adolescent experience.* New York: Wiley.

Dozier, M., Stovall, K. C., & Albus, K. (1999). Attachment and psychopathology in adulthood. In J. Cassidy & P.R. Shaver (Eds.), *Handbook of attachment: Theory, research, and clinical applications* (pp. 497–519). New York: The Guilford Press.

Dozier, M., Stovall-McClough, K. C., Albus, C., & Kathleen, E. (2008). Attachment and psychopathology in adulthood. In J. Cassidy and P. R. Shaver (eds.), *Handbook of attachment: Theory, research, and clinical applications* (2nd ed., pp. 718–744). New York: The Guilford Press.

Dryer, D. C., & Horowitz, L. M. (1997). When do opposites attract? Interpersonal complementarity versus similarity. *Journal of Personality and Social Psychology, 72*(3), 592–603.

Duck, S. (1982). *Personal relations 4: Dissolving personal relationships.* New York: Academic Press.

Duggan, M., & Brenner, J. (2013). The demographics of social media users—2012. *Pew Internet & American life project.* Retrieved from http://pewinternet.org/Reports/2013/Social-media-users.aspx

Dumka, L. E., Roosa, M. W., & Jackson, K. M. (1997). Risk, conflict, mothers' parenting, and children's adjustment in low-income, Mexican immigrant, and Mexican American families. *Journal of Marriage and the Family, 59*(2), 309–323.

Duncan, B. L., & Rock, J. W. (1993). Saving relationships: The power of the unpredictable. *Psychology Today, 26*(1), 46–51.

Dunphy, D. (1963). The social structure of urban adolescent peer groups. *Sociometry, 26,* 230–246.

Durik, A. M., Hyde, J. S., Marks, A. C., Roy, A. L., Anaya, D., & Schultz, G. (2006). Ethnicity and gender stereotypes of emotion. *Sex Roles, 54,* 429–445.

Dush, C. M., Cohan, C. L., & Amato, P. R. (2003). The relationship between cohabitation and marital quality and stability: Change across cohorts? *Journal of Marriage and Family, 65*(3), 539–549.

Eagly, A. H., & Wood, W. (2013). The nature-nurture debates: 25 years challenges of understanding the psychology of gender. *Perspectives on Psychological Science, 8*(3), 340–357.

Eastwick, P. W. (2013). Cultural influences on attraction. In J. A. Simpson & L. Campbell (Eds.), *The Oxford handbook of close relationships* (pp. 161–182). New York: Oxford University Press.

Eastwick, P. W., Finkel, E. J., Mochon, D., & Ariely, D. (2007). Selective versus unselective romantic desire: Not all reciprocity is created equal. *Psychological Science, 18,* 317–319.

Eder, D., & Evans, C. C., & Parker, S. (1995). *School talk: Gender and adolescent culture.* New Brunswick, NJ: Rutgers University Press.

Edin, K., & Reed, J. M. (2005). Why don't they just get married? Barriers to marriage among the disadvantaged. *Future of Children, 15,* 117–137.

Edwards, J. N., & Booth, A. (1994). Sexuality, marriage, and well-being: The middle years. In A. S. Rossi (Ed.), *Sexuality across the life course* (pp. 233–259). Chicago: University of Chicago Press.

Eisenberger, N. L. (2012). Broken hearts and broken bones: A neural perspective on the similarities between social and physical pain. *Association for Psychological Science, 21*(1), 42–47.

Ekman, P., & Friesen, W. V. (1994). *Unmasking the face.* Englewood Cliffs, NJ: Prentice Hall.

Elfenbein, H. A. (2013). Nonverbal dialects and accents in facial expressions of emotion. *Emotion Review, 5,* 90–96.

Elicker, J., Englund, M., & Sroufe, L.A. (1992). Predicting peer competence and peer relationships in childhood from early parent-child relationships. In R. D. Parke & G. W. Ladd (Eds.), *Family-peer relationships: Modes of linkages* (pp. 77–106). Hillsdale, NJ: Erlbaum.

Elkins, L. E., & Peterson, C. (1993). Gender differences in best friendships. *Sex Roles, 29,* 497–509.

Elliot, B. D., & Simmons, T. (2011). *Marital events of Americans: 2009.* American Community Survey Reports (ACS-13). Washington, DC: U.S. Census Bureau.

Elliott, D. B., Krivickas, K., Brault, M. W., & Kreider, R. M. (2012). *Historical marriage trends from 1890–2010: A focus on race differences.* Working Paper Number 2012–12, U.S. Census Bureau.

Ellis, R., & Kreider, R. (2011). Number, timing, and duration of marriages and divorces: 2009. *Current population reports.* Retrieved from http://www.census.gov/prod/2011pubs/p70-125.pdf

Emerson, R. (1976). Social exchange theory. In A. Inkeles, J. Colemen, & N. Smelser (Eds.), *Annual review of sociology.* Palo Alto, CA: Annual Reviews.

Emmelkamp, P. M. G., & Heeres, H. (1988). Drug addiction and parental rearing style: A controlled study. *The International Journal of the Addictions, 23*(2), 207–216.

Englert, C., Bertrams, A., & Dickhäuser, O. (2011). Dispositional self-control capacity and trait anxiety as relates to coping styles. *Psychology, 2,* 598–604.

Enzlin, P., Mathieu, C., Van Den Bruel, A., Bosteels, J., Vanderschueren, D., & Demyttenaere, K. (2002). Sexual dysfunction in women with Type I diabetes. *Diabetes Care, 25*(4), 672–677.

Erikson, E. H. (1950/1963). *Childhood and society.* New York: Norton.

Erikson, E. H. (1968). *Identity: Youth and crisis.* New York: Norton.

Erikson, E. H. (1980/1982). *Identity and the life cycle.* New York: Norton.

Erkman, F. (1992). Support for Rohner's parental acceptance-rejection theory as a psychological abuse theory in Turkey. In S. Iwawaki, Y. Kashima, & K. Leung (Eds.), *Innovations in cross-cultural psychology* (pp. 384–395). Liets, Amsterdam: Swets & Zeitlinger.

Erkman, F., & Rohner, R. P. (2006). Youth's perceptions of corporal punishment, parental acceptance, and psychological adjustment in a Turkish metropolis. In R. P. Rohner (Ed.), *Corporal punishment, parental acceptance-rejection, and youth's psychological adjustment. Cross-Cultural Research, 40,* 250–267.

Esbensen, F. A., & Carson, D. C. (2009). Consequences of being bullied: Results from a longitudinal assessment of bullying victimization in a multisite sample of American students. *Youth & Society, 41,* 209–233.

Faries, M. D., & Bartholomew, J. B. (2012). The role of body fat in female attractiveness. *Evolution and Human Behavior, 33,* 672–681.

Fattah, F. A. El. (1996). *Symptoms of depression and perception of parental acceptance and control.* Paper presented on symposium on PARTheory, Zagazig University, Egypt.

Feeney, J. A. (1994). Attachment style, communication patterns, and satisfaction across the life cycle of marriage. *Personal Relationships, 1,* 333–348.

Feeney, J. A. (1999). Adult attachment, emotional control, and marital satisfaction. *Personal Relations, 6*(2), 169–185.

Feeney, J. A. (2004). Hurt feelings in couple relationships: Toward integrative models of the negative effects of hurtful events. *Journal of Social and Personal Relationships, 21,* 487–508.

Feeney, J. (2008). Adult romantic attachment: Developments in the study of couple relationships. In J. Cassidy & P. Shaver (Eds.), *Handbook of attachment: Theory, research and clinical applications* (2nd ed., pp. 456–481). New York: The Guilford Press.

Feeney, J., Noller, P., & Hanrahan, M. (1994). Assessing adult attachment. In M. B. Sperling & W. H. Berman (Eds.), *Attachment in adults: Clinical and developmental perspectives* (pp. 128–152). New York: The Guilford Press.

Feeney, J. A., Noller, P., & Roberts, N. (2000). Attachment and close relationships. In C. Hendrick & S. S. Henderick (Eds.), *Close relationships: A sourcebook* (pp. 185–201). London: Sage.

Fehr, B. (1996). *Friendship processes.* Thousand Oaks, CA: Sage.

Fehr, B. (1999). Stability and commitment in friendships. In J. M. Adams & W. H. Jones (Eds.), *Handbook of interpersonal commitment and relationship stability* (pp. 259–280). Dordrecht, Netherlands: Kluwer.

Fehr, B. (2004). Intimacy expectations in same-sex friendships: A prototypical interaction pattern model. *Journal of Personality and Social Psychology, 86,* 265–284.

Fehr, B., & Broughton, R. (2001). Gender and personality differences in conceptions of love: An interpersonal theory analysis. *Personal Relationships, 8,* 115–136.

Feingold, A. (1990). Gender differences in effects of physical attractiveness on romantic attraction: A comparison across five research paradigms. *Journal of Personality and Social Psychology, 59,* 981–993. doi:10.1037/0022-3514.59.5.981

Feiring, C. (1996). Concepts of romance in 15-year-old adolescents. *Journal of Research on Adolescence, 6*(2), 181–200.

Feiring, C., & Lewis, M. (1996). Finality in the eye of the beholder: Multiple sources, multiple time points, multiple paths. *Development and Psychopathology, 8,* 721–733.

Fekete, E., Stephens, M. A. P., Mickelson, K. D., & Druley, J. A. (2007). Couples' support provision during illness: The role of perceived emotional responsiveness. *Families, Systems, and Health, 25,* 204–217.

Feldman, S. S., Turner, R., & Araujo, K. (1999). The influence of the relationship context on normative and personal sexual timetables in youths. *Journal of Research on Adolescence, 9,* 25–52.

Felmlee, D., & Muraco, A. (2009). Gender and friendship norms among older adults. *Research on Aging, 31*(3), 318–344.

Felmlee, D. H. (1999). Social norms in same- and cross-gender friendships. *Social Psychology Quarterly, 62,* 53–67.

Felmlee, D. H., Hilton, K., & Orzechowicz, D. (2012). Romantic attraction and stereotypes of gender and sexuality. In M. A. Paludi (Ed.), *The psychology of love* (pp. 171–184). Santa Barbara, CA: Praeger.

Felmlee, D. H., Orzechowicz, D., & Fortes, C. (2010). Fairy tales: Attraction and stereotypes in same-gender relationships. *Sex Roles, 62,* 226–240.

Field, D., & Minkler, M. (1988). Continuity and change in social support between young-old and old-old or very-old age. *Journal of Gerontology, 43,* 100–106.

Fielder, R. L., & Carey, M. P. (2010). Predictors and consequences of sexual "hook-ups" among college students: A short-term prospective study. *Archives of Sexual Behavior, 39,* 1105–1119.

Fields, J. (2004). America's families and living arrangements. *Current Population Report,* P20-553. U.S. Census Bureau, Washington, DC.

Fincham, F. D. (2003). Marital conflicts: Correlates, structures, and context. *Current Directions in Psychological Science, 12,* 23–27.

Fincham, F. D., Beach, S. R. H., & Davila, J. (2004). Forgiveness and conflict resolution in marriage. *Journal of Family Psychology, 18*(1), 72–81.

Fincham, F. D., Beach, S. R., Lambert, N., Stillman, T., & Braithwaite, S. (2008). Spiritual behaviors and relationship satisfaction: A critical analysis of the role of prayer. *Journal of Social and Clinical Psychology, 27*(4), 362–388. Retrieved from http://dx.doi.org/10.1521/jscp.2008.27.4.362

Fincham, F. D., Hall, J. L., & Beach, S. R. H. (2006). Forgiveness in marriage: Current status and future directions. *Family Relations, 55,* 415–427.

Fincham, F. D., Stanley, S. M., & Beach, S. R. H. (2007). Transformative processes in marriage: An analysis of emerging trends. *Journal of Marriage and Family, 69,* 275–292.

Fingerman, K. L., & Charles, S. T. (2010). It takes two to tango: Why old people have the best relationships. *Current Directions in Psychological Science, 19,* 172–176.

Finkel, E. J., & Campbell, W. K. (2001). Self-control and accommodation in close relationships: An interdependence analysis. *Journal Personality and Social Psychology, 81*(2), 261–272.

Finkel, E. J., Eastwick, P. W., & Matthews, J. (2007). Speed-dating as an invaluable tool for studying romantic attraction: A methodological primer. *Personal Relationships, 14,* 149–166.

Fisher, H. (2016). *Anatomy of love: A natural history of mating, marriage, and why we stray.* New York: Norton.

Fisher, H. E. (2004). *Why we love: The nature and chemistry of romantic love.* New York: Henry Holt.

Fisher, H. E., Aron, A., & Brown, L. L. (2006). Romantic love: A mammalian brain system for mate choice. *Philosophical Transactions of the Royal Society B, 361,* 2173–2186.

Fisher, R. J. (2000). Intergroup conflict. In M. Deutsch & P. T. Coleman (Eds.), *The handbook of conflict resolution: Theory and practice* (pp. 166–184). San Francisco: Jossey-Bass.

Fisher, T. D., Moore, Z. T., & Pittenger, M. (2012). Sex on the brain? An examination of frequency of sexual cognitions as a function of gender, erotophilia, and social desirability. *Journal of Sex Research, 49,* 69–77.

Fiske, S. T. (2010). *Social beings: Core motives in social psychology* (2nd ed.). Hoboken, NJ: Wiley.

Fletcher, G., & Kerr, P. (2013). *Love, reality, and illusion in intimate relationships.* In J. A. Simpson & L. Campbell (Eds.), *The Oxford handbook of close relationships.* New York: Oxford University Press.

Fletcher, G., Simpson, J. A., Campbell, L., & Overall, N. C. (2013). *The science of intimate relationships*. Chichester, UK: Wiley.

Fletcher, G. J. O., & Thomas, G. (1996). Close relationship lay theories: Their structure and function. In G. J. O. Fletcher and J. Fitness (Eds.), *Knowledge structure in close relationships: A social psychological approach* (pp. 3–24). Mahwah, NJ: Erlbaum.

Fletcher, G. J. O., Tither, J. M., O'Loughlin, C., Friesen, M., & Overall, N. (2004). Warm and homely or cold and beautiful? Sex differences in trading off traits in mate selection. *Personality and Social Psychology Bulletin, 30*, 659–672.

Floyd, K. (2006). *Communicating affection: Interpersonal behavior and social context*. New York: Cambridge University Press.

Ford, J. D., & Russo, E. (2006). Trauma-focused, present-centered, emotional self-regulation approach to integrated treatment for posttraumatic stress and addiction: Trauma adaptive recover group education and therapy (TARGET). *American Journal of Psychotherapy, 60*, 335–355.

Ford, P. (2002, April). In Europe, marriage is back. *The Cristian Science Monitor,* p. 10. Retrieved from https://secure.csmonitor.com

Fordyce, M. W. (2000). *Human happiness: Its nature and its attainment* (2nd ed.). Upper Saddle River, NJ: Prentice Hall.

Forsyth, C. J., & Copes, H. (2014). Encyclopedia of social deviance (p. 740). New York: Sage.

Fraley, R. C., & Davis, K. E. (1997). Attachment formation and transfer in young adults close friendships and romantic relationships. *Personal Relationships, 4*, 131–144.

Fraley, R. C., & Shaver, P. R. (2000). Adult romantic attachment: Theoretical developments, emerging controversies, and unanswered questions. *Review of General Psychology, 4*(2), 132–154.

Francis, D. H., & Sandberg, W. R. (2000). Friendships within entrepreneurial teams and its association with team and venture performance. *Entrepreneurship: Theory and Practice, 25*(2), 5–25.

Franks, M. M., Wendorf, C. A., Gonzalez, R., & Ketterer, M. (2004). Aid and influence: Health-promoting exchanges of older married partners. *Journal of Social and Personal Relationships, 21*, 431–445.

Franzoi, S. L., & Davis, M. H. (1985). Adolescent self-disclosure and loneliness: Private self-consciousness and parental influences. *Journal of Personality and Social Psychology, 48*, 768–780.

Fratiglioni, L., Paillard-Borg, S., & Winblad, B. (2004). An active and socially integrated lifestyle in late life might protect against dementia. *Lancet Neurology, 3*, 343–353.

Freud, S. (1949). *An outline of psychoanalysis*. New York: Norton.

Friedman, M. R., Dodge, B., Schick, V., Herbenick, D., Hubach, R. D., Bowling, J., . . . Reece, M. (2014). From bias to bisexual health disparities: Attitudes toward bisexual men and women in the United States. *LGBT Health*. doi:10.1089/lgbt.2014.0005

Frijda, N., H. (2006). *The laws of emotion.* New York: Erlbaum.

Fugère, M., Escoto, C., Cousins, A. J., Riggs, M. L., & Haerich, P. (2008). Sexual attitudes and double standards: A literature review focusing on participant gender and ethnic background. *Sexuality & Culture 12*(3), 169–182.

Fuhrman, R. W., Flannagan, D., & Matamoros, M. (2009). Behavior expectation in cross-sex friendships, same-sex friendships, and romantic relationships. *Personal Relationships, 16,* 575–596.

Fuiman, M., Yarab, P., & Sensibaugh, C. (1997). *Just friends? An examination of the sexual, physical, and romantic aspects of cross-gender friendships.* Paper presented at the biennial meeting of the International Network on Personal Relationships, Oxford, OH.

Fulcher, M., Sutfin, E. L., & Patterson, C. J. (2008). Individual differences in gender development: Associations with parental sexual orientation, attitudes, and division of labor. *Sex Roles, 58,* 330–341.

Fullerton, C. S., & Ursano, R. J. (1994). Preadolescent peer friendships: A critical contribution to adult social relatedness. *Journal of Youth and Adolescence, 23*(1), 43–64.

Fung, H., & Carstensen, L. L. (2004). Motivational changes in response to blocked goals and foreshortened time: Testing alternatives to socioemotional selectivity theory. *Psychology and Aging, 19,* 68–78.

Furman, W. (1999). Friends and lovers: The role of peer relationships in adolescent romantic relationships. In W. A. Collins & B. Laursen (Eds.), *Relationships as developmental contexts: The 29th Minnesota Symposium on Child Development* (Vol. 30, pp. 133–154). Hillsdale, NJ: Erlbaum.

Furman, W. (2002). The emerging field of adolescent romantic relationships. *Current Directions in Psychological Science, 11*(5), 177–180.

Furman, W., & Buhrmester, D. (1992). Age and sex differences in perceptions of networks of personal relationships. *Child Development, 63,* 103–115.

Furnham, A., Moutafi, J., & Baguma, P. (2002). A cross-cultural study on the role of weight and waist-to-hip ratio on female attractiveness. *Personality and Individual Differences, 32,* 729–745.

Furnham, A., Swami, V., & Shah, K. (2006). Body weight, waist-to-hip ratio and breast size correlates on ratings of female attractiveness, fecundity, and health. *Personality and Individual Differences, 41,* 443–454.

Furstenberg, F. F., & Kiernan, K. E. (2001). Delayed parental divorce: How much do children benefit? *Journal of Marriage and Family, 63,* 446–457.

Gainor, K. A. (2000). Including transgender issues in lesbian, gay, and bisexual psychology: Implications for clinical practice and training. In B. Greene & G. L. Croom (Eds.), *Education, research, and practice in lesbian, gay, bisexual, and transgendered psychology: A resource manual* (pp. 131–160). Thousand Oaks, CA: Sage.

Galati, D., Scherer, K. R., & Ricci-Bitti, P. E. (1997). Voluntary facial expression of emotion: Comparing congenitally blind with normally sighted encoders. *Journal of Personality and Social Psychology, 73,* 1363–1379.

Gallo, L. C., Troxel, W. M., Matthews, K. A., & Kuller, L. H. (2003). Marital status and quality in middle-aged women: Associations with levels and trajectories of cardiovascular risk factors. *Health Psychology, 22,* 453–463.

Galperin, A., & Haselton, M. G. (2010). Predictors of how often and when people fall in love. *Evolutionary Psychology, 8,* 5–28.

Galperin, A., Haselton, M. G., & Frederick, D. A. (2013). Sexual regret: Evidence for evolved sex difference. *Archives of Sexual Behavior, 42,* 1145–1161.

Gallup, G. H. (2003, June 24). *Current views on premarital and extramarital sex.* Gallup poll. Retrieved from www.gallup.com/poll/8704/current-views-premarital-extramarital-sex.aspx

Galupo, M. P. (2009). Cross-category friendship patterns: Comparison of heterosexual and sexual minority adults. *Journal of Social and Personal Relationships 26*(6–7), 811–831.

Galvin, K., & Brommel, B. (2000). *Family communication: Cohesion and change* (5th ed.). New York: Addison-Wesley Longman.

Gambrill, E., Florian, V., & Thomas, K. R. (2009). *Friendship across life span.* In M. Koch & J. B. Designs (Eds.), *The nature of friendship.* Kansas City, KS: Andrews McMeel.

Gangestad, S. W., Haselton, M. G., & Buss, D. M. (2006). Evolutionary foundations of cultural variation: Evoked culture and mate preferences. *Psychological Inquiry, 17,* 75–95.

Gao, G. (2001). Intimacy, passion and commitment in Chinese and U.S. American romantic relationships. *International Journal of Intercultural Relations, 25*(3), 329–342.

Garcia, L. T., & Markey, C. (2007). Matching in sexual experience for married, cohabitating, and dating couples. *Journal of Sex Research, 44*(3), 250–255.

Garcia-Falgueras, A., & Swaab, D. F. (2008). A sex difference in the hypothamaic uncinate nucleus: Relationship to gender identity. *Brain, 131,* 3132–3146.

Gardyn, R. (2003). Love stinks. *American Demographics, 25,* 10–11.

Gassanov, M. A., Nicholson, L. M., & Koch-Turner, A. (2008). Expectations to marry among American youth. *Youth & Society, 40,* 265–388.

Gates, G. J., Badgett, M. V. L., Macomber, J. E., & Chambers, K. (2007). *Adoption and foster care by gay and lesbian parents in the United States.* Los Angeles: The Williams Institute, University of California at Los Angeles.

Gaughan, M. (2002). The substitution hypothesis: The impact of premarital liaisons and human capital on marital timing. *Journal of Marriage and Family, 65,* 407–419.

Gavilano, G. (1988). *Maternal acceptance-rejection and personality characteristics among adolescents in different socio-economic sectors.* Thesis for completion of bachelor's degree, Catholic University of Peru, Lima.

Ge, X., Best, K. M., Conger, R. D., & Simon, R. L. (1996). Parenting behaviors and the occurrence and co-occurrence of adolescent depressive symptoms and conduct problems. *Developmental Psychology, 32*(4), 717–731.

Gebauer, J. E., Leary, M. R., & Neberich, W. (2012). Unfortunate first names: Effects of name- based relational devaluation and interpersonal neglect. *Social Psychological and Personality Science, 3,* 590–596. doi:10.1177/1948550611431644

Gecas, V., & Longmore, M. A. (2003). Self-Esteem. In J. J. Ponzetti Jr. (Ed.), *International encyclopedia of marriage and family relationships* (2nd ed., pp. 1419–1424). London: Macmillan.

Geiger, W., Harwood, J., Hummert, M. L. (2006). College students' multiple stereotypes of lesbians: A cognitive perspective. *Journal of Homosexuality, 51,* 165–182. doi:10.1300/J082v51n03_08

Geitsidou, A., & Giovazolias, T. (2016). Intimate partner acceptance–rejection and subjective well-being: What is the role of resilience? *Journal of Child and Family Studies, 25,* 3260–3269. doi:10.1007/s10826-016-0493-7

George, C., Kaplan, N., & Main, M. (1985). *Adult attachment interview.* Unpublished manuscript, Department of Psychology, University of California, Berkeley.

George, C., & Solomon, J. (1996). Representational models of relations. *Infant Mental Health Journal, 17,* 198–216.

Gere, J., Schimmack, U., Pinkus, R. T., & Lockwood, P. (2011). The effects of romantic partners' goal congruence on affective wellbeing. *Journal of Research in Personality, 45,* 549–559.

Gidycz, C. A., Van Wynsberghe, A., & Edwards, K. M. (2008). Prediction of women's utilization of resistance strategies in a sexual assault situation: A prospective study. *Journal of Interpersonal Violence, 23,* 571–588.

Gildersleeve, K., Haseltone, M. G., & Fales, M. R. (2014). Do women's mate preferences change across the ovulatory cycle? A meta-analytic review. *Psychological Bulletin, 140*(5), 1205–1259.

Gini, G., Pazzoli, T., Lenzi, M., & Vieno, M. (2014). Bullying victimization at school and headache: A meta-analysis of observational studies. *The Journal of Head and Face Pain, 54,* 976–986.

Giordano, P. C., Longmore, M. A., & Manning, W. D. (2006). Gender and the meaning of adolescent romantic relationships: A focus on boys. *American Sociological Review, 71,* 260–287.

Giovazolias, T. A., & Giotsa, A. (2016, June 7–10). *The mediating effect of psychological adjustment and anxiety in the relationship between parental acceptance-rejection and fear of intimacy in Greek young adults.* Presented in the 6th International Congress on Interpersonal Acceptance-Rejection, Madrid, Spain.

Gladue, B. A. (1994). Biopsychology of sexual orientation. *Current Directions, 3,* 150–154.

Glaser, C. L., Robnett, B., & Feliciano, C. (2009). Internet dater's body type preferences: Race-ethnic and gender differences. *Sex Roles, 61,* 14–33.

Glavak-Tkalic, B., Vulic-Prtoric, A., & Zoroja, A. (2016, June, 7–10). *Parental acceptance-rejection in childhood and fear of intimacy in adulthood among Croatian young adults: Moderating effects of anxiety and psychological adjustment.*

Presented in the 6th International Congress on Interpersonal Acceptance-Rejection, Madrid, Spain.

Glenn, N. D., Uecker, J., & Love, R. W. B., Jr. (2010). Later first marriage and marital success. *Social Science Research, 39*(5), 787–800. doi:10.1016/j.ssresearch.2010.06.002

Glick, P., Gangl, C., Gibb, S., Klumpner, S., & Weinberg, E. (2007). Defensive reactions to masculinity threat: More negative affect toward effeminate (but not masculine) gay men. *Sex Roles, 57,* 55–59. doi:10.1007/s11199-007-9195-3

Goetz, J. L., Keltner, D., & Thomas, E. S. (2010). Compassion: An evolutionary analysis and empirical view. *Psychological Bulletin, 36*(3), 351–374.

Goldberg, A. E. (2009). Heterosexual, lesbian, and gay pre-adoptive parents' preferences about child gender. *Sex Roles, 61,* 55–71.

Goldberg, A. E., Downing, J. B., & Sauck, C. C. (2008). Perceptions of children's parental preferences in lesbian two-mother households. *Journal of Marriage and Family, 70,* 419–434.

Goldberg, A. E., & Sayer, A. G. (2006). Lesbian couples' relationship quality across the transition to parenthood. *Journal of Marriage and Family, 68,* 87–100.

Goldberg, A. E., & Smith, J. A. Z. (2011). Stigma, social context, and mental health: Lesbian and gay couples across the transition to adoptive parenthood. *Journal of Counseling Psychology, 58*(1), 139–150.

Goldberg, S. (2000). *Attachment and development.* Hillside, NJ: The Analytic Press.

Goodwin, J. S., Hurt, W. C., Key, C. R., & Sarrett, J. M. (1987). The effect of marital status on stage, treatment and survival of cancer patients. *Journal of the American Medical Association, 258,* 3125–3130.

Gooren, L. (2006). The biology of human psychosexual differentiation. *Hormones and Behavior, 50,* 589–601.

Gordon, A. M., & Chen, S. (2014). The role of sleep in interpersonal conflict: Do sleepless nights mean worse fights? *Social Psychology and Personality Science, 5,* 168–175.

Gordon, L. (2002). *Heroes of their own lives: The politics and history of family violence.* Urbana: University of Illinois Press.

Gotlib, I. H., & Whiffen, V. E. (1991). The interpersonal context of depression: Implications for theory and research. In W. H. Jones & D. Perlman (Eds.), *Advances in personal relationships* (Vol. 3, pp. 177–206). New York: Springer.

Gott, M., & Hinchcliff, S. (2003). How important is sex in later life? The views of older people. *Social Science and Medicine, 56,* 1617–1628.

Gotta, G., Green, R. J., Blum, E. R., Solomon, S., Balsam, K., & Schwartz, P. (2011). Heterosexual, lesbian, and gay male relationships: A comparison of couples in 1975 and 2000. *Family Process, 50*(3), 353–376.

Gottman, J. M. (2010). *About relationship conflicts.* Retrieved from https://www.youtube.com/watch?v=r0OGY54yWvw

Gottman, J. M. (2011). *The science of trust: Emotional attachment for couples.* New York: Norton.

Gottman, J. (2014). *What predicts divorce? The relationship between marital processes and marital outcomes.* Hove, East Sussex, UK: Psychology Press.

Gottman, J. M. (2016). *Gottman couples & marital therapy.* The Gottman Institute. Retrieved from https://www.gottman.com

Gottman, J. M., & Levenson, R. W. (2002). A two-factor model for predicting when a couple will divorce: Exploratory analyses using 14-year longitudinal data. *Family Process, 41*(1), 105–110.

Gray, J. (2012). *Men are from Mars, women are from Venus.* New York: Harper.

Greenberger, E., & Chen, C. (1996). Perceived family relationship and depressed mood in early and late adolescence: A comparison of European and Asian Americans. *Developmental Psychology, 32,* 707–716.

Greene, K., & Faulkner, S. L. (2005). Gender, belief in the sexual double standard, and sexual talk in heterosexual dating relationships. *Sex Roles, 53*(3), 239–251. doi:10.1007/s11199-005-5682-6

Greenfield, S., & Thelen, M. (1997). Validation of the fear of intimacy scale with a lesbian and gay male population. *Journal of Social and Personal Relationships, 14,* 707–716.

Gregoire, C. (2014). Psychology of love that lasts a lifetime. *Huffinpost Healthy Living* (an online publication), The Huffingtonpost.com.

Gregoire, S. W. (2013). *Negotiating chores with your spouse.* Retrieved from http://www.focusonthefamily.com/marriage/daily-living/negotiating-chores-with-your-spouse

Grossman, M., & Wood, W. (1993). Sex differences in intensity of emotional experience: A social role interpretation. *Journal of Personality and Social Psychology, 65,* 1010–1022.

Grossmann, K. E., & Grossmann, K. (1991). Attachment quality as an organizer of emotional and behavioral responses in a longitudinal perspective. In C. M. Parkes, J. Stevenson-Hinde, & P. Marris (Eds.), *Attachment across the life cycle* (pp. 93–114). London: Routledge.

Grossmann, K. E., & Grossmann, K. (2005). Universality of human social attachment as an adaptive process. In C. S. Carter, L. Ahnert, K. E. Grossmann, S. B. Hrdy, M. E. Lamb, S. W. Porges, & N. Sachser (Eds.), *Attachment and bonding: A new synthesis. Dahlem Workshop Report 92* (pp. 199–229). Cambridge, MA: The MIT Press.

Gruder, C. L. (1971). Determinants of social comparison choices. *Journal of Experimental Social Psychology, 7*(5), 473–489. doi:10.1016/0022-1031(71)90010-2

Gueguen, N. (2012). Makeup and menstrual cycle: Near ovulation, women use more cosmetics. *Psychological Record, 62,* 541–548.

Guerrero, K. L., Anderson, A. P., & Afifi, A. W. (2007). *Close encounters: Communication in relationships.* Thousand Oaks, CA: Sage.

Guerrero, K. L., Trost, M. R., & Yoshimura, S. M. (2005). Romantic jealousy: Emotions and communicative responses. *Personal Relationships, 12,* 233–252. doi:10.1111/j. 1350-4126.2005.00113.x

Guillamon, A., Junque, C., & Gómez-Gil, E. (2016). A review of the status of brain structure research in transsexualism. *Archives of Sexual Behavior, 45,* 1615–1648.

Gunnery, S. D., Hall, J. A., & Ruben, M. A. (2013). The deliberate smile: Individual differences in expressive control. *Journal of Nonverbal Behavior, 37,* 29–141.

Guthrie, J., & Kunkel, A. (2013). Tell me sweet (and not-so-sweet) little lies: Deception in romantic relationships. *Communication Studies, 64*(2), 141–157,

Hafner, M., & Ijzerman, H. (2011). The face of love: Spontaneous accommodation as social emotional regulation. *Personality and Social Psychology Bulletin, 37,* 1551–1563.

Haidt, J. (2006). *The happiness hypothesis.* New York: Basic Books.

Halatsis, P., & Christakis, N. (2009). The challenge of sexual attraction within heterosexuals' cross-sex friendship. *Journal of Social and Personal Relationships, 26,* 919–937.

Halford, W. K., Markman, H. J., Kling, G. H., & Stanley, S. M. (2003). Best practice in couple relationship education. *Journal of Marital and Family Therapy, 29*(3), 385–406.

Halford, W. K., Markman, H. J., & Stanley, S. (2008). Strengthening couples' relationships with education: Social policy and public health perspectives. *Journal of Family Psychology, 22*(3), 497–505. doi:10.1037/a0012789

Hall, C. S., & Lindzey, G. (1978/1997). *Theories of personality.* New York: Wiley.

Hall, D. T., & Nougaim, K. E., (1968). An examination of Maslow's need hierarchy in an organizational setting. *Organizational Behavior and Human performance, 3,* 12–35.

Hall, J. A. (2011). Sex differences in friendship expectations: A meta-analysis. *Journal of Social and Personal Relationships, 28,* 723–747.

Hall, J. A. (2012). Friendship standards: The dimensions of ideal expectations. *Journal of Social and Personal Relationships, 29,* 884–904.

Hall, J. A., Larson, K., & Watts, A. (2009). *Satisfying friendship maintenance expectations: The role of friendship standards, sex, and gender.* Paper presented at the National Communication Association Conference, Chicago, IL.

Hall, J. A., Larson, K., & Watts, A. (2011). Satisfying friendship maintenance expectations: The role of friendship standards and biological sex. *Human Communication Research, 37,* 529–552.

Halpern, C. T., Oslak, S. O., Young, M. L., Martin, S. L., & Kupper, L. L. (2001). Partner violence among adolescents in opposite-sex romantic relationships: Findings from the National Longitudinal Study of Adolescent Health. *American Journal of Public Health, 91,* 1679–1685.

Halpern, C. T., Udry, J. R., Campbell, B., Suchrindran, C., & Mason, G. A. (1994). Testosterone and religiosity as predictors of sexual attitudes and activity among adolescent males: A biological model. *Journal of Biosocial Science, 26,* 217–234.

Hammond, R. J., Cheney, P., & Pearsey, R. (2014). *Sociology of the family.* Free online text and test banks.

Hansen, T., Moum, T., & Shapiro, A. (2007). Relational and individual well-being among cohabitors and married individuals in midlife: Recent trends from Norway. *Journal of Family Issues, 28,* 910–933.

Haque, A. (1988). Relationship between perceived maternal acceptance-rejection and self-esteem among young adults in Nigeria. *Journal of African Psychology, 1,* 15–24.

Hardie, J. H., & Lucas, A. (2010). Economic factors and relationship quality among young couples: Comparing cohabitation and marriage. *Journal of Marriage and Family, 72*(5), 1141–1154.

Harding, D. J., & Jencks, C. (2003). Changing attitudes toward premarital sex: Cohort, period, and aging effects. *Public Opinion Quarterly, 67,* 211–226.

Harkless, L. E., & Fowers, B. J. (2005). Similarities and differences in relational boundaries among heterosexuals, gay men, and lesbians. *Psychology of Women Quarterly, 29,* 167–176.

Harris, A. H. S., & Thoreson, C. E. (2005). Forgiveness, unforgiveness, health and disease. In E. L. Worthington (Ed.), *Handbook of forgiveness* (pp. 321–334). New York: Routledge.

Harris, T. O., Brown, G. W., & Bifulco, A. T. (1990). Depression and situational helplessness/mastery in a sample selected to study childhood parental loss. *Journal of Affective Disorders, 20,* 27–41.

Hart, C. N., Nelson, D. A., Robinson, C. C., Albano, A. D., & Marshall, S. J. (2010, July 28–31). *Italian preshoolers' peer-status linkages with sociability, and subtypes of aggression and victimization.* Paper presented at the 3rd International Congress on Interpersonal Acceptance and Rejection, Padua, Italy.

Hartup, W. W., & Stevens, N. (1999). Friendships and adaptation across the life span. *Current Directions in Psychological Science, 8,* 76–79.

Harvey, J. H., Wenzel, A., & Sprecher, S. (Eds.) (2004). *Handbook of sexuality in close relationships.* Mahwah, NJ: Erlbaum.

Harvey, S. M., & Springer, C. (1995). Factors associated with sexual behavior among adolescents: A multivariate analysis. *Adolescence, 30,* 253–264.

Haselton, M. G., and Galperin, A. (2013). Error management in relationships. In J. A. Simpson and L. Campbell (Eds.), *Handbook of close relationships* (pp. 234–254): Oxford, U. K.: Oxford University Press.

Hasse, E. (1999). The Adult Attachment Interview: Historical and current perspectives. In J. Cassidy & P. R. Shaver (Eds.), *Handbook of attachment: Theory, research, and clinical applications* (pp. 395–433). New York: The Guilford Press.

Hatfield, E., & Rapson, R., L. (2005). *Love and sex: Cross-cultural perspectives.* Lanham, MD: University Press of America.

Hatfield, E., & Rapson, R. L. (2010). Culture, attachment style, and romantic relationships. In P. Erdman & K.-M. Ng (Eds.), *Attachment: Expanding the cultural connections* (pp. 227–242). London: Routledge/Taylor and Francis.

Hatfield, E., & Rapson, R. L. (2016). Love. In D. Sander & K. Scherer (Eds.) *Oxford companion to the affective sciences* (pp. 243–245). New York: Oxford University Press.

Hatfield, E., Rapson, R. L., & Aumer-Ryan, K. (2007). Social justice in love relationships: Recent developments. *Social justice research*. New York: Springer.

Hatfield, E., Rapson, R. L, & Martel, L. D. (2007). Passionate love. In S. Kitayama & D. Cohen (Eds.), *Handbook of cultural psychology*. New York: The Guilford Press.

Hawkins, A. J., Blanchard, V. L., Baldwin, S. A., & Fawcett, E. B. (2008). Does marriage and relationship education work? A meta-analytic study. *Journal of Consulting and Clinical Psychology, 76*(5), 723–734. doi:10.1037/a0012584

Hawkins, A. J., Willoughby, B. J., & Doherty, W. J. (2012). Reasons for divorce and openness to marital reconciliation. *Journal of Divorce & Remarriage, 53,* 453–463.

Hazan, C., & Shaver, P. (1987). Romantic love conceptualized as an attachment process. *Journal of Personality and Social Psychology, 52,* 511–524.

Heaven, P. C. L., Smith, L., Prabhakar, S. M., Abraham, J., & Mete, M. E. (2006). Personality and conflict communication patterns in cohabiting couples. *Journal of Research in Personality, 40,* 829–840.

Hebl, M. R., & Heatherton, T. F. (1998). The stigma of obesity in women: The difference is black and white. *Personality and Social Psychology Bulletin, 24,* 417–426.

Heiman, J. R., Long, J. S., Smith, S. N., Fisher, W. A., Michael, S. S., & Rosen, R. C. (2011). Sexual satisfaction and relationship happiness in midlife and older couples in five countries. *Archives of Sexual Behavior, 40*(4), 741–753.

Heine, S., Foster, J., & Spina, R. (2009). Do birds of a feather universally flock together? Cultural variation in the similarity-attraction effect. *Asian Journal of Social Psychology, 12*(4), 247–258.

Heine, S. J., & Renshaw, K. (2002). Interjudge agreement, self-enhancement, and liking: Cross-cultural divergences. *Personality and. Social Psychology Bulletin, 28,* 578–587.

Heller, K. (2015). How can I improve intimacy in my marriage? *Psychology Central.* Retrieved June 29, 2016, from http://psychcentral.com/lib/how-can-i-improve-intimacy-in-my-marriage

Helms, H. M., Proulx, C. M., Klute, M. M., McHale, S. M., & Crouter, A. C. (2006). Spouses' gender typed attributes and their links with marital quality: A pattern analytic approach. *Journal of Social and Personal Relationships, 23,* 843–864.

Hendrick, C., & Hendrick, S. S. (2000). *Close relationships: A sourcebook.* Thousand Oaks: Sage.

Hendrick, S. S., & Hendrick, C. (1995). Gender differences and similarities in sex and love. *Personal Relationships, 2,* 55–65.

Hendrick, S. S., Hendrick, C., & Logue, E. M. (2010). Respect and the family. *Journal of the Family Theory & Review, 2,*126–136.

Henshaw, S. K. (2003). *Teenage pregnancy statistics with comparative statistics for women aged 20–24.* New York: Alan Guttmacher Institute.

Hergenhahn, B. R. (2000). *An introduction to the history of psychology.* Belmont, CA: Wadsworth.

Hertenstein, M. J. (2011). The communicative functions of touch in adulthood. In M. Heylens, G., De Cuypere, G., Zucker, K. J., Schelfaut, C., Elaut, E., Vanden Bossche, H., . . . T'Sjoen, G. (2012). Gender identity disorder in twins: A review of the case report literature. *Journal of Sexual Medicine, 9,* 751–757.

Hiedemann, B., Suhomlinova, O., & O'Rand, A. M. (1998). Economic independence, economic status, and empty nest in midlife marital disruption. *Journal of Marriage and Family, 60,* 219–231.

Hill, P. L., Nickel, L. B., & Roberts, B. W. (2014). Are you in a health relationship? Linking conscientiousness to health via implementing and immunizing behaviors. *Journal of Personality.* doi:10,1111/jopy.12057

Hiller, L., Harrison, L., & Warr, D. (1997). When you carry a condom, all the boys think you want it: Negotiating competing discourses about safe sex. *Journal of Adolescence, 26,* 829–837.

Hinchliff, S., & Gott, M. (2004). Intimacy, commitment, and adaptation: Sexual relationships within long-term marriages. *Journal of Social and Personal Relationships, 21*(5), 595–609.

Hines, M. (2011). Prenatal endocrine influences on sexual orientation and on sexually differentiated childhood behavior. *Front Neuroendocrinology, 32,* 170–182.

Holland, R. W., Roeder, U. R., van Baaren, R. B., Brandt, A. C., & Hannover, B. (2004). Don't stand so close to me: The effects of self-construal on interpersonal closeness. *Psychological Science, 15,* 237–242.

Holley, S. R., Haase, C. M., & Levenson, R. W. (2013). Age-related changes in demand-withdraw communication behaviors. *Journal of Marriage and Family, 75,* 822–836.

Holmberg, D., Blair, K. L., & Phillips, M. (2010). Women's sexual satisfaction as a predictor of well-being in same-sex versus mixed-sex relationships. *Journal of Sex Research, 47*(1), 1–11.

Homans, G. C. (1958). Social behavior as exchange. *American Journal of Sociology, 63,* 597–606.

Homish, G. G., & Leonard, K. E. (2008). The social network and alcohol use. *Journal of Studies on Alcohol and Drugs, 69*(6), 906–914.

Horvath, A. (2001). The alliance. *Psychotherapy: Theory, Research, Practice, Training, 38*(4), 365–372. doi:10.1037/0033-3204.38.4.365

Howard, J. A., & Hollander, J. A. (1996). *Gendered situations and gendered selves.* Thousand Oaks, CA: Sage.

Howes, C. (2011). Friendship in early childhood. In K. Rubin, W. Bukowski, & B. Laursen (Eds.), *Handbook of peer interactions, relationship, and groups* (pp. 180–194), New York: The Guilford Press.

Howes, C., Hamilton, C. E., & Matheson, C. C. (1994). Children's relationships with peers: Differential associations with aspects of the teacher-child relationship. *Child Development, 65,* 253–263.

Hoyt, T., & Yeater, E. (2011). Individual and situational influences on men's responses to dating and social situations. *Journal of Interpersonal Violence, 26*(9), 1723–1740.

Hruschka, D. J. (2010). *Friendship: Development, ecology, and evolution of a relationship.* Berkeley, CA: University of California Press.

Hsu, F. L. K. (1985). The self in cross-cultural perspective. In A. J. Marsella, G. DeVos, & F. L. K. Hsu (Eds.), *Culture and self: Asian and Western perspectives* (pp. 24–55). London: Tavistock.

Huang, K., & Uba, L. (1992). Premarital sexual behavior among Chinese college students in the United States. *Archives of Sexual Behavior, 21,* 227–240.

Hughes, S. M., & Gallup, G. G., Jr. (2003). Sex differences in morphological predictors of sexual behavior: Shoulder to hip and waist to hip ratios. *Evolution and Human Behavior, 24,* 173–178.

Hundleby, J. D., & Mercer, G. W. (1987). Family and friends as social environments and their relationship to adolescents' use of alcohol, tobacco, and marijuana. *Journal of Marriage and the Family, 49,* 151–164.

Huss, M. T. (2009). *Forensic psychology: Research, clinical practice, and applications.* Singapore: Wiley-Blackwell.

Huston, T. L., & Chorost, A. F. (1994). Behavioral buffers on the effect of negativity on marital satisfaction: A longitudinal study. *Personal Relations, 1,* 223–239.

Hyde, J. S. (2014). Gender similarities and differences. *Annual Review of Psychology, 65,* 373–398.

Ickes, W. (1993). Traditional gender roles: Do they make and then break, our relationships? *Journal of Social Issues, 49,* 71–85.

Impett, E. A., Gable, S. L., & Peplau, L. A. (2005). Giving up and giving in: The costs and benefits of daily sacrifice in intimate relationships. *Journal of Personality and Social Psychology, 89,* 327–344.

Impett, E. A., Gere, J., Kogan, A., Gordon, A. M., & Keltner, D. (2013). How sacrifice impacts the giver and the recipient: Insights from approach-avoidance motivational theory. *Journal of Personality and Social Psychology, 82*(5), 390–401. doi:10.1111/jopy.12070

Impett, E. A., Muise, A., & Peragine, D. (2014). Sexuality in the context of relationships. In D. L. Tolman, L. Diamond, J. Bauermeister et al. (Eds.), *APA handbook of sexuality and psychology* (Vol. 1, pp. 269–315). Washington DC: American Psychological Association.

Impett, E. A., & Peplau, L. A. (2006). 'His' and 'her' relationship: A review of the empirical evidence. In A. L. Vangalisti & D. Perlman (Eds.), *Cambridge handbook of personal relationships* (pp. 273–291). New York: Cambridge University Press.

Ingersoll-Dayton, B., Campbell, R., Kurokawa, Y., & Saito, M. (1996). Separateness and togetherness: Interdependence over the life course in Japanese and American marriages. *Journal of Social and Personal Relationships, 13*(3), 385–398.

Ireland, M. E., Slatcher, R. B., Eastwick, P. W., Scissors, L. E., Finkel, E. J., & Pennebaker, J. W. (2011). Language style matching predicts relationship initiation and stability. *Psychological Science, 22,* 39–44.

Itzin, C., Taket, A., & Barter-Godfrey, S. (2010). *Domestic and sexual violence and abuse.* New York: Routledge.

Ivory, A. H., Gibson, R., & Ivory, J. D. (2009). Gendered relationships on television: Portrayals of same-sex and heterosexual couples. *Mass Communication and Society, 12*(2), 170–192.

Jackson, J. B., Miller, R. B., Oka, M., & Henry, R. G. (2014). Gender differences in marital satisfaction: A meta-analysis. *Journal of Marriage and Family, 76,* 105–129. doi:10.1111/jomf.12077

Jackson, S. M., & Cram, F. (2003). Disrupting the sexual double standard: Young women's talk about heterosexuality. *British Journal of Social Psychology, 42,* 113–127.

Jakubowski, S. F., Milne, E. P., Brunner, H., & Miller, R. B. (2004). A review of empirically supported marital enrichment programs. *Family Relations, 53*(5), 528–536. doi:10.1111/j.0197-6664.2004.00062.x

James, W. (1890). *Principles of psychology.* New York: Henry Holt.

James, W. (2000). The pursuit of happiness. In G. Gunn (Ed.), *Pragmatism and other writings.* London: Penguin Books.

Jang, S. A. (2008). The effects of attachment styles and efficacy of communication on avoidance following a relational partner's deception. *Communication Research Reports, 25*(4), 300–311.

Jang, S. A., Sandi, W. S., & Timothy, R. L. (2002). To stay or to leave? The role of attachment styles in communication patterns and potential termination of romantic relationships following discovery of deception. *Communication Monographs, 69*(3), 236–252.

Jankowiak, W. R. (1995). *Romantic passion: A universal experience?* New York: Columbia University Press.

Jankowiak, W. R., & Fischer, E. F. (1992). A cross-cultural perspective on romantic love. *Ethnology, 31,* 149–155.

Jepsen, L. K., & Jepsen, C. A. (2002). An empirical analysis of same-sex and opposite-sex couples: Do "likes" still like "likes" in the '90s? *IPR Working Papers, 99-5.* Institute for Policy Research at Northwestern University, Evanston, IL.

Johnson, K. L., & Roloff, M. E. (2000). Correlates of the perceived resolvability and relational consequences of serial arguing in dating relationships: Argumentative features and the use of coping strategies. *Journal of Social and Personal Relationships, 17,* 676–686.

Johnson, S. M., & O'Connor, E. (2002). *The gay baby boom: The psychology of gay parenthood.* New York: New York University Press.

Jones, D. (1995). Sexual selection, physical attractiveness, and facial neotony: Cross-cultural evidence and implications. *Current Anthropology, 36,* 723–748.

Jose, A., Daniel O'Leary, K., & Moyer, A. (2010). Does premarital cohabitation predict subsequent marital stability and marital quality? A meta-analysis. *Journal of Marriage and Family, 72,* 105–116.

Joyner, K., & Kao, G. (2005). Interracial relationships and the transition to adulthood. *American Sociological Review, 70,* 563–581.

Judd, T., & Sajn, N. (2008). Briton faces jail for sex on Dubai beach. *Independent.* Retrieved from https//www.independent.co.uk

Juvonen, J., Wang, Y., & Espinoza, G. (2011). Bullying experiences and compromised academic performance across middle school grades. *The Journal of Early Adolescence, 31,* 152–173. Retrieved from http://dx.doi.org/10.1177 /027243160379415

Kahn, R. L., & Antonucci, T. C. (1980). Convoys over the life course: Attachment, roles, and social support. In P. B. Baltes & O. Brim (Eds.), *Life-span development and behavior* (Vol. 3). New York: Academic Press.

Kalmijn, M., & Poortman, A. R. (2006). His or her divorce? The gendered nature of divorce and its determinants. *European Sociological Review, 22*(2), 201–214.

Kalmuss, D. (1984). The intergenerational transmissions of marital aggression. *Journal of Marriage and the Family, 44,* 11–19.

Kalra, G., Subramanyam, A., & Pinto, C. (2011). Sexuality: Desire, activity, and intimacy in the elderly. *Indian Journal of Psychiatry, 53*(4), 300–306.

Kalyuga, M. (2012). Vocabulary of love. In M. A. Paludi (Ed.), *The psychology of love* (Vol. 3, pp. 75–87). Santa Barbara, CA: Praeger.

Kammrath, L. K., & Peetz, J. (2011). The limits of love: Predicting immediate versus sustained caring behaviors in close relationships. *Journal of Experimental Social Psychology, 47,* 411–417.

Kamp, D. C. M., & Taylor, M. G. (2012). Trajectories of marital conflict across the life course: Predictions and interactions with marital happiness trajectories. *Journal of Family Issues, 33,* 341–368.

Kandler, C. (2012). Nature and nurture in personality development: The case of neuroticism and extraversion. *Current Direction in Psychological Science, 21,* 290–296.

Kane, E. W. (2006). No way my boys are going to be like that! Parents' responses to children's gender nonconformity. *Gender and Society, 20,* 149–176.

Kaplan, R. M., & Kronick, R. G. (2006). Marital status and longevity in the United States population. *Journal of Epidemiology and Community Health, 60,* 760–765.

Karandashev, V. (2015). A cultural perspective on romantic love. *Online Readings in Psychology and Culture, 5*(4), 1–21. Retrieved from http://dx.doi.org/10.9707/2307-0919.1135

Karney, B. (2007). Not shifting but broadening the focus of marital research. *Journal of Marriage and Family, 69,* 310–314.

Karney, B. R., & Bradbury, T. N. (1995). The longitudinal course of marital quality and stability: A review of theory, methods, and research. *Psychological Bulletin, 118*(1), 3–34.

Karraker, A., & DeLamater, J. (2013). Past-year sexual inactivity among older married persons and their partners. *Journal of Marriage and Family, 75*(1), 142–163.

Katherine, M. (2005). *Communication theories.* New York: McGraw-Hill.

Katy, S. (2016). 1.4 Million Americans identify as transgender. *Time* (retrieved June 30, 2016).

Katz, J. M., & Schneider, M. E. (2013). Casual hook up sex during the first year of college: Prospective associations with attitudes about sex and love relationships. *Archives of Sexual Behavior, 42,* 1451–1462.

Kaur, A. (2013). Maslow's need hierarchy theory: Applications and criticisms. *Global Journal of Management and Business Studies, 3,* 1061–1064.

Keefe, K., & Berndt, T. J. (1996). Relations of friendship quality to self-esteem in early adolescence. *Journal of Early Adolescence, 16*(1), 110–129.

Kellas, J. K., Bean, D., Cunningham, C., & Cheng, K. Y. (2008). The ex-files: Trajectories, turning points, and adjustment in the post-dissolutional relationships. *Journal of Social and Personal Relationships, 25,* 23–50.

Kellas, J. K., Willer, E. K., & Trees, E. R. (2013). Communicated perspective-taking during stories of marital stress: Spouses' perceptions of one another's perspective-taking behaviors. *Southern Communication Journal, 78,* 326–351.

Kennedy, S., & Bumpass, L. (2011). *Cohabitation and trends in the structure and stability of children's family lives.* Paper presented at the annual meeting of the Population Association of America, Washington, DC.

Kennelly, S. (2012). Are married people happier? Family & couples. *The Science of Meaningful Life.* University of California, Berkeley, June 6.

Khaleque, A. (2001). *Parental acceptance-rejection, psychological adjustment, and intimate adult relationships.* Unpublished master's degree thesis, University of Connecticut.

Khaleque, A. (2003). Perceived parental control in childhood and sexual preferences of adult offspring. *Psychological Reports, 92,* 755–756.

Khaleque, A. (2004). Intimate adult relationships, quality of life and psychological adjustment. *Social Indicators Research, 69,* 351–360.

Khaleque, A. (2007). Parental acceptance-rejection theory: Beyond parent-child relationships. *Interpersonal Acceptance, 1*(1), 2–4.

Khaleque, A. (2011). An overview of the effects of divorce on culture and society within Bangladesh. In R. E. Emery & J. G. Golson (Eds.), *Cultural sociology of divorce: An encyclopedia.* New York: Sage.

Khaleque, A. (2012). Adult intimate relationships and psychological adjustment. *Psychological Studies, 57*(1), 95–100.

Khaleque, A. (2013a). Perceived parental warmth and affection, and children's psychological adjustment, and personality dispositions: A meta-analysis. *Journal of Child and Family Studies, 22,* 297–30611.

Khaleque, A. (2013b). Testing the central postulates of parental acceptance-rejection theory: An overview of meta-analyses. *Interpersonal Acceptance, 7*(1), 1–3.

Khaleque, A. (2015a, February 11). *Testing the central postulates of interpersonal acceptance-rejection theory: An overview of meta-analyses.* Rohner center faculty affiliates lecture series, Rohner and Nancy Rohner Center for the Study of Interpersonal Acceptance and Rejection, University of Connecticut.

Khaleque, A. (2015b). Parental acceptance and children's psychological adjustment. In B. Kirkcaldy (Ed.), *Promoting psychological well-being in children and families* (pp. 226–243). Basingstoke, Hampshire: Palgrave Macmillan.

Khaleque, A. (2015c). Perceived parental neglect, and children's psychological maladjustment, and negative personality dispositions: A meta-analysis of multicultural studies. *Journal of Child and Family Studies, 24,* 1419–1428.

Khaleque, A. (2017a). Perceived parental aggression, and children's psychological maladjustment, and negative personality dispositions: A meta-analysis. *Journal of Child and Family Studies, 26,* 977–988.

Khaleque, A. (2017b). IPARTheory: Progress and prospect. *Interpersonal Acceptance, 11*(1), 7–9.

Khaleque, A., & Ali, S. (2017). A systematic review of meta-analyses of research on interpersonal acceptance-rejection theory: Constructs and measures. *Journal of Family Theory and Review, 9*(4), 44–458. doi:10.1111/jftr.12228

Khaleque, A., & Rohner, R. P. (2002a). Perceived parental acceptance-rejection and psychological adjustment: A meta-analysis of cross cultural and intra-cultural studies. *Journal of Marriage and the Family, 64,* 54–64.

Khaleque, A., & Rohner, R. P. (2002b). Reliability of measures assessing the pan-cultural association between perceived parental acceptance-rejection and psychological adjustment: A meta-analysis of cross-cultural and intra-cultural studies. *Journal of Cross-cultural Psychology, 33,* 86–98.

Khaleque, A., & Rohner, R. P. (2004). Relations between partner and parental acceptance, behavioral control, and psychological adjustment among heterosexual adult women. *Proceedings of the Society for Cross-Cultural Research Conference,* San Jose, CA.

Khaleque, A., & Rohner, R. P. (2011). Transcultural relations between perceived parental acceptance and personality dispositions of children and adults: A meta-analytic review. *Personality and Social Psychology Review, 15,* 1–13.

Khaleque, A., & Rohner, R. P. (2012). Pancultural associations between perceived parental acceptance and psychological adjustment of children and adults:

A metal analytic review of worldwide research. *Journal of Cross-Cultural Psychology, 43,* 784–800.

Khaleque, A., Rohner, R. P., & Laukkala, H. (2008). Intimate partner acceptance, parental acceptance, behavioral control, and psychological adjustment among Finnish adults in ongoing attachment relationships. *Cross-Cultural Research, 42,* 35–45.

Khaleque, A., Rohner, R. P., & Rahman, T. (2011). Perceived parental acceptance, behavioral control, and psychological adjustment of children in Bangladesh and the United States. In Kourkoutas & F. Erkman (Eds.), *Interpersonal Acceptance and Rejection: Social, Emotional, and Educational Contexts.* Boca Raton, Fl.: Brown Walker Press.

Khaleque, A., Rohner, R. P., & Shirin, A. (2010, July 28–31). *Impact of fathers' power, prestige, and love in Bangladeshi families.* Third International Congress on Interpersonal Acceptance and Rejection, Padua, Italy.

Khaleque, A., Shirin, A., & Uddin, M. K. (2013). Attachment relationships and psychological adjustment of married adults. *Social Indicators Research, 110,* 237–244.

Khatun, M. N., Ali, S., Khaleque, A., & Rohner, R. P. (2017). *Perceived parental undifferentiated rejection and children's negative personality dispositions: A meta-analysis of multi-cultural studies.* Unpublished manuscript, Ronald and Nancy Rohner Center for the Study of Interpersonal Acceptance and Rejection, University of Connecticut, Storrs.

Kiefer, A. K., & Sanchez, D. T. (2007). Scripting sexual passivity: A gender role perspective. *Personal Relationships, 14,* 269–290.

King, R. B., & Bratter, J. L. (2007). A path toward interracial marriage: Women's first partners and husbands across racial lines. *Sociological Quarterly, 48,* 343–369.

King, R. B., & Harris, K. M. (2007). Romantic relationships among immigrant adolescents. *International Migration Review, 41,* 344–370.

King, V. (2002). Parental divorce and interpersonal trust in adult offspring. *Journal of Marriage and Family, 64*(3), 642–656.

King, V., & Scott, M. E. (2005). A comparison of cohabiting relationships among older and younger adults. *Journal of Marriage and Family, 67,* 271–285.

Kirkpatrick, B. L. (2015). Personality and happiness. *Undergraduate honors theses.* Dissertations at Digital@USanDiego.

Kirkpatrick, L. A., & Davis, K. E. (1994). Attachment style, gender, and relationship stability: A longitudinal analysis. *Journal of Personality and Social Psychology, 66,* 502–512.

Kitayama, S., Markus, H. R., & Kurokawa, M. (2000). Culture, emotion, and well-being: Good feelings in Japan and the United States. *Cognition and Emotion, 14*(1), **93–124.**

Kite, M. E., Deaux, K., & Haines, E. L. (2008). Gender stereotypes. In F. L. Denmark and M. A. Paludi (Eds.), *Psychology of women: A handbook of issues and theories* (2nd ed., pp. 205–236). Westport, CT: Praeger.

Kleinke, C. L. (1986). Gaze and eye contact: A research review. *Psychological Bulletin, 100,* 78–100.

Kline, S., & Stafford, L. (2004). A comparison of interaction rules and interaction frequency in relationship to marital quality. *Communication Reports, 17*(1), 11–26.

Klomek, A. B., Sourander, A., & Gould, M. (2010). The association of suicide and bullying in childhood to young adulthood: A review of cross-sectional and longitudinal research findings. *Canadian Journal of Psychiatry, 55,* 282–288.

Klusmann, D. (2002). Sexual motivation and duration of partnership. *Archives of Sexual Behavior, 31,* 275–287.

Knapp, M. L. (1984). *Interpersonal communication and human relationships.* Boston: Allyn & Bacon.

Knapp, M. L., & Vangelisti, A. L. (2009). *Interpersonal Communication and Human Relationships* (pp. 32–51). Boston: Pearson.

Kniffin, K. M., & Wilson, D. S. (2004). The effect of nonphysical traits on the perception of physical attractiveness: Three naturalistic studies. *Evolution and Human Behavior, 25,* 88–101.

Knobloch, L. K. (2008). The content of relational uncertainty within marriage. *Journal of Social and Personal Relationships, 25,* 467–495.

Knobloch, L. K., & Solomon, D. (2002). Information seeking beyond initial interaction: Negotiating relational uncertainty within close relationships. *Human Communication Research, 28,* 243–257.

Knoester, C., & Booth, A. (2000). Barriers to divorce: When are they effective? When are they not? *Journal of Family Issues, 21,* 78–99.

Kontula, O. (2002, November). *Human sexuality and aging: An empirical study.* Paper presented at the annual meeting of the Society for the Scientific Study of Sexuality, Montreal, Canada.

Korobov, N., & Thorne, A. (2006). Intimacy and distancing: Young men's conversations about romantic relationships. *Journal of Adolescent Research, 21*(1), 27–55. doi:10.1177/0743558405284035

Koyama N. F., McGain A., & Hill R. A. (2004). Self-reported mate preferences and "feminist" attitudes regarding marital relations. *Evolution and Human Behavior, 25,* 327–335.

Kozee, H. B., Tylka, T. L., & Bauerband, L. A. (2012). Measuring transgender individuals' comfort with gender identity and appearance: Development and validation of the Transgender Congruence Scale. *Psychology of Women Quarterly, 36,* 179–196. doi:10.1177/0361684312442161

Kreager, D. A., Haynie, D. L., & Hopfer, S. (2013). Dating and substance use in adolescent peer networks: A replication and extension. *Addiction, 108,* 638–647. doi:10.1111/j.1360-0443.2012.04095.x

Kreider, R. M. (2007). *Current population reports* (P70-114). Washington, DC: U.S. Census Bureau.

Kreider, R. M., & Fields, J. M. (2002). Numbers, timing, and durations of marriages and divorces: Fall 1996. *Current population reports* (pp. 70–80), Washington DC: U.S. Census Bureau.

Kupersmidt, J. B., DeRosier, M. E., Patterson, C. J., & Griesler, P. C. 1990. *Parental involvement and children's peer relationships, behavior, self-concept, and academic adjustment*. Unpublished manuscript, Department of Psychology, University of North Carolina at Chapel Hill.

Kurdek, L. A. (2004). Are gay and lesbian cohabiting couples really different from heterosexual married couples? *Journal of Marriage and Family, 66,* 880–900.

Kurdek, L. A. (2006). Differences between partners from heterosexual, gay, and lesbian cohabiting couples. *Journal of Marriage and the Family, 68,* 509–528.

Kurdek, L. A. (2008). Change in relationship quality for partners from lesbian, gay male, and heterosexual couples. *Journal of Family Psychology, 22(5),* 701–711.

Kurien, D. N. (2010). Body language: Silent communicator. *Journal of Soft Skills, 4,* 29–36.

LaBrie, J. W., Hummer, J. F., Ghaidarov, T. M., Lac, A., & Kenney, S. R. (2014). Hooking up in the college context: The event-level effects of alcohol use and partner familiarity on hookup behaviors and contentment. *Journal of Sex Research, 51(1),* 62–73. doi:10.1080/00224499.2012.714010

La Gaipa, J. J. (1987). Friendship expectations. In R. Burnett, P. McGhee, & D. Clarke (Eds.), *Accounting for relationships: Explanation, representation and knowledge* (pp. 134–157). London: Methuen.

La Greca, A. M., & Harrison, H. M. (2005). Adolescent peer relations, friendships, and romantic relationships: Do they predict social anxiety and depression? *Journal of Clinical Child and Adolescent Psychology, 34(1),* 49–61.

La Greca, A. M., & Prinstein, M. J. (1999). The peer group. In W. K. Silverman & T. H. Ollendick (Eds.), *Developmental issues in the clinical treatment of children and adolescents* (pp. 171–198). Needham Heights, MA: Allyn & Bacon.

Lam, C., & Lefkowitz, E. (2013). Risky sexual behaviors in emerging adults: Longitudinal changes and within-person variations. *Archives of Sexual Behavior, 42,* 523–532.

Lambert, N. M., & Dollahite, D. C. (2006). How religiosity helps couples prevent, resolve, and overcome marital conflict. *Family Relations, 55(4),* 439–449. Retrieved from http://dx.doi.org/10.1111/j.1741-3729.2006.00413.x

Lang, F. R., Wagner, J., Wrzus, C., & Neyer, F. J. (2013). Personal effort in social relationships across adulthood. *Psychology and Aging, 28,* 529–539.

Langlais, M. R. (2012). *Relationship deterioration: Descriptions and implications*. Unpublished master's degree thesis, University of Texas at Austin.

Langlois, J. H., Kalakanis, L., Rubenstein, A. J., Larson, A., Hallam, M., & Smoot, M. (2000). Maxims or myths of beauty? A meta-analytic and theoretical review. *Psychological Bulletin, 126,* 390–423.

Larson, R. (1983). Adolescents' daily experience with family and friends: Contrasting opportunity systems. *Journal of Marriage & the Family, 45(4),* 739–750.

Larson, R., & Lampman-Petraitis, C. (1989). Daily emotional states as reported by children and adolescents. *Child Development, 60,* 1250–1260.

Larson, R., & Richards, M. (1991). Daily companionship in late childhood and early adolescence: Changing developmental contexts. *Child Development, 62*(2), 284–300.

Larson, R. W., & Asmussen, L. (1991). Anger, worry, and hurt in early adolescence: An enlarging world of negative emotions. In M. E. Coltern & S. Gore (Eds.), *Adolescent stress: Causes and consequences* (pp. 21–41). New York: Aldine.

Larson, R. W., & Richards, M. (1998). Waiting for the weekend: Friday and Saturday night as the emotional climax of the week. In A. Crouter & R. Larson (Eds.), *Temporal rhythms in adolescence: Clocks, calendars, and the coordination of daily life.* San Francisco: Jossey-Bass.

Larson, R. W., Richards, M. H., Moneta, G., Holmbeck, G., & Duckett, E. (1996). Changes in adolescents' daily interactions with their families from ages 10 to 18: Disengagement and transformation. *Developmental Psychology, 32,* 744–754.

Laumann, E., Gagnon, J., Michael, R., & Michaels, S. (1994). *The social organization of sexuality: Sexual practices in the United States.* Chicago: University of Chicago Press.

Laumann, E. O., & Michael, R. T. (2000). *Sex, love, and health in America: Private choices and public policies.* Chicago: University of Chicago Press.

Laursen, B. (1993). Conflict management among close peers. In B. Laursen (Ed.), *Close friendships in adolescence* (pp. 39–54). San Francisco: Jossey-Bass.

Laursen, B. (1995). Conflict and social interaction in adolescent relationships. *Journal of Research on Adolescence, 5,* 55–70.

Laursen, B. (1996). Closeness and conflict in adolescent peer relationships: Interdependence with friends and romantic partners. In W. M. Bukowski, A. F. Newcomb, & W. H. Hartup (Eds.), *The company they keep: Friendship in childhood and adolescence* (pp. 186–212). New York: Cambridge University Press.

Laursen, B., Hartup, W., & Koplas, A. (1996). Towards understanding peer conflict. *Merrill-Palmer Quarterly, 42,* 76–102.

Lavner, J. A., & Bradbury, T. N. (2012). Why do even satisfied newlyweds eventually go on to divorce? *Journal of Family Psychology, 26*(1), 1–10.

Lawrence, E., Barry, R. A., Brock, R. L., Bunde, M., Langer, A., Ro, E., Fazio, E., et al. (2011). Development of an interview assessing relationship quality: Preliminary support for reliability, convergent and divergent validity, and incremental utility. *Psychological Assessment, 23,* 44–63. doi:10.1037/a0021096

Le, B., Dove, N., Agnew, C. R., Korn, M. S., & Mutso, A. A. (2010). Predicting non-marital romantic relationship dissolution: A meta-analytic synthesis. *Personal Relationships, 17,* 377–390. doi:10.1111/j.1475-6811.2010.01285

Leaper, C., & Robnett, R. D. (2011). Women are more likely than men to use tentative language, aren't they? A meta-analysis testing for gender differences and moderators. *Psychology of Women Quarterly, 35,* 129–142.

Lee, L., Loewenstein, G., Ariely, D., Hong, J., & Young, J. (2008). If I'm not hot, are you hot or not? Physical-attractiveness evaluations and dating preferences as a function of one's own attractiveness. *Psychological Science, 19,* 669–677.

Lee, K. S., & Ono, H. (2012). Marriage, cohabitation, and happiness: A cross-national analysis of 27 countries. *Journal of Marriage and Family, 74,* 953–972. doi:10.1111/j.1741-3737.2012.01001.x

Lefkowitz, E. S. (2005). "Things have gotten better": Developmental changes among emerging adults after the transition to university. *Journal of Adolescent Research, 20,* 40–63.

Lefkowitz, E. S., Boone, T. L., Aul, T. K., & Sigman, M. (2003). No sex or safe sex? Mothers' and adolescents' discussions about sexuality and AIDS/HIV. *Health Education Research, 18*(3), 341–351. doi:10.1093/her/cyf015

Lefkowitz, E. S., Shearer, C. L., Gillen, M. M., & Espinosa-Hernandez, G. (2014). How gendered attitudes relate to women's and men's sexual behaviors and beliefs. *Sex Cult, 18*(4), 833–846. doi:10.1007/s12119-014-9225-6. PMCID: PMC4244004

Lefkowitz, E. S., & Vasilenko, S. A. (2014). Healthy sex and sexual health: New directions for studying outcomes of sexual health. In E. S. Lefkowitz & S. A. Vasilenko (Eds.), *New directions for child and adolescent development: Positive and negative outcomes of sexual behavior* (pp. 87–98). San Francisco: Jossey-Bass.

Leifbroer, A., & Dourleijn, E. (2006). Unmarried cohabitation and union stability: Testing the role of diffusion using data from 16 European countries. *Demography, 43,* 203–221.

Leigh, B. C. (1989). Reasons for having and avoiding sex: Gender sexual orientation, and relationship to sexual behavior. *Journal of Sex Research, 26,* 199–209.

Lemay, E. P., Jr., & Neal, A. M. (2014). Accurate and biased perceptions of responsive support predict well-being. *Motivation and Emotion, 38,* 270–286.

Lenhart, A. (2012). *Teens & online video.* Pew Internet and American Life Project. Retrieved from http://pewinternet.org/Reports/2012/Teens-and-online-video.aspx

Lenhart, A., Madden, M., Smith, A., Purcell, K., Zickuhr, K., & Rainie, L. (2011). *Teens, kindness and cruelty on social network sites.* Pew Internet and American Life Project. Retrieved from http://pewinternet.org/Reports/2011/Teens-and-social-media.aspx

Lennon, A. P., Stewart, A. L., & Ledermann, T. (2013). The role of power in intimate relationships. *Journal of Social and Personal Relationships, 30,* 95–114.

LeVay, S. (2010). *Gay, straight, and the reason why: The science of sexual orientation.* New York: Oxford University Press.

Levin, I. (2004). Living apart together: A new family forum. *Current Sociology, 52,* 223–230.

Levin, I., & Trost, J. (1999). Living apart together. *Community, Work, & Family, 2,* 279–294.

Levinger, G. (1976). A socio-psychological perspective on marital dissolution. *Journal of Social Issues, 52,* 21–47.

Lewandowski, G. (2016). What are we fighting about? The top 15 sources of conflict in relationships. *Science of relationships.* Retrieved from http://www .scienceofrelationships.com/home/2011/10/3/what-are-we-fighting -about-the-top-15-sources-of-conflict-in.html

Lewandowski, G. W., Aron, A., & Gee, J. (2007). Personality goes a long way: The malleability of opposite-sex physical attractiveness. *Personal Relationships, 14,* 571–585.

Lewicki, R. J., & Wiethoff, C. (2000). Trust, trust development, and trust repair. In M. Deutsh & P. T. Coleman (Eds.), *The handbook of conflict resolution: Theory and practice* (pp. 86–107). San Francisco: Jossey-Bass.

Lewis, C. S. (2013). *The allegory of love: A study in medieval tradition.* Cambridge, UK: Cambridge University Press.

Lewis, M., & Feiring, C. (1989). Early predictors of childhood friendship. In T. J. Berndt & G. W. Ladd (Eds.), *Peer relationships in child development* (pp. 246–273). New York: Wiley.

Lewis, M. A., Atkins, D. C., Blayney, J. A., Dent, D. V., & Kaysen, D. L. (2013). What is hooking up? Examining definitions of hooking up in relation to behavior and normative perceptions. *Journal of Sex Research, 50,* 757–766.

Lewis, M. A., Granato, H., Blayney, J. A., Lostutter, T. W., & Kilmer, J. R. (2012). Predictors of hooking up sexual behavior and emotional reactions among U.S. college students. *Archives of Sexual Behavior, 41,* 1219–1229. doi:10.1007/s10508-011-9817-2

Li, N. P., Sing, O., & Jonason, P. K. (2012). Sexual conflict in mating strategies. T. K. Shackleford & A. T. Goetz (Eds.), *The Oxford handbook of sexual conflict in humans* (pp. 49–71). New York: Oxford University Press.

Li, N. P., Valentine, K. A., & Patel, I. (2011). Mate preferences in the US and Singapore: A cross-cultural test of the mate preference priority model. *Personality and Individual Differences, 50,* 291–294.

Li, T., & Fung, H. H. (2011). The dynamic goal theory of marital satisfaction. *Review of General Psychology, 15*(3), 246–254.

Li, X., Meier, J., & Adamsons, K. (2017). Father love and mother love: Contributions of parental acceptance-rejection to children's psychological adjustment. *Journal of Family Theory and Review* [in press].

Lichter, D. T. (2012). Childbearing among cohabiting women: Race, pregnancy, and union transitions. In A. Booth, S. L. Brown, N. Landale, W. D. Manning, & S. M. McHale (Eds.), *Early adulthood in a family context* (pp. 209–219). New York: Springer.

Lichter, D. T., Batson, C. D, & Brown, J. B. (2004). Welfare reform and marriage promotion: The marital expectations and desires of single and cohabiting mothers. *Social Service Review, 78,* 2–25.

Lichter, D. T., Qian, Z., & Mellott, L. M. (2006). Marriage or dissolution? Union transitions among poor cohabiting women. *Demography, 43,* 223–240.

Lindau, S. T., Schumm, L. P., Laumann, E. O., Levinson, W., O'Muircheartaigh, C. A., & Waite, L. J. (2007). A study of sexuality and health among older adults in the United States. *New England Journal of Medicine, 357,* 762–775.

Lindsey, C. R., & Khan, S. (2016, June 7–10). *Relationships among remembered parental acceptance, psychological adjustment, anxiety, and fear of intimacy among African American college students.* Presented in the 6th International Congress on Interpersonal Acceptance-Rejection, Madrid, Spain.

Lippa, R. A. (2009). Sex differences in sex drive, sociosexuality and height across 53 nations: Testing evolutionary and social structural theories. *Archives of Sexual Behavior, 38,* 631–651.

Little, A. C., Burt, D. M., & Perrett, D. I. (2006). What is good is beautiful: Face preference reflects desired personality. *Personality and Individual Differences, 41,* 1107–1118.

Little, A. C., Jones, B. C., & DeBruine, L. M. (2011). Facial attractiveness: Evolutionary based research. *The Royal Society Open Science.* doi:10.1098/rstb.2010.0404

Löckenhoff, C. E., & Carstensen, L. L. (2004). Socioemotional selectivity theory, aging, and health: The increasingly delicate balance between regulating emotions and making tough choices. *Journal of Personality, 72,* 1395–1424. doi:10.1111/j.1467-6494.2004.00301.x

Lofquist, D., Lugaila, T., O'Connell, M., & Feliz, S. (2012). Households and families: 2010. *2010 Census Briefs,* C2010BR-14. Retrieved January 28, 2013, from http://www.census.gov/prod/cen2010/briefs/c2010br-14.pdf

Lombardi, E. L., Wilchins, A. R., Priesing, D., & Malouf, D. (2008). Gender violence: Transgender experiences with violence and discrimination. *Journal of Homosexuality, 42*(1), 89–101. doi:10.1300/J082v42n01

Lopata, H. Z. (1988). Support systems of American urban widowhood. *Journal of Social Issues, 44,* 113–128.

Lopata, H. Z. (2010). Support systems of American urban widowhood. *Journal of Social Issues.* First published online April 2010. doi:10.1111/j.1540-4560.1988.tb02080.x

Lopez, F. G., & Brennan, K. A. (2000). Dynamic processes underlying adult attachment organization: Toward an attachment theoretical perspective on the healthy and effective self. *Journal of Counseling Psychology, 47,* 283–301.

Loscocco, K., & Walzer, S. (2013). Gender and the culture of heterosexual marriage in the United States. *Journal of Family Theory & Review, 5,* 1–14. doi:10.1111/jftr.12003

Lucas, T. W., Wendorf, C. A., & Imamoglu, E. O. (2004). Marital satisfaction in four cultures as a function of homogamy, male dominance and female attractiveness. *Sexualities, Evolution and Gender, 6,* 97–130.

Lueptow, L. B., Garovich-Szabo, L., & Lueptow, M. B. (2001). Social change and the persistence of sex typing: 1974–1997. *Journal of Consumer Research, 80*(1), 1–36.

Luo, S., & Zhang, G. (2009). What leads to romantic attraction: Similarity, reciprocity, security or beauty? Evidence from a speed-dating study. *Journal of Personality, 77,* 933–964.

Lusk, J., MacDonald, K., & Newman, J. R. (1998). Resource appraisals among self, friend and leader: Implications for an evolutionary perspective on individual differences. *Personality and Individual Differences, 5,* 685–700.

Lutz-Zois, C. J., Bradeley, A. C., Mihalik, J. L., & Moorman-Eavers E. R. (2006). Perceived similarity and relationship success among dating couples: An idiographic approach. *Journal of Social and Personal Relationships, 23,* 865–880.

Lynch, J. J. (1977). *The broken heart: The medical consequences of loneliness.* New York: Basic Books.

Lyubomirsky, S. (2008). *The how of happiness.* New York: Penguin Press.

MacCallum, F., & Golombok, S. (2004). Children raised in fatherless families from infancy: A follow-up of children of lesbian and single heterosexual mothers at early adolescence. *Journal of Psychology and Psychiatry, 45,* 1407–1419.

Maccoby, E. E. (1998). *The two sexes: Growing up apart, coming together.* Cambridge, MA: Harvard University Press.

MacNeil, S., & Byers, E. S. (2009). Role of sexual self-disclosure in the sexual satisfaction of long-term heterosexual couples. *Journal of Sex Research, 46,* 3–14. doi:10.1080/00224490802398399

Magai, C., Cohen, C., Milburn, N., Thorpe, B., McPherson, R., & Peralta, D. (2001). Attachment styles in older European American and African American adults. *The Journals of Gerontology, Social Sciences, 46B,* S1–S8.

Mahoney, A., Pargament, K. I., Jewell, T., Swank, A. B., Scott, E., Emery, E., & Rye, M. (1999). Marriage and the spiritual realm: The role of proximal and distal religious constructs in marital functioning. *Journal of Family Psychology, 13,* 1–18. Retrieved from http://dx.doi.org/10.1037/0893-3200.13.3.321

Main, M. (1995). Attachment: Overview, with implications for clinical work. In S. Goldberg, R. Muir, & J. Kerr (Eds.), *Attachment theory: Social development, and clinical perspectives* (pp. 407–474). Hillsdale, NJ: Analytic Press.

Main, M., & Goldwyn, R. (1984). *Adult attachment scoring and classification system.* Unpublished manuscript, University of California at Berkeley.

Maisel, N. C., & Karney, B. R. (2012). Socioeconomic status moderates associations among stressful events, mental health, and relationship satisfaction. *Journal of Family Psychology, 26,* 654–660.

Maisonneuve, J., & Lamy, L. (1993). *Psycho-sociologie de l'amitie.* Paris: PUF.

Maizes, V. (2015). *Integrative women's health.* Oxford, UK: Oxford University Press.

Makepeace, J. M. (1981). Courtship Violence among College Students. *Family Relations, 30(1),* 97–102, doi: 10.2307/584242

Malachowski, C. C., & Frisby, B. N. (2015). The aftermath of hurtful events: Cognitive, communicative, and relational outcomes. *Communication Quarterly, 63(2),* 187–203. doi:10.1080/01463373.2015.1012218

Malik, F., & Rohner, R. P. (2012). Spousal rejection as a risk factor for parental rejection of children. *Journal of Family Violence, 27*(4), 295–301.

Mallon, G. P., & DeCrescenzo, T. (2006). Transgender children and youth: A child welfare practice perspective. *Child Welfare, 85,* 215–241.

Mancini, A. D., & Bonanno, G. A. (2006). Marital closeness, functional disability, and adjustment in late life. *Psychology and Aging, 21,* 600–610.

Mancini, J. A., & Simon, J. (1984). Older adults' expectations of support from family and friends. *Journal of Applied Gerontology, 3,* 150–160.

Maner, J. K., Rouby, D., & Gonzaga, G. C. (2008). Automatic inattention to attractive alternatives: The evolved psychology of relationship maintenance. *Evolution and Human Behavior, 29,* 343–349.

Manning, W. D. (2013). *Trends in cohabitation: Twenty years of change, 1987–2010* (FP-13-12). National Center for Family & Marriage Research. Retrieved from http://www.bgsu.edu/content/dam/BGSU/college-of-arts-and-sciences/NCFMR/documents/FP/FP-13-12.pdf

Manning, W. D., & Cohen, J. A. (2012). Premarital cohabitation and marital dissolution: An examination of recent marriages. *Journal of Marriage and Family, 74,* 377–387.

Mansfield, P. K, Voda, A., & Koch, P. B. (1998). Predictors of sexual response changes in heterosexual midlife women. *Health Values, 19,* 10–20.

Manusov, V., & Patterson, M. L. (2006). *Handbook of nonverbal communication.* New York: Sage.

Markham, C. M., Lormand, D., Gloppen, K. M., Peskin, M. F., Flores, B., Low, B., & House, L. D. (2010). Connectedness as a predictor of sexual and reproductive health outcomes for youth. *Journal of Adolescent Health, 46,* S23–S41.

Markiewicz, D., & Doyle, A. B. (2012). Best friends. In R. J. Levesque (Ed.). *Encyclopedia of adolescence* (pp. 254–260). New York: Springer.

Markman, H. J., & Rhoades, G. K. (2012). Relationship education research: Current status and future directions. *Journal of Marital and Family Theory, 38*(1), 169–200.

Markus, H. R., & Kitayama, S. (2010). Cultures and selves: A cycle of mutual constitution. *Perspectives on Psychological Science, 5,* 420–430

Marrone, M. (1998). *Attachment and interaction.* London: Jessica Kingsley.

Marshall, T. C. (2010). Gender, peer relations, and intimate romantic relationships. In J. Chrisler & D. McCreary (Eds.), *Handbook of gender research in psychology* (Vol. 2, pp. 281–310). New York: Springer.

Marshall, T. C. (2012). Facebook surveillance of former romantic partners: Associations with post breakup recovery and personal growth. *Cyberpsychology, Behavior, and Social Networking, 15,* 521–526.

Martin, J. A., Hamilton, B. E., & Ventura, S. J. (2011). Births: Final data for 2009. National Vital Statistics Reports. U.S. Department of Health and Human Services. *National Vital Statistics System, 60,* 1.

Martin, J. A., Hamilton, B. E., Ventura, S. J., Osterman, M. J. K., Wilson, E. C., & Mathews, T. J. (2012). Births: Final Data for 2010. *National Vital Statistics*

Reports, 61(1). Hyattsville, MD: National Center for Health Statistics. Retrieved August 7, 2013, from http://www.cdc.gov/nchs/data/nvsr/nvsr61 /nvsr61_01.pdf

Martin, P. (2005). *Making happy people: The nature of happiness and its origins in child-hood.* London: Harper Collins.

Martinez, D. (2005). *Love and delusion: Real love and honest lies.* Gainesville, FL: Florida Academic Press.

Marumo, K., & Murai, M. (2001). Aging and erectile dysfunction: The role of aging and concomitant chronic illness. *International Journal of Urology, 8,* S50–S57.

Maslow, A. H. (1967). A theory of motivation: The biological rooting of the value life. *Journal of Humanistic Psychology, 7,* 93–127.

Mason, M. F., Tatkow, E. P., & Macrae, C. N. (2005). The look of love: Gaze shifts and person perception. *Psychological Science, 16,* 236–239.

Masters, W., Johnson, V., & Kolodny, R. (1994). *Heterosexuality.* New York: Harper Collins.

Matejcek, Z., & Kadubcova, B. (1984). Self-conception in Czech children from the point of view of Rohner's parental acceptance-rejection theory. *Ces-koslovenska Psychologie, 28*(2), 87–96.

Matsumoto, D., & Hwang, H. S. (2013a). Facial expressions. In D. Matsumoto, M. Frank, & H. Hwang (Eds.), *Nonverbal communications: Science and appli-cations* (pp. 15–52). Thousand Oaks, CA: Sage.

Matsumoto, D., & Hwang, H. S. (2013b). Body and gestures. In D. Matsumoto, M. Frank, & H. S. Hwang (Eds.), *Nonverbal communications: Science and applications* (pp. 75–96). Thousand Oaks, CA: Sage.

Matsumoto, D., & Hwang, H. S. (2013c). Cultural influences on nonverbal behav-ior. In D. Matsumoto, M. Frank, & H. Hwang (Eds.), *Nonverbal communi-cations: Science and applications* (pp. 97–120). Thousand Oaks, CA: Sage.

Matsumoto, D., & Hwang, H. S. (2013d). Cultural similarities and differences in emblematic gestures. *Journal of Nonverbal Behavior, 37,* 1–27.

Matthews, S. H. (1986). *Friendship through the life course.* Beverly Hills, CA: Sage.

Matthias, R. E., Lubben, J. E., Atchison, K. A., & Schweitzer, S. O. (1997). Sexual activity and satisfaction among very old adults: Results from a community-dwelling Medicare population survey. *The Gerontologist, 37,* 6–14.

Maughan, B., Pickles, A., & Quinton, D. (1995). Parental hostility, childhood behavior, and adult social functioning. In J. McCord (Ed.), *Coercion and punishment in long-term perspectives.* Cambridge, UK: Cambridge Univer-sity Press.

McAdams, D. P. (1985). *Power, intimacy, and the life story: Personological inquiries into identity.* New York: The Guilford Press.

McAllister, S., Duncan, S. F., & Busby, D. M. (2013). Exploratory analysis of factors associated with participation in self-directed and traditional marriage and relationship education. *Marriage & Family Review, 49*(7), 563–584. Retrieved from http://dx.doi.org/10.1080/01494929.2013.789461

McCabe, J., Brewster, K. L., & Tillman, H. K. (2011). Patterns and correlates of same-sex sexual activity among U.S. teenagers and young adults. *Perspectives on Sexual and Reproductive Health, 43,* 142–150.

McCabe, M. P., & Goldhammer, D. L. (2012). Demographic and psychological factors related to sexual desire among heterosexual women in a relationship. *Journal of Sex Research, 49,* 78–87.

McCoy, K. P., George, M. R. W., Cummings, E. M., & Davies, P. T. (2013). Constructive and destructive marital conflict, parenting, and children's school and social adjustment. *Social Development, 22,* 641–662.

McDonell, J., Strom-Gottfried, K. J., Burton, D. L., & Yaffe, J. (2006). *Behaviorism, social learning, and exchange theory* (pp. 349–385). In S. P. Robbins, P. Chatterjee, & E. R. Canda (Eds.), *Contemporary human behavior theory: A critical perspective for social work.* Boston: Pearson.

McDougall, P., & Valliancourt, T. (2015). Long-term adult outcomes of peer victimization in childhood and adolescence. *American Psychologist, 70*(4), 300–310.

McGinnis, S. L. (2003). Cohabiting, dating, and perceived costs of marriage: A model of marriage entry. *Journal of Marriage and Family, 65,*105–116.

McHugh, M. C., & Hambaugh, J. (2010). She said, he said: Gender, language, and power. In J. Chrisler & D. McCreary (Eds.), *Handbook of gender research in psychology* (pp. 379–410). New York: Springer.

McLanahan, S. S. (1999). Father absence and children's welfare. In E. M. Hetherington (Ed.), *Coping with divorce, single parenting, and remarriage: A risk and resiliency perspective.* Mahwah, NJ: Erlbaum.

McNulty, J. K., & Russell, V. M. (2010). When "negative" behaviors are positive: A contextual analysis of the long-term effects of problem-solving behaviors on changes in relationship satisfaction. *Journal of Personality and Social Sciences, 98,* 587–604.

Meegan, S. P., & Berg, C. A. (2002). Contexts, functions, forms, and processes of collaborative everyday problem solving in older adulthood. *International Journal of Behavioral Development, 26,* 6–15.

Meir, A. M., Carr, D. R., & Currier, J. M. (2013). Attachment anxiety and avoidance in coping with bereavement: Two studies. *Journal of Social and Clinical Psychology, 32,* 315–334.

Mendes de Leon, C. F., & Glass, T. A. (2004). The role of social and personal resources in ethnic disparities in late-life health. In N. A. Anderson, R. A. Rodolfo, & B. Cohen (Eds.), *Critical perspectives on racial and ethnic differences in health in late life* (pp. 353–405). Washington, DC: National Academies Press

Mendes de Leon, C. F., Glass, T. A., & Berkman, L. F. (2003). Social engagement and disability in a community population of older adults: The New Haven EPESE. *American Journal of Epidemiology, 157*(7), 633–642..

Mensini, E. (1997). Behavioral correlates of friendship status among Italian schoolchildren. *Journal of Social and Personal Relationships, 14*(1), 109–121.

Merino, S. M. (2013). Contact with gays and lesbians and same-sex marriage support: The moderating role of social context. *Social Science Research, 42,* 1156–1166.

Merry, J. (1972). Social characteristics of addiction to heroin. *British Journal of Addiction, 67,* 322–325.

Meston, C. M., & Ahrold, T. (2010). Ethnic, gender, and acculturation influences on sexual behaviors. *Archives of Sexual Behavior, 39,* 179–189.

Metts, S. (1994). *Relational transgressions.* In W. R. Cupach & B. H. Spitzberg (Eds.), *The dark side of interpersonal communication* (pp. 217–239). Hillsdale, NJ: Erlbaum.

Michels, R. (1983). *The scientific and clinical functions of psychoanalytic theory: The future of psychoanalysis* (A. Goldberg, Ed.). New York: International Universities Press.

Mikulincer, M., & Shaver, P. R. (2007). *Attachment in adulthood.* New York: The Guilford Press.

Mikulincer, M., & Shaver, P. R. (2008). Adult attachment and affect regulation. In J. Cassidy & P. Shaver (Eds.), *Handbook of attachment: Theory, research and clinical applications* (2nd ed., pp. 503–531). New York: The Guilford Press.

Mikulincer, M., & Shaver, P. R. (2013). The role of attachment security in adolescent and adult close relationships. In J. A. Simpson & L. Campbell (Eds.), *The Oxford handbook of close relationships* (pp. 66–89). New York: Oxford University Press.

Miller, B. C., McCoy, J. K., Olson, T. D., & Wallace, C. M. (1986). Parental discipline and control attempts in relation to adolescent sexual attitudes and behavior. *Journal of Marriage and the Family, 48,* 503–512.

Miller, B. C., Norton, M. C., Curtis, T., Hill, J. E., Schaveveldt, P., & Young, M. H. (1997). The timing of sexual intercourse among adolescents. *Youth and Society, 29,* 54–83.

Miller, P. H. (2011). *Theories of developmental psychology.* New York: Worth.

Miller, P. J. E., & Rempel, J. K. (2004). Trust and partner-enhancing attributions in close relationship. *Personality and Social Psychology Bulletin, 30,* 695–705.

Miller, R., & Perlman, D. (2008). *Intimate relationships.* New York: McGraw-Hill.

Miller, R. S. (2015). *Intimate relationships.* New York: McGraw-Hill.

Mitchell, S. A. (2002). Can love last? *The fade of romance over time.* New York: Norton.

Mooney, A., Oliver, C., & Smith, M. (2009). *Impact of family breakdown on children's wellbeing evidence review.* DCSF-RR113. London: University of London, Institute of Education, Thomas Coram Research Unit.

Monroe, W. S. (1898). Discussion and reports: Social consciousness in children. *Psychological Review, 15,* 68–70.

Monsour, M. (2000/2002). *Women and men as friends: Relationships across the life span in the 21st century.* Mahwah, NJ: Erlbaum.

Monsour, M., Harris, B., & Kurzweil, N. (1994). Challenges confronting cross-sex friendships: "Much ado about nothing?" *Sex Roles, 31,* 55–77.

Montenegro, X. P. (2004). *The divorce experience: A study of divorce at midlife and beyond.* Washington, DC: AARP Public Policy Institute.

Montesi, J. L., Fauber, R. L., Gordon, E. A., & Heimberg, R. G. (2011). The specific importance of communicating about sex to couples' sexual and overall relationship satisfaction. *Journal of Social and Personal Relationships, 28*(5), 591–609.

Montoya, R. M. (2008). I'm hot, so I say you're not: The influence of objective physical attractiveness on mate selection. *Personality and Social Psychology Bulletin, 34,* 1315–1329.

Montoya, R. M., & Horton, R. S. (2013). A meta-analytic investigation of the processes underlying the similarity-attraction effect. *Journal of Personal and Social Relationships, 30,* 64–94.

Montoya, R. M., Horton, R., & Kirchner, J. (2008). Is actual similarity necessary for attraction? A meta-analysis of actual and perceived similarity. *Journal of Social and Personal Relationships, 25,* 889–922.

Morin, R., & Cohen, D. (2008). Gender roles in the world of work. *Work exposed the blog.* Retrieved from https://workexposed.wordpress.com/2008/09/26/gender-roles-in-the-world-of-work

Morry, M. M., Kito, M., & Ortiz, L. (2011). The attraction-similarity model and dating couples: Projection, perceived similarity and psychological benefits. *Personal Relationships, 18,* 125–143.

Mott, F. L., Fondell, M. M., Hu, P. N., Kowaleski-Jones, L., & Menaghan, E. G. (1996). Adolescent population. *Family Planning Perspectives, 28,* 13–18.

Moustgaard, H., & Martikainen, P. (2009). Nonmarital cohabitation among older Finnish men and women: Socioeconomic characteristics and forms of union dissolution. *Journal of Gerontology: Social Sciences, 64B,* 507–516.

Mrug, S., Molina, B. S. G., Hoza, B., Gerdes, A. C., Hinshaw, S. P., Hechtman, L., & Arnold, L. E. (2012). Peer rejection and friendships in children with attention deficit/hyperactivity disorder: Contributions to long-term outcomes. *Journal of Abnormal Child Psychology, 40,* 1013–1026.

Muchlenhard, C. L., & Peterson, Z. D. (2011). Distinguishing between sex and gender: History, current conceptualizations, and implications. *Sex Roles, 64,* 791–803.

Muise, A., Impett, E. A., Kogan, A., & Desmarais, S. (2013). Keeping the spark alive: Being motivated to meet a partner's sexual needs sustains sexual desire in long-term romantic relationships. *Social Psychological and Personality Science, 4,* 267–273.

Mulye, T. P., Park, M. J., Nelson, C. D., Adams, S. H., Irwin, C. E., Jr., & Brindis, C. D. (2009). Trends in adolescent and young adult health in the United States. *Journal of Adolescent Health, 45*(1), 8–24. doi:10.1016/j.jadohealth.2009.03.013

Murphy, M., Glaser, K., & Grundy, E. (1997). Marital status and long-term illness in Great Britain. *Journal of Marriage and Family, 59,* 156–164.

Murry, B. M. (1996). An ecological analysis of coital timing among middle-class African-American adolescent females. *Journal of Adolescent Research, 11,* 261–279.

Murstein, B. I. (1974). *Love, sex, and marriage through the ages.* New York: Springer.

Musick, K., & Bumpass, L. (2012). Reexamining the case for marriage: Union formation and changes in well-being. *Journal of Marriage and Family, 74,* 1–18.

Musick, K., & Michelmore, K. (2015). Trends in the relative stability of marital and cohabiting unions following a first birth. *Demography, 52*(5), 1463–1485.

Myers, D. G. (2000a). The funds, friends, and faith of happy people. *American Psychologist, 55,* 56–57.

Myers, D. G. (2000b). *The American paradox: Spiritual hunger in an age of plenty.* New Haven, CT: Yale University Press.

Myers, D. G. (2007). Psychology of happiness. *Scholarpedia, 2*(8), 31–49. doi:10.4249/scholarpedia.3149.

Myers, D. G. (2010). *Psychology* (9th ed.). New York: Worth.

Myers, D. G. (2015). *Psychology* (11th ed.). New York: Worth.

Myers, H. F., Newcomb, M. D., Richardson, M. A., & Alvy, K. T. (1997). Parental and family risk factors for substance use among inner-city African American children and adolescents. *Journal of Psychopathology and Behavioral Assessment, 19,* 109–131.

National Campaign to Prevent Teen and Unplanned Pregnancy (NCTUP). (2015). *National & state data—Teen pregnancy.* Massachusetts Avenue, Washington, DC.

National Center on Domestic and Sexual Violence. (2016). *Power control wheel.* Retrieved November 2016 from www.ncdsv.org/publications_wheel.html

National Center for Injury Prevention and Control (NCIPC). (2010). *National intimate partner and sexual violence survey: 2010 summary report.* Division of Violence Prevention, Atlanta, GA. Retrieved from https://www.cdc.gov/violenceprevention

National Coalition Against Domestic Violence in the United States (NCADV). (2012). *Domestic violence national statistics.* Retrieved from https://ncadv.org/files/National%20Statistics%20Domestic%20Violence%20NCADV.pdf

National Fatherhood Initiative. (2005). *With this ring . . . A national survey on marriage in America.* Gaithersburg, MD.

National Institute on Alcohol Abuse and Alcoholism. (2002). *College drinking: Changing the culture.* Retrieved from https://www.domesticshelters.org/domestic . . . /demographics-and-domestic-violence

National Institutes of Justice. (2015). *Practical implications of current domestic violence research: For law enforcement, prosecutors and judges.* The U.S. Department of

Justice, Office of Justice Programs. Retrieved from https://www.ncjrs.gov
/ . . . /nij/ . . . /222321.pdf

National Research Council and Institute of Medicine. (2009). *Adolescent health services: Missing opportunities.* Washington, DC: The National Academies
Press.

National Survey of Families and Households. (2005). *Divorce and separation experience.* Madison, WI: University of Wisconsin Survey Center.

Newcomb, A. R., & Bagwell, C. L. (1995). Children's friendship relations: A meta-
analytic review. *Psychological Bulletin, 117,* 306–347.

Nguyen, D. (2016). Virginity in different cultures. *Love and sex.* Retrieved from
https//www.futurescopes.com/love-and-sex/9846/virginity-different
-cultures

Noller, P. (2012). Conflicts in family relationships. In P. Noller & G. C. Karantzas
(Eds.), *The handbook of couples and family relationships.* Hoboken, NJ: Wiley.

Office for National Statistics. (2013). *Life satisfaction and anxiety levels,* UK.
Retrieved from http://www.ons.gov.uk

Ogolsky, B. G., & Bowers, J. R. (2013). A meta-analytic review of relationship
maintenance and its correlates. *Journal of Social and Personal Relationships,
30*(3), 343–367.

O'Leary, K. D., Acevedo, B. P., Aron, L., Huddy, L., & Mashek, D. (2012). Is long-
term love more than a rare phenomenon? If so, what are its correlates?
Social Psychological and Personality Science, 3(2), 241–249.

Oliver, M. B., & Hyde, J. S. (1993). Gender differences in sexuality: A meta-
analysis. *Psychological Bulletin, 114,* 29–51.

Olson, D. H., & Olson, A. K. (2000). *Empowering couples: Building on your strengths.*
Minneapolis: Life Innovations.

O'Meara, D. (1994). Cross-sex friendship opportunity challenge: Uncharted ter-
rain for exploration. *Sex Roles, 21,* 525–543.

Ong, A. D., Bergeman, C. S., Bisconti, T. L., & Wallace, K. A. (2006). Psychological resilience, positive emotions, and successful adaptation to stress in later
life. *Journal of Personality and Social Psychology, 91*(4), 730–749.

Onsager, M. (2014). Understanding the importance of non-verbal communication.
Body Language Dictionary, New York. Retrieved October 26, 2014, from
http://www.bodylanguageproject.com/dictionary

Ooms, T. J., & Wilson, P. C. (2004). The challenges of offering couples and marriage education to low income couples. *Family Relations, 53,* 440–446.

Orbuch, T. L., & Sprecher, S. (2003). Attraction and interpersonal relationships.
Handbook of social psychology. New York: Kluwer Academic/Plenum.

Orina, M. M., Collins, W. A., Simpson, J. A., Salvatore, J. E., Haydon, K. C., &
Kim, J. S. (2011). Developmental and dyadic on commitment in adult
romantic relationships. *Psychological Science, 22,* 908–915.

Orlofsky, J. L. (1993). Intimacy status rating manual. In J. E. Marcia, A. S. Water-
man, D. R. Matteson, S. L. Archer, & J. L. Orlofsky, *Ego identity: A handbook for psychology and social research.* New York: Springer.

Ortega, G. (2006). *Happiness skills theory.* Retrieved from http://www.thehappi nessshow.com/HappiestCountries.htm

Osborne, C., Manning, W., & Smock, P. (2007). Married and cohabiting parents' relationship stability: A focus on race and ethnicity. *Journal of Marriage and Family, 69*(5), 1345–1366.

Ostrom, E., & Walker, J. (Eds.). (2003). *Trust and reciprocity: Interdisciplinary lessons from experimental research.* New York: Russell Sage Foundation.

O'Sullivan, L. F., Cheng, M. M., Harris, K. M., & Brooks-Gunn, J. (2007). I wanna hold your hand: The progression of social, romantic and sexual events in adolescent relationships. *Perspectives on Sexual and Reproductive Health, 39,* 100–107.

O'Sullivan, L. F., Wadiya Udell, W., Montrose, V. A., Antoniello, P., & Hoffman, S. (2010). A cognitive analysis of college students' explanations for engaging in unprotected sexual intercourse. *Archive of Sexual Behavior, 39*(5), 1121–1131.

Oswald, D. L., Clark, E. D., & Kelly, C. M. (2004). Friendship maintenance: An analysis of individual and dyad behaviors. *Journal of Social and Clinical Psychology, 23*(3), 413–441.

Oswald, D. L., & Russell, B. L. (2006). Perceptions of sexual coercion in heterosexual dating relationships: The role of initiator gender and tactics. *Journal of Sex Research, 43,* 87–95.

Overall, N. C., Girme, Y. U., Lemay, E. P., Jr., & Hammond, M. D. (2014). Attachment anxiety and reactions to relationship threat: The benefits and costs of inducing guilt in romantic partners. *Journal of Personality and Social Psychology, 106,* 235–256.

Overall, N. C., Simpson, I. A., & Struthers, H. (2013). Buffering attachment related avoidance: Softening emotional and behavioral defenses during conflict discussions. *Journal of Personal and Social Psychology, 104,* 854–871.

Palomares, N. A. (2009). Women are sort of more tentative than men, aren't they? How men and women use tentative language differently, similarly, and counter stereotypically as a function of gender salience. *Communication Research, 36,* 538–560.

Papalia, D. (2012). *Adult development and aging.* New York: McGraw-Hill.

Papp, L. M., Goeke-Morey, M. C., & Cummings, E. M. (2013). Let's talk about sex: A diary investigation of couples' intimacy conflicts in the home. *Couple and Family Psychology: Research and Practice, 2*(1), 60–72. doi:10.1037/ a0031465

Paris, G. (1883). Études sur les romans de la table ronde: Lancelot du lac. II: Le conte de la charrette. *Romania, 12,* 459–534.

Parker, G., Kiloh, L., & Hayward, L. (1987). Parental representations of neurotic and endogenous depressives. *Journal of Affective Disorders, 13,* 75–82.

Parker, J. G., & Seal, J. (1996). Forming, losing, renewing, and replacing friendships: Applying temporal parameters to the assessment of children's friendship experiences. *Child Development, 67,* 2248–2268.

Parker, K., & Wang, W. (2013). *Modern parenthood*. Pew Research Center. Retrieved March 10, 2015, from http//www.pewsocialtrends.org

Parker, R., & Pattenden, R. (2009). *Strengthening and repairing relationships: Addressing forgiveness and sacrifice in couples education and counselling*. Australian Institute of Family Studies. Retrieved from https://aifs.gov.au/cfca

Parmar, P., Ibrahim, M., & Rohner, R. P. (2008). Relations among perceived spouse acceptance, and remembered parental acceptance in childhood, and psychological adjustment among married adults in Kuwait. *Cross-Cultural Research, 42*(1), 67–76.

Parmar, P., & Rohner, R. P. (2005). Relations among perceived intimate partner acceptance, and remembered parental acceptance, and psychological adjustment among young adults in India. *Ethos, 33*(3), 402–413.

Parmar, P., & Rohner, R. P. (2008). Relations among perceived spouse acceptance, and remembered parental acceptance in childhood, and psychological adjustment among married adults in India. *Cross-Cultural Research, 42*(1), 57–66.

Parmar, P., & Rohner, R. P. (2010). Perceived teacher and parental acceptance and behavioral control, school conduct, and psychological adjustment among school-going adolescents in India. *Cross-Cultural Research, 44*(3), 253–265.

Parrinder, G. (1996). *Sexual morality in the world's religions*. New York: Oxford University Press.

Parrott, Les, & Parrott, Leslie. (2013). *The good fight*. Brentwood, TN: Worthy.

Pascoal, P. M., Narciso, I. S. B., & Pereira, N. M. (2014). What is sexual satisfaction? Thematic analysis of lay people's definitions. *The Journal of Sex Research, 51*, 22–30.

Patterson, C. J. (2000). Family relationships of lesbians and gay men. *Journal of Marriage and Family, 62*, 1052–1069.

Patterson, C. J. (2013). Sexual orientation and family lives. In G. W. Peterson & K. R. Bush (Eds.), *The handbook of marriage and the family*. New York: Springer.

Patterson, C. J., & Riskind, R. G. (2010). New developments in the field to be a parent: Issues in family formation among gay and lesbian adults. *Journal of GLBT Family Studies, 6*, 326–340.

Paunonen, S. V., (2006). You are honest, therefore I like you and find you attractive. *Journal of Research in Personality, 40*(3), 237–249.

Pedersen, W. (1994). Parental relations, mental health, and delinquency in adolescents. *Adolescence, 29*, 975–990.

Peplau, L. A, & Fingerhut, A. W. (2007). The close relationships of lesbians and gay men. *Annual Review of Psychology, 58*, 405–424.

Peplau, L. A., Fingerhut, A., & Beals, K. P. (2004). Sexuality in the relationships of lesbians and gay men. In J. Harvey, A. Wenzel, & S. Sprecher (Eds.), *Handbook of sexuality in close relationships* (pp. 350–369). Mahwah, NJ: Erlbaum.

Peplau, L. A., & Garnets, L. D. (2000). A new paradigm for understanding women's sexuality and sexual orientation. *Journal of Social Issues, 56*(2), 329–350.

Percell, C. H., Green, A., & Gurevich, L. (2001). Civil society, economic distress, and social tolerance. *Sociological Forum, 16,* 203–230.

Perilloux, C., & Buss, D. M. (2008). Breaking up romantic relationships: Costs experienced and coping strategies developed. *Evolutionary Psychology, 6,* 164–181.

Perilloux, H. K., Webster, G. D., & Gaulin, S. J. C. (2010). Signals of genetic quality and maternal investment capacity: The dynamic effects of fluctuating asymmetry and waist-to-hip ratio on men's ratings of women's attractiveness. *Social Psychology and Personality Science, 1,* 34–42.

Perlman, D. (2007). The best times, the worst times: The place of close relationships in psychology and our daily lives. *Canadian Psychology, 48,* 7–18.

Perlman, D., & Duck, S. (2006). The seven seas of the study of personal relationships. In A. L. Vangelisti & D. Perlman (Eds.), *The Cambridge handbook of personal relationships.* Cambridge, UK: Cambridge University Press.

Perry, D. G., Perry, L. C., & Kennedy, E. (1992). Conflict and the development of antisocial behavior. In C. U. Shantz & W. Hartup (Eds.), *Conflict in child and adolescent development* (pp. 301–329). New York: Cambridge University Press.

Peters, B., & Ehrenberg, M. F. (2008). The influence of parental separations and divorce on father-child relationships. *Journal of Divorce and Remarriage, 49,* 96–97.

Petersen, J. L., & Hyde, J. S. (2010). A meta-analytic review of research on gender differences in sexuality, 1993–2007. *Psychological Bulletin, 136,* 21–38.

Peterson, D. R. (2002). Conflict. In H. H. Kelley et al. (Eds.), *Close relationships* (pp. 265–314). Clinton Corners, NY: Percheron Press.

Peterson, D. R. (2007). *Cultural diversity and intergroup conflict: Social prejudice and intercultural understanding.* Retrieved from http://gsappweb.rutgers.edu /facstaff/dynamic/profile.php?ID=49

Pew Research Center. (2013). *In gay marriage debate, both supporters and opponents see legal recognition as inevitable.* Retrieved from http://www. people.press .org

Pew Research Center. (2014a). *Global views on morality.* Retrieved from http://www .pewglobal.org/2014/04/15/global-morality

Pew Research Center. (2014b). *Gay marriage around the world.* Retrieved from http// www.pew.forum.org

Pew Research Center (2014c). *Record share of Americans have never married.* Pew Research Center's survey, May 22–25 and May 29–June 1. 1615 L Street, NW, Suite 800, Washington, DC.

Pienta, A. M., Hayward, M. D., & Jenkins, K. R. (2000). Health consequences of marriage for the retirement years. *Journal of Family Issues, 21,* 559–586.

Piercy, F. P., & Piercy, S. K. (1972). Interpersonal attraction as a function of pro-pinquity in two sensitivity groups. *Psychology: A Journal of Human Behavior, 9*(1), 27–30.

Pitts, M. K., Smith, A. M. A., O'Brien, M., & Misson, S. (2004). Who pays for sex and why? An analysis of social and motivational factors associated with male clients of sex workers. *Archives of Sexual Behavior, 33*(4), 353–358.

Pokorski, M., & Kuchcewicz, A. (2012). Quality of cohabiting and marital relationships among young couples. *International Journal of Humanities and Social Science, 2*(24), 191–195.

Poortman, A., & Sheltzer, J. A. (2007). Parents' expectations about childrearing after divorce: Does anticipating difficulty deter divorce? *Journal of Marriage and Family, 69,* 254–269.

Porges, S. W. (2011). *The polyvagal theory: Neurophysiological foundations of emotions, attachment, communication, and self-regulation.* New York: Norton.

Pottharst, K. (Ed.). (1990). *Explorations in adult attachment.* New York: Peter Lang.

Prager, K. J., Shirvani, F. K., Garcia, J. J., & Coles, M. (2013). Intimacy and positive psychology. In M. Hojjat & D. Cramer (Eds.), *Positive psychology of love* (pp. 16–29). New York: Oxford University Press.

Pratto, F., Stallworth, L. M., Sidanius, J., & Siers, B. (1997). The gender gap in occupational role attainment: A social dominance approach. *Journal of Personality and Social Psychology, 72,* 37–53.

Preciado, P., Snijders, T., Burk, W. J., Stattin, H., & Kerr, M. (2011). Does proximity matter? Distance dependence of adolescent friendships. *Social Networks, 34,* 18–31.

Prejean, J., Song, R., & Hernandez, A. (2011). Estimated HIV incidence in the United States, 2006–2009. *PLOS ONE, 6,* e17502. doi:10.1371/journal.pone.0017502

Previti, D., & Amato, P. R. (2003). Why stay married? Rewards, barriers, and marital stability. *Journal of Marriage and Family, 65*(3), 561–573.

Prigerson, H. G., Maciejewski, P. K., & Rosenheck, R. A. (2000). Preliminary explorations of the harmful interactive effects of widowhood and marital harmony on health, health service use, and health care costs. *The Gerontologist, 40,* 349–357.

Proulx, C. M., Helms, H. M., Buehler, C. (2007). Marital quality and personal well-being: A meta-analysis. *Journal of Marriage and Family, 69,* 576–593. doi:10.1111/j.1741-3737.2007.00393.x

Purdie, M. P., Norris, J., Davis, K. C., Zawacki, T., Morrison, D. M., George, W. H., Kiekel, P. A. (2011). The effects of acute alcohol intoxication, partner risk level, and general intention to have unprotected sex on women's sexual decision making with a new partner. *Experimental and Clinical Psychopharmacology, 19*(5), 378–388. Retrieved from http://dx.doi.org/10.1037/a0024792

Quiñones, E. (2006). *Link between income and happiness is mainly an illusion*. News at Princeton University, August, 4, 2016. Princeton, NJ 08544.

Rakovec-Felser, Z. (2014). Domestic violence and abuse in intimate relationship from public health perspective. *Health Psychology Research, 2*(3), 1821–1831.

Raley, R. K., Crissey, S., & Muller, C. (2007). Of sex and romance: Late adolescent relationships and young adult union formation. *Journal of Marriage and Family, 69,* 1210–1226.

Raley, R. K., Durden, T. E., & Wildsmith, E. (2004). Understanding Mexican-American marriage patterns using a life-course approach. *Social Science Quarterly, 85,* 872–890.

Rasulo, D., Christensen, K., & Tomassini, C. (2005). The influence of social relations on mortality in later life: A study on elderly Danish twins. *The Gerontologist, 45,* 601–608.

Rauer, A. J., Karney, B. R., Garvan, C. W., & Hou, W. (2008). Relationship risks in context: A cumulative risk approach to understanding relationship satisfaction. *Journal of Marriage and Family, 70*(5), 1122–1135.

Reed, J. (2007). Anatomy of a breakup: How and why do unmarried couples with children break up? In P. England & K. Edin (Eds.), *Unmarried couples with children* (pp. 133–156). New York: Russell Sage Foundation.

Reeder, H. (2000). "I like you as a friend": The role of attraction in cross-sex friendship. *Journal of Social and Personal Relationships, 7,* 329–348.

Reeder, H. (2003). The effect of gender role orientation on same and cross-sex friendship formation. *Sex Roles, 49*(3/4), 143–152.

Regan, P.C. (2015). Sexual desire: Conceptualization, correlates, and causes. In W. Hofmann & L. F. Nordgren (Eds.), *The psychology of desire* (pp. 347–381). New York: Guilford.

Rehman, U. S., Janssen, E., Newhouse, S., Heiman, J., Holtzworth-Munroe, A., Fallis, E., & Reiber, C., & Garcia, J. R. (2010). Hooking up: Gender differences and pluralistic ignorance. *Evolutionary Psychology, 8,* 390–404.

Reich, S. M., Subrahmanyam, K., & Espinoza, G. (2012). Friending, IMing, and hanging out face-to-face: Overlap in adolescents' online and offline social networks. *Developmental Psychology, 48,* 356–368.

Reijntjes, A., Kamphuis, J. H., Prinzie, P., Boelen, P. A., van der, Schoot, M., & Telch, M. J. (2011). Peer vicitimization and internalizing problems in children: A meta-analysis of longitudinal studies. *Child Abuse and Neglect, 34,* 244–253. Retrieved from http://dx.doi.org/10.1016/j.chiabu.2009.07.009

Reinhold, S. (2010). Reassessing the link between premarital cohabitation and marital instability. *Demography, 47,* 719–733.

Reis, H. T. (2013). Relationship well-being: The central role of perceived partner responsiveness. In C. Hazan & M. I. Campa (Eds.), *Human bonding: The science of affectional ties* (pp. 283–307). New York: The Guilford Press.

Reis, H. T. (2014). Responsiveness: Affective interdependence in close relationships. In M. Mikulincer & P. R. Shaver (Eds.), *Mechanisms of social connection: From brain to group* (pp. 255–271), Washington, DC: American
Psychological Association.

Reis, H. T., Lin, Y., Bennet, M. E., & Nezlek, J. B. (1993). Changes and consistency in social participation during early adulthood. *Developmental Psychology, 29*(4), 633–645.

Reis, H. T., Maniaci, M. R., Caprariello, P. A., Eastwick, P. W., & Finkel, E. J.
(2011). In live interaction, does familiarity promote attraction or contempt?
Reply to Norton, Frost, and Ariely (2011). *Journal of Personality and Social
Psychology, 101*(3), 575–578.

Rempel, J. K., Holmes, J. G., & Zanna, M. P. (1985). Trust in close relationships.
Journal of Personality and Social Psychology, 49, 95–112.

Rheingold, H., & Eckerman, C. (1970). The infant separates himself from his
mother. *Science, 168,* 78–83.

Rhoades, G. K., Stanley, S. M., & Markman, H. J. (2010). Should I stay or should
I go? Predicting dating relationship stability from four aspects of commitment. *Journal of Family Psycholology, 24*(5), 543–550. doi:10.1037/a0021008

Rhoades, G. K., Stanley, S. M., & Markman, H. J. (2012). A longitudinal investigation of commitment dynamics in cohabiting relationships. *Family Issues,
33*(3), 369–390. doi:10.1177/0192513X11420940

Rhynard, J., Krebs, M., & Glover, J. (1997). Sexual assault in dating relationships.
Journal of School Health, 67, 89–93.

Rice, F. P., & Dolgin, K. G. (2005). *The adolescent: Development, relationships, and
culture.* Boston: Pearson.

Rice, F. P., & Dolgin, K. G. (2008). *The adolescent: Development, relationship, and
culture.* Boston: Allyn and Bacon.

Richter, J. (1994). Parental rearing and aspects of psychopathology with special
reference to depression. In C. Perris, W. A. Arrindell, & M. Eisemann
(Eds.), *Parenting and psychopathology* (pp. 235–251). Chicester, England:
Wiley.

Rick, S. L., Small, D. A., & Finkel, E. J. (2011). Fatal (fiscal) attraction: Spend-
thrifts and tightwads in marriage. *Journal of Marketing Research, 48,*
228–237.

Rigazio-DiGilio, S. A., & Rohner, R. P. (2008). Clinical adaptation of parental
acceptance-rejection theory questionnaires as interactive assessment and
treatment tools in relational therapy. In F. Erkman (Ed.), *Acceptance: The
essence of peace. Selected papers from the First International Congress on Interpersonal Acceptance and Rejection* (pp. 3–23). Istanbul: Turkish Psychology Association.

Ripoll-Núñez, K. (2016, June 6–10). *Relationship quality: An organizing construct for
research on adult intimate relations.* Paper presented at the 6th International
Congress of Interpersonal Acceptance and Rejection Society, Madrid,
Spain.

Ripoll-Núñez, K., & Alvarez, C. (2008). Perceived intimate partner acceptance, remembered parental acceptance, and psychological adjustment among Colombian and Puerto Rican youths and adults. *Cross-Cultural Research, 42*, 23–34.

Ripoll-Núñez, K., & Carrillo, S. (2016). Adult intimate relationships: Linkages between interpersonal acceptance-rejection theory and adult attachment theory. *Online Readings in Psychology and Culture, 6*(2). Retrieved from http://dx.doi.org/10.9707/2307-0919.1149

Rising, D. G. (1999). *The influence of perceived parental acceptance-rejection, parental control, and psychological adjustment on job instability among men.* Unpublished doctoral dissertation, Northern Illinois University.

Riskind, R. G., & Patterson, C. J. (2010). Parenting intentions and desires among childless lesbian, gay, and heterosexual individuals. *Journal of Family Psychology, 24*(1), 78–81.

Rizkalla, L., Wertheim, E. H., & Hodgson, L. K. (2008). The roles of emotion management and perspective taking in individuals' conflict management styles and disposition to forgive. *Journal of Organizational Behavior, 22*, 645–690.

Roazen, P. (1997). *Erick H. Erikson: The power and limits of his vision.* New York: Free Press.

Roberts, L., & Pragner, K. J. (1997). *Intimacy diaries and videotape: Conceptualizing and measuring intimacy.* Roundtable presented at the annual meeting of the International Network on Personal Relationships, Oxford, OH.

Roberts, S. G. B., & Dunbar, R. I. M. (2011). The cost of family and friends: An 18-month longitudinal study of relationship maintenance and decay. *Evolution of Human Behavior, 32*, 186–197.

Robinson, L., Segal, J., & Smith, M. A. (2015). How to make close friends? HelpGuide. Org. Last updated, August 2015.

Rodgers, J. L., Rowe, D. C., & Harris, D. F. (1992). Sibling differences in adolescent sexual behavior. Inferring process models from family composition patterns. *Journal of Marriage and the Family, 54*, 142–152.

Rodriquez, C., Jr., & Moore, M. B. (1995). Perceptions of pregnant/parenting teens: Reframing issues for an integrated approach to pregnancy problems. *Adolescence, 30*, 685–706.

Rohner, R. P. (1960). *Child acceptance-rejection and modal personality in three Pacific societies.* Unpublished master's degree thesis, Stanford University.

Rohner, R. P. (1975). *They love me, they love me not: A worldwide study of the effects of parental acceptance and rejection.* New Haven, CT: HRAF Press.

Rohner, R. P. (1984/1991). *Handbook for the study of parental acceptance and rejection.* Center for the Study of Parental Acceptance and Rejection, University of Connecticut at Storrs.

Rohner, R. P. (1986/2000). *The warmth dimension: Foundations of parental acceptance-rejection theory.* Newbury Park, CA: Sage. [Reprinted by Rohner Research.]

Rohner, R. P. (1990). *Handbook for the study of parental acceptance and rejection.* Storrs, CT: Rohner Research.

Rohner, R. P. (1994). Patterns of parenting: The warmth dimension in cross-cultural perspectives. In W. J. Lonner & R. S. Malpass (Eds.), *Readings in psychology and culture.* Needham Heights, MA: Allyn and Bacon.

Rohner, R. P. (1998). Father love and child development: History and current evidence. *Current Directions in Psychological Science, 7,* 157–161.

Rohner, R. P. (1999). *Similarities and differences between attachment theory and PARTheory.* Unpublished manuscript. University of Connecticut, Storrs.

Rohner, R. P. (2001). *Bibliography of writings using parental acceptance and rejection.* Retrieved from http://vm.uconn.edu/~rohner

Rohner, R. P. (2004). The parental acceptance-rejection syndrome: Universal correlates of perceived rejection. *American Psychologist, 59,* 827–840.

Rohner, R. P. (2005). *Glossary of significant concepts in parental acceptance-rejection theory.* Retrieved February 18, 2015, from http://www.cspar.uconn.edu/Glossary.pdf

Rohner, R. P. (2006). *Introduction to PARTheory studies of intimate partner relationships.* Paper presented at the 1st International Congress on Interpersonal Acceptance and Rejection, Istanbul, Turkey.

Rohner, R. P. (2007). Intimate Relationship Questionnaire (IARQ). In R. P. Rohner, *Measures for use in parental acceptance-rejection theory research.* Unpublished manuscript, University of Connecticut, Storrs, CT.

Rohner, R. P. (2008). Parental acceptance-rejection theory studies of intimate adult relationships. In R. P. Rohner & T. Melendez (Eds.), Parental acceptance-rejection theory studies of intimate adult relationships [Special issue]. *Cross-Cultural Research, 42,* 5–12.

Rohner, R. P., Khaleque, A., Shamsuddin, E., & Sabina, S. (2010). The relationship between perceived teacher and parental acceptance, school conduct, and the psychological adjustment of Bangladeshi adolescents. *Cross-Cultural Research, 44,* 239–252.

Rohner, R. P. (2014). Parental power and prestige moderate the relationship between perceived parental acceptance and offspring's psychological: Introduction to the international father acceptance-rejection project. *Cross-Cultural Research.* doi:10.1177/1069397114528295

Rohner, R. P. (2015). *Introduction to interpersonal acceptance-rejection theory, methods, evidence, and implications.* Retrieved September 25, 2015, from University of Connecticut, Ronald and Nancy Rohner Center for the Study of Interpersonal Acceptance Rejection website: http://csiar.uconn.edu

Rohner, R. P., & Britner, P. A. (2002). Worldwide mental health correlates of parental acceptance-rejection: Review of cross-cultural and intracultural evidence. *Cross-Cultural Research, 36,* 16–47.

Rohner, R. P., & Chaki-Sircar, M. (1988/2000). *Women and children in a Bengali village.* Hanover, NH: University Press of New England.

Rohner, R. P., Kean, K. J., & Cournoyer, D. E. (1991). Effects of corporal punishment, perceived caretaker warmth, and cultural beliefs on the psychological adjustment of children in St. Kitts, West Indies. *Journal of Marriage and the Family, 53,* 681–693.

Rohner, R. P., Khaleque, A. (2003). Reliability and validity of the Parental Control Scale: A meta-analysis of cross-cultural and intra-cultural studies. *Journal of Cross-Cultural Psychology, 34,* 643–649.

Rohner, R. P., & Khaleque, A. (2005). *Handbook for the study of parental acceptance and rejection.* Storrs, CT: Rohner Research.

Rohner, R. P., & Khaleque, A. (2008). Relations between perceived partner and parental acceptance. In J. K. Quinn & I. G. Zambini (Eds.), *Family relations: 21st century issues and challenges.* New York: Nova Science.

Rohner, R. P., & Khaleque, A. (2010). Testing the central postulates of parental acceptance-rejection theory (PARTheory): A meta-analysis of cross-cultural studies. *Journal of Family Theory & Review, 2,* 73–87.

Rohner, R. P., & Khaleque, A. (2014). Essentials of parenting: Parental warmth, behavioral control, and discipline. In K. D. Keith (General Ed.), *The encyclopedia of cross-cultural psychology.* Malden, MA: Wiley-Blackwell.

Rohner, R. P., & Khaleque, A. (2015a). Parental acceptance-rejection and life-span development: A universalist perspective. In W. Friedlmeir (Ed.), *Readings in psychology and culture.* Center for Cross-Cultural Research, Western Washington University.

Rohner, R. P., & Khaleque, A. (2015b). *Introduction to interpersonal acceptance-rejection theory, methods, evidence, and implications.* Retrieved September 25, 2015, from University of Connecticut, Ronald and Nancy Rohner Center for the Study of Interpersonal Acceptance Rejection website: http://csiar.uconn.edu

Rohner, R. P., & Melendez, T. (2008). Parental acceptance-rejection theory studies of intimate adult relationships. *Cross-Cultural Research, 42*(1), 77–86.

Rohner, R. P., Melendez, T., & Kraimer-Rickaby, L. (2008). Intimate partner acceptance, parental acceptance, and psychological adjustment among American adults in ongoing attachment relationships. *Cross-Cultural Research, 42*(1), 13–22.

Rohner, R. P., & Pettingill, S. M. (1985). Perceived parental acceptance-rejection and parental control among Korean adolescents. *Child Development, 56*(2), 524–528.

Rohner, R. P., & Rohner, E. C. (1980). Worldwide tests of parental acceptance-rejection theory. *Behavioral Science Research, 15,* 1–21.

Rohner, R. P., Roll, S., & Rohner, E. C. (1980). Perceived parental acceptance-rejection and personality organization among Mexican and American elementary school children. *Behavior Science Research, 15,* 23–39.

Rohner, R. P., Uddin, M. K., Shamsunnaher, M., & Khaleque, A. (2008). Intimate partner acceptance, parental acceptance in childhood, and psychological adjustment among Japanese adults. *Cross-Cultural Research, 42,* 87–97.

Rohner, R. P., & Veneziano, R. A. (2001). The importance of father love: History and contemporary evidence. *Review of General Psychology, 5,* 382–405.

Rollie, S. S., & Duck, S. W. (2006). Stage theories of marital breakdown. In J. H. Harvey and M. A. Fine (Eds.), *Handbook of divorce and dissolution of romantic relationships* (pp. 176–193). Mahwah, NJ: Erlbaum.

Rollins, B. C., & Feldman, H. (1970). Marital satisfaction over the family life cycle. *Journal of Marriage Family, 32,* 20–28.

Rosenberg, C. M. (1971). The young addict and his family. *British Journal of Psychiatry, 118,* 469–470.

Rosenbluth, S. C., & Steil, J. M. (1995). Predictors of intimacy for women in heterosexual and homosexual couples. *Journal of Social and Personal Relationships, 12*(2), 163–165.

Rosenfeld, M. J., Thomas, R. J., & Falcon, M. (2015). *How couples meet and stay together* (waves 1, 2, and 3 version 3.04; wave 4 supplement version 1.02; wave 5 supplement version 1.03). Stanford, CA: Stanford University Libraries.

Rosenthal, D. A., Biro, F. M., Succop, P. A., Bernstein, D. I., & Stanberry, L. (1997). Impact of demographics, sexual history, and psychological functioning on the acquisition of STDs in adolescents. *Adolescence, 32,* 757–770.

Rosenthal, D. A., Moore, S. M., & Brumer, I. (1990). Ethnic group differences in adolescent responses to AIDS. *Australian Journal of Social Science, 25,* 77–88.

Rosenthal, N. L., & Kobak, R. (2010). Assessing adolescents' attachment hierarchy: Differences across developmental periods and association with individual adaptation. *Journal of Research on Adolescence, 20,* 678–706.

Rosenthal, S. L., Biro, F. M., Cohen, S. S., Succop, P. A., & Stanberry, L. R. (1995). Strategies for coping with sexually transmitted diseases by adolescent females. *Adolescence, 30*(119), 655–666.

Rowe, J. W., & Kahn, R. L. (1998). *Successful aging.* New York: Random House.

Ruan, F. F. (1991). *Sex in China: Studies in sexology in Chinese culture.* New York: Plenum Press.

Rubin, K. H., & Andrea, T. (2003). *Friendship factor: Helping our children navigate their social world—and why it matters for their success and happiness.* New York: Penguin Books.

Rubin, K. H., Bukowski, W., & Parker, J. G. (1998). Peer interactions, relationships, and groups. In W. Damon & N. Eisenberg (Eds.), *Handbook of child psychology: Social, emotional, and personality development* (pp. 619–700). New York: Wiley.

Rubin, L. (1985). *Just friends.* New York: Harper & Row.

Rudder, C. (2014). *Dataclysm: Who we are when we think no one is looking.* New York: Crown.

Rudman, L. A., Fetterolf, J. C., & Sanchez, D. T. (2013). What motivates the sexual double standard? More support for male versus female control theory. *Personality and Social Psychology Bulletin, 38,* 734–746.

Rudman, L. A., & Phelan, J. E. (2007). The interpersonal power of feminism: Is feminism good for romantic relationships? *Sex Roles*. doi:10.1007/s11199-007-9319-9

Ruppel, E., & Curran, M. A. (2012). Relational sacrifices in romantic relationships: Satisfaction and the moderating role of attachment. *Journal of Social and Personal Relationships, 29,* 508–529. doi:10.1177/0265407511431190

Rusbult, C. E., Agnew, C. R., & Arriaga, X. B. (2012). The investment model of commitment processes. In P. A. M. Van Lange, A. W. Kruglanski, & E. T. Higgins (Eds.), *Handbook of theories of social psychology* (Vol. 2, pp. 218–231). Los Angeles: Sage.

Rusbult, C. E., Coolsen, M. K., Kirchner, J. L., & Clarke, J. A. (2006). Commitment. In A. L. Vangelisti & D. Perlman (Eds.), *The Cambridge handbook of personal relationships* (pp. 615–635). Cambridge, UK: Cambridge University Press.

Russell, V. M., Baker, L. R., & McNult, J. K. (2013). Attachment insecurity and infidelity in marriage. *Journal of Family Psychology, 27,* 242–251.

Saavedra, J. M. (1980). Effects of perceived parental warmth and control on the self-evaluation of Puerto Rican adolescent males. *Behavior Science Research, 15,* 41–54.

Sabin, E. P. (1993). Social relationships and mortality among elderly. *Journal of Applied Gerontology, 12,* 44–60.

Sacerdote, B., & Marmaros, D. (2005). *How do friendships form?* National Bureau of Economic Research, Working Paper Series. Retrieved from http://nber.org/papers/w11530

Saffrey, C., & Ehrenberg, M. (2007). When thinking hurts: Attachment, rumination, and postrelationship adjustment. *Personal Relationships, 14,* 351–368.

Sager, D. E., & Sager, W. G. (2005). SANCTUS marriage enrichment. *The Family Journal, 13*(2), 212–218. Retrieved from http://dx.doi.org/10.1177/1066480704273223

Salami, S. (2011). Personality and psychological well-being of adolescents: The moderating role of emotional intelligence. *Social Behavior and Personality, 39*(6), 785–794. doi:10.2224/sbp.2011.39.6.78

Salkind, N. J. (2004). *An introduction to theories of human development.* Los Angeles: Sage.

Samter, W. (2003). Friendship interaction skills across the life span. In J. O. Green & B. R. Burleson (Eds.), *Handbook of communication and social interaction skills* (pp. 637–684). Mahwah, NJ: Erlbaum.

Sanchez, D. T., Fetterolf, J. C., & Rudma, L. A. (2012). Eroticizing inequality in the United States: The consequences and determinants of traditional gender role adherence in intimate relationships. *Journal of Sex Research, 49*(2–3), 168–183.

Sanchez, D. T., Phelan, J. E., Moss-Racusin, C. A., & Good J. J. (2012). The gender role motivation model of women's sexually submissive behavior and satisfaction in heterosexual couples. *Personality and Social Psychology Bulletin, 38*(4), 528–539. doi:10.1177/0146167211430088

Sanchez-Fuentas, M. M., Santos-Iglosias, P., & Sierra, J. C. (2014). A systematic review of sexual satisfaction. *International Journal of Clinical and Health Psychology, 14*(1), 67–75.

Santos-Iglesias, P., Sierra, J. C., & Vallejo-Medina, P. (2013). Predictors of sexual assertiveness: The role of sexual desire, arousal, attitudes, and partner abuse. *Archives of Sexual Behavior, 42,* 1043–1052.

Sapadin, L. A. (1988). Friendships and gender: Perspectives of professional men and women. *Journal of Social and Personal Relationships, 5,* 387–403.

Sartin, R. M., Hansen, D. J., & Huss, M. T. (2006). Domestic violence treatment response and recidivism: A review and implications for the study of family violence. *Aggression and Violent Behavior, 11,* 425–440.

Sassler, S. (2004). The process of entering into cohabiting unions. *Journal of Marriage and Family, 66,* 491–505

Sassler, S. (2010). Partnering across the life course: Sex, relationships, and mate selection. *Journal of Marriage and Family, 72*(3), 557–575.

Savic, I., & Lindström, P. (2008). PET and MRI show differences in cerebral asymmetry and functional connectivity between homo- and heterosexual subjects. *Proceedings of the National Academy of Science, USA, 105,* 9403–9408.

Savin-Williams, R. C. (2006). *The new gay teenager.* Cambridge, MA: Harvard University Press.

Saxena, V. (1992). Perceived maternal rejection as related to negative attention-seeking classroom behavior among primary school children. *Journal of Personality and Clinical Studies, 8*(1–2), 129–135.

Sbarra, D. A. (2006). Predicting the onset of emotional recovery following nonmarital relationship dissolution: Survival analyses of sadness and anger. *Personality and Social Psychology Bulletin, 32,* 298–312.

Sbarra, D. A., & Emery, R. E. (2005). The emotional sequelae of nonmarital relationship dissolution: Analysis of change and interindividual variability over time. *Personal Relationships, 12,* 213–232.

Schacher, S., Auerbach, C. F., & Silverstein, L. B. (2005). Gay fathers. Expanding the possibilities for all of us. *Journal of GLBT Family Studies, 1*(3), 31–52.

Schick, V., Rosenberger, J. G., Herbenick, D., Calabrese, S. K., & Reece, M. (2012). Bidentity: Sexual behavior/identity congruence and women's sexual, physical and mental well-being. *Journal of Bisexuality, 12,* 178–197.

Schmitt, D. P. (2005). Sociosexuality from Argentina to Zimbabwe: A 48-nation study of sex, culture, and strategies of human mating. *Behavioral and Brain Sciences, 28,* 247–275.

Schmitt, D. P. (2008). Attachment matters: Patterns of romantic attachment across gender, geography, and cultural forms. In J. P. Forgas & J. Fitness (Eds.), *Social relationships: Cognitive, affective, and motivational processes* (pp. 75–100). New York: Psychology Press.

Schmitt, D. P. (2016). Fundamentals of human mating strategies. In D. M. Buss (Ed.), *The evolutionary psychology handbook* (pp. 294–316). New York: Wiley.

Schmitt, D. P., & Shackelford, T. K. (2008). Big Five traits related to short-term mating: From personality to promiscuity across 46 nations. *Evolutionary Psychology, 6,* 246–282.

Schmitt, D. P., Youn, G., Bond, B., Brooks, S., Frye, H., Johnson, S., Klesman, J., Peplinski, C., Schoebi, D., Karney, B. R., & Bradbury, T. N. (2012). Stability and change in the first 10 years of marriage: Does commitment confer benefits beyond the effects of satisfaction? *Journal of Personality and Social Psychology, 102*(4), 729–742.

Schoebi, D., Wang, Z., Ababkov, V., Perrez, M. (2010). Affective interdependence in married couples' daily lives: are there cultural differences in partner effects of anger? *Family Science, 183*–92. 10.1080/19424620903471681

Schover, L. R., Fouladi, R. T., Warnecke, C. L., Neese, L., Klein, E. A., Zippe, C., et al. (2004). Seeking help for erectile dysfunction after treatment for prostate cancer. *Archives of Sexual Behavior, 33,* 443–454.

Schumm, W. R. (2016). A review and critique of research on same-sex parenting and adoption. *Psychological Reports, 3,* 641–760.

Schwartz, S. J., Zamoanga, B. L., Revert, R. D., Kim, S. Y, Weisskirch, R. S., Williams, M. K., et al. (2009). Perceived parental relationships and health-risk behaviors in college-attending emerging adults. *Journal of Marriage and Family, 71,* 727–740.

Schwarz, S., & Hassebrauck, M. (2008). Self-perceived and observed variations in women's attractiveness throughout menstrual cycle—A dairy study. *Evolution and Human Behavior, 29,* 282–288.

Scollon, C. N., Diener, E., Oishi, S., & Biswas-Diener, R. (2005). An experience sampling and cross-cultural investigation of the relation between pleasant and unpleasant affect. *Cognition and Emotion, 19*(1), 27–52.

Scott, M. E., Steward-Streng, N. R., Manlove, J., Schelar, E., & Cui, C. (2011). *Characteristics of young adult sexual relationships: Diverse, sometimes violent, often loving.* Washington, DC: Child Trends.

Scott-Jones, D., & White, A. B. (1990). Correlates of sexual activity in early adolescence. *Journal of Early Adolescence, 10,* 221–238.

Scott-Sheldon, L. A., Huedo-Medina, T. B., Warren, M. R., Johnson, B. T., & Carey, M. P. (2011). Efficacy of behavioral interventions to increase condom use and reduce sexually transmitted infections: A meta-analysis, 1991 to 2010. *Journal of Acquired Immune Deficiency Syndrome, 58,* 489–498.

Seem, S. R., & Clark, M. D. (2006). Healthy women, healthy men, and healthy adults: An evaluation of gender role stereotypes in the 21st century. *Sex Roles: A Journal of Research, 55,* 247–258.

Segal, N. L. (2012). *Born together-reared apart: The landmark Minnesota twin study.* Cambridge, MA: Harvard University Press.

Segal-Caspi, L., Roccas, S., & Sagiv, L. (2012). Don't judge a book by its cover, revisited: Perceived and reported traits and values of attractive women. *Psychological Science, 23,* 1112–1116.

Selman, R. L. (1980). *The growth of interpersonal understanding.* London: Academic Press.

Selman, R. L. (2007). *Promotion of social awareness: Powerful lessons from the partnership of developmental theory and classroom practice.* New York: Russell Sage.

Seltzer, J. A. (2000). Families formed outside of marriage. *Journal of Marriage and Family, 62,* 1247–1268.

Senchak, M., & Leonard, K. E. (1992). Attachment styles and marital adjustment among newlywed couples. *Journal of Social and Personal Relationships, 9,* 51–64.

Shackelford, T. K., & Goetz, A. T. (2004). Men's sexual coercion in intimate relationships: Development and initial validation of the Sexual Coercion in Intimate Relationships Scale. *Violence and Victims, 19,* 541–556.

Shallcross, A. J., Ford, B. Q., Floerke, V. A., & Mauss, I. B. (2013). Getting better with age: The relationship between age, acceptance, and negative affect. *Journal of Personality and Social Psychology, 104*(4), 734–749.

Shaver, P., Furman, W., & Buhrmester, D. (1985). Transition to college: Network changes, social skills, and loneliness. In S. Duck & D. Perlman (Eds.), *Understanding personal relationships: An interdisciplinary approach* (pp. 193–219). London: Sage.

Shaver, P. R., Belsky, J., & Brennan, K. A. (2000). The Adult Attachment Interview and self-reports of romantic attachment: Associations across domains and methods. *Personal Relationships, 7,* 25–43.

Shaver, P. R., & Clark, C. L. (1994). The psychodynamics of adult romantic attachment. In J. M. Masling & R. F. Bornslein (Eds.), *Empirical perspectives on object relations theory* (Vol. 5, pp. 105–56). Washington DC: American Psychological Association.

Shaver, P. R., & Fraley, R. C. (2008). Attachment, loss and grief: Bowlby's views and current controversies. In J. Cassidy & P. Shaver (Eds.), *Handbook of adult attachment: Theory, research and clinical applications* (2nd ed., pp. 48–77). New York: The Guilford Press.

Shaver, P. R., & Hazan, C. (1988). A biased overview of the study of love. *Journal of Social and Personal Relationships, 5,* 473–501.

Shaver, P. R., & Mikulincer, M. (2008). An overview of adult attachment theory. In J. H. Obegi & E. Berant (Eds.), *Attachment theory and research in clinical work with adults* (pp. 17–45). New York: The Guilford Press.

Shedler, J., & Block, J. (1990). Adolescent drug use and psychological health: A longitudinal inquiry. *American Psychologist, 45*(5), 612–630.

Shelley-Sireci, L. M., & Ciano-Boyce, C. B. (2002). Becoming lesbian adoptive parents: An exploratory study of lesbian adoptive, lesbian birth, and heterosexual adoptive mothers. *Adoption Quarterly, 6,* 33–43.

Sherman, L. E., Michikyan, M., & Greenfield, P. M. (2013). The effects of text, audio, video, and in-person communication on bonding between friends. *Cyberpsychology: Journal of Psychosocial Research on Cyberspace, 7*(2), article 1. doi:10.5817/CP2013-2-3

Sherman, M. D., & Thelen, M. H. (1996). Fear of Intimacy Scale: Validation and extension with adolescents. *Journal of Social and Personal Relationships, 13,* 507–521.

Shiota, M. N., Campos, B., Conzaga, B., Kelthner, D., & Peng, K. (2010). I love you but: Cultural differences in complexity of emotional experience during interaction with a romantic partner. *Cognition and Emotion, 24*(5), 786–799.

Shrier, L., Pierce, J., Emans, S., & Du Rant, R. (1998). Gender differences in risk behaviors associated with force or pressured sex. *Archives of Pediatrics and Adolescent Medicine, 152,* 57–63.

Shuang Xia, B. M. (2013). *An investigation about relationship maintenance strategies after the discovery deception about infidelity.* Unpublished master's degree thesis, Texas Technical University.

Shulman, S., Elicker, J., & Sroufe, L. A. (1994). Stages of friendship growth in preadolescence as related to attachment history. *Journal of Social and Personal Relationships, 11,* 341–361.

Shulman, S., & Laursen, B. (2002). Adolescent perceptions of conflict in interdependent and disengaged friendships. *Journal of Research on Adolescence, 12,* 353–372.

Sias, P. M., Heath, R. G., Perry, T., Silva, D., & Fix, B. (2004). Narratives of workplace friendship deterioration. *Journal of Personal and Social Relationships, 21*(3), 321–340.

Siegler, E. (2013). Marriage linked to better survival in middle age. *Annals of Behavioral Medicine.* doi:10.1007/s12160-012-9457-3

Sieving, R., McNeely, C., & Blum, R. (2000). Maternal expectations, mother-child connectedness, and adolescent sexual debut. *Archives of Pediatrics and Adolescent Medicine, 154,* 809–816.

Sigle-Rushton, W., & McLanahan, S. S. (2004). Father absence and child well-being: A critical review. In D. P. Moynihan, T. Smeeding, & L. Rainwater (Eds.), *The future of the family* (pp. 116–155). New York: Russell Sage Foundation.

Simon, R. W., & Barrett, A. E. (2010). Nonmarital romantic relationships and mental health in early adulthood: Does the association differ for women and men? *Journal of Health and Social Behavior, 51,* 168–182.

Simon, V., Aikins, J., & Prinstein, M. (2008). Romantic partner selection and socialization during early adolescence. *Child Development, 79,* 1676–1692.

Simpson, J. A. (1990). The influence of attachment styles on romantic relationships. *Journal of Personality and Social Psychology, 59,* 971–980.

Simpson, J. A. (2007a). Psychological foundation of trust. *Current Directions in Psychological Science, 16,* 264–268.

Simpson, J. A. (2007b). Foundations of interpersonal trust. In A.W. Kruglanski & E.T. Higgins (Eds.), *Social psychology: Handbook of basic principles* (2nd ed., pp. 587–607). New York: The Guilford Press.

Simpson, J. A., & Belsky, J. (2008). Attachment theory within a modern evolutionary framework. In J. Cassidy & P. Shaver (Eds.), *Handbook of attachment: Theory, research and clinical applications* (2nd ed., pp. 131–157). New York: The Guilford Press.

Simpson, J. A., Collins, W. A., Tran, S., & Haydon, K. C. (2007). Attachment and the experience and expression of emotions in romantic relationships: A developmental perspective. *Journal of Personality and Social Psychology, 92*(2), 355–367.

Simpson, J. A., & Rholes, W. S. (1998). *Attachment theory and close relations*. New York: The Guilford Press.

Singh, D. (1995). Female judgment of male attractiveness and desirability for relationships: Role of waist-to-hip ratio and financial status. *Journal of Personality and Social Psychology, 69,* 1089–1101.

Singh, R., & Ho, S. Y. (2000). Attitudes and attraction: A new test for the attraction, repulsion, and the similarity-dissimilarity asymmetry hypotheses. *British Journal of Social Psychology, 39*(2), 197–211.

Skakoon-Sparling, S., & Cramer, K. (2014). Paratelic/telic state, sexual arousal, and sexual risk-taking in university students. *Journal of Motivation, Emotion, and Personality, 2,* 32–37.

Skinner, B. F. (1953). *Science and human behavior.* New York, NY: Simon & Schuster.

Skinner, K. B., Bahr, S. J., Crane, D. R., & Call, V. R. A. (2002). Cohabitation, marriage, and remarriage: A comparison of relationship quality over time. *Journal of Family Issues, 23,* 74–90.

Slade, A. (2008). The implications of attachment theory and research for adult psychotherapy: Research and clinical perspectives. In J. Cassidy & P. Shaver (Eds.), *Handbook of attachment: Theory, research and clinical applications* (2nd ed., pp. 762–782). New York: The Guilford Press.

Slavin, R. E. (2012). *Educational psychology.* Boston: Allyn and Bacon.

Slee, P. (2002). *Child, adolescent and family development.* Cambridge, UK: Cambridge University Press.

Smith, G., Mysak, K., & Michael, S. (2008). Sexual double standards and sexually transmitted illnesses: Social rejection and stigmatization of women. *Sex Roles, 58,* 391–401. doi:10.1007/s11199-007-9339-5

Smith, M., & Segal, J. (2014). Domestic violence and abuse: Signs of abuse and abusive relationships. *Helpguide.org.* Retrieved from http://www.helpguide.org/articles/abuse/domestic-violence-and-abuse.htm

Smith, P. K., Talmelli, L., Cowie, H., Naylor, P., & Chauhan, P. (2004). Profiles of non-victims, escaped victims, continuing victims, and new victims of school bullying. *British Journal of Educational Psychology, 74,* 565–581.

Smith, T. W. (1994). *The demography of sexual behavior.* Menlo Park, CA: Henry J. Kaiser Family Foundation.

Smith, T. W. (2006). Sexual behavior in the United States. In R. D. McAnulty & M. M. Burnette (Eds.), *Sex and sexuality* (pp. 103–131). Westport, CT: Praeger.

Snell, W. E., Jr., & Belk, S. S. (2002). On assessing "equity" in intimate relationships. In W. E. Snell, Jr. (Ed.), *New directions in the psychology of intimate relations: Research and theory.* Cape Girardeau, MO: Snell.

Soboleswki, J. M. (2007). Parents' discord and divorce, parent-child relationships and subjective well-being in early adulthood: Is feeling close to two parents always better than feeling close to one? *Social Forces, 85,* 1105–1124.

Solano, C. H. (1986). People without friends: Loneliness and its alternatives. In V. J. Derlega & B. Winstead (Eds.), *Friendship and social interaction* (pp. 225–246). New York: Springer.

Sollier, P. (2005). *Listening for wellness: An introduction to the Tomatis method.* Walnut Creek, CA: The Mozart Center Press.

Solomon, D., & Theiss, J. A. (2008). A longitudinal test of the relational turbulence model of romantic relationship development. *Personal Relationships, 15,* 339–357.

Solomon, D., & Theiss, J. (2013). *Interpersonal communication: Putting theory into practice.* New York: Routledge.

Solomon, S. E., Rothblum, E. D., & Balsam, K. F. (2005). Money, housework, sex, and conflict: Same-sex couples in civil unions, those not in civil unions, and heterosexual married siblings. *Sex Roles, 52,* 561–575.

Soto, C. J., John, O. P., Gosling, S. D., & Potter, J. (2011). Age differences in personality traits from 10 to 65: Big five domains faces in a large cross-sectional sample. *Journal of Personality and Social Psychology, 100,* 330–338.

Spangle, M., & Isenbart, M. (2003). *Negotiation communication for diverse settings.* Thousand Oaks, CA: Sage.

Spitzberg, B. H. (1999). An analysis of empirical estimates of sexual aggression, victimization and perpetration. *Violence and Victims, 14,* 241–260.

Spitzberg, B. H. (2013). Intimate partner violence. In J. G. Oetzel & A. Ting-Tomey (Eds.), *The Sage handbook of conflict communication.* Thousand Oaks, CA: Sage.

Sprecher, S. (2002). Sexual satisfaction in premarital relationships: Association with satisfaction, love, commitment, and stability. *Journal of Sex Research, 39,* 190–196.

Sprecher, S. (2014). Evidence of change in men's versus women's emotional reactions to first sexual intercourse: A 23-year study in a human sexuality course at a Midwestern university. *Journal of Sex Research, 51,* 466–472.

Sprecher, S., Aron, A., Hatfield, E., Cortese, A., Potapova, E., & Levitskaya, A. (1994). Love: American style, Russian style, and Japanese style. *Personal Relationships, 1,* 349–369.

Sprecher, S., Barbee, A., & Schwartz, P. (1995). "Was it good for you too?" Gender differences in first sexual intercourse experiences. *Journal of Sex Research, 32,* 3–15.

Sprecher, S., & Fehr, B. (2011). Dispositional attachment and relationship-specific attachment as predictors of companionate love for a partner. *Journal of Social and Personal Relationships, 28,* 558–574.

Sprecher, S., Schmeeckle, M., & Felmlee, D. (2006). Inequality in emotional involvement in romantic relationships. *Journal of Family Issues, 27,* 1255–1280.

Sprecher, S., & Sedikides, C. (1993). Gender differences in perception of emotionality: The case of close heterosexual relationships. *Sex Roles, 28,* 511–530.

Sprecher, S., & Toro-Morn, M. (2002). A study of men and women from different sides of earth to determine if men are from Mars and women are from Venus in their beliefs about love and romantic relationships. *Sex Roles: A Journal of Research, 46(5/6),* 131–147.

Sprecher, S., Treger, S., & Sakaluk, J. K. (2013). Premarital sexual standard and socio-sexuality: Gender, ethnicity, and cohort differences. *Archives of Sexual Behavior, 42,* 1395–1405.

Sroufe, A. (1995). *Emotional development: The organization of emotional life in the early years.* New York: Cambridge University Press.

Sroufe, L. A. (1983). Individual patterns of adaptation from infancy to preschool. In M. Perlmutter (Ed.), *Minnesota symposium in child psychology* (Vol. 16, pp. 41–85). Hillsdale, NJ: Erlbaum.

Sroufe, L. A., Carlson, E. A., & Shulman, S. (1993). Individuals in relationships: Development from infancy through adolescence. In D. C. Funder, R. D. Parke, C. Tomlinshon-Keasey, & K. Widaman (Eds.), *Studying lives through time: Personality and development* (pp. 315–342). Washington DC: American Psychological Association.

Sroufe, L. A., & Fleeson, J. (1986). Attachment and the construction of relationships. In W.W. Hartup & Z. Rubin (Eds.), *The nature of relationships* (pp. 51–71). Hillsdale, NJ: Erlbaum.

Stacey, J. (2006). Gay parenthood and the decline of paternity as we knew it. *Sexualities, 9,* 27–55.

Stackert, R. A., & Bursik, K. (2003). Why am I satisfied? Adult attachment style, sexed irrational relationship beliefs, and young adult romantic relationship satisfaction. *Personality and Individual Differences, 34,* 1419–1429.

Stafford, L. (2003). Maintaining romantic relationships: A summary and analysis of one research program. In D. J. Canary & M. Dainton (Eds.). *Maintaining relationships through communication* (pp. 59–78). Mahwah, NJ: Erlbaum.

Stafford, L., David, P., & McPherson, S. (2014). Sanctity of marriage and marital quality. *Journal of Social and Personal Relationships, 31,* 54–70.

Stanley, S. M. (2001). Making a case for premarital education. *Family Relations, 50,* 272–280.

Stanley, S. M., Amato, P. R., Johnson, C. A., & Markman, H. (2006). Premarital education, marital quality, and marital stability: Findings from a large, random household survey. *Journal of Family Psychology, 20*(1), 117–126.

Statista. (2012). *Reasons for opposing same-sex marriage in the United States.* Retrieved from http://www.statista.com/statistics/248079/reasons-for -opposing-same-sex-marriage-in-the-united-states

Statista. (2016). *Americans' opinion on the legalization of same-sex marriages from 1996–2015.* Retrieved from http://www.statista.com/statistics/217962/ opinion-of-legalization-of-same-sex-marriages-in-the-us

Statistical abstract of the United States (2009): 2009-Census Bureau. https://www .census.gov/uat/facets-publications/2008/compendia/statab/128ed.html

Stephenson, K. R., Ahrold, T. K., & Meston, C. M. (2011). The association between sexual motives and sexual satisfaction: Gender differences and categorical comparisons. *Archives of Sexual Behavior, 40,* 607–618.

Sternberg, R. J. (1987). Liking versus loving: A comparative evaluation of theories. *Psychological Bulletin, 102,* 331–345.

Sternberg, R. J. (1988a). *The triangle of love.* New York: Basic.

Sternberg, R. J. (1988b). Triangulating love. In R. J. Sternberg & M. L. Barnes (Eds.), *The psychology of love* (pp. 119–138). New Haven, CT: Yale University Press. Copyright © 1988 by Yale University Press.

Sternberg, R. J. (2006). A duplex theory of love. In R. J. Sternberg & K. Weis (Eds.), *The new psychology of love* (pp. 184–199). New Haven, CT: Yale University Press.

Sternberg, R. J. (2013). Searching for love. *The Psychologist, 26*(2), 98–101.

Sternberg, R. J., & Weis, K. (2006). *The new psychology of love.* New Haven, CT.: Yale University Press.

Stevens, M., Golombok, S., Beveridge, M., & Team, T. A. S. (2002). Does father absence influence children's gender development? Findings from a general population study of preschool children. *Parenting: Science and Practice, 2,* 47–60.

Stewart, S., Stinnett, H., & Rosenfeld, L. B. (2000). Sex differences in desired characteristics of short-term and long-term relationship partners. *Journal of Social and Personal Relationships, 17,* 843–853.

Stone, L. (1989). Passionate attachments in the West in historical perspective. In W. Gaylin & E. Person (Eds.), *Passionate attachments: Thinking about love* (pp. 15–26). New York: Touchstone.

Strohm, C. Q., Seltzer, J. A., Cochran, S. D., & Mays, V. M. (2009). "Living apart together" relationships in the United States. *Demographic Research, 21,* 177–214.

Strough, J., & Margrett, J. (2002). Overview of the special section on collaborative cognition in later adulthood. *International Journal of Behavioral Development, 26,* 2–5.

Stulp, C., Buunk, A. P., & Pollet, T. V. (2013). Women want taller men more than men want shorter women. *Personality and Individual Difference, 54,* 877–883.

Subrahmanyam, K., Reich, S. M., Waechter, N., & Espinoza, G. (2008). Online and offline social networks: Use of social networking sites by emerging adults. *Journal of Applied Developmental Psychology, 29,* 420–433.

Sukel, K. (2013). Do men and women have sex for different reasons? *This is your brain on sex. New York: Free Press.*

Sullivan, H. S. (1953). *The interpersonal theory of psychiatry.* New York: Norton.

Suls, J., & Wheeler, L. (2012). Social comparison theory. In P. A. M. Van Lange, A. W. Kruglanski, & E. T. Higgin (Eds.), *Handbook of social psychology* (pp. 460–481). Los Angeles: Sage.

Sultana, S., & Khaleque, A. (2016). Differential effects of perceived maternal and paternal acceptance on male and female adult offspring's psychological adjustment. *Gender Issues, 33*(1), 42–52. doi:10.1007/s12147 -015-9147-0

Swaab, D. F. (2003). *The human hypothalamus: Basic and clinical aspects. Part I: Nuclei of the human hypothalamus.* Amsterdam: Elsevier.

Swain, S. O. (1992). Men's friendships with women: Intimacy, sexual boundaries, and the informant role. In P. M. Nardi (Ed.), *Men's friendships* (pp. 153– 171). Newbury Park, CA: Sage.

Swami, V., Furnham, A., Chamorro-Premuzic, T., Akbar, K., Gordon, N., Harris, T., Finch, J., & Tovee, M. J. (2010). More than just skin deep? Personality information influences men's ratings of the attractiveness of women's body sizes. *The Journal of Social Psychology, 150*(6), 628–674.

Sweeney, M. M. (2002). Two decades of family change: The shifting economic foundations of marriage. *American Sociological Review, 67,* 132–147.

Sweeney, M. M., & Phillips, J. A. (2004). Understanding racial differences in marital disruption: Recent trends and explanations. *Journal of Marriage and Family, 66,* 239–250.

Tafoya, M. A., & Spitzberg, B. H. (2007). The dark side of infidelity: Its nature, prevalence, and communicative functions. In B. H. Spitzberg & W. R. Cupach (Eds.), *The dark side of interpersonal communication* (pp. 201– 242). Mahwah, NJ: Erlbaum.

Tappé, M., Bensman, L., Hayashj, K., & Hatfield, E. (2013). Gender differences in receptivity to sexual offers: A new research prototype. *Interpersonal Relations, 7*(2). doi:10.5964/ijpr.v7i2.121

Taraban, C. B., Hendrick, S. S., & Hendrick, C. (1998). Loving and liking. In P. A. Andersen & L. K. Guerrero (Eds.), *Handbook of communication and emotion* (pp. 331–351). San Diego, CA: Academic Press.

Taylor, L. S., Fiore, A. T., Mendelsohn, G. A., & Cheshire, C. (2011). "Out of my league": A real-world test of the matching hypothesis. *Personality and Social Psychology Bulletin, 37*(7), 942–954.

Taywaditep, K. J. (2001). Marginalization among the marginalized: Gay men's anti-effeminacy attitudes. *Journal of Homosexuality, 42,* 1–28. doi:10.1300/ J082v42n01_01

Teachman, J. (2003). Premarital sex, premarital cohabitation, and the risk of subsequent marital dissolution among women. *Journal of Marriage and Family, 65*(2), 444–455.

Terrell, J. E. (2014). *A talent for friendship: Rediscovery of a remarkable trait.* Oxford, UK: Oxford University Press.

Teti, D., & Abalard, K.E. (1989). Security of attachment and infant-sibling relationships: A laboratory study. *Child Development, 60,* 1519–1528.

Thompson, L., & Walker, A. J. (1989). Gender in families: Women and men in marriage, work, parenthood. *Journal of Marriage and the Family, 51,* 845–871.

Thompson, R. A. (1998). Early socio-personality development. In W. Damon (Series Ed.) & N. Eisenberg (Vol. Ed.), *Handbook of child psychology: Social, emotional, and personality development* (pp. 25–104). New York: Wiley.

Thompson, R. A. (2008). Early attachment and later development: Familiar questions, new answers. J. Cassidy & P. Shaver (Eds.), *Handbook of adult attachment: Theory, research and clinical applications* (2nd ed., pp. 348–365). New York: The Guilford Press.

Thompson, R. G., & Auslander, W. F. (2011). Substance use and mental health problems as predictors of HIV sexual risk behaviors among adolescents in foster care. *Health & Social Work, 36,* 33–43.

Thompson, S. (2015). *Types of interpersonal conflict.* Retrieved from http://www.livestrong.com/article/133713-types-interpersonal-conflict

Thornhill, R., Chapmen, J. F., & Gangestad, S. W. (2013). Women's preferences for men's scents associate with testosterone and cortisol levels: Patterns across the ovulatory cycle. *Evolution and Human Behavior, 34,* 216–221.

Thors, C. L., Broeckel, J. A., & Jacobsen, P. B. (2001). Sexual functioning in breast cancer survivors. *Cancer Control, 8,* 442–448.

Tidwell, N. D., & Eastwick, P. W. (2013). Sex differences in succumbing to sexual temptations: A function of impulse or control? *Personality and Social Psychology Bulletin, 39,* 1620–1633.

Toma, C. L., & Hancock, J. T. (2010). Looks and lies: The role of physical attractiveness in online dating self-presentation and deception. *Communication Research, 37,* 335–351. doi:10.1177/0093650209356437

Totenhagen, C. J., Butler, E. A., & Ridley, C. A. (2012). Daily stress, closeness, and satisfaction in gay and lesbian couples. *Personal Relationships, 19,* 219–233.

Totenhagen, C. J., Curran, M. A., Serido, J., & Butler, E. A. (2013). Good days, bad days: Do sacrifices improve relationship quality? *Journal of Social and Personal Relationships, 30,* 881–900.

Townsend, J. M., & Wasserman, T. H. (2011). Sexual hookups among college students: Sex differences in emotional reactions. *Archives of Sexual Behavior, 40,* 1173–1181.

Treas, J. (2002). How cohorts, education, and ideology shaped a new sexual revolution on attitudes toward non-marital sex, 1972–1998. *Sociological Perspectives, 45,* 267–283.

Treas, J., & De Ruijter, E. (2008). Earnings and expenditures on household services in married and cohabiting unions. *Journal of Marriage and Family, 70,* 796–805.

Troy, M., & Sroufe, L.A. (1987). Victimization among preschoolers: The role of attachment relationship history. *Journal of American Academy of Child Psychiatry, 26,* 186–172.

Trudel, G., Turgeon, L., & Piche, L. (2000). Marital and sexual aspects of old age. *Sexual & Relationship Therapy, 15*(4), 381–406.

Tryon, W. W., & Tryon, G. S. (2011). No ownership of common factors. *American Psychologist, 66*(2), 151–152.

Tucker, P., & Aron, A. (1993). Passionate love and marital satisfaction at key transition points in the family life cycle. *Journal of Social and Clinical Psychology, 12*(2), 135–147.

Tucker, J. S., Friedman, H. S., Wingard, D. L., & Schwartz, J. E. (1996). Marital history at midlife as a predictor of longevity: Alternative explanations to the protective effect of marriage. *Health Psychology, 15,* 94–101.

Tudge, J. R. H., Mokrova, I., Hatfield, B. E., & Karnik, R. B. (2009). Uses and misuses of Bronfenbrenner's bioecological theory of human development. *Journal of Family Theory & Review, 1,* 198–210.

Turner, P. H., & Welch, K. J. (2012). *Parenting in contemporary society.* Boston: Pearson.

Twenge, J. M. (2014). *Generation me: Why today's young Americans are more confident, assertive, entitled—and more miserable than ever before* (2nd ed.). New York: Atria Books.

Twenge, J. M., Sherman, R. A., & Wells, B. E. (2015). Changes in American adults' sexual behavior and attitudes, 1972–2012. *Archives of Sexual Behavior, 44,* 2273–2285. doi:10.1007/s10508-015-0540-2

Uchino, B. N., Cacioppo, J. T., & Kielcolt-Glaser, J. K. (1996). The relationship between social support and physiological process: A review with emphasis on underlying mechanisms and implications for health. *Psychological Bulletin, 119,* 488–531. Family, 71, 727–740.

Uddin, M. K., Khaleque, A., Aktar, R., Hossain, M. A., & Roy, K. (2016, June 7–10). *Parental rejection in childhood predicts fear of intimacy in adults of Bangladesh.* Presented in the 6th International Congress on Interpersonal Acceptance-Rejection, Madrid, Spain.

Uecker, J. E. (2008). Religion, pledging, and the premarital sexual behavior of married young adults. *Journal of Marriage and Family, 70,* 728–744.

Uecker, J. E., & Stockes, C. E. (2008). Early marriage in the United States. *Journal of Marriage and Family, 70,* 835–846.

Ueno, K., Gayman, M. D., Wright, E. R., & Quartz, S. D. (2009). Friends' sexual orientation, relationship quality, and mental health among gay, lesbian, & bisexual youth. *Personal Relations, 16,* 659–670.

Umberson, D. (2005). Stress in childhood and adulthood: Effects on marital quality over time. *Journal of Marriage and Family, 67*(4), 1332–1347.

Umberson, D., Williams, K., Powers, D., Chen, M. D., & Campbell, A. (2005). As good as it gets? A life course perspective on marital quality. *Social Forces, 84,* 493–511.

Umberson, D., Williams, K., Powers, D. A., Liu, H., & Needham, B. (2006). You make me sick: Marital quality and health over the life course. *Journal of Health and Social Behavior, 47,* 1–16.

U.N. Demographics and Social Statistics Division. (2015). *Countries with highest divorce rate.* New York: Statistics Division, United Nations.

Underwood, N. K., Kupersmidt, J. B., & Coie, J. D. (1996). Childhood peer sociometric status and aggression as predictors of adolescent childbearing. *Journal of Research on Adolescence, 6,* 201–223.

U.S. Bureau of Labor Statistics. (2013). Marriage and divorce: Patterns by gender, race, and educational attainment. *Monthly Labor Review,* October 2013.

U.S. Census Bureau. (2000). *Marital status by sex, unmarried partners households, and grandparents and caregivers: 2000* [Online].

U.S. Census Bureau. (2003). *Marital status: 2000.* Washington, DC: U.S. Department of Commerce.

U.S. Department of Health and Human Services (USDHHS). (2013). Overview: Teen pregnancy and Childbearing. *Reproductive Health.* Retrieved from http://www.hhs.gov

Vagianos, A. (2015). 30 shocking domestic violence statistics that remind us it's an epidemic. *The Huffington Post.* TheHuffingtonPost.com.

Vaillant, C. O., & Vaillant, G. E. (1993). Is the U-curve of marital satisfaction an illusion? A 40-year study of marriage. *Journal of Marriage and Family, 55*(1), 230–239.

Valkenburg, P. M., & Peter, J. (2009). Social consequences of the Internet for adolescents: A decade of research. *Current Directions in Psychological Science, 18,* 1–5.

Vandell, D. L., Owen, M. T., Wilson, K. S., & Henderson, V. K. (1988). Social development in infant twins: Peer and mother-child relationships. *Child Development, 59,* 168–177.

Vander-Drift, L. E., Agnew, C. R., & Wilson, J. E. (2009). Nonmarital romantic relationship commitment and leave behavior: The mediating role of dissolution consideration. *Personality and Social Psychology Bulletin, 35,* 1220–1232.

Van der Kolk, B. A. (2010). *Developmental trauma disorder: Towards a relational diagnosis for children with complex trauma histories.* Unpublished manuscript.

Vanfraussen, K., Ponjaert-Kristoffersen, I., & Brewaeys, A. (2003). Family functioning in lesbian families created by donor insemination. *American Journal of Orthopsychiatry, 73,* 78–90.

Vangelisti, A. L., & Perlman, D. (2006). *The Cambridge handbook of personal relationships.* Cambridge, UK: Cambridge University Press.

Van Ijzendoorn, M., & Sagi-Schwartz, A. (2008). Cross-cultural patterns of attachment. In J. Cassidy & P. Shaver (Eds.), *Handbook of adult attachment: Theory, research and clinical applications* (2nd ed., pp. 880–905). New York: The Guilford Press.

Van Laningham, J., Johnson, D. R., & Amato, P. (2001). Marital happiness, marital duration, and the U-shaped curve: Evidence from a five-wave panel study. *Social Forces, 79,* 1313–1323.

Van Lear, C. A., Koerner, A., & Allen, D. M. (2006). Relationship typologies. In A. L. Vangelisti & D. Perlman (Eds.), *The Cambridge handbook of personal relationships* (pp. 91–110). New York: Cambridge University Press.

Vannier, S. A., & O'Sullivan, L. F. (2011). Communicating interest in sex: Verbal and nonverbal initiation of sexual activity in young adults' romantic dating relationships. *Archives of Sexual Behavior, 40*(5), 961–969.

Vaquera, E., & Kao, G. (2005). Private and public displays of affection among interracial and intra-racial adolescent couples. *Social Science Quarterly, 86,* 484–508.

Varan, A., Rohner, R. P., & Eryuksel, G. (2008). Intimate partner acceptance, parental acceptance in childhood, and psychological adjustment among Turkish adults in ongoing attachment relationships. *Cross-Cultural Research, 42,* 46–56.

Veneziano, R. A. (2003). The importance of paternal warmth. *Cross-Cultural Research, 37,* 265–281.

Veneziano, R. A. (2008, July 3–6). *The relative importance of fathers versus mothers for offspring's behavior: Theory and implications for future research.* Paper presented at the Second International Congress on Interpersonal Acceptance and Rejection, University of Crete, Rethymno, Greece.

Ven-hwei, L., So, C. Y. K., & Guoliang, Z. (2010). The influence of individualism and collectivism on internet pornography exposure, sexual attitudes, and sexual behavior among college students. *Chinese Journal of Communication, 3,* 10–27.

Ventura, S. J., Mosher, W. D., Curtin, M. A., Abma, J. C., & Henshaw, S. (2001). Trends in pregnancy rates for the United States, 1976–1997: An update. *National Vital Statistics Reports, 49,* 1–9.

Verhaegen, P. (1979). *Work satisfaction in the present-day working life: Ergonomics and work satisfaction.* In R. G. Sell & P. Shipley (Eds.), *Satisfaction in work design: Ergonomics and other approaches* (pp. 81–88). London: Taylor and Francis.

Vernon, M. (2006). *The philosophy of friendship.* London: Palgrave Macmillan.

Vescio, T. K., Schlenker, K. A., & Lenes, J. G. (2010). Power and sexism. In A. Guinote & T. Vescio (Eds.), *The social psychology of power* (pp. 363–380). New York: The Guilford Press.

Vespa, J. (2014). Historical trends in the marital intentions of one-time and serial cohabitors. *Journal of Marriage and Family, 76,* 207–217.

Veves, A., Webster, L., Chen, T., Payne, S., & Boulton, A. (1995). Aetiopathogenesis and management of impotence in diabetic males: Four years experience from combined clinic. *Diabetic Medicine: A Journal of the British Diabetic Association, 12*(1), 77–82.

Vigil, J. M. (2007). Asymmetries in the friendship preference and social styles of men and women. *Human Nature, 18,* 143–161.

Vincent, J. P., Peterson, J. L., & Parrott, D. J. (2009). Differences in African American and White women's attitudes toward lesbian and gay men. *Sex Roles, 61,* 599–606.

Voracek, M., & Fisher, M. L. (2006). Success is all in the measures: Androgenousness, curvaceousness, and starring frequencies in adult media actresses. *Archives of Sexual Behavior, 35,* 297–304.

Voracek, M., Hofhansl, A., & Fisher, M. L. (2005). Clark and Hatfield's evidence of women's low receptivity to male strangers' sexual offers revisited. *Psychological Reports, 97,* 11–20.

Vrangalova, Z. (2014). Does casual sex harm college students' well-being? A longitudinal investigation of the role of motivation. *Archives of Sexual Behavior.* doi:10.1007/s10508-013-0255-1

Vrasti, R., Eisemann, M., Podea, D., Olteanu, I., Scherppler, D., & Peleneagra, R. (1990). Parental rearing practices and personality in alcoholics classified according to family history. In C. N. Stefanis, C. R. Soldatos, & A. D. Rabavilas (Eds.), *Psychiatry: A world perspective* (Vol. 4, pp. 359–364). Amsterdam: Elsevier Science.

Vucheva, E. (2013). Social affairs: Europeans marry older, less often. Retrieved September 5, 2013, from Euobserver.com

Waite, L. J., & Joyner, K. (2001). Emotional satisfaction and physical pleasure in sexual unions: Time horizon, sexual behavior and sexual exclusivity. *Journal of Marriage and the Family, 63,* 247–264.

Walczak, D. (2015). The process of exchange, solidarity and sustainable development in building a community of responsibility. *Mediterranean Journal of Social Sciences, 6.* doi:10.5901/mjss.2015.v6n1s1p506

Walker, R. B., & Luszcz, M. A. (2009). The health and relationship dynamics of late-life couples: A systematic review of the literature. *Ageing & Society, 29,* 455–480.

Wallen, K. (1989). Mate selection: Economics and affection. *Behavioral and Brain Sciences, 12*(1), 37–38. Retrieved from http://dx.doi.org/10.1017/S0140525X00024250

Wallerstein, J. S., & Lewis, J. (2000). *The unexpected legacy of divorce: A 25 year landmark study.* New York: Hyperion.

Wang, H. Y., Kao, G., & Joyner, K. (2006). Stability of interracial and intraracial romantic relationships among adolescents. *Social Science Research, 35,* 435–453.

Wang, W., & Parker, K. (2014). *Record share of Americans have never married: As values, economics and gender patterns change.* Pew Research Center report, September 24. Washington, DC.

Warren, S. L., Huston, L., Egeland, B., & Sroufe, L. A. (1997). Child and adolescent anxiety disorders and early attachment. *Journal of the American Academy of Child and Adolescent Psychiatry, 36,* 637–644.

Waters, E., Hamilton, C. E., & Weinfield, N. S. (2000). The stability of attachment security from infancy to adolescence and early adulthood: General introduction. *Child Development, 71*(3), 678–683.

Watson, J. B. (1913). Psychology as the behaviorist views it. *Psychological Review, 20,* 158–177.

Watson, D., Beer, A., & McDade-Montez, E. (2014). The role of active assortment in spousal similarity. *Journal of Personality, 82,* 116–129. doi:10.1111/jopy.12039

Watson, D., Hubbard, B., & Wiese, D. (2000). General traits of personality and affectivity as predictors of satisfaction in intimate relationships: Evidence from self- and partner-ratings. *Journal of Personality, 68,* 413–449.

Watson, D., Klohnen, E. C., Casillas, A., Nus Simms, E., Haig, J., & Berry, D. S. (2004). Match makers and deal breakers: Analyses of assortative mating in newlywed couples. *Journal of Personality, 72,* 1029–1068. doi:10.1111/j.0022-3506.2004.00289.x

Watson, R. J. (2017). LGBTQ definitions every good ally should know. *USA Today,* June 15.

Webster, R. (1996). *Why Freud was wrong: Sin, science and psychoanalysis.* London: Harper Collins.

Weinbender, M. L. M., & Rossignol, A. M. (1996). Lifestyle and risk of premature sexual activity in a high school population of seven-day adventists: Value genesis, 1989. *Adolescence, 32,* 265–281.

Weiss, L., & Lowenthal, M. F. (1975). Life course perspectives on friendship. In M. Lowenthal, M. Thurnher, & D. Chiriboga (Eds.), *Four stages of life.* San Francisco: Jossey-Bass.

Welch, S., & Rubin, R. B. (2002). Development of relationship stage measures. *Communication Quarterly, 50,* 24–40.

Wells, B. E., & Twenge, J. M. (2005). Changes in young people's sexual behavior and attitudes, 1943–1999: Across-temporal meta-analysis. *Review of General Psychology, 9,* 249–261.

Welzel, C. (2013). *Freedom rising: Human empowerment and the quest for emancipation.* Cambridge, UK: Cambridge University Press.

Wentzel, K. R., & Feldman, S. S. (1996). Relations of cohesion and power in family dyads to social and emotional adjustment during early adolescence. *Journal of Research on Adolescence, 6,* 225–244.

Wertheim, E. H., Love, A., Peck, C., & Littlefield, L. (2006). *Skills for resolving conflict: Creating effective solutions through co-operative problem solving.* Melbourne: Eruditions.

West, L., Anderson, J., & Duck, S. (1996). Crossing the barriers to friendships between men and women. In J. Wood (Ed.), *Gendered relationships* (pp. 111–127). Mountain View, CA: Mayfield.

West, M. L., & Sheldon-Keller, A. E. (1992). The assessment of dimensions relevant to adult reciprocal attachment. *Canadian Journal of Psychiatry, 37,* 600–606.

West, R. L., & Turner, L. H. (2007). *Introducing communication theory* (pp. 186–187). New York: McGraw-Hill.

Whitbeck, L. B., Conger, R. D., & Kao, M. Y. (1993). The influence of parental support, depressed affect, and peers on the sexual behavior of adolescent girls. *Journal of Family Issues, 14*(2), 261–278.

Whitton, S., Stanley, S., & Markman, H. (2002). Sacrifice in romantic relationships. In A. L. Vangelisti, H. T. Reis, & M. A. Fitzpatrick (Eds.), *Stability and change in relationships.* Cambridge, UK: Cambridge University Press.

Whitton, S., Stanley, S., & Markman, H. (2007). If I help my partner, will it hurt me? Perceptions of sacrifice in romantic relationships. *Journal of Social and Clinical Psychology, 26*(1), 64–92.

Widmer, E. D., Treas, J., & Newcomb, R. (1998). Attitudes toward nonmarital sex in 24 countries. *Journal of Sex Research, 35,* 349–358.

Wilcox, W. B., & Nock, S. (2006). What's love got to do with it? Equality, equity, commitment and women's marital quality. *Social Forces, 84*(3), 1321–1345.

Wiley, A. R. (2007). Connecting as a couple: Communication skills for healthy relationships. *The Forum for Family and Consumer Issues, 12*(1), 1–9.

Willetts, M. C., Sprecher, S., & Beck, F. D. (2004). Overview of sexual practices and attitudes within relational contexts. In J. H. Harvey, A. Wenzel, & S. Sprecher (Eds.), *The handbook of sexuality in close relationships* (pp. 57–85). Mahwah, NJ: Erlbaum.

Wills, T. A. (1981). Downward comparison principles in social psychology. *Psychological Bulletin, 90*(2), 245–271. doi:10.1037/0033-2909.90.2.245

Wilson, R. S., Boyle, P. A., Levine, S. R., Yu, L., Anagnos, S. E., Buchman, A. S., Schneider, J. A & Bennett, D. A. (2012). Emotional neglect in childhood and cerebral infarction in older age. *Neurology, 79*(15), 1534–1539

Wilson, S. M., & Medora, N. P. (1990). Gender comparisons of college students' attitudes toward sexual behavior. *Adolescence, 25,* 615–627.

Winch, R. F., Ktsanes, T., & Ktsanes, V. (1955). Empirical elaboration of the theory of complementary needs in mate-selection. *The Journal of Abnormal and Social Psychology, 51*(3), 508–513.

Winslett, A. H., & Gross, A. M. (2008). Sexual boundaries: An examination of the importance of talking before touching. *Violence Against Women, 14,* 542–562. doi:10.1177/1077801208315527

Winstead, B. A., Derlega, V. J., Montgomery, M. J., & Pilkington, C. (1995). The quality of friendships at work and job satisfaction. *Journal of Social and Personal Relationships, 12*(2), 199–215.

Wirth, J. H., Sacco, D. F., Hugenberg, K., & Williams, K. D. (2010). Eye gaze as relational evaluation: Averted eye gaze leads to feelings of ostracism and relational devaluation. *Personality and Social Psychology Bulletin, 36,* 869–882.

Wiseman, J. P. (1986). Friendship: Bonds and binds in a voluntary relationship. *Journal of Social and Personal Relationships, 3,* 191–211.

Wolfinger, N. H. (2003). Family structure homogamy: The effects of parental divorce on partner selection and marital stability. *Social Science Research, 32*(1), 80–97.

Wong, J. S., & Schonlau, M. (2013). Does bully victimization predict future delinquency? A propensity score matching approach. *Criminal Justice and Behavior, 40,* 1184–1208.

Wood, D., & Brumbaugh, C. (2009). Using revealed mate preferences to evaluate market force and differential preference explanations for mate selection. *Journal of Personality and Social Psychology, 96,* 1226–1244.

World Health Organization (WHO). (2013). *Global and regional estimates of violence against women: Prevalence and health effects of intimate partner violence and non-partner sexual violence.* Retrieved from http://apps.who.int/iris/bitstream/10665/85239/1/9789241564625_eng.pdf

World Health Organization (WHO). (2016). *Violence against women.* Retrieved from www.who.int/iris/bitstream/10665/85239/1/9789241564625_eng.pdf

Wright, P. H. (1998). Toward an expanded orientation to the study of sex differences in friendship. In D. J. Canary & K. Dindia (Eds.), *Sex differences and similarities in communication* (pp. 41–64). Mahwah, NJ: Erlbaum.

Wright, P. H. (2006). Toward an expanded orientation to the comparative study of women's and men's same-sex friends. In K. Dindia & D. J. Canary (Eds.), *Sex differences and similarities in communication* (2nd ed., pp. 37–57). Mahwah, NJ: Erlbaum.

Wrzus, C., Hanel, M., Wagner, J., & Neyer, F. J. (2013). Social network changes and life events across the life span: A meta-analysis. *Psychological Bulletin, 139,* 53–80.

Yabiku, S., & Gager, C. T. (2009). Sexual frequency and the stability of marital and cohabiting unions. *Journal of Marriage and Family, 71*(4), 983–1000.

Yagil, D., Karnieli-Miller, O., Eisikovits, Z., & Enosh, G. (2006). Is that a "No"? The interpretation of responses to sexual harassment. *Sex Roles, 54*(3–4), 251–260.

Yan, W., Wu, Q., Liang, J., Chen, Y., & Fu, X. (2013). How fast are the leaked facial expressions: The duration of micro-expressions. *Journal of Nonverbal Behavior, 37,* 217–230.

Yang, Y. (2008). Social inequalities in happiness in the United States, 1972 to 2004: An age-period-cohort analysis. *American Sociological Review, 73,* 204–226.

Yeh, H. C., Lorenz, F. O., Wickrama, K. A. S., Conger, R. D., & Elder, G. H., Jr. (2006). Relationships among sexual satisfaction, marital quality, and marital instability at midlife. *Journal of Family Psychology, 20,* 339–343.

Yeung, R., & Leadbeater, B. J. (2010). Adults make a difference: Protective effects of parent and teacher emotional support on emotional and behavioral problems of peer victimized adolescents. *Journal of Community Psychology, 38,* 80–98. Retrieved from http://dx.doi.org/10.1002/jcop.20353

Young, E. W., Jensen, L. C., Olsen, J. A., & Cundick, B. P. (1991). The effects of family structure on the sexual behavior of adolescents. *Adolescence, 26,* 977–986.

Youngblade, L. M., & Belsky, J. (1992). Parent-child antecedents of 5-year-olds' close friendships: A longitudinal analysis. *Developmental Psychology, 28,* 700–713.

Youniss, J., & Smollar, J. (1985). *Adolescent relations with mothers, fathers, and friends.* Chicago: University of Chicago Press.

Youniss, J., and Volpe, J. (1978). A relational analysis of children's friendships. In W. Damon (Ed.), *Social cognition.* San Francisco: Jossey-Bass.

Yucel, C., & Eroglu, K. (2013). Sexual problems in postmenopausal women and coping methods. *Sexuality and Disability, 31*(3), 217–228.

Yucel, D., & Gassanov, M. A. (2010). Exploring actor and partner correlates of sexual satisfaction among married couples. *Social Science Research, 39*(5), 725–738.

Zawacki, T. (2011). Effects of alcohol on women's risky sexual decision making during social interactions in the laboratory. *Psychology of Women Quarterly, 35,* 107–118.

Zeidner, M., & Kloda, I. (2013). Emotional intelligence (EI), conflict resolution patterns, and relationship satisfaction: Actor and partner effects revisited. *Personality and Individual Differences, 54,* 278–283.

Zentner, M. R. (2005). Ideal mate personality concepts and compatibility in close relationships: A longitudinal analysis. *Journal of Personality and Social Psychology, 89*(2), 242–256.

Zhang, F., & Labouvie-Vief, G. (2004). Stability and fluctuation in adult attachment style over a 6-year period. *Attachment and Human Development, 6*(4), 419–437.

Zhang, S., & Kline, S. L. (2009). Can I make my own decision? A cross-cultural study of perceived social network influence in mate selection. *Journal of Cross-Cultural Psychology, 40,* 3–23.

Zhang, Y. T., & Van Hook, J. (2009). Marital dissolution among interracial couples. *Journal of Marriage and Family, 71,* 95–107.

Zhang, Z., & Hayward, M. D. (2006). Gender, the marital life course, and cardiovascular disease in late midlife. *Journal of Marriage and the Family, 68,* 639–657.

Zhou, J. N., Hofman, M. A., Gooren, L. J., & Swaab, D. F. (1995). A sex difference in the human brain and its relation to transsexuality. *Nature, 378,* 68–70.

Zimmerman. M. A. (2000). Empowerment theory: Psychological, organizational, and community levels of analysis. In J. Rappaport & E. Seidman (Eds.), *Handbook of community psychology* (pp. 43–63). New York: Springer.

Zwierzynska, K., Wolke, D., & Lereya, T. (2013). Peer victimization in childhood and internalizing problems in adolescence: A prospective longitudinal study. *Journal of Abnormal Psychology, 41*(2), 309–323.

Index

Page numbers followed by *f* or *t* indicate figures or tables, respectively.

About the Author

Abdul Khaleque, PhD, is an adjunct professor in the Department of Human Development and Family Studies and a senior scientist in the Ronald and Nancy Rohner Center for the Study of Interpersonal Acceptance and Rejection at the University of Connecticut. He was a professor of psychology at the University of Dhaka in Bangladesh, and a visiting faculty in the Department of Psychology at the University of Otago in New Zealand, a visiting fellow in the Department of Psychology at the University of Delhi in India, and a visiting professor in the Department of Applied Psychology at the University of the Punjab in Pakistan. He is a past president of the International Society for Interpersonal Acceptance and Rejection, and Bangladesh Psychological Association, and a past secretary general of the South Asian Association of Psychologists. He is a current member of the American Psychological Association, and a life member of the Human Factors Society of America. He has also been serving as a member of the editorial board and as a reviewer of about a dozen international journals. He has authored or coauthored some 120 research articles, 40 book chapters, and authored/edited 12 books in psychology and human development. Khaleque earned a BA with Honors in Philosophy from the University of Dhaka, Bangladesh, an MSc in Applied Psychology from the University of the Punjab in Pakistan, an MA in Family Studies from the University of Connecticut, and a PhD in Psychology from the Catholic University of Leuven in Belgium.